Home/Front

Home/Front

The Military, War and Gender in Twentieth-Century Germany

Edited by
**Karen Hagemann and
Stefanie Schüler-Springorum**

Oxford • New York

First published in 2002 by
Berg
Editorial offices:
150 Cowley Road, Oxford, OX4 1JJ, UK
838 Broadway, Third Floor, New York, NY 10003–4812, USA

Originally published in German as
Heimat – Front
by
Campus Publishers, Frankfurt

Berg is an imprint of Oxford International Publishers Ltd.

Library of Congress Cataloging-in-Publication Data
Heimat-Front. English
   Home/front : the military, war, and gender in twentieth-century
Germany / edited by Karen Hagemann and Stefanie Schüler-Springorum.
      p. cm.
Includes bibliographical references and index.
      ISBN 1-85973-665-3 (Cloth) — ISBN 1-85973-670-X (Paper)
   1. Women and the military—Germany—History—20th century.
2. Women and war—Germany—History—20th century.   3. Sociology,
Military—Germany.   4. Germany–Social conditions–20th century.
5. Germany—History, Military—20th century.   I. Hagemann, Karen.
II. Schüler-Springorum, Stefanie.   III. Title.
U21.75 .H45 2002
355'.0082'09430904—dc21

                                                                2002014677

British Library Cataloguing-in-Publication Data
A catalogue record for this book is available from the British Library.

ISBN 1 85973 665 3 (Cloth)
      1 85973 670 X (Paper)

Typeset by JS Typesetting Ltd, Wellingborough, Northants.
Printed in the United Kingdom by Biddles Ltd, Guildford and King's Lynn.

Contents

Contents

Contents

Preface

When gender historians and military historians met for the first time in November 1997 for an international colloquium on 'Military, War and the Gender Order in Historical Transition (16th–19th Century Germany),' both sides initially regarded the attempt with a great deal of skepticism. But the skepticism soon gave way to curiosity when it was discovered how much both sides could profit from each other. The conference highlighted the far-reaching correlations between the transformations in the military and warfare and changes in the gender order over the course of four centuries. The results of this successful experiment, which was a co-operation of the Center for Interdisciplinary Women's and Gender Studies at the Technical University of Berlin and the 'Working Group on the Military and Society in the Early Modern Period', were documented in an expanded volume.[1]

Since that time, gender history has forged a path into the history of war and military. The history of the military has begun to change and is now opening up to new questions and approaches. Conversely, historical research on women and gender is discovering the relevance of the military and war for the formation of gender relations. In particular, our understanding of the military and society before, during and after the First and Second World Wars has gained new perspectives from historical studies of gender, because these wars were 'total wars' that mobilized both the 'front' and the 'homeland'. They were characterized by a tendency towards the 'total' mobilization and ideological indoctrination of the entire nation and the incorporation of the services of men and women for the requirements of industrialized mass war. 'Front' and 'home' were intimately related. An expression of this is the concept of the 'home front', which was created in the very first months of the First World War in German propaganda. The 'home front' was to become the backbone of the troops in the field. Thus, the constantly emphasized traditional borders between military and civilian society, between 'front' and 'home' became increasingly blurred, particularly during the Second World War. 'Home' was turned into a 'front' during the bombing as the civilian population became the direct target of military violence. Even the lines separating war and peace were blurred as a result of both World Wars. Long before these wars broke out, they were prepared for both politically and culturally. Long after the declared end of these wars the societies involved had to cope with the long-lasting consequences, which affected all aspects of the economy and society, politics and culture.

This volume on the military, war and gender in twentieth-century Germany focuses on the relationships between war and peace, military and civilian society, home and front, and men and women. The punctuation of the title, *Home/Front*, is meant to underline the variety of these relationships. The book presents the results of an international conference that took place in Berlin in October 1999 and was intended as a continuation and a completion of attempts at a gendered rewriting of the history of the military and war in the German-speaking region from the sixteenth to the twentieth century. Again, the initiative came from the Center for Interdisciplinary Women's and Gender Studies at the TU Berlin, which co-operated this time with the 'Military History Study Group'. More than 120 scholars from ten different countries came together for two days. Three topics stood at the center of the discussions and frame the focus of this book: first, the connections between gender images and the national, social, racist and ethnic concepts of the enemy in the two World Wars; second, gender relations and hierarchies in the military and war during this period; and third, the experiences, perceptions, and memories of the First and Second World War.

Roger Chickering's assertion that 'Total War requires total history'[2] may represent an impossible demand, but it accurately describes the problem that confronts any research on the age of the World Wars and which was very evident in the conference discussions. Because these wars were characterized by a tendency towards 'total' mobilization, we must try to write the history of the era of World Wars as a 'total' history that not only pays equal attention to the economy, society, culture and politics, but also self-evidently includes 'gender' as a central 'socio-cultural category' of historical analysis alongside others. The basic assumption of this volume is that we cannot possibly understand the dynamics of the historical development of the period of 'total wars', the relationship between 'home' and 'front', the economic, social and cultural functions of the 'home front', or indeed the so-called "general" political and military developments of the era, without integrating gender. Based on this assumption, a productive cooperation between and complementing of gender history and the history of the military and war is not only possible but also indispensable. We expect that the systematic integration of gender perspectives will yield new interpretations that will modify the general representation and interpretation of both world wars.

Preface

The essays rest on the most recent research and explore the intersections of the military, war and gender in twentieth-century Germany from a variety of perspectives. The contributors investigate the relevance of the military and war for the formation of gender relations and their representation as well as for the construction of the individual and social agency of both genders in civil society and in the military. They inquire into the origins and development of gendered images as they were shaped by war. They expound upon the multifarious mechanisms that served to reconstruct gender relations in the two postwar periods. They analyze the participation of women and men in the creation of wars as well as the gender-specific meaning of their respective roles. And lastly, they investigate the different ways of remembering and coming to terms with the two great military conflicts in the extremely violent twentieth century. The contributions represent a breadth of research approaches and methods, from social and political history to literary and cultural history. This breadth and openness is typical of current research on the military, war, and gender, because this highly complex relationship is best approached from multiple perspectives and (sub)disciplines. The most fruitful and innovative studies in the field appear to be those that, like a number of contributions in this volume, combine various approaches and perspectives and thus, for example, ground a discourse analysis in social history, place a history of the body in a political context, or combine oral history analysis with reflections from social psychology and cultural studies.

The essays in the volume are organized chronologically. The introduction on 'The Military, Violence and Gender in the Age of the World Wars' by Karen Hagemann will suggest the main lines of development, indicate potential areas for future research, discuss research problems and introduce and contextualize the contributions to the volume. It thus seeks to outline the investigative space for a gendered rewriting of the history of the military and war in Germany in the age of the World Wars. The introduction is complemented by a selected bibliography on 'The Military, War and Gender in Nineteenth- and Twentieth-Century Germany' at the end of this volume, which highlights the most relevant recent publications in the field. The bibliography is intended to provide a general orientation to the topic.

Before we conclude, we would like to thank all of the institutions, colleagues and friends who supported this project, starting with the institutions that generously financed the conference – the German Research Foundation, the Gerda Henkel Foundation and the Technical University of Berlin. More debts have accumulated in the process of transforming the conference into a book. First and foremost, we would like to thank

Preface

Karin Hausen, director of the Center for Interdisciplinary Studies on Women and Gender at the Technical University of Berlin, and Wilhelm Deist, chairman of the 'Military History Study Group', for their constant support. The discussions that took place during the conference and afterwards made it possible for the editors and the authors to revise their contributions. The finished volume has benefited from the generosity of all conference participants, especially the commentators. The organizational skills of Marcus Funck, with whom we organized the conference, and the tireless support of the student group headed by Stefan Grob helped to make the conference a success. The Gerda Henkel Foundation and the Johanna und Fritz Buch Gedächtnis Stiftung have provided further financial support for the printing of this volume. Kathleen May has been a constructive and sympathetic editor. Last but not least, we would like to thank Kathrin Hoffmann-Curtius, who lent us the reproduction for the cover illustration and provided us with information about this painting by the Berlin artist Elisabeth Voigt, which was shown at the Great Berlin Art Exhibition in the National Gallery in 1942 under the title 'Collecting Wool'.

Karen Hagemann
Stefanie Schüler-Springorum
Toronto and Hamburg, September 2002

Notes

1. See *Landsknechte, Soldatenfrauen und Nationalkrieger. Militär, Krieg und Geschlechterordnung im historischen Wandel,* ed. Karen Hagemann and Ralf Pröve (Frankfurt a.M., New York, 1998).
2. Roger Chickering, 'Total War. The Use and Abuse of a Concept,' in *Anticipating Total War. The German and American Experiences, 1871–1914,* ed. Manfred F. Boemeke et al. (Cambridge, 1999), 13–28, 27.

Home/Front

The Military, Violence and Gender Relations in the Age of the World Wars

Karen Hagemann

In January 1943 *Westermanns Monatshefte* printed a black and white reproduction of a painting by the Berlin artist Elisabeth Voigt entitled *Collecting Wool (Die Wollsammlung)* which had been shown one year earlier at the Great Berlin Art Exhibition in the National Gallery.* The renowned cultural history magazine[1] introduced the picture to its educated, mainly conservative readership[2] as a visual incarnation of the 'valorous *Volk* community' in the midst of 'total war'. This 'total war' had been officially declared by the Nazi state in a decree of the Führer of 13 January 1943,[3] and was publicly announced by Minister of Propaganda Goebbels in his notorious speech at the Sports Palace in Berlin five weeks later. In light of the enormous losses suffered by the Wehrmacht at Stalingrad[4] the last reserves had to be mobilized, for which reason the decree of 13 January ordered a 'comprehensive deployment of men and women for the purposes of defending the Reich.' With the objective of freeing up all 'men capable of military service for deployment at the front' women were to be increasingly employed on the 'home front' in all areas of the economy relevant to the war effort.[5] Therefore the decree called upon all 'German women' to make a 'sacrifice for the imperiled *Volk* community.' At least since the defeat of the First World War, it had become clear to every leading military officer and most politicians that a victory at the front needed to be won on the home front as well.

This complex relationship between home and front, which was accompanied during the war by new demands upon both men and women, is partially reflected in the painting, which the magazine author commented upon as follows:

---

*Only the reproduction of the painting came down to us. We chose it for the cover of this book because of its complexity and ambivalence, as will be developed in the following.

Its timeless arrangement lifts it above the [present] day. It lends a universal meaning to the sacrifice. But the masses surging back and forth before the arched wall that symbolically separates home and abroad recall a very particular event that crowned the sacrifices of the past weeks. The field-gray marching wall behind the arch allows us to see nothing of the distance but the reddened sky, in which the squadrons thunder off to battle. In the foreground, the group of girls and women lends the finest expression to the image of the protected and caring homeland.[6]

At first glance, 'Collecting Wool', with its trivialization of war as an idyll, indeed appears to represent in a timelessly 'universal' manner the traditional stereotype of the relationship between 'home' and 'front', between women and men in wartime society. The men – in our picture, the steel-helmeted soldiers in the background – go off to war as 'defenders of the fatherland' and protect and preserve the 'caring homeland' embodied by women. The women – in the painting represented by the folklorically dressed group in the foreground – support the war not just mentally, by bolstering men's courage and will to fight, and seeing to order and morality at home, but also practically, through their self-sacrificing actions, by working voluntarily to equip and arm the warriors and the war machine and to provide wartime welfare and medical services. This model of the wartime gender order appears to have been highly functional for mobilizing for war under the conditions of universal conscription. Otherwise, it would be hard to explain why it was propagated so massively over a period of nearly 150 years in every German war of the nineteenth and twentieth centuries, adapted in each case to the specific circumstances and needs of the time.[7]

It was precisely because this model was not specific to National Socialism that it was also propagated by the respected culture magazine. It had willingly placed itself at the disposal of the Nazis in 1933 and regarded its task, as a self-portrait of the magazine noted in September 1934, as combining the 'administration and cultivation of the most valuable traditions,' with the 'promotion and realization of the new will to expand out of spirit and blood.'[8] The painting 'Collecting Wool' was eminently suited to this mission. The magazine could expect the wartime gender order propagated in the painting to meet with the approval of its bourgeois readership since it had such a long tradition.

On closer scrutiny, however, Elisabeth Voigt's painting reveals more than old familiar images. It also shows us something new and specific to its time, although not necessarily to National Socialism. We see not only the largely female '*Volk* community' on the home front mobilized to collect and process used clothing in the center of the picture. The magazine's commentary implicitly points to collections by the Winter Relief, which was not invented by the National Socialists, but organized to perfection by Nazi People's Welfare as a mass relief effort.[9] There is more, though; in the background, behind the arch, we can see quite small combat aircrafts. The author interprets the 'thundering squadrons' as signs of the strong male protection of the homeland.[10] But the combat squadrons in the background of the picture (inadvertently) refer to more, namely to the real, contemporary war, a bombing war in which the homeland was no longer clearly separate from the front, and indeed had become a 'second front', which could not be protected by men's willingness to fight. This is a fact that must have been familiar in the winter of 1942/43 to most viewers and readers, who were increasingly learning how little German air defense could do to stop the Allied air attacks that had intensified since 1942.[11]

Thus, in the contemporary context, Elisabeth Voigt's painting showed a great deal more than the magazine editors were willing to see. Paradoxically, it pointed out, mediated by the perceptions of beholders, that the old gender images, which had symbolized a fundamental social order, no longer functioned in the reality of 'total war'. More than any previous conflict, this form of war called the peacetime gender order into question. The conscripted men no longer functioned as 'breadwinners'. As the war went on they also became increasingly ineffective as 'protectors'. The women left behind were forced more and more to replace the men, not just in the wartime economy but also by assuming responsibility for the livelihood and survival of their families.[12] In addition, they were entrusted with public functions that considerably expanded their scope of action and responsibilities.[13] This tension between traditional gender images and new expectations appears to have been viewed with mixed feelings by men and women alike. This, at least, is what many soldiers' letters home from the First and Second World War indicate.[14] Women appear to have felt overwhelmed both physically and mentally by the various new demands that everyday life during wartime placed upon them.[15] Men, in turn, feared a loss of authority within the family.[16] At the same time, at the front they frequently faced quite contradictory and often bewildering experiences that called their traditional self-image as men into question.[17]

After both world wars, the respective political elites of the postwar societies did everything in their power to counteract the de facto expansion of women's scope of action during the war by intensively propagating a gender order centered on the traditional model of the 'breadwinner-housewife family.'[18] What is more, practical politics, too, aimed to stabilize this model and even to generalize it still further. An example is the demobilization policy of the Weimar Republic, whose primary goal was to stabilize the social and political order by reintegrating former soldiers into occupational life. This aim could only be attained by dismissing female workers from those areas of the economy in which they had taken jobs during wartime previously reserved for men.[19] There is much evidence that both postwar societies were historical developmental phases in which the process of 're-gendering' the social order proceeded with great intensity.[20] After the war, the gender order, which had been disrupted by the particular requirements of total war, was reestablished with a vengeance (albeit on a different level adapted to the new circumstances of the age) because of its central significance for stabilizing the entire social order. After all, the gender order is a basic structure that runs through all areas of the economy, society and politics and links the individual with the collective and the 'personal' with the 'political'.

The painting *Collecting Wool* and its location in the contemporary context thus stands paradigmatically for the model of a 'double helix' that Margaret and Patrice Higonnet develop in the introduction to their path breaking 1987 essay collection *Behind the Lines: Gender and the Two World Wars*. This model allows us to perceive the lines of continuity in the gender order and gender images that are evident in the era of the world wars, running parallel to all the changes in the position and situation of women.[21] These parallels are visible in all states that were involved in the First and Second World War. Obviously, the general demands of highly industrialized 'total war' meant that, despite all national differences in the economy, society, politics and culture, and, what is more, despite the differences between the allied blocks, not only the gender order and the gender images of wartime society, but also the forms of female wartime participation were similar.[22] A comparison of the discourses and politics in all of the states involved in the two world wars is an important scholarly task that remains to be undertaken. Only such a comparison would allow us to examine the hypothesis offered above. In the following introduction my aim will be more limited.[23] I begin with reflections on the central term 'total war', which has shaped recent discussions about the age of the world wars. In a second step, I suggest the main lines of historical development, indicate potential areas for future research, discuss research problems, and introduce and contextualize the contributions to the volume. I thus seek to outline the scholarly space for a *rewriting* of the history of the military and war in Germany in the age of the world wars from the perspective of social, cultural, and gender history. Like all of the authors in this volume, I will use the term 'gender' to refer to a socially and culturally formed relational and context-specific category of social scientific and historical analysis, whose function can only be adequately understood in interaction with other categories of differentiation such as class, race, ethnicity and religion, but also age, marital status and sexual orientation. Such an understanding naturally includes the analysis of constructions of masculinity.[24]

The Age of the World Wars as an Epoch of 'Total Wars'

If, as Roger Chickering recently put it, what distinguishes a 'total war' from earlier forms of war is mainly 'its peculiar intensity and extension' and its tendency to abolish the boundaries that distinguish the front from the homeland (that is, it fulfills the following conditions: first, its theaters of war extend simultaneously into large segments of the world and it is conducted with mass armies made up of 'citizens in uniform who were passionate because ideologically motivated'; second, the 'mobilization for war no longer stops at the borders of civilian life', 'because all members of the belligerent states' participate more or less in the mighty efforts necessary to conduct a war successfully; third, 'all members of the belligerent states are now the legitimate targets of military action', 'whether by blockade,' occupation, looting and requisitioning or aerial bombing; and fourth, the 'war aims are accordingly directed towards the extermination of the enemy'),[25] then the age of the world wars was the classic period of 'total war', even if we need to do much more comparative research and define precisely what distinguished these two great twentieth-century wars from their predecessors.[26]

If we adopt a comparative historical perspective, it should be possible to show that the Revolutionary and Coalition Wars between 1792 and 1815, the first to be conducted as 'national wars' with mass armies, already displayed 'total' tendencies. They extended far beyond Europe to encompass for a time not just parts of Africa and Asia but also North America.[27] The number of casualties, at least five million, was also comparable, relative to the size of the European population at the time, to that of World War I.[28] Even mobilization for war in the print media attained previously unknown dimensions.[29] To make such an argument is to ignore neither the lasting transformations in the military and warfare in the nineteenth and twentieth centuries and the new quality of technologization and mass extermination in the First, and more particularly the Second World War, nor the unimaginable dimensions of the will to destruction that underlay the Holocaust. It does require us to sharpen our perceptions of the far-reaching structural consequences of the universal mobilization for war, not just for the military itself, but also for the conduct of war, the relationship between 'front' and 'homeland' and soldiers and civilians, and indeed between the state and the nation and men and women.[30] This connection remains invisible, however, if we restrict our analysis to the military and warfare in the narrow sense. Rather, we must broaden our investigation to include society as a whole, and systematically incorporate the gender dimension, which is, after all – and this is the thesis underlying the present volume – a central indicator of the 'totality' of a war. It most clearly marks the erasure of the lines separating the military and civilian realms – the more or less pronounced chief characteristic of any 'total' war – that results from the interplay among the four ideal-typical elements of a 'total war': the 'totality' of war aims, methods, mobilization, and control.

To speak of 'total war' is not to assume that these wars were, in reality, as truly 'total' as the ideal typical definition of present-day military historians might suggest, or as the totalitarian claims of early military and nationalist protagonists of the term, which first became fashionable in the 1920s, demanded.[31] Actual practice was marked by ambivalence, frictions, ruptures, and contradictions. This is true even of the Second World War, where the tendency to 'totalize' warfare was most pronounced, especially on the German side, since the political leadership of the 'Third Reich' aimed at the total extermination of the 'enemy' in the Holocaust and the Wehrmacht participated in this policy. Even the link between war and genocide is not specific to the Second World War, however. This has correctly been pointed out in the current discussion of the concept of 'total war', prompting the question of whether genocide more generally was not the most logical and radical, if by no means necessary, consequence of the tendency toward total war.[32]

The term 'age of the world wars', too, requires some qualification: it suggests the unity of an epoch that cannot be so clearly defined as such. This already begins with the simple question of when this 'age' began and when it ended.[33] The political and cultural groundwork for both world wars was laid long before they began, and because of their profound totality, which encompassed the political, economic and social spheres, the effects continued to be felt long after hostilities had ended. We have chosen the term 'age of the world wars' for this volume in order to emphasize the connections between mobilization and demobilization, between preparations for war, war itself, and its consequences, and how they have been processed. At the same time, we would like to direct attention to continuities and ruptures. In our view, all of this becomes especially apparent when we systematically integrate the gender dimension into our research.

The First World War

What was new about the First World War was not primarily the fact that it was conducted as a 'total war' in the sense outlined above, but rather the circumstance that it was conducted, more resolutely and radically than any previous war since the introduction of universal conscription, as a 'total war' with huge mass armies. The precondition was the massive deployment of the most up-to-date transportation and weapons technology, which led to an industrialization of war and to an unprecedented destruction of people and material within a short period of time. This industrialization of war had multiple effects not just on the conduct of war itself and thus on the war experience of soldiers and officers, which came to resemble less and less the heroic nineteenth-century image of war, but also on the involvement of the homeland.[34]

Industrialized mass warfare demanded an unprecedented degree of patriotic national mobilization among both soldiers and civilians. The traditional lines between the military and civilian society, which the military elites, in particular, had vigorously defended in Imperial Germany, became increasingly blurred by the altered demands of warfare. This occurred in part even before the war, as Marcus Funck's contribution 'Ready for War? Conceptions of Military Manliness in the Prusso-German Officer Corps before the First World War' demonstrates. Funck elaborates the substantial repercussions for the hegemonic ideal of military masculinity of changes in the social composition of the Prussian officer corps, and hence in its professional self-understanding, in the four peacetime decades before 1914.

Increasingly, serving the 'valorous nation' and 'specialist military work' became values in their own right, alongside service to the monarchical social order. At the same time, the aristocratic concept of the officer that had dominated representations of the officer corps after 1871 was increasingly stigmatized as 'effeminate'. The general staff involved in planning the next war, in particular, favored an image of the officer and of masculinity characterized by 'cool professionalism', which drew its claims to exclusivity from an understanding of military leadership as an esoteric science based on expert knowledge. This was accompanied by a 'hardening' and 'masculinization' of the model of the officer and a growing mental, but paradoxically deficient practical, preparation of the officers of the imperial army for war, which would become evident soon after the beginning of the First World War. Funck's essay is an example of the extent to which a further development of gender history in the direction of a men's history that investigates the mutually referential and simultaneous nature of competing models of masculinity can enrich our knowledge of how the military functions as a central social and cultural institution. At the same time, his contribution points to the ambivalence and fragility of even 'hegemonic models of masculinity.'[35]

Recent studies on Imperial Germany have shown how poorly prepared the German empire as a whole was for the altered demands of industrialized mass warfare, despite the arms buildup and bellicose rhetoric.[36] Compared to other European states, Germany possessed a highly developed mobilization technology even before the First World War,[37] but since the political, and to a lesser extent the military leadership in 1914/15 still expected a *Blitzkrieg* ending in quick victory, they anticipated only a brief interruption to the peacetime economy and took only improvised measures at best. The inaccuracy of this assessment, and the dire consequences of underestimating the economic and social dimensions of warfare, soon became all too apparent. As the war continued, industrialized mass warfare demanded an increasing regulation of the economy. For this reason a number of new government departments and agencies needed to be created in which representatives of the private sector were given extensive planning and executive powers under the direction of the military. While the regulation of production and consumption was tightened ever more, the political leadership was prepared, in light of the '(social) truce' (*Burgfrieden*) declared at the beginning of the war, on the one hand to make concessions to the trade unions, and on the other to offer profit incentives to industrial enterprises in the form of generously calculated prices for all goods necessary for outfitting and provisioning the armed forces.[38]

During the First World War the homeland was for the first time explicitly referred to as a home front – a term coined, not coincidentally, at the beginning of the war by official German propaganda. As it became increasingly industrialized, the war depended more than ever before on the willingness of civilians at home, both male and female, to support the war effort, not just by making material sacrifices and participating in war relief and nursing but above all by working in war-relevant industry. The 'second front' at home was expected to provide a steady supply of men and material for the war on the first front, and at the same time to process losses both materially and mentally. For that reason the war was increasingly conducted in the economic arena, among other things by the Allied blockade policy, which dramatically worsened the supply of everyday goods to the German civilian population, and in the cultural arena, not least by propaganda about the enemy. The German side was particularly active here, seeking to sell its war of aggression as a defensive war, since only such a conflict was guaranteed the broad support that has attracted so much attention as the 'experience of August 1914'.[39] To this end, political and military leaders coined the term 'preventive defensive war.' This term, like the rhetoric of a 'social truce' associated with it, was very useful in mobilizing the 'home front', which institutionally integrated not just the middle-class women's movement but, for the first time, the organized working class and with it the Social Democratic women's movement as well.[40]

How great the misgivings that had to be overcome were, despite all the propaganda about a universal readiness for war, is evident in the ideological onslaught on soldiers in the German armed forces press, which Robert L. Nelson addresses in his contribution 'German Comrades – Slavic Whores. Gender Images in the German Soldier Newspapers of the First World War.' He points out that the circa 115 forces newspapers that appeared between September 1914 and the end of the war in November 1918 not only far exceeded anything ever seen before, but also disseminated propaganda far more intensely among soldiers than the military newspapers of any of Germany's enemies. For British and French soldiers, it was far more self-evident to view the conflict begun by Germany as a defensive war, and thus it was apparently not necessary to agitate among them to the same degree. The German soldiers' newspapers sought to mobilize their readers on the one hand by the gender images they sketched, and on the other by traditional and stereotypical national, ethnic and racist images of the enemy, which were always also overlaid with gender connotations. Similarly complex constructed images of the enemy could also be found in the general press, in leaflets, brochures and on posters. How strongly gender images and racist stereotypes were interwoven and referred to each other as complements becomes clear in Christian Koller's contribution, 'Race and Gender Stereotypes in the Discussion on Colonial Troops. A Franco-German Comparison, 1914–1923.' He also shows the lasting aftereffects of images of the enemy formulated during and for the war.[41]

This intense war propaganda was not ineffective. From the beginning, the war was actively supported by the middle-class women's movement organized under the umbrella of the Federation of German's Women's Associations (BDF), and by the Social Democratic labor movement. The BDF had founded the National Women's Service (*Nationaler Frauendienst*) on 31 July 1914 with the aim of mobilizing women for 'patriotic work on the home front'. At first, the National Women's Service concentrated on helping to organize wartime nursing care, food supplies and relief for the family of soldiers and for those made jobless by war. Soon, though, it widened its scope. Gradually it became more active in child and youth welfare, protection for infants and new mothers and homeless relief.[42] The National Women's Service was only able to handle this wide range of activities because, by 7 August 1914, the Women's Secretariat of the SPD party executive and the Women Worker's Secretariat of the General Commission of the Free Trade Unions had become members, relinquishing for the first time the principle of strict separation between them and the BDF. This cooperation was intended to prevent a scattering of energies. The declared hope was that women would be given the vote in recognition of their achievements on the home front.[43]

As the war went on, mobilizing women for the wartime economy and arranging employment became key fields of activity for the National Women's Service. The enormous casualties of the great battles of the summer of 1916 compelled the government to free men of military age for front duty and to step up arms production. To this end it had the Reichstag pass a 'Patriotic Auxiliary Service Act' (*Hilfsdienstgesetz*) on 6 December 1916, which obliged all men between the ages of seventeen and sixty to work in the wartime economy.[44] Women were explicitly excluded from this law. Since it soon became obvious that the hoped-for success was not forthcoming, however, it was decided that they should increasingly be recruited as volunteers for the war industry. The enforcement of the Relief Service Law was turned over to the War Office, which was set up in 1 November 1916. A Central Office for Women's Labor was established there to coordinate the employment and deployment of the female workers needed for the armaments industry. Leading representatives of the National Women's Service headed the Central Office for Women's Labor.[45]

Beginning in the spring of 1917, the Central Office for Women's Labor promoted not only women's work in the war industry, but also military service 'behind the lines'. The so-called army auxiliaries (*Etappenhelferinnen*) were supposed to free soldiers in the communications zone for service at the front. In strategic and actual terms, the communications zone was directly behind the front. They had to provision an army group, secure new supplies, and organize day-to-day needs. Thus women came very close to the combat zone.[46] As Bianca Schönberger's paper 'Motherly Heroines and Adventurous Girls. Red Cross Nurses and Women Army Auxiliaries in the First World War' shows, a remarkably large number of women grasped this new opportunity to do war work. Alongside nursing, service in the communications zone rapidly became an important form of female participation in the war. At the end of the conflict, in addition to the 28,000 military nurses, more than 20,000 women were working as army auxiliaries. In her analysis of the discourse on the possibilities and limits of women's participation in the war, Schönberger emphasizes the importance of notions of gender and class in evaluating women's war work, determining their scope of action and defining their contributions in relation to those of men. She shows that Red Cross nurses, whom collective memory during the Weimar Republic placed in the foreground as a complement to the image of the soldier at the front, had already been viewed far more positively during the First World War. The fact that women had long cared for sick and wounded soldiers will doubtless have played a role here.[47] Army auxiliaries, unlike nurses, directly replaced soldiers and thus also posed a greater challenge to the gender order. During the war the public already sought to neutralize this challenge by accusing auxiliaries of 'egotism' and 'immorality'. The disparate perceptions of army auxiliaries and nurses were apparently heightened by the different origins of the two groups. While the auxiliaries largely came from the lower and middle classes, the nurses included many women from the upper middle class and the aristocracy. Women of the first group were repeatedly accused of only wanting to work in the communications zone because of the relatively good pay and independent way of life. The latter, in contrast, were assumed to be acting out of 'female patriotism'.[48]

In light of the absence of a quick victory and the dramatically rising numbers of dead and wounded soldiers at the front, but also of the increasingly catastrophic supply situation at home,[49] the 'social truce' declared when the war began soon began to crumble, and social protest and opposition to the war grew. New social differences, such as those between so-called war profiteers and war victims, arose alongside old, reemerging political ones. The press denounced as war profiteers anyone who earned money from the war, who did not go hungry, or who made no 'sacrifice'. This group included agricultural producers in particular, along with merchants and the well-heeled who could afford to buy on the burgeoning black market. 'War victims' included not just fallen or disabled soldiers and widows and orphans but also the working wives of soldiers, mainly working-class women with children, who continued to do perform their 'duties' in the family and the workplace despite hunger and cold. In her contribution 'Homefront. Food, Politics and Women's Everyday Life in the First World War,' Belinda J. Davis examines the significance of this social difference in contemporary public discourse. Using an analysis of surveillance reports by the Berlin police, among other sources, she shows that the increasing protests by working-class women against food shortages met with far more sympathy than the strikes for higher wages led by armaments workers, both male and female. Her explanation is that shortages of food and fuel affected people with middle incomes as well.[50] Only after defeat and revolution was the 'stab-in-the-back legend' constructed and propagated, mainly by leading military officers. This legend claimed that people in the homeland caused the German defeat by failing to hold out and adequately support those at the front and by harboring growing antiwar sentiments. The military used this argument to explain its own lack of success and project responsibility onto its political opponents. In this way, working-class women's hunger protests also came under fire from reactionary critics. Those once viewed as the victims of the war were now held responsible for Germany's defeat.[51]

The Interwar Period

The war lived on into the postwar period, at first as part of the necessary process of coping with its consequences. Apart from political debates over responsibility for the defeat,[52] which was linked to the collapse of the political and social order of Imperial Germany, the focus in the first years after the war was on the issue of economic and social demobilization. The far-reaching political, economic, social and cultural after-effects of the war, which affected large segments of the population, but in very different ways according to region, class, sex, marital status, age, etc., also had to be addressed. As during the war, those who suffered most from the economic and social consequences of the conflict – food, fuel and housing shortages and inflation – were the urban poor. The situation of many war victims was and remained precarious as well: 1.69 million soldiers had died in the war. They left behind 371,800 widows and 113,600 mothers who had lost their sons, as well as 1,031,400 fatherless children. In addition, 2.7 million men had been made disabled.[53] The material support they received from the crisis-ridden Weimar state was inadequate and also mirrored the hierarchy of values in wartime society. Former soldiers were better provided for than war widows and orphans.[54] Nevertheless, the situation of disabled veterans in postwar society was also difficult, since their very physical appearance was a permanent reminder to contemporaries of a war they sought to forget and repress as quickly as possible.

In her contribution 'Body Damage. War Disability and Constructions of Masculinity in Weimar Germany,' Sabine Kienitz analyzes the medical and social scientific discourse on the male body destroyed by war, which had already begun during the First World War.[55] This discourse not merely constructed new body images defined as genuinely 'masculine', but also established new standards for the male body. In the case of disabled veterans, this led to a paradoxical development: on the one hand, engineers intensively considered the problems of the economic deployment of the disabled, and tried with the help of new technologies, a different organization of labor, and prostheses, to turn 'war cripples' into 'whole men' capable of performing normal work. On the other hand, these very norms and standardizations, as well as the increased use of technology, repeatedly called veterans' attention to their own diminished capacities and thus masculinity. Their prostheses were a daily reminder of their physical deficiencies. What is more, in order to enforce their official claims to benefits, they were compelled to emphasize their handicaps over and over again and point to their origins in wartime service. This was highly precarious to their masculine self-image, since in the Weimar welfare state only a man who could fulfill his role as a breadwinner was deemed a 'real man'. In contrast to the situation after the nineteenth-century wars of liberation and unification, the military service evident in their disability was no longer a generally recognized mark of manliness.[56]

Sabine Kienitz's essay is one example of the variety and contradictions of models of masculinity in the interwar period, a subject also addressed in the essays by Thomas Kühne, Birthe Kundrus and Stefanie Schüler-Springorum. They show that the ideal of 'martial masculinity' that was invoked above all in German-national circles in the Weimar Republic was just one among many. This ideal, which Klaus Theweleit described and interpreted so impressively in his 1980 *Male Fantasies*,[57] arose as part of a postwar culture of war shaped mainly by men, who continued to glorify war as a 'bath of steel' which would turn men 'feminized' by civilian society into tough, self-disciplined and remasculinized warriors.[58] This image was intended to keep alive the 'warrior spirit' and to prepare society mentally for the next war. At the same time, it transported the myth, cultivated at first in the *Freikorps* and the *Reichswehr*[59] and later increasingly also in the many published war memoirs, in war literature and war movies,[60] of the male bonding and comradeship of the front. This image of men was accompanied by demands for a clear complementarity and hierarchy in gender relations. The best-known protagonist of this 'soldierly nationalism' was the writer Ernst Jünger.[61] In recent years, his highly expressive texts have been repeatedly analyzed and interpreted by historians and cultural and literary scholars and cited as evidence of the 'brutalization' of the hegemonic image of masculinity in the Weimar Republic.

The generalized thesis of the dominance of the image of 'martial masculinity' adopts the one-sided perspective of those survivors who, like Ernst Jünger, managed to reinterpret the war, despite military defeat, as an affirmation of their philosophy of life. It does more than simply ignore the destructive emasculating effects of the war for many men, and not just for disabled veterans. It also overlooks competing models of masculinity that emerged at the same time out of the labor, women's, peace, youth, sports, life and sexual reform movements. Men and women close to these future-oriented movements were among those who, as Birthe Kundrus emphasizes in her essay, 'Gender Wars. The First World War and the Construction of Gender Relations in the Weimar Republic,' experienced the war as a radical break, to be sure, but also regarded the defeat and the ensuing establishment of the parliamentary republic as a great opportunity and a new beginning that would facilitate far-reaching reforms in all areas of the economy, society, culture and politics. These hoped-for changes included more comradely relationships between men and women. The terms 'woman as a comrade' and 'comradely marriage' marked this position in contemporary discourse. At the time, these phrases did not mean that man and woman were considered equal. Rather, they too contained the idea of complementarity: men and women were regarded as different 'by nature' and thus 'equally valuable but not the same'. Both were expected to make specific contributions to the economy, society and politics as well as within marriage and the family on the basis of their 'different natures'. What is more, at least from the male perspective, this emphasis on 'different natures' continued to imply a gender hierarchy, as became clearly evident especially in concrete political and social practice.[62]

This position, which was typical of the liberal and left-wing political spectrum of the Weimar Republic, was less influential in the broader society than more conservative views. Many men appear to have regarded even the moderate model of 'comradeship between the sexes' as a challenge to or even an assault on their masculine power and identity, and quite a few women also found it overwhelming. Particularly towards the end of the Weimar Republic, a reactionary climate of opinion asserted itself against the background of a drastic international economic crisis with its unprecedented levels of mass unemployment. In this political context, the experiences of the First World War were increasingly glorified, and the image of the 'iron-hard front soldier' idealized. Calls to 'straighten out' relations between the sexes went hand in hand with this climate, and were expressed in the campaign against so-called dual earners, married women who worked outside the home.[63] This development was intensified by a specific line of continuity in the public processing of the First World War: From the beginning, 'the front and veterans of the front were accorded unrestricted economic, social and cultural priority'[64] not just in memorial services and rituals, literature and films,[65] but also, as mentioned earlier, in social policy measures designed to deal with the consequences of war.[66]

Even alternative models of military masculinity did not fundamentally challenge this national hierarchy of values or the gender order, as Stefanie Schüler-Springorum's contribution 'Flying and Killing. Military Masculinity in German Pilot Literature, 1914 – 1939' demonstrates. She shows how the ideal of the 'heroic airman' emerged amidst the technologization and industrialization of war as an alternative to the image of the 'iron-hard front soldier'.[67] This ideal glorified the pilots of the new elite fighting force as 'knights of the air.' It linked the officer corps' traditional aristocratic values and codes of conduct with modern abilities and behaviors, above all a deft grasp of the newest technology and a playful and athletic casualness that was also expressed in dress and lifestyle. It permitted men not only to retain their individuality amidst mass warfare, but also to become war heroes as individuals. Schüler-Springorum's chronological analysis of the genesis and transformation of the image of the 'heroic airman' in pilot literature shows that its construction tended initially to be an open and heterogeneous process. Each generation of men expressed the image in different ways specific to their time. This very openness seems to have represented part of its attraction, since it made 'the airman' a potential figure of identification for very different men. Depending upon the social and political context, the military or the civilian side of the image would be emphasized more strongly. During the 1920s, however, the image of the airman was also increasingly co-opted by masculinist 'soldierly nationalism'. This began a process that persisted into the 'Third Reich' of erasing the individuality so long emphasized in this image.

Parallel to the creation of a climate of opinion that glorified the front experience of the First World War, the violence of this war experience was 'socialized' within postwar society well beyond the 100,000 professional soldiers to which the imperial army had been reduced. Increasingly, violence became an instrument of politics.[68] This process began in the November Revolution of 1918, when the Majority Social Democratic Party (MSPD) government ordered the deployment of the *Reichswehr* against the workers' and soldiers' councils and the mobilization of the *Freikorps* and citizen guards (*Einwohnerwehren*). It continued with the establishment of paramilitary 'protection units' by almost the entire spectrum of political groupings[69] and the militarization of demonstration culture, including the wearing of uniforms.[70] It culminated in meeting-hall and street terror and political assassinations.[71] It is striking that in all political camps it was mainly younger men who became violent. It was not the generation of war veterans but their younger brothers and sons who largely drove forward a process that ended in the militarization of political culture and the acceptance of violence as a political means.[72] We need to study more closely which factors shaped this process, what role war experience played and what motives inspired the supporters of various political camps who pursued it more or less actively. An important aspect appears to be the growing popularity of an image of men that connoted masculinity with strength and a readiness to fight and regarded a uniform and a military appearance as signs of it. This image, its specific shape and social and political variants, require more precise analysis. Apparently it became popular – and this was new – not just in the national-conservative camp and among supporters of the Nazi Party, but also in growing segments of the Social Democratic and Communist labor movements in the second half of the Weimar Republic. Remarkably, it does not seem to have contradicted the ideal of 'woman as comrade', since this ideal referred primarily to the 'inside world' of marriage and family, while the image of men referred to presence and action in the 'outside world' of politics.

This militarization and brutalization of political culture produced a paradoxical phenomenon that has received little attention from scholars up until now: On the one hand, the Weimar constitution guaranteed women's legal equality for the first time. They were able to vote and stand for election for the first time on 19 January 1919, and in the period that followed attained more influence in all parties, although it soon became evident that the high hopes that both the middle-class and the Social Democratic women's movements had placed in political equality were not to be fulfilled. On the other hand, the transformation of political culture increasingly tended to prevent women from visibly demanding their rights in public space, on the streets. The more the demonstrations and rallies of the second half of the Weimar Republic became uniformed, militarized marches, the more often they ended in violent clashes with political opponents, in veritable street battles, the fewer women appear to have taken part in them. In the course of this transformation of Weimar political culture women were also increasingly excluded from spontaneous protests such as the hunger riots that working-class women, in particular, had used quite successfully during wartime and even, occasionally, after the war.[73] Another consequence of the growing militarization and brutality of political culture was a desire among growing segments of the population for quiet and order, for the exclusion of those who disturbed the peace from the national community. This longing was accompanied by a growing acceptance of the use of force by the state.

The more political debates became irrevocably polarized, and the more bewildering and violent political circumstances became, the stronger the desire for a strong man at the helm of a strong state appears to have become.

These connections between gender-specific experiences of violence and the willingness and ability to engage in violence should be pursued far more carefully by scholars, for the National Socialist movement and state could build on the mental disposition towards and acceptance of violence formed during the Weimar Republic. This could also lead us to a better view of the problems of political and cultural demobilization and mobilization, which are always also problems of demobilizing violence, and of their gender and body history dimensions. In this context we need to study more closely not just the individual experience of wartime violence and how it was processed mentally, but also the collective experience, perception, and processing of public violence during and after the First World War. In order to obtain a complex picture of the contradictory developments during and after the First World War, it seems especially important to keep our eye on the competing forces and movements involved, that is, on both those parts of society that formed the postwar culture of war and those that were committed to international disarmament and peace and opposed on principle to the use of violence.[74] From this 'holistic' perspective, the period between the end of the war in 1918 and the beginning of the war in 1939 would be perceived far more strongly as a conflictual and contradictory post- and pre-war period. This would allow us to pay more attention to the cultural preparations that preceded the Second World War, which were a decisive precondition for the broad and lasting support of huge segments of the German population. If, as Michael Geyer suggested in 1995, the history of war in the narrow sense of the word should be written in future as 'a history of organized deadly force,' a history of killing and being killed, of mass violence and mass death,[75] then the dimension of violence, which was generally exercised and suffered in gender-specific ways, should also be a central focus of a social and gender history of the military and war.[76]

The Second World War

The Second World War, even more obviously than the First, was prepared for long before the conflict itself began. A first striking signal was the reintroduction of universal conscription, in violation of the Treaty of Versailles, in the Defense Law of 21 May 1935, which also provided the legal basis for compulsory service for women. Its introductory stipulations noted that 'in case of war, above and beyond compulsory military service, every German man and every German woman is obliged to serve the fatherland.'[77] A second important signal was the arms buildup policy that began in 1936, accompanied by the introduction of a 'Four Year Plan' and the extension of the state regulation of the economy on the eve of the Second World War. A third signal was the *Mobilmachungsplan für das Heer* regulating the army's preparations for mobilization, which went into effect on 5 October 1937.[78] It was supplemented that same year by the 'Mobilization Book for the Civilian Administrations,' which declared 'the military preparedness of the entire nation' to be the 'prerequisite for the effective defense of the Reich' and called for the 'mobilization of all the nation's personnel and material resources.'[79] Thus from the very beginning the Nazi state and the Wehrmacht planned and prepared the next war as a 'total war'.

Accordingly, the Second World War, far more than the First, was marked by the deployment of large masses of people, the large-scale use of highly developed military technology (tanks, aircraft, artillery and automatic weapons), powerful equipment (particularly motor vehicles of all types) and new communications technology. A rough comparison between the numbers involved in the First and Second World War soon makes the dimensions clear: from 1914 to 1918 thirty-eight states were at war, in which a total of 60–70 million men were called up; from 1939 to 1945, seventy-two states and 80–110 million soldiers were involved.[80] During the First World War, the war zone encompassed a 'mere' ca. four million km^2, in the Second, twenty-two million km^2. During the First World War all of the states combined spent about 208 billion dollars on the direct costs of war, while in the Second the figure was 1,117 billion.[81] Its very dimensions rendered the consequences of the Second World War incomprehensible: eleven million people of different nationalities were murdered in prisons and concentration and extermination camps. While during the First World War a total of some ten million soldiers from all countries involved died, in the Second World War the figure was some thirty-two million. Twenty million disabled veterans after 1918 compared to thirty-five million after 1945. During the First World War around eight million soldiers were taken prisoner, compared to about eighteen million during the Second. Countless civilians died in air raids.[82]

The enormous proportions of the Second World War and its effects resulted from the war's specific character. While the First World War was still shaped by the old, nineteenth-century lines of conflict, and bore strong marks of an imperial war, the Second World War was a war of conquest and annihilation legitimated primarily by racist motives. A murderous will to destruction characterized the Third Reich's conduct of war, which cannot be separated from the Holocaust, as many scholars did for far too long. Omer Bartov has rightly pointed out that the Holocaust could only be carried out within the context of a war of annihilation legitimated by racism.[83] Scholarship is revealing more and more how deeply involved the *Wehrmacht* was in the Holocaust.[84] One of the most horrifying aspects of the 'barbarization of warfare' between 1939 and 1945 is the fact that the *Wehrmacht* was a conscript army. Setting aside the heroic stereotypes of warrior manhood and the comradeship of the front that served as a common substratum, this was an army made up of all sorts of men from the most various regional, social, cultural and political contexts. At the beginning of the war 4.7 million soldiers were called up. Some 17.3 million soldiers joined the German army, air force and navy and 900,000 the Waffen-SS.[85] Not all Wehrmacht soldiers were involved in the murderous logic of the war of annihilation and the Holocaust, but very many participated when confronted with a relevant situation, albeit for different reasons. In his contribution 'Comradeship. Gender Confusion and Gender Order in the German Military, 1918–1945,' Thomas Kühne points to the significance of 'comradeship' for the integration of 'normal' men into the Wehrmacht, and indeed for their exercise of military violence. The model of comradeship could fulfill this function above all because it tended to be open and also to include 'soft', 'womanly' elements of masculinity. On the one hand, this allowed men at the front to communicate verbally about the tensions between the heterosexual norm and the sublimated homosexuality characteristic of any male community, thus safeguarding the men's individual and biographical identities. On the other, it also facilitated communication with those back home, since it incorporated the idea of 'comradeship' between the homeland and the front. This made it easier to symbolically bridge disparate experiences. At the same time, according to Kühne, it functioned as a 'symbolic hinge between violence and harmony, war and peace.' Among other things, it bridged the contradiction between military violence and the civilian norm of non-violence and offered soldiers emotional relief from their violent 'duties' at the front.

Few men tried to escape military service, for example by self-mutilation, or deserted. We know far too little about these groups of men. During the Second World War 10,000 Wehrmacht soldiers alone were convicted of 'self-mutilation' by a military tribunal. More than half of them were sentenced to death. The law on special military tribunals (*Kriegssonderstrafgerichtsordnung*) treated self-mutilation as fulfilling the offense of 'undermining military strength' (*Wehrkraftzersetzung*). Feigning illness for the purpose of avoiding military service either permanently or temporarily also counted as self-mutilation. Allied counter-intelligence appears to have recognized quite early on the opportunity to encourage enemy soldiers to simulate illness or even injure themselves in order to weaken the fighting strength and morale of the German troops. To this end leaflets were distributed beginning in 1940 that contained veiled instructions and advice. The convicted soldiers were mainly very young enlisted men from poor social backgrounds with little education. It is unclear whether they were typical of the men who tried to avoid service in this way, or were simply less adept at deception and were caught for that reason.[86] A much more careful investigation of the group of soldiers who deserted or tried in other ways to avoid military service would be desirable. What motivated them? Who supported them? How did they define their identities as men in wartime and postwar societies that regarded desertion, 'malingering', and self-mutilation as undermining military strength, 'cowardly, unmanly' behavior, and indeed treason?[87]

During the Second World War, more than in the First, the boundary between the front and the homeland was abolished. In a dual sense, the homeland also became a front, a home front without whose support the war could not be won, and a battlefront that was itself imperiled by the war in the form of both bombing raids and Allied ground troops. The political, moral, economic and military significance of the home front for victory increased still further with this erasure of the lines between military and civilian spheres. The leaders of the Nazi state and the Wehrmacht were well aware of this. In order to prevent the homeland's much-feared 'stab in the back', they never fully implemented the compulsory service for women permitted by the Defense Law of 1935. The Nazi state filled the gap left by the male breadwinner's military service far more successfully than the imperial German government had done. In so doing, it sought to preserve even in wartime the model of the 'breadwinner-housewife' family, which also formed a key foundation of the economic and social system and the hierarchical gender order under National Socialism.[88] Accordingly, Nazi propaganda clung to the pre-war model of womanhood, which permitted unmarried but not married 'German women' to work outside the home. The latter were relegated to their duties as housewives and mothers.[89]

As a consequence of this policy, at first mainly young unmarried women were obliged to perform wartime service. The 'Law on the Implementation of Reich Labor Service for Female Youth' of 4 September 1939 stipulated that all girls between seventeen and twenty-five who were not in full-time employment, school, or occupational training and were not needed as 'helping family members' in agriculture must join the Reich Labor Service (RAD). During the first two years of the war they were deployed mainly in agriculture and gardening, as well as in the household and the care of children, the elderly and the sick. With the invasion of the Soviet Union and the opening of a second military front in June 1941 the need for personnel in the armaments industry and the Wehrmacht grew considerably. The numbers of dead and wounded soldiers also rose, and more and more men of military age were conscripted. For that reason the 'Decree on the Further Wartime Deployment of the Reich Labor Service for Female Youth' of 29 June 1941 allowed the use of RAD girls for 'auxiliary war service'. They were now conscripted for twelve months as 'Auxiliary War Service Girls' (*Kriegshilfsdienstmädchen*) and attached to the Wehrmacht. There they worked mainly in clerical and communications positions, increasingly performing tasks previously reserved for soldiers. By the winter of 1941/42 some 150,000 RAD girls were on duty.[90]

For all other women and girls, obligatory war service was facilitated by the Emergency Service Law of 15 October 1938, which regulated the recruitment of workers to 'combat public emergencies'. The first implementation law of 15 September 1939 stipulated that all Germans, both men and women, between the ages of fifteen and seventy were obliged to serve if they did not have two or more children under fifteen at home, were not at least six months pregnant or generally incapable of working. Only employees in the medical professions or other areas essential to the war effort were exempt from this compulsory service. Those who refused to do paid emergency service faced imprisonment or fines.[91] This law was not applied consistently during the early years of the war. For quite some time, compulsory service for adult women was hindered by fears that increasing pressure on them might not just sour the mood on the 'home front' but also, via the military post, affect the morale of the troops.[92] Only in the face of the dramatic defeat of the Wehrmacht at Stalingrad did it become necessary from early 1943 on to mobilize the last reserves for wartime service, which led to the above-cited decree of 13 January 1943.[93] An implementing regulation of 27 January 1943 stipulated that all men between sixteen and sixty-five and all women between seventeen and forty-five had to report to their local employment office for labor service. Exceptions were made for mothers-to-be and women with one pre-school age child or two or more children under fourteen.[94] In a second decree of 29 July of the following year this order was extended to women between forty-five and fifty.[95]

This compulsory service for women between seventeen and fifty without small and school-age children proved necessary, since many of them could not be moved to volunteer for work in the wartime economy. Corresponding recruitment campaigns had had little success, not least because the Nazi state had done such a good job since the beginning of the war in securing the livelihood of soldiers' wives. In contrast to the situation during the First World War, the wives of soldiers received support that allowed them to care for their families without taking on paid work. Moreover, since the guidelines stipulated that family benefits be cut by the amount that women earned, in practice this policy actually encouraged some women to give up paid employment.[96] The Nazi state was, however, highly selective in its support for soldiers' families, in accordance with its racial and class politics. Thus while better off women with children were so well provided for that they did not have to work for money at all during the war and also managed through connections and excuses to avoid compulsory service, as the war went on working-class mothers were forced more and more to do war work. This led to growing dissatisfaction among both civilians and soldiers.[97]

During the war years these labor market and family policies, which were shaped by population and racial policy motives on the one hand[98] and the demands of the wartime economy on the other,[99] were possible only because of the massive deployment of forced laborers who kept the wartime economy going. To be sure, prisoners of war and civilians had already been used as forced labor during the First World War, but in the Second World War compulsory labor attained unprecedented quantitative and qualitative dimensions. By May 1941 some 1,753,500 civilians deported from the occupied countries and 1,316,000 prisoners of war were working in the German wartime economy.[100] Another central component of Nazi wartime policy for the pacification of the home front emerged from the lessons of the First World War. Adequate food supplies at home were ensured at the expense of the conquered and pillaged eastern territories.[101] Most Germans began to suffer from hunger and cold only during the final year of the war, but especially after it was over. This doubtless contributed decisively to stabilizing the mood at home.[102]

It is remarkable that, despite heavy losses at the front and the constant bombing of German cities, Nazi war policy succeeded in maintaining the stability of the home front until the end of the war.[103] According to recent studies, a total of 5.3 million Wehrmacht soldiers were killed during the Second World War. More than 50 per cent of them died on the eastern front, an average of more than 2,000 every day, rising to up to 5,000 in the autumn of 1944. At the front, as at home, exact casualty figures were unavailable, but like the soldiers and officers who experienced death on a daily basis, family members in Germany also heard of the heavy death toll. Almost every family mourned the death of at least one soldier. The increasingly intense mobilization of the last reserves after the invasion of the Soviet Union made the extent of the losses in the final two years of the war abundantly clear.[104] This development, like the massive Allied bombing campaign, which brought destruction and suffering to the cities especially after 1943, increasingly pointed to the hopelessness of the war. Countless people in Germany were made homeless by air raids and many were severely injured. By the end of the war some 410,000 civilians had fallen victim to the bombing.[105] In the final years of the war the necessary air defense measures affected the entire civilian population. Millions of women and men were active in the 'Reich Air Defense Association'. Hundreds of thousands assisted the bombed out, evacuees and refugees as part of 'People's Welfare'[106] and supported the *Kinderlandverschickung*, a program in which five million children from the large and middle-sized cities most at risk from air raids were evacuated to less dangerous parts of the country and cared for there.[107]

But the 'home front' held up, despite the disastrous course of events. Women's persistent readiness to function in the everyday life of wartime and thus to support the 'home front' meant that they bore substantial responsibility for the continuation of the war and with it the racist policy of murder, even if most of them were not actively involved in the regime of terror and extermination.

This connection between the homeland and the front, and with it the issue of women's responsibility and culpability needs to be studied far more closely. The so-called *Historikerinnenstreit* among women historians that began in the late 1980s and revolved around the question of women's role as victims or perpetrators[108] led to a number of research projects on women in National Socialism.[109] Their authors were and are largely concerned to overcome the unproductive 'moral dichotomization' between victims and perpetrators that initially dominated the debate, and to arrive at more complex answers. The objective today is to examine a broad spectrum of behaviors, since social practice in National Socialism was made up 'not just of deliberate deeds, but also of everyday dirty work and shows of approval, of indifference and sympathy, compliance and resistance.' Most women, like most men,

> indeed had a choice of how they wanted to pursue their professional careers and rise socially or not, in which ways they exerted influence on their husbands, sons, daughters, relatives and friends, whom they stood by and whom they

avoided, when they watched or listened with interest and when they consciously looked away or preferred not to have heard something.[110]

The breadth and variety of women's possible behavior during the Second World War is evident among other places in a group of biographical studies.[111] They leave us with an ambivalent picture. What emerges is that even women who were not actively involved in the Nazi system, and indeed at least partially distanced themselves from it, nonetheless bore substantial responsibility for the functioning of the system and the continuation of the war. By focusing their attentions as well as their concerns and activities on their immediate families and friends, they stabilized the home front and with it the front proper. It was precisely the conscious detachment of 'high politics' from 'private everyday life' that rendered their everyday actions political.

A significant number of women also supported the war actively, however. In the Second World War they were deployed for military service to a far greater extent than they had been in the First World War, and not just as 'War Auxiliary Service Girls'. Around 15,000 Red Cross nurses[112] and 450,000 to 500,000 'Wehrmacht auxiliaries' served in the various areas of the military–one woman to every twenty soldiers. Only one-third of these women were performing compulsory service. A central area of deployment was air defense in Germany proper, the so-called *Altreich*, which, except for leadership positions, was largely in the hands of women in 1944/45.[113] What kind of women were they? What motivated them? What role did they play in the Wehrmacht? To what extent were they involved in occupation policy? We cannot answer these questions satisfactorily at the moment. Studying them will also force us to reflect on why women's participation in the *Wehrmacht* was one of the best-repressed subjects in postwar Germany. Did women's involvement perhaps illustrate most clearly the everyday participation of the many?[114]

At present we have neither a study of women's military service that meets current historiographic standards nor a precise investigation of their participation in the Nazi regime of occupation and extermination. Elizabeth Harvey makes a start with her research on the deployment of women in occupied Poland. Her contribution 'Remembering and Repressing. German Women's Recollections of the 'Ethnic Struggle' in Occupied Poland during the Second World War' shows the extent to which 'normal German women' were part of the occupying power and thus of the German society of perpetrators. The women she studies were not obvious perpetrators such as the female employees of the SS troop task forces, SS telecommunications and staff auxiliaries, SS doctors and nurses and SS concentration camp guards.[115] Nor does she look at the spouses who followed their husbands to the occupied regions, such as the many SS wives whose outstanding importance for the functioning of the system of extermination Gudrun Schwarz describes in her book *Eine Frau an seiner Seite. Ehefrauen in der SS-Sippengemeinschaft*. Rather, she analyzes the motives that led young, single 'German women' to go to occupied Poland to work as teachers and counselors for the ethnic German community as part of the 'ethnic struggle' (*Volkstumskampf*) against Poland's 'non-German' population.[116] Harvey makes it clear that these women went to Poland because working within the occupation regime promised them a wider scope of action, more responsibility, and greater privileges than employment in Germany proper. In her exemplary analysis of four interviews, Harvey shows how strongly these women's memories were influenced by their personal biographies on the one hand, and by their individual ways of dealing with the collective memory of the National Socialist period after 1945 on the other. She emphasizes how difficult this makes it to interpret the interviews. Since the women she interviewed still have largely positive memories of their activities in occupied Poland and are not very critical of the work they did, it seems unlikely that they questioned it at the time either. Like many women on the home front, they focused their attention and awareness on their narrow personal interests, daily tasks and duties, and ignored the wider social context.

The occupation regime is an area that, by and large, has only quite recently begun to be studied from the perspective of social history and the history of everyday life. This work has not only drawn attention to the everyday functioning of dictatorship, but also addresses collaboration, defiance, and armed resistance on the part of the occupied, although the gender dimension has not been sufficiently incorporated up until now.[117] One of the first studies devoted to relations between male occupiers and the female occupied is Ebba D. Drolshagen's *Ungeschoren davongekommen. Das Schicksal der Frauen in den besetzten Ländern, die Wehrmachts-soldaten liebten*. Her analysis, however, is limited to the autobiographical recollections of women from Western and Northern Europe.[118] The inclusion of the occupied regions of Eastern Europe would certainly yield a very different, less positive picture, since the concrete occupation policies in northern, southern, and western Europe differed markedly from those applied in the east, less as a result of the respective economic, social and political conditions than of racist images of the enemy and the different objectives that arose from them.

The substantial differences in occupation policy are amply evident in Birgit Beck's contribution 'Rape. The Military Trials of Sexual Crimes

Committed by Soldiers in the Wehrmacht, 1939–1944,' which treats a largely unwritten chapter in the history of war crimes.[119] Even those publications that focus on the many atrocities and other acts of violence committed by the Wehrmacht or the SS in occupied Eastern Europe during the Second World War pay scant attention to acts of sexual violence such as rape and forced prostitution.[120] In her essay, Beck tries to qualify the generalizing view, dominant until now, that German soldiers 'deployed rape systematically in order to spread terror'[121] and that these perpetrators could expect 'to get off scot-free.'[122] By studying Wehrmacht court-martial records she succeeds not just in refuting the thesis that rapes by soldiers went unpunished, but also in showing how differently such offenses were dealt with by military tribunals on the eastern and western fronts, reflecting the respective intentions of occupation policy. She finds that on the western front courts-martial dealt harshly with rapists, passing long prison sentences on German soldiers in part for reasons of discipline, but mainly out of concern for the reputation of the Wehrmacht. On the eastern front, in contrast, far fewer rapes were reported, which reflects not the frequency of such acts of violence but rather the anticipated unwillingness of the authorities to pursue the perpetrators. These few reported cases were also only vigorously punished when military interests appeared to be seriously endangered or the act could be expected to have a negative effect on esprit de corps. On both the eastern and western fronts sentencing was strongly influenced by the racist thinking and gender images of the judges, who primarily represented the interests of the Wehrmacht and its male members. This circumstance is reflected in the more severe punishment of far less serious crimes against property because they were considered to 'undermine military strength.' Beck ultimately concludes that rapes were not part of the 'Nazi strategy of war.' It is to be hoped that further empirical studies will follow that deal more intensively with the problem of sexual violence in the First and Second World War. Until now, such research has succeeded only in fixing in the public mind the mass rapes of German women by soldiers of the Red Army at the end of the war in 1945, which became a portent of defeat and capitulation in the collective memory of the German nation.[123]

The Postwar Period in the Two Germanies

Many Germans experienced the defeat of 1945 as even more traumatic than that of 1918, since it was associated with expulsion, mass flight, and occupation. The Third Reich, the Holocaust, and the racist war of annihilation that was its precondition cast their shadows over all areas of divided

Germany.[124] Postwar society in the two Germanies was marked by a 'stigma of violence.'[125] It was not simply 'a "post-fascist" society,' but also a society marked by the consequences of war. These two aspects were intertwined, but also associated with their own dimensions of meaning and aftereffects.[126] In both Germanies, postwar society focused first of all on destruction, hardship and suffering and how to cope with them practically in everyday life.[127] At the same time, society grappled with the individual and collective perception, recognition, assessment, and processing of wartime and postwar experience. This was the case not least because so much depended on it: one's social and political position, access to limited economic and social resources, and political influence over the shaping of the economy and society.

Subsequently, considerations of the Nazi past and the Second World War in both German states were marked by a 'victimization discourse' conducted on many levels, which split off individual responsibility and culpability and delegated it to 'the German people' as a whole, or at least stylized individual groups of the population as surrogate victims, who explicitly or implicitly entered a 'competition of suffering' with actual victims of the Nazis.[128] Susanne zur Nieden's contribution 'Erotic Fraternization. The Legend of German Women's Quick Surrender' analyzes one example of the 'victimization discourse.' It examines the topos of the *Ami-Liebchen* (Yank sweetheart) which became widespread after the end of the war.[129] This was a term used to refer to German women who had relationships with American soldiers in violation of the US Army ban on 'fraternization'. In the immediate postwar years, these women seem to have become a focus for the rage and shame felt by many Germans. Even in retrospect, they were often judged extremely harshly.[130] The *Ami-Liebchen* was constructed as a negative counter-image to the positive figure of the *Trümmerfrau*, the 'rubble-clearing woman' who symbolized the pragmatic 'can-do' attitude and will to rebuild of the postwar period, which sought to 'cope' with the past by repression and future-oriented activity.[131] Zur Nieden concludes that the myth of German women's quick surrender was a variation on the stab-in-the-back legend of the First World War. In light of the unconditional surrender of the Wehrmacht it was impossible to perpetuate this myth in the old form. The drama of the moral 'stab-in-the-back' of those fighting at the front by those who remained at home was thus rewritten and heightened to apply to the gender question. Her thesis is that this made it possible, despite the unconditional military capitulation, to uphold the image of a stalwartly fighting army that was ultimately defeated, after a long struggle, by the superior strength of its enemies. Certainly the image of the *Ami-Liebchen* offered a means of processing the perilously unbalanced gender order of wartime society. As during the First World War, here, too, the accusation of sexual infidelity directed at women who had stayed home served to rein in the independence they had gained during the war and restrict their scope of action. What is more, men could gain relief by distancing themselves from the humiliation and shame that many of them felt in the face of the mass rapes of German women after the end of the war, given their obvious failure to function as male protectors. They aggressively reversed these feelings and projected them onto those women who voluntarily entered into relationships with occupying soldiers. The precondition for this projection appears, even before the war ended, to have been a displacement of the legitimation for the war. Particularly during the phase of retreat, men were fighting less and less for the 'fatherland' and more and more exclusively to defend 'home' and family.

The 'victimization discourse' dominated other areas of opinion-making in the postwar period as well. Irene Stoehr examines a second example in her contribution 'Cold War Communities. Women's Peace Politics in Postwar (West) Germany, 1945–1952.' She studies the phenomenon of 'female pacifism'[132] in the postwar Germanies. This pacifism, too, was marked by a delegation of responsibility and a simultaneous feeling of women's failure. The conviction that the two world wars were largely the responsibility of men combined with the admission that women had done nothing to stop them. That was also the reason why women in particular must now do everything in their power to prevent another war. This attitude appears to have been consensus across party lines. In conjunction with the initially universal goal of non-partisan cooperation among all women, it not only ensured that most of the women's organizations established or reestablished immediately after 1945 would not refuse former National Socialists as members, but also hindered an active and self-critical confrontation with the Nazi past. In women's peace politics, particularly among western-oriented women's organizations, this stance meant that their arguments proceeded not from the experience of National Socialism and the Second World War, but from the fears of nuclear war, which only became acute in 1945. This approach could also be readily reconciled with the growing exclusion of the German Democratic Women's League, which was deemed 'communist' and continued to stress the close connections between women and peace. Its peace politics emphasized women's interest in peace as mothers. The association of motherliness with peace seems to have fallen on fertile soil, since it permitted women not just to delegate responsibility for the war, but also to maintain solidarity as a community of victims within a conquered people.[133]

It was no accident that the 'victimization discourse' in the two German postwar societies was strongly 'gendered'. There is much evidence that the process of 'gendering' the social order as part of coping with reconstruction and the aftermath of war was pursued more intently after the capitulation of 1945 than after the defeat of 1918. The gender order that had been 'disrupted' during the Second World by the special demands of a society involved in a 'total' war of annihilation had to be redefined after the war, albeit in distinct ways adapted to the different times and the specific situations in the two Germanies. In the West, the family, and the family policy pursued in order to stabilize it, played a decisive role, whose chief objective was the absolute reestablishment of the 'breadwinner-housewife' family. Published discourse glorified the family as a foundation of social reconstruction and a haven of stability 'unsullied' by National Socialism. The churches in particular pursued a policy of re-stabilizing the family and re-christianizing society. Families were supposed to heal the wounds left by war. It was above all the duty of women to integrate men returning from the war and POW camps into the family and, via the family, into a civil society still in the process of reconstruction. Marriage and the family thus became 'private arenas for coping with the aftermath of war.'[134] Although they were scarcely equal to this challenge, as is evident, among other things, in the high divorce rates of the immediate postwar years, the majority held up remarkably well despite all the strains and the violence they had experienced.[135] An important prerequisite for the 'familialization' of West German postwar society in the 1950s was the successful economic reconstruction that allowed a growing number of families to experience the 'breadwinner-housewife' model for the first time in their everyday lives. In East Germany the counter-model of the 'two breadwinner-housewife' family was imposed, primarily owing to economic constraints, but secondarily in accordance with political programs of emancipation.[136]

The lasting consequences for the social position of women have been studied relatively thoroughly, above all for the Federal Republic. Scholars have devoted less attention to the consequences of the Second World War and of postwar developments for the social position of men. Frank Biess's essay 'Men of Reconstruction – The Reconstruction of Men. Returning POWs in East and West Germany, 1945–1955' addresses this question. He focuses on the relationship between coming to terms with the consequences of war and the 'remasculinization' of postwar society.[137] He analyzes this relationship with regard to the two million veterans who returned to the two postwar societies between 1945 and 1955 from battle and Soviet POW camps.[138] By directly comparing East and West, Biess reveals the specific aftereffects of the violent war of annihilation on the two German postwar societies and the respective conditions and opportunities for processing them.[139] He focuses on the one hand on societal perceptions of the returning veterans in East and West Germany, and on the other on the men's reactions to their reception. Biess shows that returning veterans, as 'men in their prime', played a central role as a projection surface for the formulation of a new postwar masculinity. Because veterans returning from the Soviet Union in particular were perceived in both German postwar societies as the population group – apart from ethnic Germans expelled from Eastern Europe – who had been most strongly affected by war and defeat, their successful integration was considered the example *par excellence* of successful coping with the aftermath of war.[140] With their strong will to survive and to rebuild the country they were stylized as models for all men.[141]

One of the central questions that historians have only just begun to ask in this context is whether we can speak of a specific German attitude towards war, the military, and masculinity, and if so, to what extent it was shaped by the experiences of the First World War, but above all by those of the Second World War. As heirs to the Third Reich, both German postwar states struggled to find new models of masculinity appropriate to the most recent past and the altered circumstances of the time, and new heroes who could represent these models. The history of both states includes a process of 'remasculinization' during the 1950s and early 1960s, which appears to have been a key component of the necessary (re)formation of the nation. To what extent was this process intensified in the course of the reintroduction of universal military conscription in the two German states? How far did it go? After all, both German states experienced a mental 'demilitarization' around the same time, which can be located, among other places, in the widespread uneasiness that surrounded rearmament. In West Germany the pacifist protest movements – the 'Count me out movement' (*Ohne-mich-Bewegung*) of the early 1950s, the 'Fight Nuclear War' movement of 1958 with its mass demonstrations, the Easter March movement of the 1960s and 1970s, and the peace movement of the 1980s – are evidence of a profound change in public opinion, at least in the West.[142] In the GDR the establishment of the National People's Army encountered reservations and misgivings among a large segment of young people.[143] The contrast to Imperial Germany and the Weimar era is remarkable: In those periods pacifism was broadly rejected and appeared incompatible with 'true' manliness. This difference signals a far-reaching transformation in Germans' relationship to the nation and the military as well as to hegemonic notions of masculinity that remain to be studied more closely.[144] We must not forget, however, that above all in the West a military and nationalist sub-culture persisted in cultivating the myth of the front soldier and idealizing the Wehrmacht,[145] whose participation in the crimes of the Nazi regime was publicly long denied.[146]

Conclusion

In conclusion, I would like to suggest how a *rewriting* of the history of the era of the world wars would need to be organized as social and thus also as gender history. First, it appears very useful to regard the period before, during, and after both world wars as a single epoch, and to heed the continuities and discontinuities, common ground, and differences. Second, it is important to bring out the ambivalence, ruptures, and contradictions of this period, which can best be achieved with a multi-perspective approach. For this reason, methodological pluralism and (sub)disciplinary openness are key to the study of the military, war, and gender. Third, it has proven productive, particularly in regard to the dimensions of cultural history and the history of experience, to keep long lines of historical development in mind and to compare different periods. Fourth, it is necessary to pursue the history of these two 'total wars' according to Roger Chickering's call for a 'total history'. If we take this rather lofty term down a few pegs and speak instead of an 'integrative history' of the era of the world wars that equally encompasses the economy and society, culture and politics, as well as the military and warfare, then the inclusion of gender history must be self-evident, given that it is far more nowadays than a history of women. 'Gender' is a central 'socio-cultural category' of historical analysis alongside others, without which we cannot possibly understand the dynamic of the historical development of this period, the relationship between 'home' and 'front', or indeed the so-called general political and military development of the era in question. Fifth, and finally, it is about time we began studying the history of the military, war and gender in the twentieth century from a comparative perspective. We need to ask which of the problems and contexts addressed here were specific to Germany, the instigator of the two twentieth-century world wars, and which of them can be observed in quite similar form in the other belligerent nations.[147]

Notes

I would like to thank Pamela Selwyn for her translation and Wilhelm Deist, Stig Förster and Björn Hennings for their critical reading of the manuscript.

In order to keep the notes to a minimum, I will provide only short references (author and year of publication) here for all titles listed in the Selected Bibliography at the end of this volume.

1. *Westermanns Monatshefte* appeared uninterruptedly from 1856 to 1987 and were intended 'primarily to satisfy the popular interest in cultural history.' See Barbara Weiß, *Weiblichkeitsbilder in Zeitschriften zur ästhetischen Erziehung im Nationalsozialismus erarbeitet an 'Westermanns Monatsheften' und 'Koralle,'* MA thesis (Tübingen, 1991), 10ff.
2. 'Der Bunte Bogen,' *Westermanns Monatshefte* 173, vol. 144. (Jan. 1943): 233.
3. Erlaß Hitlers. Umfassender Einsatz von Männern und Frauen für Aufgaben der Reichsverteidigung, 13.1.1943. Reproduced in Gersdorff (1969), 375–377.
4. On Stalingrad see Hettling (1995); Michael Kumpfmüller, *Die Schlacht von Stalingrad. Metamorphosen eines deutschen Mythos* (Munich, 1995).
5. Erlaß Hitlers. Umfassender Einsatz von Männern und Frauen für Aufgaben der Reichsverteidigung, 13.1.1943. Reproduced in Gersdorff (1969), 375–377.
6. 'Der Bunte Bogen,' *Westermanns Monatshefte* 173, vol. 144 (Jan. 1943), 233.
7. See Hagemann (1997) and (2002); Hagemann and Pröve (1998); Quataert (2001); Thébaud (1994); Rupp (1980); and Reder (1998).
8. Foreword to *Westermanns Monatshefte* 79 (Sept. 1934), I–II.
9. Josef Franz Zimmermann, *Die NS-Volkswohlfahrt und das Winter-hilfswerk des Deutschen Volkes als die vom Hauptamt für Volkswohl-fahrt der Reichsleitung der NSDAP betreuten Sozialgemeinschaften des Dritten Reiches* (Würzburg, 1938).
10. See Reder (1998); Quataert (2001).
11. Olaf Groehler, *Bombenkrieg gegen Deutschland* (Berlin, 1990).
12. See Gersdorff (1969); Winkler (1977); Hachtmann (1993); Kundrus (1995), 211–394; Gerber (1996).
13. See u.a. Reese (1989); Koonz (1991); Gehmacher (1998).

14. A number of editions of soldiers' letters home, as well as theoretical and methodological contributions on their analysis, have now been published. Two of the most recent are Ulrich (1994) and Latzel (1997).
15. See Dörr (1998), vol. 2; zur Nieden (1993).
16. See Latzel (1998), 337–352; Jureit (1999).
17. See Thomas Kühne's contribution in this volume as well as Kühne (1996), (1998) and (1999).
18. See Karin Hausen, 'Frauenerwerbstätigkeit und erwerbstätige Frauen. Anmerkungen zur historischen Forschung,' in *Frauen arbeiten. Weibliche Erwerbstätigkeit in Ost- und Westdeutschland nach 1945*, ed. Gunilla-Friederike Budde (Göttingen, 1997), 19–45, 21–24.
19. See Hagemann (1990), 430–445; Rouette (1993) and (1997).
20. Christine Eifler, 'Nachkrieg und weibliche Verletzbarkeit. Zur Rolle von Kriegen für die Konstruktion von Geschlecht,' in Eifler (1999), 155–186, 157.
21. Margaret R. Higonnet and Patrice L.-R. Higonnet, 'The Double Helix,' in Higonnet (1987), 31–50, 39.
22. See Thébaud (1986); Higonnet (1999). More literature on other European countries, mainly Britain and France see the selected bibliography.
23. See for an overview on the research on Germany: most recently: Epkenhans (1998); Hämmerle (2000); Hagemann (2001); Kühne (1999) and (2001); Kundrus (1996), (1999) and (2000); Nonn (2001).
24. Still useful as an introduction to this approach to gender history is Joan W. Scott, *Gender and the Politics of History* (New York, 1988), 2; and 'Gender: A Useful Category of Historical Analysis,' in: ibid., 28–50. On the theoretical and methodological discussion surrounding 'men's history,' see Michael Roper and John Tosh, 'Introduction. Historians and the Politics of Masculinity,' in *Manful Assertions. Masculinities in Britain since 1800*, ed. Roper and Tosh (London, 1991), 1–14; John Tosh (1998), 'What should Historians do with Masculinity,' *History Workshop* 38 (Autum 1994): 179–202. For general literature on the military, war and gender see the selected bibiography in this volume.
25. Roger Chickering, 'Militärgeschichte als Totalgeschichte im Zeitalter des totalen Krieges,' in Kühne and Ziemann (2000), 301–312, 306; see Chickering (1999), 'Total War. The Use and Abuse of a Concept,' in Boemekc (1999), 13–28; Förster (1999).
26. See the 'Total War' conference series organized by the German Historical Institute, which is intended to include five conferences.

The following volumes have already appeared: Förster and Nagler (1997); Boemeke (1999); Chickering and Förster (2000).

27. Stig Förster, 'Der Weltkrieg, 1792–1815. Bewaffnete Konflikte und Revolutionen in der Weltgesellschaft,' in *Kriegsbereitschaft und Friedensordnung in Deutschland 1800–1814*, ed. Jost Dülffer (Münster, 1995), 17–38.

28. David Gates, *Napoleonic Wars 1803–1815* (London and New York, 1997), 272.

29. See Hagemann (2002).

30. For an extensive account see Hagemann (2002).

31. See Stig Förster, ed., *An der Schwelle zum Totalen Krieg. Militärische Fachzeitschriften und die Debatte über den Krieg der Zukunft, 1919– 1939* (Paderborn, 2002).

32. See Bartov (2000).

33. This is revealed particularly strikingly in the debate around postwar society in the two Germanies, whose end is defined completely differently by different scholars. See Klaus Naumann, Einleitung, in Naumann (2001), 9–28; and 'Die Frage nach dem Ende: Von der unbestimmten Dauer der Nachkriegszeit,' *Mittelweg* 36 (1999): 21–32.

34. As introductions to the history of the First World War, see Kocka (1984); Chickering (1998); Ferguson (1999). On the experience of the First World War see, among others, Lipp (1996); Hirschfeld (1997); Ziemann (1997); Koller (2000).

35. On the key term 'hegemonic masculinity,' see Robert W. Connell, *Gender and Power. Society, the Person and Sexual Politics* (Cambridge, 1987), 183–188; and *Masculinities* (Cambridge, 1995).

36. See, among others, Wilhelm Deist, 'Organisationsformen der Heimatfront in beiden Weltkriegen,' in Thoss (2002).

37. See Bernhard R. Kroener, 'Mobilmachungspläne zwischen 1930 und 1939 im Lichte der Erfahrungen des Ersten Weltkrieges,' in Thoss (2002).

38. On the policy of truce (*Burgfrieden*) Wolfgang Kruse, *Krieg und nationale Integration. Eine Neuinterpretation des sozialdemokratischen Burgfriedensschlusses 1914/15* (Essen, 1993); more generally, see Kocka (1984).

39. See, most recently, Verhey (2000).

40. On women's activities during the First World War see, among others, Seidel (1979); Gutmann (1989); Hämmerle (1992) and (1997); Bauer (1995) and (1998); Quataert (2000).

41. See also Maas (2001). For a comparison with Britain and France: Harris (1993); Gullace (1997); Levine (1998); Stovall (1998).

42. On the National Women's Service, see Barbara Greven-Aschoff, *Die bürgerliche Frauenbewegung in Deutschland 1894–1933* (Göttingen 1981), 150–158; Hagemann (1990), 523–528; Kundrus (1995), 98–123.
43. Hagemann (1990), 523ff.
44. See Feldman (1992); on the administrative enforcement of the law and its effects on the female workforce, see Daniel (1997).
45. Gersdorff (1969), 15–37, 26ff.
46. Ibid., 27–30.
47. On the activities of the patriotic women's associations during the wars against Napoleon, see Reder (1998); on later developments, see Quataert (1997), (2000) and (2001); Jakob Vogel, 'Samariter und Schwestern. Geschlechterbilder und -beziehungen im "Deutschen Roten Kreuz" vor dem Ersten Weltkrieg,' in Hagemann and Pröve (1998), 322–344; on the history of the Red Cross see Riesenberger (1992). For a comparison with Britain before 1914, see Summers (1988).
48. On the image of the war nurse see also Schulte (1996). On the British Women's Auxiliary Corps during the First World War: see Grayzel (1997).
49. For an extensive account see Bonzon and Davis (1997).
50. On the activities and perceptions of women on the 'home front' in Britain, see Thom (1998); Kennedy (1999); Lomas (2000).
51. See also Davis (2000); and more generally on gender relations during and after the Second World War, Domansky (1990) and (1996); Thébaud (1994).
52. See Ulrich and Ziemann (1997); Ulrich (1999); Duppler and Groß (1999).
53. Hausen (1987), 128; see also Hausen (1994); Geyer (1983).
54. See Whalen (1984); Hausen (1987) and (1994); Geyer (1983).
55. See also: Kienitz (1999) and (2001). For a comparison with Britain, see Bourke (1996); Cohen (2001); also interesting are studies on 'war neurosis'. See Malleier (1996); Lerner (1996) and (1998).
56. See Hagemann, ed. (2001).
57. See Theweleit (1987).
58. See also Mosse (1990) and (1996).
59. See Theweleit (1980).
60. See among others Prümm (1976); Amberger (1984); Behrenbeck (1996).
61. See among others Seifert (1995); Kämper (2000); Weisbrod (2000).
62. See Hagemann (1990), 325ff and 528ff.

63. See Hagemann (1990), 458–465.
64. Thébaud (1994), 57; See also Bessel (1993).
65. See Benjamin Ziemann, 'Die Erinnerung an den Ersten Weltkrieg in den Milieukulturen der Weimarer Republik,' in Schneider (1999), 249–270, 259–261.
66. See Kundrus (1995), 398–400.
67. See Gabriele Mentges, 'Cold, Coldness, Coolness: Remarks on the Relationship of Dress, Body and Technology,' *Fashion Theory* 4 (2000): 27–48.
68. See Bessel (1991); Weisbrod (1992).
69. See among others: Berghahn (1966); Rohe (1966); Diehl (1977); Ziemann (1998).
70. See Hagemann (1993).
71. See Rosenhaft (1983); Weitz (1997).
72. See Bessel (1995); Schuhmann (2001).
73. See Hagemann (1993).
74. See Davy (1999).
75. See Geyer (1995).
76. See also Schuhmann (1997).
77. Gersdorff (1969), 29.
78. Mobilmachungsplan für das Heer vom 12. März 1937 ('Mob.-Plan Heer'), Berlin 1937, see Gersdorff (1969), 45ff.
79. Mobilmachungsbuch für die Zivilverwaltungen (Berlin, 1939) (reprint).
80. Rüdiger Overmans, 'In der Hand des Feindes'. Geschichtschreibung zur Kriegsgefangenschaft von der Antike bis zu Zweiten Weltkrieg, in Overmanns (1999), ed., 1–19, 7 and 15.
81. Zweiter Weltkrieg, *Wörterbuch zur Deutschen Militärgeschichte*, vol. 2 (Berlin, 1985), 1072–1088, 1087.
82. See Zweiter Weltkrieg, 1087.
83. See Bartov (1997).
84. See Bartov (1991); Browning (1992); Heer and Naumann (1995); Herbert (1998); Müller and Volkmann (1999); Pohl (1999).
85. See Overmans (1999), Verluste, 293.
86. See Seidler (1977), 233–277.
87. See Wette (1995); Benjamin Ziemann, 'Flüchten aus dem Konsens zum Durchhalten. Ergebnisse, Probleme und Perspektiven der Erforschung soldatischer Verweigerungsformen in der Wehrmacht 1939–1945,' in Müller and Volkmann (1999), 589–613; on the Second World War: Jahr (1998); in general: Bröckling and Sikora (1998).
88. See Kundrus (1995), 322–351, and (1997); Pine (1997).

89. See Rupp (1980); Irmgard Weyrather, *Muttertag und Mutterkreuz. Der Kult um die 'deutsche Mutter' im Nationalsozialismus* (Frankfurt a.m., 1993); Pine (1997); Heinemann (2001).
90. See Seidler (1977), 44–50. See auch Seidler (1979).
91. See Seidler (1977), 46f.
92. See Kroener (1988), 772.
93. Erlaß Hitlers. Umfassender Einsatz von Männern und Frauen für Aufgaben der Reichsverteidigung, 13.1.1943, reproduced in Gersdorff (1969), 375–377.
94. Verordnung über die Meldung von Männern und Frauen für Aufgaben der Reichsverteidigung, 27.1.1943, *Reichsgesetzblatt* (1943): 67. For an extensive account of the potentials and limits of women's deployment in the wartime economy during the Nazi period, see Gersdorff (1969); Winkler (1977); Hachtmann (1993); Gerber (1996). On the First World War: Daniel (1997).
95. Letter from the Reich Minister and head of the Reich Chancellery, 'Erweiterung der Meldepflicht für Frauen,' 29 July 1944, reproduced in Gersdorff (1969), 430.
96. See Kroener (1988), 770ff; Kundrus (1995), 245–296.
97. See Gersdorff (1969), 56–60 and 342–349; Rupp (1980).
98. See, in particular, Gisela Bock, 'Frauen und Geschlechterbeziehungen in der nationalsozialistischen Rassenpolitik,' in Wobbe (1992), 99–134; Bock (1986).
99. On this see Pine (1997); Hachtmann (1993).
100. See Kroener (1998), 774f; Herbert (1985) and (1991); Spanger (1999).
101. On occupation policy as economic policy, see Gerlach (1999); on the war in the East and the plunder that took place there, see also Boog (1983); on its significance for the wartime economy, see: Kroener (1988) and (1999); Heer (1999).
102. On this see Deist (forthcoming 2002).
103. See Kundrus (1997).
104. Overmans (1999), 294, 303.
105. See *Zweiter Weltkrieg*, 1087.
106. See Michael Krause, *Flucht vor dem Bombenkrieg, 'Umquartierungen' im Zweiten Weltkrieg und die Wiedereingliederung der Evakuierten in Deutschland 1943–1963* (Düsseldorf, 1997).
107. See Kock (1997).
108. For overviews of the *Historikerinnenstreit*, see Dagmar Reese and Carola Sachse, 'Frauenforschung zum Nationalsozialismus. Eine Bilanz,' in Gravenhorst and Tatschmurat (1990), 73–106; Saldern

(1994); Ulrike Weckel et al., *Einleitung*, in Heinsohn et al. (1997), 7–23.

109. For a recent overview of the literature on women in National Socialism, Kundrus (1996) and (2000).

110. Weckel et al (1997), 12.

111. See zur Nieden (1993); Hammer and zur Nieden (1992); Dörr 1998.

112. Kroener (1999), 835.

113. See Gersdorff (1969), 49–77; Seidler (1972), 35–202; Tuten (1982); Willmot (1985); Zipfel (1995); Kundrus (1999); Hagemann (2002), *Militäreinsatz*. For a comparison on women's military service in Britain, see Stone (1999); Summerfield and Peniston (2000).

114. See Zipfel (1997).

115. See Ebbinghaus (1987).

116. See also Harvey (1998); Stephenson (1981), 190–193; Wobbe (1992).

117. See Chiari (1998); for a review of the literature see Chiari (1995). For an example of an analysis that integrates the gender dimension, see Bunting (1996). On the role of women in the armed resistance in Eastern Europe, see Strobl (1989).

118. See Drolshagen (1998). The German title *Ungeschoren davongekommen* is a play on words, meaning both 'escaped unscathed' and 'escaped unshorn,' a reference to the practice of shaving the heads of women in occupied countries who were believed to have had relationships with German soldiers.

119. See also Beck (1996) and (1999).

120. On (forced) prostitution, see Seidler (1977), 135–192; Paul (1994); Meinen (1999).

121. Brownmiller (1976).

122. Sander and Johr (1995), 70.

123. See Sander and Johr (1995); Teo (1996); Grossmann (1998); Mühlhäuser (1999) and: 'Vergewaltigung in Deutschland 1945. Nationaler Opferdiskurs und individuelles Erinnern,' in Naumann (2001), 384–408; Petö (1999).

124. See among others Rosenthal (1987); Danyel (1995); Barnouw (1996); Frei (1996); Domansky (1997); Herf (1997); Hartmann (1999); Moeller (1996) and (2001).

125. Geyer (1995).

126. Naumann (2001), 9.

127. Particularly on women's everyday lives after 1945 see Meyer and Schulze (1985), *Wie wir das alles*, and (1985), *Von Liebe*; Bandhauer-Schöffmann and Hornung (1990); Baumgartner (1994); Berger and

Holler (1994); Neumann (1998). For comparison with other European countries: Duchen and Bandhauer-Schoffmann (2000).

128. See most recently, Moeller (2001); sowie: Svenja Goltermann, 'Im Wahn der Gewalt. Massentod, Opferdiskurs und Psychiatrie 1945–1956, in Naumann (2001), 343–363.

129. See also Boyer and Woller (1983); Bauer (1996); Domentat (1998); Heide Fehrenbach, '"Ami-Liebchen" und "Mischlingskinder". Rasse, Geschlecht und Kultur in der deutsch-amerikanischen Begegnung,' in Naumann (2001), 178–205.

130. See Lutz Niethammer, 'Heimat und Front,' in *'Die Jahre weiß man nicht, wo man die heute hinsetzen soll.' Faschismuserfahrungen im Ruhrgebiet. Lebensgeschichte und Sozialkultur im Ruhrgebiet 1930 bis 1960,* ed. Niethammer and Alexander von Plato, vol. 1 (Berlin, 1983), 163–232, 229; Domentat (1998), 182–200.

131. On the many-layered image of the 'Trümmerfrau,' see Berger and Holler (1994); but in particular Bandauer-Schöffmann and Hornung (1999).

132. See Annette Kuhn, 'Frauen suchen neue Wege der Politik,' in *Frauen in der deutschen Nachkriegszeit*, ed. Kuhn, vol. 2 (Düsseldorf, 1986).

133. On women's politics after the war see also Möding (1988); Genth (1996); Stoehr (1997) and: 'Phalanx der Frauen? Wiederaufrüstung und Weiblichkeit in Westdeutschland 1950–1957,' in Eifler and Seifert (1999), 187–205.

134. Naumann (2001), 25.

135. On inner–familial tensions and how they were processed publicly, see Franka Schneider, '"Einigkeit im Unglück"? Berliner Eheberatungsstellen zwischen Ehekrise und Wiederaufbau,' in Naumann (2001), 206–226.

136. See above all Gesine Obertreis, *Familienpolitik in der DDR 1945–1980* (Opladen, 1986); Klaus-Jörg Ruhl, *Verordnete Unterordnung. Berufstätige Frauen zwischen Wirtschaftswachstum und konservativer Ideologie in der Nachkriegszeit (1945–1963)* (Munich, 1994); Moeller (1997); Elisabeth Heinemann, *What Difference does a Husband Make? Women and Marital Status in Nazi and Postwar German* (Berkeley, 1999); Lukas Rolli-Alkemper, *Familie im Wiederaufbau. Katholizismus und bürgerliches Familienideal in der Bundesrepublik Deutschland, 1945–1965* (Paderborn, 2000).

137. In her study of the USA after the Vietnam War Susan Jeffords defines 'remasculinization' as 'regeneration of the concepts, constructions, and definitions of masculinity . . . and of the gender

system for which [they are] formulated.' See Jeffords (1989), 51; see also Robert Moeller , 'The "Remasculinization" of Germany: An Introduction,' *SIGNS* 24 (1998): 101–106; Fehrenbach (1998); Poiger (1998) and: 'Krise der Männlichkeit. Remaskulinisierung in beiden deutschen Nachkriegsgesellschaften,' in Naumann (2001), 227–266.

138. On prisoners of war and returning veterans after 1945 see also Biess (1999), (2000) and (2001); and: '"Russenknechte" und "Westagenten". Kriegsheimkehrer und die (De)Legitimierung von Kriegsgefangenschaftserfahrungen in Ost- und Westdeutschland nach 1945,' in Naumann (2001), 59–89; Moeller (1998); Goltermann (1999); Hilger (2000).

139. Klaus Naumann, 'Nachkrieg: Vernichtungskrieg, Wehrmacht und Militär in der deutschen Wahrnehmung nach 1945,' *Mittelweg 36*, 7 (1997): 1–16; Geyer (1995).

140. More recent work on the social history of the postwar period, however, revises the dominant picture of the 'quick integration' of the expelled in West Germany. See Paul Lüttinger, 'Der Mythos der schnellen Integration. Eine empirische Analyse zur Integration der Vertriebenen,' *Zeitschrift für Soziologie* 15 (1987): 20–36; Michael Schwartz, 'Vertreibung und Vergangenheitspolitik. Ein Versuch über geteilte deutsche Nachkriegsidentitäten,' *Deutschland Archiv* 30 (1997): 177–195; on war veterans and victims after 1945: Diehl (1993) and (1997). As a general overview on the research see: Anselm Doering-Manteuffel, 'Deutsche Zeitgeschichte nach 1945. Entwicklung und Problemlagen der historischen Forschung,' *Vierteljahreshefte für Zeitgeschichte* 41 (1993): 1–29.

141. On this see also Moeller (1998); and his contribution 'Heimkehr ins Vaterland. Die Remaskulinisierung Westdeutschlands in den fünfziger Jahren,' in Hagemann (2001), Nach – Kriegs – Helden.

142. See Michael Geyer, 'Der Kalte Krieg, die Deutschen und die Angst. Die westdeutsche Opposition gegen die Wiederbewaffnung und Kernwaffen,' in Naumann (2002), 267–318. On the anti-militarist opposition in West Germany more generally, see Fritz Krause, *Antimilitaristische Opposition in der BRD 1949–55* (Frankfurt a.M.,1971).

143. See Mary Fulbrook, *Anatomy of a Dictatorship. Inside the GDR 1949–1989* (Oxford, 1995), 135–136.

144. For more on these reflections see Richard Bessel, 'Was bleibt vom Krieg? Deutsche Nachkriegsgeschichte(n) aus geschlechtergeschichtlicher Perspektive – Eine Einführung,' in Hagemann (2002), Nach – Kriegs – Helden; Kühne (2000), Von der Kriegskultur.

145. On the image of the front soldier in the illustrated magazines, see Schornstheimer (1995); in war novels: Klaus F. Geiger, *Kriegsromane in der BRD*. *Inhalt und Funktionen* (Tübingen, 1974); on the subculture of Wehrmacht veterans, see Diehl (1993); Jörg Echternkamp, 'Mit dem Krieg seinen Frieden schließen – Wehrmacht und Weltkrieg in der Veteranenkultur (1945–1960),' in Kühne (2000), Kriegskultur, 80–95; Alaric Searle, 'Veterans' Associations and Political Radicalism in West Germany, 1951–54. A Case Study,' *Canadian Journal of History* 8 (1999): 221–248.
146. How long-lived the myth of the 'clean Wehrmacht' was is evident among other things in the continuing controversy over the exhibition on the Wehrmacht mounted by the Hamburg Institut für Sozialforschung, on this, see Thiele (1997); Klundt (2000).
147. As an attempt at comparison see Thebaud (1994); also stimulating are Higonnet and Higonnet (1987); and Joan W. Scott, 'Rewriting History,' in Higonnet (1987), 31–50. For an initial overview of the important studies on the military, war and gender in France, Britain and the United States see the Selected Bibliography.

Ready for War?

Conceptions of Military Manliness in the Prusso-German Officer Corps before the First World War

Marcus Funck

At first glance it all appears quite simple. Whether it be in the most dramatic and bombastic metaphorical language in the glossy literature of the Wilhelmine period or the sarcastic, harshly drawn caricatures and satires of *Simplicissmus*, contemporary German representations of the Wilhelmine officer portray the stereotypical eternal lieutenant: tall and tightly fitted, in a perfect, self-assured stance with a dashing coolness in the facial expression, which is strengthened by the Caesarean nose with a monocle resting upon it. The outer uniformed appearance reflects the inner composure, which is the unmistakable aristocratic nature of the officer. This disposition was based upon a solid set of aristocratic and military virtues that supposedly went back generations: princely loyalty and patriotism, a natural gift for leadership and willpower, discipline and sense of duty, fearlessness of death and heroic courage, composure and honorableness. These virtues, to which the officers corps and to a growing extent the entire male society were subjugated, were held together by the idea of military manliness. The public officer was an exclusive object of art, a *Gesamtkunstwerk*,[1] which had to be reinforced and newly created by a continous stream of homogenous depictions, which were in stark contrast to the non-officer and the ordinary man. Before taking a second look at the matter, it is important to state that this Wilhelmine officer never existed in its purest form, but contemporaries and even historians have drowned themselves in the flood of words and pictures found in the numerous self-depictions and contemporary accounts.[2]

As strong as this image of the Wilhelmine officer still is today, at the time it was frail and disputed. Aside from the various military and socio-cultural traditions of the regimental milieus, there was an increasing differentiation and specialization throughout the entire officer corps. This in turn brought about a reorganization within the hierarchy of military planners and decision-makers, placing the General Staff officers at the top. Equally important, a broadening of the recruitment base, i.e. the repercussions of universal conscription, and the mechanization of warfare were decisive factors within the army for the development of rival concepts of the officer in the individual units in the German Empire. Furthermore, the officer and his caricature moved from the periphery, where they had been banished (due in part to self-denial) into the 1860s, to the center of the Wilhelmine society. A drawback to the popularization of the officer, following the Wars of German Unification in 1864, 1866 and 1870/71, was that their position – certainly with heavy limitations like the position of the Kaiser as commander-in-chief – was publicly open to discussion and thus open to attack.[3] The officer became an object of all sorts of attributions, a projection surface for wishes and desires, fears and aversions, hopes and expectations. At the same time a subject and object of public yearning, the officer had a theatrical responsibility along with his military work. These roles, even if they pleased him, could also be thrust upon him by the non-military society.

Lying to rest firstly the idea of the Prusso-German officer corps before 1914 as a homogenous block extracted from the historical transformation, as a *rocher de bronze*,[4] a door to new research perspectives is opened. The gradual disintegration of the homogenous officer's world created sources of friction within the corps. This spurred rivalries as well as a general need among the officers for role model after which they could orient themselves, and, consequently, the possibility of new hegemonies opened up. This leads us to three levels of investigation, which conform to the general discussions of men's history.[5]

While it was by no means certain that the concept of the aristocratic Prussian officer could impose itself upon the entire German Empire after 1870-71 due to regional resistance[6], a concept of military manliness that was based on the principle of social inequality did prevail – also among men – as the highest form of justice; one officer was not equal to another officer, one man was not equal to another man. Beyond the description of this concept, it is necessary to look for its respective attractiveness to various military and social groups. The plausibility and appeal of this essentially aristocratic officer's concept for a significant portion of bourgeois society appears at first to be the result of a much more complex tapestry of conditions, as the theory of bourgeois re-feudalization suggests.[7] On the other hand this concept was in no way steadfast, rather it was subject to the ever-changing dynamics of bourgeois and masculine society of the German Empire. The predominant image of the aristocratic officer was only able to sustain itself as long as the military and civil society believed in its superiority.

This reveals a general fragility in the concept of manliness and, in the case of pre-First World War military manliness, potential sources of friction, which resulted from different interpretations by aristocratic and bourgeois officer groups. Moreover, this was a result of differences between the cultural model and the subjective experiences in everyday social life. The well-known example of the Eulenburg Scandal in 1907/8, which heightened the lesser-known smoldering crisis in the masculine military society, demonstrates the existence of rivaling concepts as well as the softening and breaking up of an apparently rigid hierarchy of masculinities. This hierarchical reorganization of images of masculinity, i.e. the 'turn to toughness', did not mean that all the elements of the Prussian-aristocratic design had become passé. Quite the opposite occurred with a number of them being smoothly integrated, while others simply fell away. In the first decade of the twentieth century one finds a highly charged mixture of differing concepts of manliness, whose representatives were no longer distinguishable along the conventional social lines between the nobility and the bourgeoisie.

Not only written descriptions, but also the experience of manhood in everyday life should receive our attention. It is not enough to simply analyze the literary production of images and stereotypes of masculinity. Investigating the practice of adopting and portraying manhood and taking seriously the differing, deviant, and even alternative behavior will open up new perspectives on the so-called hegemonic masculinities. From behind the rigid surface of the Wilhelmine officer, an amazing multitude of behavioral patterns comes to light. Taking a look at the officer's casinos or at everyday regimental life, the contours of the stereotypical dichotomy of gender roles – hardened, invulnerable masculinity here and domestic femininity over there – becomes unclear. Additionally, ascribing gender roles becomes rather questionable, especially when one considers that officer's wives were not denied entry into the barracks and played a significant role in the social life of the regimental officer. With the equally important inclusion of reciprocal relationships between structural conditions and social actions, not only the gender concepts of contemporaries will be examined, but also the suitability of static models of historical interpretation. Thus, it becomes clear that the images of gender depicted in the literature were fragile and constantly threatened and, consequently, military masculinity had to be continually renewed and stabilized. On the other hand, if there is no correspondence between the contemporary images of gender and what we know of everyday behavior during the period, doubts as to the value of purely historical discourse analysis arise.

In this article I will build up a two-pronged base of sources. The use of normative literature makes possible an organization of detailed data on the production of the reigning official images of military masculinity. This includes the semi-official and official *Standespflichten* from the highest cabinet order to the multitude of informational brochures from the military publishing machinery, as well as from non-governmental distribution agencies. Still, the range of explanation offered by these sources is limited. In order to gain a view of social practices as well as subjective experiences and, consequently, deviations from the norm, it is imperative to utilize all types of written sources from the contemporaries themselves. Having said this, I have supported my research primarily with autobiographical literature. The stylization in the autobiographies offers valuable information about the day-to-day life of the officer, which is seldom found in the semi-official and official documents. Furthermore, they present the historian with a glimpse into the military society from the writer's point of view.[8]

In the new and innovative literature on Prusso-German military history, and in particular the work on the history of military masculinity, officers play only a secondary role.[9] Studies of the 'ordinary man' in the wave of 'military history from below', as well as in studies of the military and social consequences following the introduction of conscription in Germany during the nineteenth century, have experienced a flux in recent years. Along with studies of the production of war images and concepts of masculinity that were largely created by the educated middle-class, these areas of research have taken priority. This has been in large part due to an obvious need to catch up in these areas. However, a two-folded discrepancy has arisen, which can certainly not be corrected in this article alone. Firstly, the extensive new developments in military history in Germany have, until now, only partially handled the officer corps as a subject of research. Their history has been based on studies that have become classics in the field and follow very conventional methods and lines of argument. Important starting points for new interpretations, however, have at this point only marginally been accepted and have been routinely placed in appendices.[10] Secondly, in some studies of the 'ordinary man' in the military and war, it is often completely forgotten that the military organization is a strict hierarchy based on the interaction of discipline and obedience. Of course, today no serious historian would want to maintain that the 'spirit of the army' rested in its officers. For the pre-1914 times, however, it is obvious that the aura surrounding the military was strongly marked by the image of the officer. The above-mentioned 'catalogue of military virtues' had, for example, its social and cultural base in the officer corps before it found entry into other military and bourgeois social groups.

'At the Court and in the Field': The Officer as an Aristocrat

In the search for aristocratic traditions in the officer corps and a specific aristocratic concept of the officer, it makes sense to begin with the Guards regiments, which had rather close ties to the court. However, this should not lead one to draw general conclusions on the officer corps based on the particular case of the Prussian Guards. In his reminiscence of the Franco-German War, which he experienced as commander of the Guard's artillery, the aristocratic Prince Kraft zu Hohenlohe-Ingelfingen comments on the infantry captain von Chappius in the Kaiser Franz Guard-Grenadiers. He describes how the captain, under heavy artillery fire, '[. . .] went fully erect in an elegant pace, as if he was leading the dance at court, up and down, one could clearly recognize his figure, and [. . . exhorted] his men to remain calmly lying down, to calmly take aim and shoot'.[11] In fact, von Chappius pursued a double carrier as premier dancer at the Potsdam court and as an officer in Berlin. Kaiser William I is supposed to have sent von Chappius into the field in January 1864 with the words, 'My dear Chappius, you were always the first one here on the parquet, you will also be the first in the sconce.'[12] Such anecdotal peace-time stories of war lead us directly to the center of the aristocratic military code: military service was understood as royal service and, consequently, professional military and courtly behavior did not hinder each other, rather they were understood as one and the same. The learning and mastering of this distinct code as part of a proper upbringing or military sociability was considered an indispensable condition for an officer's carrier. It contained everything that appeared to be the defining elements of the officer. The image of the officer, standing upright and dancing, under enemy fire and in front of the soldiers, who were lying on the ground, presented an impressive display of certainty and honorableness, intrepidity and willpower, strong leadership qualities and superiority. This ensemble of values made the officer not only capable in war but equally acceptable for the court, separating him, as a warrior, from the female gender and, as a courtier, from the mass of soldiers. Through this distinction, he was allowed to claim a special position in both the female and male society.

This model of doubled gender inequality ran through a multitude of accepted behavioral codes for the officers, as can be found in its original formulation in the *Einleitungsordre zur Ehrengerichts-Verordnung* of May 2, 1874.[13] The basis and point of orientation of this order was the officer's special *point d' honneur*, which was drawn from the 'tried and tested traditions in the chivalric sense of the officer class'. Aside from the references to damage done to 'military competence' and to the cracks in the base of the aristocratic officer through a 'softening up of the way of life', which William I suspected as resulting from luxurious consumption outside of the court, the order offers no concrete indications as to the gender of the *point d' honneur* or its military meaning; these are taken for granted as a given. In this document, the general guidelines for an officer corps in their transition from war to peace were laid out. The interpretation of these guidelines was taken up by countless semi-professional interpreters inside and outside the officer corps.[14] Under the title 'The Officer: Modern Knighthood', in 1889 the *Militär-Wochenblatt* tried in the spirit of the 1874 order not only to define this distinguished chivalry, but also to present specific behavioral guidelines for social occasions. With reference to Scheibert's much published, decisive *Officer's Brevier*:

> Nothing is more becoming of the young officer than a clever, moral courteous behavior in social dealings with the beautiful gender, to whom he offers his adoration with knightly veneration. The women are for him supposedly untouchable creations; but he holds himself back shyly from the untouchables; [. . .] The helpless lady, who entrusts herself to his protection, as a man of honor, would be just as safe inside the walls of an abbey. He is equally polite, tender and attentive towards the simple middle class woman and the blossom of aristocracy, as well as towards the old matron and the young sprouting bud of girlhood. In more than 20 battles and skirmishes, my experiences have shown that the merry dancers of the ballroom were also the best and most exquisite leaders in the bloody dance of war.[15]

Competence in war resulted from a combination of military achievement and distinguished sociability, also with the female gender. One was unthinkable without the other. In the officer's world, built up around the aristocracy, the man of honor was at the same time a protector and admirer of the lady. The service in peace and war was, at the end of the day, a modern form of knightly homage to the unattainable lady; for the accessible woman (die 'Antastbaren', das 'Weib') remained only contempt and sexual use. An inner military counterpart to this was the camaraderie among the officers. It was the specifically male aristocratic officer's honor that should regulate and control the dealings 'between the son of a count or prince and a subordinate civil servant or trader [. . .] between an 18 year-old and 33 year-old lieutenant'. In view of the expansion of the recruitment basis and the functional differentiation of the officer corps, a reminder of the earlier self-evident truths appears to have been necessary. According to the view the officers had of themselves, it was certain that the individual officer stood under a banner of comradeship as a potentially equal member of the privileged class of men: 'With the same responsibilities and dispositions, based on equal honor and similar upbringing they are all socially equal.' Also according to the Wilhelmine aristocratic officer's concept, comradeship had the function of a motor in building a closed male community,[16] but, of course, only the socially acceptable men were included.

In strict distinction to the non-officer ranks, all facets of the inner relationship among the officers was regulated by varying degrees of intimacy and distance, thus making possible behavior that would have been unthinkable outside the aristocratic military sphere. In his autobiography, the Saxon lieutenant in the King's Regiment 100, Arnold Vieth von Golßenau, remembered a special ball held in the officer's mess of his Dresden Regiment around 1900:

> The tall orderly brought the champagne bucket, in which there were two bottles, and set the tall glasses before us. Every one of our officers had his own large glass in the casino, on which his coat of arms was engraved and with his name on the base (. . .). An orderly came running and bowed to Ehrenthal with his hands pressed against the seams of his trousers: 'Herr Lieutenant Graf of Münster-Langelage is drinking to Herr Lieutenant and his banquet.' (. . .) In the hall, a few had risen and were standing around with their glasses in hand. As a waltz began, the Lieutenant von Tschammer and Osten came to me in hard footsteps: 'Do you dance?' Seydewitz and Hauk were already dancing. It was always the best dancers who began to dance at the banquets in order to be seen by the older officers; we did not think very much of their old-fashioned style of dancing.[17]

All male dance evenings were, at least in regiments at court, not at all unusual.[18] In such aristocratically molded luxury regiments, the male body could be put on display among equals without getting into difficulties, but not in public. The reason for this is found in the idea of the aristocratic officer's body as a sex-free zone and its disassociation from sexually loaded masculinity: Whoever was a *Herr* and an officer did not have to prove himself as a man and was not permitted to engage in emotional dilemmas. Controlled by the genuine aristocratic code of behavior, the officer was able to move freely between the contexts of court life and the military without having to continually check his sexualized mascul-inity.[19] What counted as unmanly or even homosexual by moral codes in the civilian middle-class society and in any case as behavior unfit for war was, in fact, nothing more than a transference of the dancing military officers' behavior onto the context of peaceful circumstances. What appears to us today as a paradox – the unity of military professionalism and neo-feudal representation – was self-evident for the aristocratic officer. In 1893 the young regimental adjutant Friedrich von der Schulen-burg sneered at the 'wild dancing that numbs the intellect'[20] at the court; however, he used this central location of social life to secure his personal image and military advancement. After being called to the General Staff in 1899, his further career stages as military attaché in London (1904), commander of the regiment Garde du Corps (1913), and Chief of the General Staff of the Crown Prince Army Group (1916) show that he knew how to smoothly integrate aristocratic habitude and professional military work.

Obviously, the officers did not only dance with their equals, even though according to their self-portrayals they stayed, for the most part, amongst themselves. The frequency and intensity with which wives were mentioned in the autobiographies was far behind that of the officers' favorite horses and, at best, they were described as 'best friend and comrade'.[21] The forced absence of women contrasts with the valuation of military service as a service for women.

Contrary to the retrospective marginalization of the officers' wives in everyday social life and the limitation of their activities to the realm of charity, the wives and daughters, especially those of the older officers, used the possibilities available to them to influence the non-military everyday life within the military. There was multitude of occasions for controlled social encounters between the sexes: court and society balls, regiment banquets and receptions. The conventions of the aristocratic concept of military masculinity required active social cooperation also on the part of women in regimental affairs. But this did not mean that the division of men and women described by Ute Frevert as an integral part of nineteenth-century bourgeois society would be permanently dis-mantled.[22] The regiment, the actual social and cultural point of reference of the aristocratic officer's concept, was thought of as an extended family comprised of the officers and their families. The officers' wives and daughters ran the house and represented the masculine officer corps outside of the professional military sphere. They were thus considered, in their special function, as members of the regiment. Given the significance of social life for the officers' careers, it is no wonder that the wives could intervene in judgments of taste and personal decisions. The house of the commander was a marriage market and a place of social observation and scrutiny. In the military humoresque 'Die Frau Oberst' from 1914, the writer, Freiherr von Schlicht, presents a *commandante* who goes behind the back of her husband, the regimental commander, to transform the awkward association between her daughter and a lieutenant of the regiment into a class-befitting engagement. Confronted with accusations from her husband, 'the Frau Oberst scolded her husband for punishing one of his officers without notifying her, for she, as *commandante*, was the next to know what was happening in the regiment'.[23] Inversely, if an officer over-involved himself in intrigues with the ladies and went against this strict etiquette, it could cost him his career regardless of the military qualities he had to offer. A heightened nervousness overcame the officers not only in the moment of truth when they were invited to a social event at the commander's house or even to the court, but also when the officer's casino was opened to women.[24] It was the ladies, the officers' wives and daughters, who carefully oversaw the affair, making sure that the cotillion and quadrille were performed properly.[25] In a few cases, the highborn ladies were even allowed to break through the strict polarity of the gender order. Ladies from princely houses, for example, who presided at official events as 'owner' of the regiment wore the regiment uniform. Of all people, the 'Empress Friedrich', a suspected liberal who was not very highly respected in Prussian officer's circles, attracted attention to herself by wearing the hussar uniform of her regiment.[26] Many officers' wives were invited to take part in the frequent official and unofficial regiment hunting trips, where they not only wore uniforms, but also participated in the hunt in order to display their shooting skills.[27] Secured by the strict conventions, the aristocratic concept of the officer and of masculinity integrated women with the appropriate behavior and status with the expectation that they implement the behavioral code and report offences of the code, and thus stabilize the system of double gender inequality.

While the mixed-gender company in the officers' social circles was earlier regulated by genuine aristocratic convention, this was no longer possible after the massive entry of the bourgeoisie into the officer corps. In official and semi-official brochures, officers' wives of questionable class standing were offered advice as to the organization of everyday life among the officer's ranks, which included information on everything from arranging formal balls and dinners to recipes. Even the *Deutsches Offiziersblatt* published by the *Deutscher Offiziersverein* included from 1897 onwards the section, 'The Practical Officer's Wife'. What had earlier been attained simply by origin was now a form of knowledge that had to be learned by heart. To the dismay of a number of officers, there was a noticeable fall in regimental sociability; far more decisive, however, was the re-shaping of military masculinity connected to this. Certainly, one can find enough examples from the everyday experience of the officer, especially from those stationed in garrisons in larger cities, who had contradicted the aristocratic concept of gender relations much earlier. Breaking away from sexual inhibitions such as masturbation, brothel visits and adultery (although not with the wives of other officers) was quietly tolerated, as long as the occurrence was not too frequent, was limited to the rank of lieutenant, and did not become public and therefore potentially scandalous. In the crisis years of aristocratic-military masculinity, all of this was no longer guaranteed and after the turn of the century would lead to the collapse of the ideal of masculinity in the officer corps dominant until then.

Crisis and Collapse of the Aristocratic Concept of the Officer

In the cultural magazine *Der Morgen* in 1907, the cultural philosopher Rudolf von Delius defended the aristocratic habitus of the officer class by pointing to the unique position of the officer within society. Because the life of the career officer consisted of the preparation for war and for death, he was rewarded for this by being raised to the highest class. The outward, generally accepted social preeminence was a counter to the servitude and forced collectivity in military society. As special class honor, von Delius understood nothing more than a surrogate, which would be prepared by civil society. On the one hand, this was in order to make the deprivation of the officers more tolerable and on the other hand, in order to get control over the members of the entire corps, 'including the woman one marries, the bars where one can be seen'.[28] Von Delius remained close to the traditional aristocratic conception of the officer, but there are two remarkable shifts in his defense of the aristocratic officer. Firstly, he placed the officer's possible death in battle, which followed the principle of co-operative representation and bound the general field marshal with the youngest lieutenant,[29] at the beginning and center of his argumentation. Only the lifelong commitment to the form of death with which they had been brought up, the 'bitter core' of his existence, resulted in the officer's right to exclusivity: 'The actual redemption of this debt the officers have to the people – the debt accrued because they are permitted to play high society without actually being it – can only be redeemed in battle by leading the way into death.'[30] Secondly, the power of attribution rested no longer in the hands of the officers alone. The principle of replacing forbidden individuality with a class personality took shape according to the 'superficial feeling of being at one with the masses'. It touched upon the recognition and belief of others, and was, therefore, no longer self-referential. Von Delius blenched away from the logical conclusion, namely, that the attributes of military masculinity would be subject to historical transformation: 'They can only become something different if the officer class changes its very roots. In my view this is impossible.' Even as he was writing this in 1907, the roots of the officer class had already been chopped off.

The fragility of the aristocratic officer concept in the bourgeois era became obvious during the scandal revolving around the 'Kaiser's best friend', Philipp Prince von Eulenburg-Hertefeld, between 1906 and 1908 – a crisis that eventually grew to be a crisis for the entire guard corps. In the criticism of the *Ancien Régime*, the enlightened bourgeoisie of the eighteenth century had already declared the absolutist court, the most sensitive place in aristocratic society, their target of attack. The opponents of the exclusive court society combined criticism of class principles based on birthright and the facade of etiquette and ceremony with a comment on extravagance, sexual immorality, as well as effeminate behavior – all of which they contrasted with their own civilized morality and with bourgeois virtues.[31] In the nineteenth century, this was taken even further by arguments, principally from the educated middle class, in which this supposed moral dilapidation was conjured up as a national danger and eventually scandalized in the media of the rising mass culture. The debates over luxury in the army, the criticism of the aristocratic privilege and the scandals based on individual cases of homosexuality in the officer corps after 1871 are to be viewed in this context. These three related topics were borne by an involuntary alliance between the military-based ideals of old Prussia, the new bourgeois right and social democracy, each having their own motivations and interests.[32] What connected these sides in this matter was an agreement on the need for restructuring the hierarchy of military masculinity as well as the social hierarchy. Whether it was active or inactive officers or civilians who were openly debating issues such as luxuries, the Guard's regiments, or homosexuality – the later it got, the more shrill the debate – the abuses were given sexually coded character traits: effeminate, sickly, weak, unmanly, and, finally, unsuitable for the military: not warlike. In the heated political atmosphere during crises years – along with the Eulenburg-Scandal came the Daily Telegraph Affair and the Morocco crisis that shattered the Wilhelmine establishment – an accusation of weakness and unsuitability for war resulted in a devastating court ruling. It was not by chance that Maximilian Harden, the driving force behind the scandalization of individual cases of 'deviant' sexual behavior among those close to the Kaiser, labeled the Kaiser himself 'Wilhelm the Peaceful'. From this point on the rhetoric took a turn to mud slinging. Even the correspondent for the *Berliner Tageblatt*, the liberal critic of the aristocracy Colonel (ret.) Richard Gädke, took a sharp accusatory tone against those officers accused of homosexuality. He cursed them with words such as 'boil' and 'putrefier' and demanded their 'ruthless expulsion'.[33]

The course and political fallout of these scandals have been thoroughly described and analyzed in a number of studies.[34] The far-reaching consequences for the officer corps and the hierarchy of military masculinity have been correctly alluded to. In Nicolaus Sombart's swan song to the last Kaiser, homosexuality is presented as a phenomenon that had no place in Prussian military tradition and was being combated by the career officers. In 1907 Wilhelm's abdication, according to Sombart, had already been initiated and had only to be constitutionally completed in 1918. Isabell Hull sees the significance of the scandal in the changing of the royal entourage – turning from a predominantly civilian to a military dominated group – and in the militarization of the Kaiser's politics resulting from this change.[35] Both interpretations are similar in that they point to the military as the decisive factor and, in the end, the victor in these scandals. Which military do they mean? Harden's attacks on the civilian 'Kamarilla', the political clique at court, and at the same time on the Kaiser himself tend to upstage other scandals. One should not forget that the course of the Eulenburg Scandal and its wake constituted an explosive social conflict centered around the conception of the officer and military masculinity. The aristocratic career officers did not preside over policies that were too soft, rather they were themselves the object of the courts.

Nothing was more feared by the aristocratic officer corps than the public, which is why an attempt was made at the beginning of the crisis to find an inner-military solution so that it would not come to 'ugly proceedings'.[36] Spinning out of control, the conflict mobilized the Wilhelmine public sphere – from the daily papers all the way to the Parliament – and was thus able to influence the definition of military masculinity. The officers themselves had only the option of letting this continue or taking part in the dismantling of the image of the aristocratic officer; the majority of them chose the latter.

The individual cases of supposed or actual homosexuality – which aside from the 'Liebenberger Roundtable' concerned, above all, the

Prussian guard corps and individual cavalry regiments – are nothing more than of voyeuristic interest. Much more important is the acknowledgement of the public accusations of homosexuality being flung in all directions as a political weapon, which could be used to push through a new ideal of masculinity. The private ballet program of Eberhard Count Hülsen-Haeseler, influential chief of the Prussian Military Cabinet, for which he donned his little ballet outfit, would have been turned into a mockery had he not died of an aneurism. Middle-class commentators (and later also historians) who made this incident public towards the end of 1907 did not do this; rather they pointed to the incident as a further piece of evidence for the moral decay of the aristocratic officer.

The public proceedings and honorary court processes against high-ranking officers were led by a systematic cleansing of the 'pink regiments', which were considered to be the most distinguished, most expensive and most aristocratic in the Prussian army: the First Guard-Dragoons Regiment, the Dragoons Regiment No. 2, or the Potsdam Regiment, Garde du Corps, whose soldiers were forbidden to wear black boots and tight white trousers due to the erotic impression they made. The uncertainty on the part of the commanders in the involved regiments went so far that they enlisted the expert knowledge of the Berlin police president Hans von Tresckow and even the sex scientist Magnus Hirschfeld: 'Almost daily the commanders of the Berlin and Potsdam regiments come to me and request advice on how they could combat the pederasty among their soldiers.'[37]

The continued attacks on 'Hohenau, Lynar and consorts' were definitely directed at the individual officers, but there was much more at stake: 'The system that is carried by the leading men is an unhealthy one that is deeply damaging the army. For this reason, these men must leave the positions which they are unable to fulfill.'[38] With the 'system', Gädke meant nothing less than the Military Cabinet, the Ministry of War, as well as the commanders of the guard corps. For him, these were three institutions that represented in equal capacity the aristocratic privileges and the softening of the army and in his eyes bore the responsibility for the lack of military preparedness. For the Social Democrats, August Bebel stressed on 29 November 1907 before the Reichstag that 'entire regiments' were 'infested' and demanded, probably knowing full well that only the Guard Regiments were involved, the ruthless expulsion of those involved and a full public inquiry. Although Bebel was among the first to sign a parliamentary petition against paragraph 175 of the penal code and had loose ties to Magnus Hirschfeld's scientific-humanitarian committee, for reasons of political tactics and because of inner conviction he instrumentalized the crisis of the male Wilhelmine society as an attack on the aristocratic dominance in the Prussian officer corps.[39] To the chagrin of the career officers, he placed the disgrace in connection with the Guards not outside of the officer corps, but rather within it. The Prussian Minister of War, Karl von Einem, however, referred to the 'attacks of the scoundrels from civilian circles', but also turned against the 'sick part of the otherwise healthy body' of the officer corps:

> Such a man should never become an officer. Such a man is susceptible to going against his oath; he does not bring out the best, but rather the very worst through his behavior. Such a man buries the discipline, such a man forces his troops to disobey his superiors. Wherever there might be such a man with such feelings biding his time in the army, I would like to call to him: take your leave, remove yourself, for you do not belong in our ranks! Should he be caught instead, gentlemen, whoever it might be and wherever he might be standing and in whatever location he finds himself, there he must be annihilated.[40]

These examples demonstrate that not only 'the specific Wilhelmine nationalism and militarism pressed for a ban on homosexuality',[41] but rather completely different social and political groups made use of the 'homosexualization of the enemy'.[42] In the logic of the aristocratic concept of the officer, the transfer of military command to the court was unquestioned, like that of the two first lieutenants Count Wendt zu Eulenburg and the Count Moritz zu Innhausen-Knyphausen as the premier dancers at the Potsdam Court. This was from now on branded by both the left and right political opposition as incompatible with the military training.[43] The times in which dancing officers set the tone both on the social parquet floor and in the military organization were over. The liberal-democratic oriented Württemberger daily newspaper, *Der Beobachter*, summed up the change in the political climate: 'There where good work is presumed to be done, there are no aristocratic officers.'[44]

Obviously, the homophile tendencies of individual officers had already been known. The Kaiser's entourage was occasionally sneered at, for it often advanced militarily incapable men to the highest posts, but this criticism remained, for the most part, private.[45] The interpretation of this concept of military masculinity as being a soft, unsoldierly femininity, as well as its links to protest against the striking social inequalities in the Prussian army, was founded on the traditional criticism of the military and aristocracy among the educated classes. Yet the Wilhelmine mass public sphere and the growing media market first raised these accusations to scandals of national importance during a phase of war hysteria and war fantasies. The success of this action was a result of the susceptibility of the 'decorative militarism' to the accusation of being unsuitable for war. For many privileges which the officer class claimed over the civilian society were derived from their expert preparation and execution of military operations. The public's trust in the ability of the military and the social glitter of the aristocratic officer concept on which the existence of the officer's image mostly depended had been shaken to its core, as the expertise in industrialized war was no longer an affair for a small, exclusive group, but rather for the entire society.

Hardening, or the Search for Character

As early as 1907 Gädke claimed in the *Berliner Tageblatt*: 'It is not reprimands that we need, nor cabinet orders, but rather men, other men, real men!'[46] By this he was not only indicating the need for an exchange of personnel, but in general a new officer concept. Referring to the dangers of the long periods of peace unavoidably leading to luxurious lifestyles and the softening up of the officer corps, people on all sides, both in and outside military circles, were searching for a new warlike concept of the officer. Leaving behind the luxury regiments, this new concept had to be one of 'real men'. Essentially, this was an attempt to find a new, universally acceptable meaning for an old term that had been in widespread use since the beginning of the nineteenth century: *character*.

Wilhelm II had already indicated in an edict of 29 March 1890 that in view of the new recruiting base, it was of the utmost importance to rouse character and then to develop it. What he meant by character in the edict remains uncertain, but it is clearly a conceptual medium which did not contain the factors of origin or knowledge and was equally attractive for a large part of the middle class as well as the militarily influenced aristocrats.[47] Two factors that explain the integrating force of the term 'character' deserve mention in this context: its sexual codification and the militaristic charge it carries. Both of these are again connected to the 'turn to hardness'.[48] As character had, for the most part, been freed of its attachment to social origin and scientific military training and had instead risen to indicate something about male upbringing and military discipline, the term and concept could now find a wide base of acceptance within society. The attractiveness of 'hardened masculinity' accelerated the eroding of the habitual aristocratic dominance in the officer corps and increased the chances of mobilizing the masses. Especially in the most powerful right-wing national organizations such as the *Alldeutscher Verband* (Pan-German League), *Flottenverein* (Naval League) and the *Deutscher Wehrverein* (German Army League), origin and royalist convictions played a secondary role compared to that of character and national conviction.[49] Nevertheless, the image of the officer as an educator of the masculine nation remained unscathed.[50] It was precisely this endurance of the officer's claim to being the lone responsible figure for male discipline in the national classroom, which made necessary a division between the purely decorative side of military leadership and the training for modern war. How could one believably convey the characteristic ideals of military manliness to the recruits when deviant behavior had already been found in the ranks of the military leaders? The crux of the dilemma on the eve of the First World War was that the masculine attributes which for decades had carried over to the civilian society were now being brought in a radicalized form back into the military and into the officer corps.

The change led to a range of military reforms which took the conditions of modern warfare into account and made the readiness for war visible for everyone. This included a variety of individual reforms, such as the inclusion of realistic war scenarios in the annual imperial maneuvers, a gradual increase in the role played by technical units, the introduction of the field-gray uniform, and the intensification of paramilitary training for young men in the *Jungdeutschlandbund*. The professional military leadership willingly made concessions to the overheated demands of the mass organizations and even instrumented them in internal military discussions, as long as they were able to be brought under the formalized technocratic leadership model of the general staff.

Of course, this aroused resistance against the 'sham and fashion buffoonery', 'the pomaded steeds of Potsdam', and the 'fairytale princes' within the officer corps where one could assume a certain degree of aristocratic solidarity. Precisely this so-called aristocratic *Alt-Preußentum* consolidated its history and its present into a one-sided, military-based hard masculinity. The emphasis now rested upon purely military terms like *toughness, endurance, service,* and *duty*, which had much more to do with the realities of modern warfare than with the image of a caste of aristocratic warriors. Memoirs of life in the cadet corps, for example, always refer to the manly toughness of military training: 'There is no question that life in the cadet corps displayed a hefty masculine quality, which tolerates no weakness, laziness, and hypocrisy and it was quite a blessing. The capable man came out, once he made it through the strictness, and was acknowledged. There was no lack of bodily hardening.'[51] The demand from all sides for 'new men' rang throughout the military society. The attractiveness of the officer's concept, which stressed and required a manly character, was due to the fact that one could read much into it. It was also appealing, as it appeared to jump the bounds of the tensions among the officers, tensions which had been increasingly interpreted as burdensome. In the innumerable publications which followed and promoted this change, rarely is the connection between 'hardened masculinity and future warfare' missing,[52] while at the same time both internal and external enemies were marked as feminine.

A seldom but nevertheless important future-oriented variant of the newly formed gender relations was that of the 'worker bees', who developed an expert ability in military questions in the service of the General Staff. The self-imposed warrior image of masculinity was certainly not foreign to them, and they employed it freely in their public stylization; but as a way of life in their everyday work, it must have been rather hindering. For the General Staff officers, the wives were neither representatives of a highly valued class nor comrades with specific wifely duties, but rather diligent, competent workers in important military questions. After 1918, these women were demonized and their unhealthy influence on their husbands reproved; names such as Eliza von Moltke, Margarethe Ludendorff, and Dorothea von Seeckt come to mind. It was not seen as improper in the General Staff circles before 1914 and even in the German headquarters during the First World War to continue work in the family circles after the General Staff office hours.[53] With its justification based in a marital-private community of workers, the concept of the professional officer that had developed out of the work of the General Staff created a division of labor in military questions. In the barracks, one did not go dancing anymore, but rather stayed home together to work. But this new form of gender relations, which contradicted the military and its masculine traditions, remained hidden from the public up until recently. While even the men who were typified as the toughest and manliest could not withstand the challenges of the coming war, as can be seen in the rather high number of nervous breakdowns in the military leadership, the General Staff soldiers formed the nucleus of the future military elite.[54]

Conclusion

In more than four decades of peace between 1871 and 1914, the Prussian officer corps changed in a dramatic way in its social composition and in its understanding of itself as a professional institution. These changes had tremendous repercussions on the ideal of military masculinity. This development manifested itself in the public debates, in which the officer and his manhood were transformed through open discourse, as well as in the experiences and everyday routines of the officer. This in turn was reflected in the military as well as in the social transformation before 1914. For the respective officer groups and generations, the defense of the nation and the specialized military work increased in value and became equal to that of service to the monarchial social order, which had considerable effects on the officer's picture of himself as the masculine educator of the masculine nation.

Accelerated by the crisis of military masculinity in the opening decade of the twentieth century, the dominance of the aristocracy in the external perception of the officer was stigmatized as 'soft' or 'effeminate' and banned to the periphery of society. Two designs that were elements of the old variant of *officerdom* in the public eye were now pushed to the forefront, but they were legitimated in a fundamentally different way. For one, in the loud variety of 'inflamed soldiery' of right-wing nationalist groups with their countless number of retired officers, which was a manly movement supposedly aiming at the exclusion of everything weak and unmanly. In support of the rediscovered, one-sided historical example stemming from the changes within the military, this self-righteous community reclaimed for itself the old and newly formed definitions for tough manhood and war readiness. Secondly, there was the concept of the General Staff and its 'cool professionalism' that derived its right to exclusivity from its understanding of military leadership as a secret science based on expert knowledge. For those planners and organizers the manly, warlike adventurism and the uncontrolled saber-rattling were as foreign as the pompous and ostentatious neo-feudal self-representation. Through these two alternative concepts, the social inequality within the officer corps was not to be corrected, but under the banner of toughened manhood it was now open to public discussion, as well as to attack.

In everyday military life, these three concepts of the officer ranks and military masculinity were mixed together and broken up, which also loosened their associations with specific social groups. For this reason one should be careful with interpretations which too strongly suggest a linear development from the courtier to the warrior or a schematic dualism between the old and the new militarism.[55] Neither was the collapse of the aristocratic officer's concept complete, nor did the toughening of the masculine ideal before the First World War guarantee hardened, war-crazed men. Instead – and much more decisive for the military order after 1914/15 – the parallel existence of competing models for the ideal officer and for masculinity suggest a strain in the wide-reaching, hegemonic concept of masculinity, as well as excessive demands on the officers to fulfill the expectations of this ideal. With the variety of expectations put upon them by the civil society, the officer before the First World War ultimately had to have the abilities of an actor. As the courtly model on the parquet floor, as the erotic object of (feminine) desires, as the represent-ative of the monarchial-militaristic rule over subordinates, or as organizer and military specialist, the officer was expected to have the appropriate manly behavior. At the same time, he was becoming less and less capable of meeting these expectations. Behind the thin layer of military-oriented representations of social power and manly-oriented representations of preparedness, which most historians until recently have regarded as the nucleus, there was an uncertainty among the overworked and a presumpt-uousness among the imperious commanders. For the numerous concepts of masculinity presented here, the use of military force was regarded as a natural fact of life, as a reason for being, and went so far as to become a militaristic obsession. With each of the individual, partly contradictory, motives, methods and goals, not only was the close connection between masculinity and military force strengthened, but it also came in line with the requirements of modern war. In none of these concepts, whether the aristocratic, radical nationalist, or the professional, was there a potential for restraint which could have channeled the forces that unleashed the First World War. The manly officer, representing a *Gesamtkunstwerk*, had, however, already been demystified after the first months of the war and soon broke into individual pieces.

Notes

1. Angelika Tramitz, 'Nach dem Zapfenstreich. Anmerkungen zur Sex-ualität des Offiziers,' in *Willensmenschen. Über deutsche Offiziere*, ed. Ursula Breymayer, Bernd Ulrich and Karin Wieland (Frankfurt a. M.,1999), 211–226.
2. The tension between the neo-feudal facade and the professional normal working day in the Wilhelmine officer corps has been recently brought out, but since then the construction of the officer's image has at best been simply repeated. See Michael Geyer, 'The Past as Future, The German Officer Corps as Profession,' in *German Professions, 1800–1950*, ed. Geoffrey Cocks and Konrad Jarausch (New York, 1990), 183–212.

Marcus Funck

3. Ute Frevert, 'Das jakobinische Modell: Allgemeine Wehrpflicht und Nationsbildung in Preußen-Deutschland,' in *Militär und Gesellschaft im 19. und 20. Jahrhundert*, ed. Frevert (Stuttgart, 1997), 17–47, here: 46.

4. Wilhelm Deist, 'Zur Geschichte des preußischen Offizierkorps 1888–1918,' in *Das deutsche Offizierkorps 1860–1960*, ed. Hanns Hubert Hoffmann (Boppard, 1980), 39–57. The author cautiously refers to the fragmentation of the Prussian/German officer corps along the lines of military specialization.

5. One can still start with: John Tosh, 'What Should Historians Do with Masculinity? Reflections on Nineteenth-Century Britain,' *History Workshop Journal*, no. 38 (1994), 179–202. An introduction to the present research in German-speaking countries is: Christa Hämmerle, 'Von den Geschlechtern der Kriege und des Militärs,' in *Was ist Militärgeschichte?*, ed. Thomas Kühne and Benjamin Ziemann (Paderborn, 2000), 229–262.

6. On this topic, the following work is as yet unsurpassed: Hermann Rumschöttel, *Das bayerische Offizierkorps 1866–1914* (Berlin, 1973).

7. For example, Martin Kitchen, *The German Officer Corps 1890–1914* (Oxford, 1968); Hartmut John, *Das Reserveoffizierkorps im Deutschen Kaiserreich 1890–1914. Ein sozialgeschichtlicher Beitrag zur Untersuchung der gesellschaftlichen Militarisierung im Wilhelminischen Deutschland* (Frankfurt a. M./New York, 1981).

8. Compare with Marcus Funck and Stephan Malinowski, 'Masters of Memory. The Strategic Use of Autobiographical Memory by the German Nobility,' in *The Work of Memory. New Directions in the Study of German Society and Culture*, ed. Alon Confino and Peter Fritzsche (Urbana, 2002), 86–103.

9. A very successful exception is Sabina Brändli, 'Von "schneidigen Offizieren" and "Militärcrinolinien": Aspekte symbolischer Männlichkeit am Beispiel preußischer und schweizerischer Uniformen des 19. Jahrhunderts,' in *Militär und Gesellschaft*, ed. Ute Frevert, 201–228.

10. For a history of the Prusso-German officer corps I am thinking of Michael Geyer, *The Past as Future* as well as Geoff Eley, 'State, Army, and Civil Society: Revisiting the Problem of German Militarism,' in *From Unification to Nazism, Reinterpreting the German Past*, ed. Eley (Boston, 1990), 85–109; and the more up-to-date Mark Stoneman, 'Bürgerliche und adlige Krieger: Zum Verhältnis zwischen sozialer Herkunft und Berufskultur im wilhelminischen Armee Offizierkorps,'

in *Adel und Bürgertum in Deutschland II. Entwicklungslinien und Wendepunkte im 20. Jahrhundert*, ed. Heinz Reif (Berlin, 2001), 25–63.

11. Prinz Kraft zu Hohenlohe-Ingelfingen, *Aus meinem Leben* (Berlin, 1897), 316.

12. Hermann von Chappius, *Bei Hofe und im Felde* (Berlin, 1902), 16.

13. Einleitungsordre zu der Ehrengerichts-Verordnung from 2 May 1874, found in Karl Demeter, *Das deutsche Offizierkorps in Gesellschaft und Staat 1650–1945* (Frankfurt a. M., 1962), 269–272. Wilhelm II took this up in his cabinet order on the occasion of his taking of the command of the army on 5 July 1888 and in his edict on the expansion of the officer corps on 29 March 1890. Both can be found in Hans Meier-Welcker, ed. *Offiziere im Bild von Dokumenten aus drei Jahrhunderten* (Stuttgart, 1964), 195–198.

14. A small collection of the often republished *Offiziersratgeber*: Justus Scheibert, *Offiziers-Brevier. Ein Festgeschenk für den jungen Kameraden von einem alten Offizier* (Berlin, 1879); Camill Schaible, *Standes- und Berufspflichten des deutschen Offiziers. Für angehende und junge Offiziere des stehenden Heeres und des Beurlaubtenstandes* (Berlin, 1891); Kurt v. Rabenau, *Die deutsche Land- und Seemacht und die Berufspflichten des Offiziers. Ein Handbuch für Offiziere des aktiven Dienststandes und des Beurlaubtenstandes sowie Fähnriche, Einjährig-Freiwillige und Vizefeldwebel der Reserve* (Berlin, 1914).

15. Anonymous, 'Der Offizier. Das moderne Rittertum,' *Militär-Wochenblatt* 74, no. 62 (1889): 1311–1326 and 1451–1456.

16. Thomas Kühne, '"Kameradschaft – das beste im Leben des Mannes." Die deutschen Soldaten des Zweiten Weltkriegs in erfahrungs- und geschlechtergeschichtlicher Perspektive,' in *Geschichte und Gesellschaft* 22 (1996): 504–529.

17. Ludwig Renn, *Adel im Untergang* (Berlin,1948), 124–126.

18. At least for the bourgeois officers, who were outsiders, like the young second lieutenant Wilhelm Heye, who had been sent from Saarbrücken to the Infantry-Lehr-Battalion in Potsdam. His disconcertment over this practice was weaker than the charisma of the Guard regiment: 'Most often I, the youngest, danced with Colonel v. Plessen, who was later the most loyal companion of Wilhelm II.' BA-MA Freiburg No. 18/1 (Heye papers), *Mein Lebenslauf*, 70.

19. Herein lies the key difference from the primitive and perverse sexualization of the battle among the representatives of the 'military nationalism' of the 1920s so vividly described by Theweleit. Compare with Klaus Theweleit, *Male Fantasies*, vol. 2 (Minneapolis, 1987/89).

Marcus Funck

In this respect one must re-examine the ground-breaking study by Nicolaus Sombart, *Die deutschen Männer und ihre Feinde, Carl Schmitt – ein Schicksal zwischen Männerbund und Matriarchatsmythos* (Munich/Vienna, 1991). See also: Brändli, 'Von schneidigen Offizieren," 220–226.

20. A letter to Graf Dietloff v. Arnim-Boitzenburg from 1.12.1892 (private collection).

21. Paul v. Hindenburg, *Aus meinem Leben* (Berlin, 1920), 51.

22. Ute Frevert, 'Soldaten, Staatsbürger. Überlegungen zur historischen Konstruktion von Männlichkeit,' in *Männergeschichte als Geschlechtergeschichte, Männlichkeit im Wandel der Moderne*, ed. Thomas Kühne (Frankfurt a. M./New York, 1996), 69–87.

23. Freiherr v. Schlicht [i.e. Wolf Graf Baudissin], *Die Frau Oberst. Militärhumoresken* (Berlin, 1914), 25.

24. Letter from Wanda v. Eulenburg about the Garde du Corps banquet on 8.22.1889, in Christoph v. L'Estocq, *Fünf Eulenburgs aus dem Hause Wicken im alten Ostpreußen*, manuscript in Deutsches Adelsarchiv Marburg, 36. Compare with Renn, *Adel im Untergang*, 306.

25. An example of this is *Tagebuch der Baronin Spitzemberg. Aufzeichnungen aus der Hofgesellschaft des Hohenzollernreiches*, ed. Rudolf Vierhaus (Göttingen, 1960), which is littered with both praiseful and spiteful commentaries on the successful and unsuccessful balls.

26. Philipp Fürst zu Eulenburg-Hertefeld, *Aus 50 Jahren: Erinnerungen, Tagebücher und Briefe aus dem Nachlaß des Fürsten Philipp zu Eulenburg-Hertefeld*, ed. Johannes Haller (Berlin, 1923), 29.

27. Joachim Dissow [i.e. v. Rantzau], *Adel im Übergang* (Stuttgart, 1961), 18.

28. Rudolf v. Delius, 'Der Offizier,' *Der Morgen*, no. 24 (1907): 773.

29. Marcus Funck, 'The Meaning of Dying: East Elbian Noble Families as "Warrior-Tribes" in the Nineteenth and Twentieth Centuries,' in *Sacrifice and National Belonging in 20th Century Germany*, ed. Greg Eghigian and Matt Berg (Arlington, 2002), 26–63.

30. Delius, 'Der Offizier,' 774.

31. Michael Maurer, *Die Biographie des Bürgers. Lebensformen und Denkweisen in der formativen Phase des deutschen Bürgertums (1618–1815)* (Göttingen, 1996), 236–254.

32. For the reform-oriented criticism from German Social Democrats see: Bernhard Neff, '"Dekorationsmilitarismus". Die sozialdemokratische Kritik eines vermeintlich nicht kriegsgemäßen Militärwesens (1890–1911),' in *Militarismus in Deutschland 1871 bis 1945. Zeitgenössische Analysen und Kritik* (Jahrbuch für historische Friedensforschung vol. 8), ed. Wolfram Wette, 128–145.

33. Richard Gädke, 'Wo sind die Schuldigen?' *Berliner Tageblatt* 36, no. 552 (1907).

34. For example John C.G. Röhl, 'Graf Philipp zu Eulenburg – des Kaisers bester Freund,' in *Kaiser, Hof und Staat. Wilhelm II. und die deutsche Politik*, ed. John C.G. Röhl (Munich, 1988). As a summary: Wolfgang J. Mommsen, 'Homosexualität, aristokratische Kultur und Weltpolitik,' in *Große Prozesse. Recht und Gerechtigkeit in der Geschichte*, ed. Uwe Schultz (Munich, 1996), 279–288. Not only colorful in the title of the respective chapter 'Pink Prussia': Giles MacDonough, *Prussia. The Perversion of an Idea* (London, 1996), 204–230.

35. Nicolaus Sombart, *Wilhelm II. Sündenbock und Herr der Mitte* (Berlin, 1996); Isabell V. Hull, *The Entourage of Kaiser Wilhelm II* (Cambridge, 1982).

36. Hans v Tresckow, *Von Fürsten und anderen Sterblichen* (Berlin, 1922), 165 (diary entry from 7 May 1907).

37. Tresckow, *Fürsten*, 185 (diary entry from 3 July 1907); compare with: Magnus Hirschfeld, *Von einst bis jetzt. Geschichte einer homosexuellen Bewegung 1897–1922*, ed. Manfred Herzer, James Steakley (Berlin, 1986), 145–149.

38. Richard Gädke, 'Hohenau, Lynar und Konsorten,' *Berliner Tageblatt* 36, no. 577 (1907).

39. *Goodbye to Berlin? 100 Jahre Schwulenbewegung*, ed. Schwules Museum Berlin and Akademie der Künste Berlin (Berlin, 1997), 37–41.

40. Speeches by August Bebel and Karl von Einem in: *Verhandlungen des Reichstages*, vol. 229, 61; Session from 11.29.1907, 1909–1916.

41. Andrea Taeger and Rüdiger Lautman, 'Sittlichkeit und Politik. §175 im Deutschen Kaiserreich (1871–1918),' in *Männerliebe im alten Deutschland. Sozialgeschichtliche Abhandlungen* (Berlin, 1992), 260.

42. Jens Dobler, 'Von Fürsten und anderen Sterblichen. Porträts zur ersten Zusammenarbeit zwischen Schwulenbewegung und Polizei,' in *Schwule, Lesben, Polizei. Vom Zwangsverhältnis zur Zweck-Ehe?* (Berlin, 1996), 25–60, here: 46.

43. *Verhandlungen des Reichstages*, vol. 235, 226. Session from 17 March 1909, 7547.

44. Newspaper article from *Der Beobachter*, no. 167 (1910), in the Württembergisches Hauptstaatsarchiv Stuttgart, M 1/3 (Kriegsministerium-Zentralabteilung), no. 793, vol. 39.

45. Spitzemberg, *Aufzeichnungen*, 436 (diary entry from 25 November 1903):

There is quite a bit of discussion over the summoning of Kuno Moltke to the Kaiser, his being named general and especially chief of the second (historic) division of the General Staff [. . .] though he is completely incapable for such a position, earning such a high salary and *klavicymbeling* to his Master. The Berliner or better yet an army joke says he has been summoned in order to found the soon to be created music division of the General Staff and later as its chief to direct the European concert!

46. *Berliner Tageblatt* 36 (1907), no. 552.
47. Roger Chickering, *We Men Who Feel Most German. A Cultural Study of the Pan-German League 1886–1914* (Boston, 1984); Marcus Funck and Stephan Malinowski, '"Charakter ist alles!" Erziehungsideale und Erziehungspraktiken in deutschen Adelsfamilien des 19. und 20. Jahrhunderts,' *Jahrbuch für historische Bildungsforschung*, vol. 6 (2000): 71–91.
48. Joachim Radkau, *Das Zeitalter der Nervosität. Deutschland zwischen Bismarck und Hitler* (Munich/Vienna, 1998), 357.
49. For more on this subject read the relevant works by the loudest agitators: Daniel Frymann [i.e. Heinrich Class], *Wenn ich der Kaiser wär! Politische Wahrheiten und Notwendigkeiten* (Leipzig, 1911); August Keim, *Erlebtes und Erstrebtes* (Hannover, 1925).
50. The expression 'nation in arms' does not refer to a *Volksbewaffnung* in the sense of equality among free men, but rather the introduction of the mobilization of the entire bourgeois society within the confines of the military organization. Colmar von der Goltz, *Das Volk in Waffen. Ein Buch über Heerwesen und Kriegführung unserer Zeit* (Berlin, 1883).
51. According to Colmar v. d. Goltz, *Denkwürdigkeiten*, ed. Friedrich Freiherr v. d. Goltz (Berlin, 1932), 26, in the section with his youth and childhood memories, which were written before 1914, but were nevertheless rather beautified. On the cadet institutions see: John Moncure, *Forging the King's Sword. Military Education Between Tradition and Modernization. The Case of Royal Prussian Cadet Corps 1871–1918* (New York/Berlin, 1993).
52. The influential book: Friedrich v. Bernhardi, *Deutschland und der nächste Krieg* (Berlin/Stuttgart, 1912) is littered with such references.
53. Bundesarchiv-Militärarchiv Freiburg, N 87/41 (Otto v. Below papers), *Erinnerungen*, vol. 4, 356; Wilhelm Groener, *Lebenserinnerungen. Jugend, Generalstab, Weltkrieg*, ed. Friedrich Freiherr Hiller von Gaetringen (Göttingen, 1957), 70.
54. In spite of this, a multitude of authors projected their concepts of a renewed military masculinity in the person of General Ludendorff

after 1918, which despite his nervous breakdown in the fall of 1918 were considered the incarnation of the *Führer* in the age of mechanized warfare. 'Ludendoff, who was always factual, strong and full of ideas, was often with me. He always discussed the situation with me openly. In war he was the most loved and most hated officer. All of his co-workers loved him, the system of the collapse hated him and was hated by him. Everything about Ludendorff was manly.' Karl v. Einem, *Erinnerungen eines Soldaten* (Leipzig, 1933), 186. Similarly: Bundesarchiv-Militärarchiv Freiburg, N 5/27 (Stülpnagel papers), *Erinnerungen*, 64; and also the ardent descriptions in: Edith Salburg [i.e. Freifrau. v. Krieg-Hochfelden], *Erinnerungen einer Respektlosen* (Leipzig, 1927), 74; compare with the distanced acknowledgement from the homosexual reserve officer and former *Landrat* Joachim v. Winterfeld-Menkin, *Jahreszeiten des Lebens* (Berlin, 1941), 253.

55. Stig Förster, *Der doppelte Militarismus. Die deutsche Heeresrüstungspolitik zwischen Status-Quo-Sicherung und Aggression 1890–1913* (Wiesbaden, 1985).

–2–

German Comrades – Slavic Whores

Gender Images in the German Soldier Newspapers of the First World War
Robert L. Nelson

The propagandistic use of gendered imagery during the First World War was intended both to identify 'friends' and 'enemies', as well as to define the necessary wartime roles of men and women, at the front and at home. A central medium of war propaganda was provided by the soldier newspapers, which were created and distributed within the army, and appeared in great numbers. Through an analysis of this medium, the articles and sketches produced by both officers and lower ranks, conclusions can be drawn regarding images of the self, the enemy and the foreigner. Here, the degree to which national and social identity was constructed by gender becomes apparent. Through the use of gendered attributes various groups could be differentiated and set into a hierarchy. With the ascription of what were deemed positive gender traits, one's own nation could be rendered worthy, while other nations, through negative connotations, could be deemed less respectable. This practice was most evident in the soldier newspapers of the First World War. These journals were replete with gender-specific formulations of both friend and foe, and these renditions will be analyzed in examples below. This study thus contributes to two areas in the growing field of 'new cultural history'-oriented research of war and the military. The first encompasses the analysis of martial images, experiences and perceptions. The second pertains to the research into gender and nationalism from a historical point of view, which, among other things, seeks to define the connections between nation, war and gender. In the German-speaking world, these themes have been explored in the pioneering work of Karen Hagemann for the era of the Napoleonic Wars, and Thomas Kühne for the Second World War. Similar studies for the First World War do not exist.[1]

The findings developed below result from my analysis of the German soldier newspapers of the First World War. This vast, rich and rarely used source, produced at or near the front by and for soldiers, provides valuable insight into the language and semantics of the officers and lower-rank soldiers of this period.[2] The journals varied greatly in size, distribution and production from the large army newspapers (*Armeezeitungen*) to the small trench journals (*Schützengrabenzeitungen*). Of the ca. 115 titles that appeared between September 1914 and the end of the conflict, twenty-one were army newspapers, fifteen were at the corps and divisional level, and more than sixty appeared ranging from the regimental level down through various smaller units to the 'company' trench journals. The largest and most influential of the army newspapers, the *Liller Kriegszeitung* in the West and the *Zeitung der 10. Armee* in the East, had circulations averaging around 80,000 and 30,000 respectively, while sometimes only a few copies of the smallest journals would appear, to be passed around within a company by hand. Some of the largest army newspapers appeared several times a week, while the smaller trench journals were typically published once a month. Printing presses in occupied territory were often commandeered to produce the newspapers. If this was not possible, the finished plates would be sent to the closest German press for printing. Distribution of most soldier newspapers occurred via the military postal system, as well as through sale at bookshops and canteens. The newspapers were financed by soldier subscriptions (with different prices for officers and lower ranks), home front subscriptions and donations, and, very rarely, money from the military when a paper was in serious financial need.[3]

There was, of course, a certain amount of censorship and military control over the content of the soldier newspapers. It was the oft-stated purpose of these newspapers to provide news about the war in general alongside local coverage, and to raise and maintain the mood of the soldier audience. The provision of news was the major difference between the soldier newspapers of the two main fronts, as those units far out in the East had little access to home front newspapers and thus more space was devoted to the war in general. Additionally, the eastern front newspapers contained many more articles about the local, alien populations than the newspapers in the West. The manners and customs of occupied populations in the western regions seemed to have been much more familiar to the soldiers than what they observed in the East. The soldier newspapers were thus a significant, and often the only, source of information for the soldiers wishing to learn about the lands and peoples under their control.

What limited information exists on the editorial teams of the newspapers indicates an even split between officers and lower ranks, with a large number of these men listing the newspaper business as their prewar employment. The larger the newspaper, the larger the percentage of officers on the editorial staff. In 1916, an army press authority was set up to more closely monitor the content of the soldier newspapers, as well as to provide approved articles on a weekly basis to be appropriated by the editorial staffs, should they so choose. Although this formal censorship, as well as the self-censorship exhibited by the editors, severely limited the free expression of soldiers' ideas and beliefs, the fact remains that these newspapers were bought in vast numbers, were read (sometimes aloud) and shared by virtually all soldiers who served in the war. This clearly indicates their usefulness as a guide to interpreting the discursive worlds shared by the soldiers and officers on the eastern and western fronts in the First World War.

The following analysis of gender imagery in the German soldier newspapers of the First World War will begin with the model they propagated of the 'German soldier'. At the center of this analysis is the concept of comradeship. Then, throughout the remainder of the study, both complementary and opposing images will be examined, firstly the imagery of enemy soldiers on the western and eastern fronts, secondly the description of German women on the home front, and thirdly the portrayal of women in the occupied areas of the West and East. At the same time, the connection between gender imagery and ethnic traits will be analyzed. In the conclusion, a comparison will be made with the soldier newspapers of the Allied armies.

German Comrades

The many soldier newspaper articles with simple headings such as 'Comradeship' or 'Comrades' contained various stories or poems which loosely referred to some shared notion of what comradeship meant at the front between 1914 and 1918. Oftentimes these columns took the form of a straightforward description of what kind of behavior was to be expected of comrades. An article with the title 'Gedanken über Kameradschaft', in the *Liller Kriegszeitung* of 26 July 1917, for example, gave some pointers, all in the form of aphorisms, such as, 'He who is most honest and faithful to you, and who also cheerfully and openly tells you your mistakes, he is your best comrade!'[4] Along with the constant invocations to 'do one's duty' (*Pflicht*), work hard, and be faithful (*treu*), these 'rules' would sometimes tend toward the petty and sophomoric, such as in the article 'Kameradschaft', in the 26 May 1918 edition of the *Champagne-Kamerad*, which asked the men not to tease, or talk behind each other's backs.

Another column, 'Sei ein Mann!' in the *Zeitung der 10. Armee* of 12 October 1916, demanded that the soldiers 'be men' and not pay attention to what others were saying about them.[5] A central component of 'comradeship' was the myth of the reciprocity of loyalty and fraternity unto death, the conviction that comrades were ready and willing to put their life in danger to rescue a friend. This myth was related through the popular 'rescue story'. Almost invariably the tale concerned a German raid which had left the body, alive or dead, of a comrade in No Man's Land. A hero, usually an officer, then returned to recover the wounded/dead man in the face of extreme danger.[6]

Alongside the virile, military-heroic conception of comradeship, considerable space was given in the soldier newspapers to describing the 'soft, feminine' side of soldier relationships. Stories of men extending a 'loving hand' like 'mother' to ease the pain of the dying[7] existed alongside articles that dealt with the heart-wrenching loss of an extremely close comrade in battle.[8] Indeed, in a few articles, most often with the title 'Friendship', the soldier newspapers moved into the terrain of the homoerotic. One example was the article 'Freundschaft', that appeared in the 29 June 1916 edition of the *Kriegszeitung der 4. Armee*. After describing the death of a friend in battle, Staff Sergeant Rudolf Hölbing portrays their friendship as having been 'much more [. . .] than love'. He continued, 'I know that I was one with him. We belonged together like blossom and root. One takes root [*wurzelt*] in the other, one blossoms, living in the other.'[9] Another article, 'Von der Freundschaft' in the 21 April 1918 issue of the same newspaper, argued that the 'faithfulness and honesty' of friendship between men is greater than that of marriage. Its author, stretcher-carrier Hünich, goes on in this piece to describe how friendship is one-on-one, while comradeship is between many. If one is lucky, he says, friendship will result from the latter.[10] And in a very suggestive article of 6 June 1915 from the eastern front newspaper *Deutsche Kriegszeitung in Polen*, the 'reversing game' (*Widerspiel*) of nature that occurred in war was invoked to describe the strong love found between men far from home, 'on cold earth' and 'deep in the trenches'.[11] This negotiated idea of German comradeship indicates that the concept was a complicated mixture of both masculine and feminine components. The stress however was always upon what were considered to be the truly masculine traits: battle-readiness, duty, pride, hard work, honesty and loyalty.

The projection of such tight-knit relationships to something resembling a 'front community' also occurred in the soldier newspapers. The article 'Kameradschaft' in the May 1916 *Vogesenwacht* for instance, stated that there was a community at the front, but identified it mainly as a group of people who, unlike those at home, knew the truth of what was happening, specifically, how terrible the war was.[12] Constructed as such, this common experience brought the men at the front together, and helped to erase divisions of class and age. For the most part, such articles were somewhat realistic in their depiction of everyday life at the front. Sometimes however the level of description was elevated to the sacred, as in the 7 September 1916 poem 'Kriegskameraden' in the *Kriegszeitung der 4. Armee*, where images of 'blood', 'mud', and comradeship, invoked a 'holy union' along the lines of the postwar, mythical 'front community'.[13] Other articles extended the concept of comradeship to include both the martial contribution of those at the front as well as those at home. The author of 'The Real Fatherland Party' in the 18 November 1917 *Champagne-Kamerad*, stated that, unlike the new political party of that name, the 'real' Fatherland Party consisted of all those comrades working together for victory, both the men at the front, as well as the old people, women and children at home.[14] Such stories, requesting that all social and political differences at home and at the front should be forgotten during the war, were incessantly repeated in the soldier newspapers. This message was emphasized and taken further in the article 'Kameradschaft' in the *Somme-Wacht* of 7 September 1917, which argued that the *Burgfrieden* (truce among political factions in Germany) and comradeship were 'necessary' for Germany to win the war. Afterwards, differing political parties would return and resume squabbling as before, only this time, hoped the author, after the experience of war, without any 'personal' hatred for one another.[15]

These positive images of German soldiers and comrades were contrasted with the negative depiction of 'shirkers'. The men who had not entered the military were featured in the soldier newspapers as weak, cowardly and feminine. A good example was the sketch in the 28 April 1915 issue of the *Liller Kriegszeitung* which portrayed a rather 'womanly' man, thin with fine clothing, strolling through town with all passers-by staring at him. The caption read 'exempt from military duty'.[16] Another article, 'What We Soldiers Want' in the 24 September 1917 *Liller Kriegszeitung*, berated members of parliament for 'staying with mother'.[17] More varied was the reporting on the munitions workers whose participation was considered necessary for the war effort. The semblance of unity was disrupted, however, during the strikes of January 1918, when the strains and complexity of this relationship became apparent in the soldier newspapers. Many newspapers reined in their criticism and merely reminded the workers of their fraternal 'duty', which involved their continued support of the soldiers in the fight against the Allies. Other newspapers, however, unleashed aggressive and demeaning articles about the strikers. The major complaint was that the military's most important workers on the home front had broken the comradely bond of loyalty with the soldiers at the front, and that the soldiers' back was thus falling in.[18]

Gendered descriptions, though, were not limited to contrasting the 'comrades' at the front from the 'shirkers' at home. The editors and authors of the soldier newspapers also used gendered imagery in many other combinations, likely because they were aware that this was a powerful tool with which to create a hierarchy of groups. Already existing prejudices could thus be strengthened. This was most apparent with the images of friends, foreigners and enemies. Utilizing gender-specific connotations, a long tradition of ethnic stereotyping was deepened, and in such a manner, a hierarchy of nations was depicted in the soldier newspapers of the First World War. The examples that follow will demonstrate the manner in which three groups were thus portrayed: enemy soldiers, German women on the home front and foreign women in occupied lands.

Enemy Soldiers

The *Champagne-Kamerad* of 9 December 1917 carried a fascinating article entitled 'Masculine and Feminine Peoples'. The author argued that, as was the case in nature, different nations (*Völker*) were divided into masculine and feminine groups. The Germanic people were manly, meaning they were active and independent. The Slavs and the Celts were womanly, meaning passive, always needing to be told what to do. Pure masculine breeds, like the Swabians of southwestern Germany, were so independent-minded that they had trouble following orders. The Prussians, on the other hand, with a mix of Germanic and Slavic blood, were perfect at both getting things done, and at taking orders when need be. The British were characterized in the same manner, a mix of effeminate Celtic and masculine Anglo-Saxon blood.[19]

The characterization of one's enemy as effeminate was not new in the First World War. In fact, there already existed a tradition which extended back to the era of the Wars of Liberation 1813–15, a struggle which had recently been depicted as a time of heroes during the 100th anniversary celebrations. Images of both friend and enemy from the earlier wars were now echoed in the soldier newspapers, most clearly with the depiction of the French nation as cowardly and 'womanly' (*weibisch*).[20] This tradition was further seized upon for the negative portrayal of those to the East; Slavs were represented in the frontline press as the most womanly of all peoples, so utterly dependent that they required and longed for conquest.

They were depicted as a lazy, dirty, primitive, barefoot and begging 'race'.[21]

The general tendency to effeminize enemy nations, especially the civilian populations of conquered and occupied regions, differed noticeably when it came to depicting enemy soldiers. They received softer criticism. This was especially the case for French and British soldiers. The French soldiers were ridiculed, just as was their nation, for being superficial and fashion-conscious. An example of this appeared in the 19 February 1916 *Liller Kriegszeitung*, with the cartoon: 'Peace dream of a Frenchman on watch'. It depicted a slumbering *poilu* dreaming of a brand new suit.[22] However, one could also find a rather masculine description of occasional French heroism, such as that which appeared in the 21 November 1915 issue of *Der Schützengraben*.[23] There were very few references to British troops in the German soldier newspapers. Despite the rampant 'Hate England' campaign of the home front newspapers, the few sketches of British prisoners depicted these combatants of a well-respected world power looking extremely manly in their tin hats, well-shaven, pipe in mouth. The only fault found with the Empire appeared in the occasional accusation of 'ungentlemanly' behavior by the British with regard to their 'beastly' treatment of their dark-skinned colonial troops.[24]

The description of Russian soldiers was less flattering. What is significant, however, is that negative depictions of Russian troops virtually only appeared in western front newspapers. There, the 7 April 1915 *Kriegszeitung für das XV. Armeekorps* made reference to the poor quality and dirtiness of the Russians' trenches,[25] and in the 1 October 1915 *Liller Kriegszeitung*, 'Mutig "vorwärts"' featured two Russian soldiers marching 'forward' toward St. Petersburg because they could not read the road sign.[26] Later, in the 12 August 1917 *Wacht im Westen*, 'Russian Offensive Power' was mocked with a sketch of a large tractor stuck in the mud.[27] In the eastern front newspapers the Russian troops were not cast so negatively, and there was even a positive description of Russian military culture: A 9 April 1916 article in the largest eastern front newspaper, the *Zeitung der 10. Armee*, contained a glowing evaluation of Russian soldier songs, arguing that only Germans and Russians could sing.[28] A possible explanation for this lack of criticism in the East may be that, unlike the occupied civilian populations, the Russians opposite the Germans' eastern trenches were daily encountered as *soldiers*, and were thereby fulfilling the most masculine of roles imaginable. This is an instance of negotiation in the newspapers; the readership would not stand for the transformation into passive 'sissies' the men who successfully killed and wounded German soldiers. Although it is not clear whether or not this resulted from some sense of 'respect' toward one's fellow warrior, recognition of the fact that the Germans had not been victorious may have been in play. The portrayals of both the Russian and French soldiers were sometimes marred by the sudden intrusion of a more overt propaganda, namely in the form of describing the 'ungentlemanly', or 'uncomradelike' behavior of these soldiers. In order to demonize the Russians, articles recalled their alleged barbarity in raping civilians in East Prussia,[29] and the French, for their part, were charged with operating atrociously inhumane prisoner of war camps.[30] The increasing number of prisoner of war atrocity stories toward the end of the war likely had less to do with denouncing the enemy, however, than frightening the growing number of German soldiers away from the decision to desert.

German *Kameradinnen*

The imagery of wives, girlfriends, mothers and sisters on the 'home front' in the soldier newspapers combined new ideas with old. Here, a tradition that reached back at least as far as the Wars of Liberation (1813–15) was seized upon. Already in the propaganda of these earlier hostilities, wars which first in Prussia and later in other German states introduced universal conscription, women were promoted as representing a crucial aspect of the war economy. In this era of 'national' wars, success required the waging of a *Volkskrieg*, a struggle which pursued national interests supported equally by both the military and civilian components of the nation. In her studies of this period, Karen Hagemann argues that the image of the 'valorous *Volk* family' was propagated with the goal of defining the specific tasks of men and women, according to their class, age and marital status within a clear gender order appropriate to the war economy. Women were to support the wars of liberation as 'heroic mothers, war brides and magnanimous nurses'. Within the family this meant that women should support the courage and fighting spirit of the men going off to war, and maintain their female honor during the separation. Specifically, they were to uphold their morality and loyalty. In the public sphere, in wartime they were to join the newly founded patriotic women's leagues. There, among other things, they were to raise money for the equipping of their 'national warriors', as well as provide care for the wounded and sick, and comfort to invalids, widows and orphans. Correspondingly, the main task of those men liable for military service was defined as the protection of family, home and fatherland. Onto their shoulders fell the responsibility to actively defend female honor, and to protect girls and women from the sexual attacks of enemy soldiers. Manly honor was thus inextricably linked to the readiness to do one's duty in defending family, home and fatherland.[31]

The propaganda of the First World War seized upon this tradition. Accordingly, in the pages of the soldier newspapers, the women on the home front were described as loyal and heroic mothers, soldiers' wives, and 'war brides'. In numerous articles, brave German women were described as sitting patiently at home, waiting for their lover or husband, and putting up with the troubles and difficulties of the war just as stoically as they performed their duties. In the 30 July 1916 issue of the *Kriegszeitung der 4. Armee*, an article described 'The Proper Soldier's Wife' as a caring mother and loyal wife, who never sent 'bitching letters' (*Jammerbriefe*) to her man at the front, and instead strengthened his will to hold out.[32] Many articles attempted to raise the morale of the troops by providing assurances that, despite their many problems, women at home proudly supported their fighting men.[33] Again and again the soldier newspapers referenced the 'loyalty', or *Treue*, of the girlfriends and wives, indicating that this was something exceptionally important to the men. In terms of comradeship, *Treue* was a major component in the constitution of worthy individuals, and thus German women, or *Kameradinnen*, could join in the 'holy union', albeit not as equals, for the ultimate comrades could only be fellow men fighting and dying in the field.[34]

A key aspect of the imagery of the comradeship of home and front, of soldiers' wives and warriors, was however new. With the movement of women into traditionally male occupations on a scale never before seen in Germany, German women became a part of the war effort to such a degree that they began to be physically 'masculinized' in the pictures of the soldier newspapers. They had become the providers for their families, and in taking on such difficult labor, they became, in the sketches of the soldier newspapers, 'de-feminized'. 'Farewell', in the 21 July 1917 *Zeitung der 10. Armee*, depicted a large, strong woman with rippling tendons, standing with her child in a field, while German soldiers marched in the distance.[35] This, like other sketches and references to women diligently ploughing fields, was meant to indicate that these asexual mothers were going to take the place of the absent men, while keeping the home front strong and remaining loyal to their husbands.[36] This evidence corresponds with the research of Belinda Davis on the public perception of women on the home front.[37] The new image of German women was brought about by a 'total war' economy which forced women to move into strange, previously male occupations, while learning to cope with a poorly organized state system of food rationing, and intensifying their already burdensome household production.

This development threatened to overcome the gender order because it put into question the previously dominant perception that the division of labor was naturally ordered. The uncertainty that this brought about in the men was rarely explicit in the soldier newspapers, but appeared repeatedly in implicit forms. A two frame cartoon in the *Drahtverhau* of January 1918, entitled 'Women's Auxiliary Service', depicted, in the first frame, a group of dowdy, overcoated, grumpy women getting on a commuter train during the week. The second frame, with the caption 'Sundays', had the same women dressed attractively in slim-fitting outfits being hit on by the same men who were only the day before shoving them onto the train.[38] In a story about home-leave, 'On the Train' in the 8 July 1917 edition of the *Kriegszeitung der 4. Armee*, a soldier, while changing trains at the station in Aachen, is startled when he encounters a young blonde woman, clearly dressed like a boy, working for the rail service. He trades some bread for a kiss, and remarks that everything in Germany is fine and happy, and that any rumors of a revolution should be dispelled.[39] In this manner, not only was potentially morale-sapping and politically undesirable news from the home front rendered innocuous, but male angst about a threatened gender role reversal was mollified.

Lovers and Whores

The women of the conquered and occupied lands were cast as the opposites of the German women on the home front. Further, these women were set into a hierarchy with the women of France depicted in a much more positive fashion than their counterparts in the East. Although not portrayed as especially hardworking or loyal like German women, French women were sometimes shown to be doing a certain amount of 'women's work', be it sewing or helping around field hospitals. Significantly, they were never begging. They were also clean and well-dressed. However, French women were criticized for their lack of morality and loyalty, and their tendency to frivolity and materialism. They were depicted flirting with the German soldiers, showing no desire to wait faithfully for the end of the war and the return of their husbands. Thus, it was suggested that French women were providing sex for the occupying soldiers, but, importantly, they were not simply portrayed as whores. Instead, despite their many faults, they were the declared 'girlfriends' of the soldiers. They were not, however, 'comrades' like German women, for it was clear in most cases that the relationships were temporary and convenient. Yet, the undeniably 'advanced' state of French culture and civilization, made most apparent by the ability of many educated German soldiers to speak the language, resulted in the recognition of the respectability of French women through the existence of rudimentary relationships.[40]

The image of Slavic women in the soldier newspapers of the eastern front was completely different. The cultural practices of Poles and Russians were as despised as their languages were unfamiliar. Such devaluation and rejection was evidenced in the depiction of the occupied female population. These women were portrayed as the polar opposites of everything manly, or 'properly' feminine: they were dirty, wore rags and walked barefoot; they were indolent, and were often depicted begging or smuggling; and it was clear that they were available for 'faithless' sex. In the 18 May 1917 issue of the *Zeitung der 10. Armee*, there was a joke letter written by one 'Marinnja' to her Russian husband. Having been asked by him how it is that their baby was born in June when the husband was on leave only in January, she writes that a certain 'Herr Hoffmann' had told her she was pretty. She then signs the letter 'Yours faithfully, Marinnja'.[41] In one of the most sexually implicit cartoons to be found in the German soldier newspapers, the 11 August 1917 *Kriegs-Zeitung von Baranowitschi* depicted two *Landser* walking past a little Polish house. A buxom young woman stands in the doorway, her little brother on the front step. 'Come in, Good Gentlemen!' the boy calls, 'Would you like to drink a glass of tea with sugar?'[42] What little respect the women of the East received in the newspapers existed in the occasional sketch of a pretty Slavic woman, and in one atypical photo, from the 8 November 1916 edition of the *Zeitung der 10. Armee*, of four German soldiers standing among five Polish girls in head-scarves. The caption read, 'Separate Peace' (*Sonderfrieden*).[43]

It was in the depiction of women in the occupied territories that the ambiguity and double standard of the concept of loyalty was most apparent. While for German women it was understood that female loyalty meant monogamy, this was not expected of either the women of the enemy or of the German soldiers themselves. There was no attempt in the soldier newspapers to disguise the fact that the German men were being sexually 'disloyal' to their partners all the time. The only evidence of disapproval of this kind of behavior can be found in the occasional article about venereal disease, informing the German soldier that it was his 'duty' not to sleep with prostitutes because this would leave him sick, and unable to fight for the fatherland. It is clear that loyalty in the soldier newspapers meant something different for men than it did for women. For women loyalty was extended to the men they were engaged or married to. For men, loyalty was to the nation and to fellow male soldiers: it was their duty to defend the home front and fatherland, and to stand fast with their comrades. Ute Frevert has addressed the 'complementarity' of male and female 'honor'. Through her loyalty, a woman protects not only her own honor, but that of her husband as well. He must protect her honor from any and all attacks. If he fails as a protector, he fails as a man.[44]

Closing Remarks: War Propaganda and Gender Imagery

In her essay, 'Masculinity and Nationalism: Gender and Sexuality in the Making of Nations', Joanne Nagel claims that: 'the culture and ideology of hegemonic masculinity [goes] hand in hand with the culture and ideology of hegemonic nationalism [...] Terms like honour, patriotism, cowardice, bravery and duty are hard to distinguish as either nationalistic or masculinist, since they seem so thoroughly tied both to the nation and to manliness.'[45] She further claims that the 'microculture' of masculinity in daily life mirrors the demands of the military, war and nation. This is confirmed in the analysis of the soldier newspapers of the First World War. The depictions of self and enemy were permeated with gendered attributes. Male imagery was always cloaked in either friendly or foreign renderings of femininity as well as various versions of masculinity. Both the images of men and women were seldom purely 'masculine' or 'feminine'.[46] This becomes most clear in the complementary image of German men and women, on the front and at home. The manly image of comrades at the front was a mixture of both 'hard' bravery in battle and 'soft' love when among close friends. The model of wife-comrades blended feminine love and loyalty with autonomy, strength and great patience. The relatively unambiguous prewar gender imagery that had been founded upon a clear bifurcation of masculine and feminine duties in society had been broken down and modified by the exigencies of industrialized mass warfare, a form of conflict that necessitated the commitment of the entire population if victory were to be achieved. Women at home entered in great number occupations that had formerly been associated with the male population, and thus in many cases German women became the breadwinners for their families. This overall development appeared to many men – the soldiers at the front – as a threatening and deeply unsettling experience. This crisis of the gender order, which more than anything was a crisis of masculinity, appeared throughout the pages of the soldier newspapers. Paradoxically, it was present most clearly in the insistence upon the 'manliness' of German soldiers at the front, their honor and stalwart defense.[47]

If the changes on the home front were the sole reason for the constant reference to masculinity and honor in the German soldier newspapers, then one should expect to find the same in the soldier newspapers of the Allied armies,[48] for their domestic fronts were undergoing similar adjustments. Yet, the French and British soldier newspapers were strangely mute when it came to declarations of manliness and honor. Words such as 'comradeship' rarely if ever appeared. What then could account for such a radically different tone in the soldier newspapers of the two conflicting forces? The results of my research thus far support a general thesis which is reinforced by the frequent appearance of 'honorable masculinity' in the German soldier newspapers. It would seem as though the rank and file of the German army had doubts as to the legitimacy of the military's position. Unlike their opponents, the German soldier newspapers were forced to spend an inordinate amount of time 'justifying' the existence of German armies on foreign soil. It would have been obvious to anyone looking at a map that Germany had not been invaded, and thus, in order to feel at ease, the myth of a Germany on the defensive was created through constant reference to aggressive and unfair enemy nations. In addition, a heavy emphasis was placed on the great need for German colonization of the 'immature' East. The doubts that more than a few German soldiers seemed to have had were tirelessly countered in the propaganda of the soldier newspapers, journals whose stated purpose was to strengthen the morale of the fighting men. British and French soldiers and officers however, perceiving themselves as clearly defending against German aggression on French and Belgian soil, saw little need to justify their actions. With regard to the actual defense of their own 'fatherlands', their honor and masculinity never stood in doubt.[49]

Notes

I thank Stefanie Schüler-Springorum and above all Karen Hagemann for intensive criticism and revision.

1. See Karen Hagemann, 'A Valourous *Volk* Family. The Nation, the Military, and the Gender Order in Prussia in the Time of the Anti-Napoleonic Wars, 1806-15,' in *Gendered Nations. Nationalisms and Gender Order in the Long Nineteenth Century*, ed. Ida Blom, et al. (Oxford, 2000), 179–205; Karen Hagemann, 'Of "Manly Valor" and "German Honor": Nation, War, and Masculinity in the Age of the

Robert L. Nelson

Prussian Uprising Against Napoleon,' *Central European History* 30 (1998): 187–220; Karen Hagemann, *'Mannlicher Muth und Teutsche Ehre'. Nation, Militär und Geschlecht zur Zeit der Antinapoleonischen Kriege Preußens* (Paderborn, 2002). See also: Ute Frevert, ed., *Militär und Gesellschaft im 19. und 20. Jahrhundert* (Stuttgart, 1997); Karen Hagemann and Ralf Pröve, eds., *Landsknechte, Soldatenfrauen und Nationalkrieger. Militär, Krieg und Geschlechterordnung im historischen Wandel* (Frankfurt, 1998); Thomas Kühne, 'Zwischen Männerbund und Volksgemeinschaft: Hitlers Soldaten und der Mythos der Kameradschaft,' *Archiv für Sozialgeschichte* 38 (1998): 165–189; Thomas Kühne, 'Kameradschaft – "Das Beste im Leben des Mannes". Die deutschen Soldaten des Zweiten Weltkriegs in erfahrungs- und geschlechtergeschichtlicher Perspektive,' *Geschichte und Gesellschaft* 22 (1996): 504–529; see also his contribution to this volume.

This article is informed by the methodological approaches utilized in recent research into British colonialism, such as: Graham Dawson, *Soldier Heroes. British Adventure, Empire and the Imagining of Masculinity* (New York, 1994); Mrinali Sinha, *Colonial Masculinity. The 'Manly Englishman' and the 'Effeminate Bengali' in the Late Nineteenth Century* (Manchester, 1995); David Omissi, *The Sepoy and the Raj. The Indian Army, 1860–1940* (London, 1994).

2. See Anne Lipp, 'Friedenssehnsucht und Durchhaltebereitschaft: Wahrnehmung und Erfahrungen deutscher Soldaten im Ersten Weltkrieg,' *Archiv für Sozialgeschichte* 36 (1996): 279–292; Anne Lipp, 'Heimatwahrnehmung und soldatisches "Kriegserlebnis",' in *Kriegserfahrungen: Studien zur Sozial- und Mentalitätsgeschichte des Ersten Weltkriegs*, ed. Gerhard Hirschfeld, et al. (Essen, 1997), 225–242. The only earlier publication I have found which uses German soldier newspapers as a major source of historical evidence is Dennis E. Showalter, 'The Homesick Revolutionaries: Soldiers' Councils and Newspaper Propaganda in German-Occupied Eastern Europe, 1918–1919,' *Canadian Journal of History* 11 (1976): 69–88. The German soldier newspapers of the Second World War are discussed in Heinz-Werner Eckhardt, *Die Frontzeitungen des deutschen Heeres. 1939–1945* (Stuttgart, 1975).

3. The production and censorship of the soldier newspapers is extensively described in: Karl Kurth, *Die deutschen Feld- und Schützengrabenzeitungen des Weltkrieges* (Leipzig, 1937), 207–247. This and the following two paragraphs rely heavily on Kurth. I found 67 titles (ca. 7 000 individual issues) for the western front, and 48 titles (ca. 5 000 individual issues) for the eastern and southeastern fronts. This corresponds

closely to what Kurth lists in his dissertation, and it is unlikely that there were too many more titles that escaped his notice. Today, large collections of the soldier newspapers can be found in the Library of Contemporary History in Stuttgart, the Military Archives in Freiburg and the most complete collection in the German Library in Leipzig.

4. 'Gedanken über Kameradschaft,' *Liller Kriegszeitung*, 26 July 1917.

5. 'Sei ein Mann!,' *Zeitung der 10. Armee*, 12 October 1916.

6. A good example can be found in 'Kameradschaft,' *Kriegszeitung für das XV. Armeekorps*, 22 May 1915.

7. 'Ich hatt' einen Kameraden . . .,' *Deutsche Kriegs-Zeitung von Baranowitschi*, 17 June 1916.

8. 'Ich hatt' einen Kameraden,' *Liller Kriegszeitung*, 7 February 1917.

9. 'Freundschaft,' *Kriegszeitung der 4. Armee*, 29 June 1916.

10. 'Von der Freundschaft,' *Kriegszeitung der 4. Armee*, 21 April 1918.

11. 'Freundschaft,' *Deutsche Kriegszeitung in Polen*, 6 June 1915.

12. 'Kameradschaft,' *Vogesenwacht*, May 1916.

13. 'Kriegskameraden,' *Kriegszeitung der 4. Armee*, 7 September 1916.

14. 'Die wahre Vaterlandspartei,' *Champagne-Kamerad*, 18 November 1917.

15. 'Kameradschaft,' *Somme-Wacht*, 7 September 1917.

16. 'Der Militäruntaugliche,' *Liller Kriegszeitung*, 28 April 1915.

17. 'Was wir Soldaten fordern,' *Liller Kriegszeitung*, 24 September 1917.

18. See 'Streik in Berlin!,' *Champagne-Kamerad*, 17 February 1918. Also: 'Der Streik,' *Drahtverhau*, February 1918. Anne Lipp argues that both levels of newspapers were thoroughly damning of the strikes, but that many lower-rank soldiers were sympathetic to the strikers, and that the larger newspapers were responsible for perpetuating the myth of a 'stab-in-the-back' by striking workers. See Lipp, 'Friedenssehnsucht und Durchhaltebereitschaft,' 291. The evidence she cites suggests otherwise. The larger newspapers were clearly trying to maintain a *Burgfrieden*, being critical but diplomatic, while the most unrestrained venom came from the smallest journals. For a discussion of complex soldier attitudes towards strikers, see Wolfgang Kruse, 'Krieg und Klassenheer. Zur Revolutionierung der deutschen Armee im Ersten Weltkrieg,' *Geschichte und Gesellschaft* 22 (1996): 530–561.

19. 'Männliche und Weibliche Völker,' *Champagne-Kamerad*, 9 December 1917. The author was Otto von Bismarck.

20. For an explanation of the nuances differentiating 'weiblich' from 'weibisch' at the time of the Napoleonic Wars, see Hagemann, 'Volk Family'. See also Michael Jeismann, *Das Vaterland der Feinde:*

Robert L. Nelson

Studien zum nationalen Feindbegriff und Selbstverständnis in Deutschland und Frankreich 1792–1918 (Stuttgart, 1992).

21. See for example, 'Das Panjehaus,' *Zeitung der 10. Armee*, 28 January 1917.

22. 'Friedenstraum eines französischen Vorpostens,' *Liller Kriegszeitung*, 19 February 1916.

23. 'Das Franzosengrab,' *Der Schützengraben*, 21 November 1915.

24. See 'Gefangener Engländer,' *Somme -Wacht*, 25 February 1917; 'Englischer Gefangener,' *Somme-Wacht*, 1 April 1917; 'Gefangener Engländer,' *Somme-Wacht*, 24 June 1917. The treatment of race in the German newspapers is far too large and complex for this brief paper. The French and German discussion of the use of colonial troops, as well as the German imagery of Eastern Jews is discussed at length in my forthcoming PhD dissertation, 'German Soldier Newspapers of the First World War,' (Cambridge University). See also Christian Koller's contribution to this volume.

25. 'Deutsche und russische Schützengrabenarbeit,' *Kriegszeitung für das XV. Armeekorps*, 7 April 1915.

26. 'Mutig "Vorwärts"', *Liller Kriegszeitung*, 1 October 1915.

27. 'Die russische Offensivkraft,' *Wacht im Westen*, 12 August 1917.

28. 'Russische Soldatenlieder,' *Zeitung der 10. Armee*, 9 April 1916.

29. Among many examples: 'Ostpreußen-nummer,' *Zeitung der 10. Armee*, 3 February 1917.

30. See for example, 'Der französische Soldat,' *Liller Kriegszeitung*, 9 September 1918.

31. See Hagemann, 'Volk Family'; Karen Hagemann, *Mannlicher Muth*. For more on gender-specific definitions of honor, see: Ute Frevert, *'Mann und Weib, und Weib und Mann'. Geschlechter-Differenzen in der Moderne* (Munich, 1995), 166–222.

32. 'Die rechte Soldatenfrau,' *Kriegszeitung der 4. Armee*, 30 July 1916.

33. Among many examples, see 'Frau und Krieg,' *Zeitung der 10. Armee*, 20 October 1916; 'Heldentum,' *Kriegszeitung der 4. Armee*, 26 May 1915; 'Heldenfrauen,' *Seille-Bote*, 4 June 1916.

34. Among others, 'Einer treuen Frauenhand,' *Kriegszeitung der 4. Armee*, 14 May 1915; 'Treue,' *Liller Kriegszeitung*, 4 September 1916; 'Die Kriegersfrau,' *Zeitung der 10. Armee*, 13 February 1917.

35. 'Abschied,' Zeitung der 10. Armee, 21 July 1917. See also: 'Weiblicher Hilfsdienst,' *Der Drahtverhau*, August 1917.

36. An article, 'Ein Erntegruß deutscher Frauen – ins Feld!' in the 20 August 1916 *Kriegszeitung der 4. Armee*, tellingly equated women's work with that of the front; a female-tilled piece of earth was referred to as a 'Field of Honor' (*Ehrenfeld*).

37. Belinda Davis, *Home Fires Burning. Food, Politics, and Everyday Life in World War I Berlin* (Chapel Hill/London, 2000); see also her contribution to this volume.
38. 'Weiblicher Hilfsdienst,' *Der Drahtverhau*, January 1918.
39. 'Auf der Eisenbahn,' *Kriegszeitung der 4. Armee*, 8 July 1917.
40. There are numerous articles and sketches in western front newspapers illustrating this. Among others: 'Eifersucht,' *Schützengrabenzeitung*, Christmas 1915; 'Lillerin,' *Somme-Wacht*, 25 February 1917; 'Das Wunder,' *Liller Kriegszeitung*, 24 July 1918.
41. 'Schnurrpfeifer,' *Zeitung der 10. Armee*, 18 May 1917.
42. Untitled, *Kriegs-Zeitung von Baranowitschi*, 11 August 1917.
43. Untitled, *Zeitung der 10. Armee*, 8 November 1916.
44. See Frevert, *Mann und Weib*, 216.
45. Joanne Nagel, 'Masculinity and Nationalism: Gender and Sexuality in the Making of Nations,' *Ethnic and Racial Studies* 21 (1998): 249–252.
46. Karen Hagemann comes to a rather similar conclusion concerning the construction of national and military gender imagery in the period of the Napoleonic Wars. See her *Männlicher Muth*.
47. Karen Hagemann has discussed such a paradox in her 'Venus und Mars. Reflexionen zu einer Geschlechtergeschichte von Militär und Krieg,' in Hagemann/Pröve, *Landsknechte*, 13–48, 27ff.
48. Studies of the Allied soldier newspapers can be found in the following: Stéphane Audoin-Rouzeau, *Men at War, 1914–1918: National Sentiment and Trench Journalism in France during the First World War* (Providence, 1992); Jean-Pierre Turbergue, ed., *1914–1918. Les journeaux de tranchées* (Paris, 1999); J.G. Fuller, *Troop Morale and Popular Culture in the British and Dominion Armies, 1914–1918* (Oxford, 1990). See also F. Bertrand, *La presse francophone de tranchée au front belge, 1914–1918* (Brussels, 1971), and Mario Isnenghi, *Giornali di trincea 1915–1918* (Turin, 1977). A reference to patriotic journals for Russian soldiers is in footnote 36 on page 186 of Hubertus Jahn, *Patriotic Culture in Russia during World War One* (Ithaca, 1995).
49. On the British defense of a 'way of life', see Fuller, *Troop Morale*.

–3–

Motherly Heroines and Adventurous Girls

Red Cross Nurses and Women Army Auxiliaries in the First World War

Bianca Schönberger

My two brothers have volunteered and they have been gone since September, my father will still have to go and so I don't want to sit at home and be idle while so many men out there lay down their lives for the fatherland. I, too, have German blood running through my veins and I want to have a closer relation to the war. Here in our industrial town of Fürth the war is hardly noticeable.[1]

These words were written in August 1915 by the 18-year-old Anna Sauter in her petition to King Ludwig of Bavaria. Like her, many women expressed their desire to participate more directly in the war and to share the male war experience near the front. In the First World War this wish, however, came true for only two groups of women: for the nurses and for the women army auxiliaries who were employed in the rear-echelons and in the General Administrations.[2] The first-time orchestrated incorporation of nurses in the army medical services and of the women army auxiliaries in the military administrations during the First World War created an official working place for thousands of women in the army. A discussion of the contemporary discourse on the forms and limits of women's participation in war will highlight the influence of class and gender on the assessment of women's war work, on their scope of action and on the definition of their contribution to the war effort relative to men. Although the actual work they performed – nursing and clerical work – was 'feminine' enough, the fact that women were employed 'in the field' – a sphere with a genuinely male connotation – played an important role in the social and cultural formation of gender images in the war society. The analysis is based on contemporary publications, press-releases of the Red Cross, biographies and previously largely unused military sources – in particular from the Bavarian and Württemberg Armies and their respective Ministries of War.

A study of women army auxiliaries and nurses in the First World War is located at the interface of gender history and military history; as a result these women's services have been largely ignored by both disciplines.[3] Only very recently German historiography has begun to explore the inter-relations of the military, war and the gender order in more detail.[4] These studies demonstrate pointedly that war culture and gender are inseparably connected. Much more is known about women who worked as nurses and army auxiliaries with the armies of other combatant powers in the First World War. American and British historians in particular have developed more nuanced images of societies at war for many years by including women army auxiliaries and nurses in the picture. Besides editions of autobiographical testimonies[5] and more descriptive literature[6] there are numerous studies on the British women army auxiliaries and nurses which cover aspects such as the origins of the service,[7] class relations,[8] patriotism (or the lack of it),[9] gender order and gender images.[10] Susan Zeiger has studied the class and gender dynamics at the work place of American women army auxiliaries in France.[11] Hanna Hacker has written about the women in the Austro-Hungarian army with a methodological approach that owes much to queer studies.[12] French women's role in the orderly rooms and hospital wards has been researched by Margaret H. Darrow.[13]

The Red Cross Nurses[14]

For the Red Cross nurses their employment beyond the homefront from August 1914 onwards was neither unexpected nor unprepared for. Since the mid-nineteenth century, numerous local Patriotic Women's Associ-ations of the Red Cross, headed by the Empress, had offered 'women of higher and the highest ranks'[15] the possibility to engage in philanthropic work. The Women's Associations, born out of military nursing in the wars of 1866 and 1870/71, and the Red Cross sisterhoods, in which Red Cross nurses lived in convent-like 'mother-houses'[16] modelled on the religious sisterhoods, played a central role in the health services and local welfare provision. Although in the decades before the outbreak of the First World War the Women's Associations were mainly involved in civilian philan-thropy such as girls' education and employment, children's welfare, and support for the local poor and sick,[17] this work was – at least rhetorically – always put in context of the preparation for a future war. Volunteer Nursing (*Freiwillige Krankenpflege*) in wartime was conceptualized as women's counterpart to men's bravery on the battlefield.[18] According to the conservative gender image of the Red Cross, the fairer sex was principally gifted for nursing as it gave 'women's nature, the driving force behind women's life, what it needs: to be able to care, love and give, hence creating true happiness, inner peace and everlasting satisfaction'.[19]

When the war broke out, the Red Cross handed its trained nurses over to the military for service in the rear-echelons. The Medical Service in War Act (*Kriegssanitätsordnung*) of 1878 gave the Red Cross nurses a role in military nursing according to which they had to go into action in the rear of the fighting army 'incorporated into the State organism' and 'headed by State authorities'.[20] The Red Cross also called upon the female population as early as August 1914 to train as nurses and nursing aides, as a substantial lack of nursing personnel was already foreseeable.[21] The appeal of the Prussian Women's Associations of the Red Cross was met with a very good response in all parts of society, while nursing 'fresh wounds' on the 'blood-spattered battlefield' was seen as particularly attractive.[22] 'The rush of female volunteers in the days of mobilization was everywhere indeed enormous, especially the volunteering of women and girls for the nursing of casualties, particularly in the rear area and even in the rear of the fighting army [. . .].'[23] The number of female nurses employed beyond the homefront as part of Volunteer Nursing soon attained dimensions unknown in any previous war as more and more male army nursing staff was drafted for fighting and had to be replaced by nurses. Until the autumn of 1918 more than 28,000 nurses worked behind the front and in the occupied territories where the professional nurses were soon outnumbered by the nursing aides who had been trained in the war.

The initial wave of female volunteers for the military hospitals came from various social classes. In the course of the war, however, a self-selection by social class evolved, particularly after the rapid deterioration of food supplies in Germany. Only a certain group of women could afford to learn nursing unpaid and to work for a salary of 70 pfennig[24] per day, when employment in factories could earn them a salary four to eight times as high.[25] The 22-year-old orphan Anna Murr from Munich, for example, asked the Bavarian King in a letter in June 1918 'to help her find a job as a Red Cross nurse'. She claimed she could not raise the costs herself, 'the obstacle is the four-week course; then the self-catering and the clothes, I cannot afford it. I am a poor girl [. . .].'[26] Financial pressure, therefore, kept an increasing number of women from volunteering for the Red Cross, and the commitment to Volunteer Nursing was left largely to bourgeois and noble women as had already been the case before the war.[27]

The Women Army Auxiliaries

The nurses in the rear-echelons had competitors for the first time in the spring of 1917. Before the outbreak of the war and during its first two years, the idea of integrating women into the army in a non-medical capacity[28] would have been considered simply absurd. In the face of a growing lack of able-bodied men, however, this changed in the winter of 1916. As a result of the enormous loss of lives in the major battles of the previous summer, the government was forced to pass the Patriotic Auxiliary Service Act (*Gesetz über den Vaterländischen Hilfsdienst*) through Parliament. According to this law all men on the homefront between the age of 17 and 60 were obliged to do compulsory labour in the war industries and in orderly rooms in order to set soldiers free for service at the front and to enhance the production of munitions.[29] But all law-making and administrative attempts to make good the manpower shortage were unsuccessful. The only positive response to the Patriotic Auxiliary Service Act came from women who – although they themselves had been exempted from the act – soon outnumbered the men liable under the act in replacing able-bodied men in the industry and in orderly rooms on the homefront.[30] The number of replacements, however, was still too small. Thus from the spring of 1917 onwards the first organized large-scale replacement of soldiers by women army auxiliaries in the occupied territories was started.[31] This was not only a reaction to the failure of the Patriotic Auxiliary Service Act and the ongoing lack of able-bodied men for front service, but it was also intended to stop the increasing 'uncoordinated employment' of female office staff in both the General Administrations and – more and more – in the rear-echelons.[32]

The women in the newly founded War Office (*Kriegsamt*) in Berlin, and in the local War Office Bureaux (*Kriegsamtsstellen*) with the Deputy General Commands who were given the task to organize the employment of women army auxiliaries, were almost all members of the bourgeois women's movement. Marie-Elisabeth Lüders, a long-standing member of the Federation of German Women's Associations (*Bund Deutscher Frauenvereine*, BDF) was the head of the newly founded Women's Department in the War Office until the winter of 1917; Agnes von Harnack, also an influential member of the BDF, became her successor. Gertrud Bäumer, chairwoman of the BDF, Alice Salomon and Elisabeth Altmann-Gottheiner, both members of the BDF standing committee, headed the Women's Departments in their respective local War Office Bureaux. The BDF had already made a contribution to the militarization of the female 'homefront-army' by organizing the National Women's Service (*Nationaler*

Frauendienst).[33] Their new task was in fact 'a somewhat foolhardy under-taking'[34] as Alice Salomon recapitulated, because never before had there been an orchestrated mobilization of women to replace soldiers in the occupied territories. Women between the age of twenty and forty who were neither employed in administration nor in a war industry or agricul-ture could apply for a place in the rear-echelon as a civilian in the 'army entourage' with her local War Office Bureau, where she had to hand in numerous references including a health certificate, work reports and a character reference.[35] The number of women army auxiliaries grew con-stantly, and by the end of the war more than 20,000 women were working in the orderly rooms from Sedan to Sevastopol.

The women army auxiliaries were decidedly different from the nurses in regard to social class, as they were mainly lower middle-class and – to a smaller extent – working-class.[36] The War Office employed women army auxiliaries in 'higher positions' in orderly rooms, in field book-shops, as postal supervisors or in the management of small economic enterprises. A smaller number also worked in kitchens and laundries. General Ludendorff – since 1916 Head of General Staff in the Third Supreme Command – had already declared in July 1917 that in regard to women auxiliaries 'female relatives of officers and senior officials [. . .] were generally not considered for this service'.[37] There was, therefore, only a small group of ladies with experience in social work to be employed as matrons for the dormitories or as female consultants in the rear-echelons, responsible for the supervision of the women army auxiliaries.

Women's War Service and Gender Images

In the wartime popular press the nurses working alongside the soldiers – brave and resolute – displayed 'not male heroism, but [. . .] motherliness, which implied self-sacrifice and devoted care, "motherly" heroism'. This was true for all nurses 'even if they had not been mothers themselves'.[38] This elevation of the nurses in the media as the ideal of 'sacrifice and selfless fulfilment of women's duty'[39] imperceptibly picked up the Red Cross's prewar propaganda which had interwoven the image of the Red Cross nurse with idealized female characteristics and the motif of the religious sisters. Hence sentimental stories in magazines like *Die Woche*, which was published in Berlin, featured nurses who smiled 'wise and sweet like a mother'.[40] In the iconography and in the literature nurses also often resembled nuns, angels or the Madonna.

Inside an old gothic church. Candlelight glides silently along the wall, it makes the colours of the paintings shine, it nuzzles around the Madonna at the altar, so that the eyes of Mary Mother of God and of the child on her arm come to life. The soft light shines on the blood-covered straw, it shines on bullet-wounded, quiet and moaning people. Like silent shadows, the nurses move between them, helping, caring, tending.[41]

These reports were further enhanced with images of noblewomen dressed in the costume of the Red Cross nurse (often combined with religious accessories such as a rosary). In these images the class status and the costume unified likewise into the ideal of nun-like serenity and motherly care. Furthermore, captions like 'Red Cross Sister Stephanie' (Countess of Lonyay)[42] suggested that in principle every sister could be a hidden 'lady'. It does not come as a surprise, therefore, that the Red Cross nurses – especially those working near the frontlines[43] – enjoyed the highest prestige in the eyes of the general public in wartime society and that they embodied the objective of many women's wish for participation in the war.[44] The Red Cross also enabled women to 'play an active part' in the nation at the time of national emergency.[45] A poem published in the *Deutsche Tageszeitung* in the autumn of 1914 read:

No less brave than the men's companies
Who are called to the bloody struggle
Not caring about trouble or imminent danger
You are going into the fields making sacrifices.[46]

It was thus not only the publications of the Red Cross that praised the nursing of wounded in this way – as a selfless patriotic service for the fatherland, free from monetary interest and with a high personal risk.

This idealization of an actual or imagined incorporation of women into the patriotic 'companies' of 'men' and their departure 'into the fields', however, did not remain undisputed. As the nurse personified female participation in the war effort, she became the target for all those critics who suspected the patriotically motivated women in the war to be an onslaught on the male monopoly of warfare or an attack on the existing gender order. Not surprisingly, it was the more conservative circles of society that led the way in discrediting the nurses.[47] The 'Historical-Political Papers of Catholic Germany' (*Historisch-politische Blätter des Katholischen Deutschland*), the journalistic spearhead of the Catholic intelligentsia and clergy, wrote in September 1915 a 'Religious Review and Outlook after the First Year of War' in this spirit.

Womanhood does not seem at her best at the moment. One interjects this opinion by pointing out what she has achieved by the nursing of the wounded. Remarkable indeed. One cannot help to think, however, that very, very much of this is done only to create a pretence or for selfish reasons. [. . .] when one sees the wounded in the parks surrounded by the most immature of our youth and when one hears the even sadder reports of the state of affairs behind the front one cannot help to think of Isaiah 4,1: On that day seven women will take hold of one man and say, 'We shall provide our own food and clothing if only we may bear your name. Take away our disgrace!⁴⁸

Isaiah 4,1, in fact, alludes to the previous verse 3, 25: 'Zion, your men will fall by the sword, your warriors in battle.' Hence it refers to women whose husbands were killed in war and who are begging other men to marry them in order to put them out of their misery of widowhood – again an innuendo on the theme of nurses' pursuit of matrimony amongst the sick and wounded.[49] In addition stories of nurses' affairs with soldiers and – even worse – with prisoners of war as well as of the apparent snobbery of nurses were spread in the papers. Already in the autumn of 1914 the *Saarbrücker Volkszeitung* asked ironically with an allusion to nurses' proposed preference for wounded officers: 'Are these women nurses?'[50] The *Berliner Zeitung* answered this question in its own way – it wrote about a group of prostitutes 'disguised' as nurses who had been arrested by the police.[51]

Nurses denigrated in this way embodied the eroticized counterpart of the 'sacrificing nurse' and hence threatened the fragile imagined balance between the wounded soldier and the asexually connoted nurse. The suggestion that nurses saw the soldiers not as patients but as men – as potential lovers or even future husbands – was associated with stereotypes of female frivolity, vice and gender chaos. The critics of female Volunteer Nursing suggested that many women 'played nurses' out of indecent motifs, while soldiers selflessly devoted themselves to the fatherland. This criticism denied women's patriotic feelings and also diminished their contribution to the war effort in the spirit of those who wanted to save the war as the 'last exclusively male show'.[52]

This criticism of the nurses has also to be seen in the context of increasingly virulent social conflict in the army and on the homefront.[53] Nurses, and particularly nursing aides, often shared their social background with the officers, and they were often treated by these officers particularly courteously. This made them a target for soldiers' defamatory statements, which were then swept from the front to the home-front. Hence in June 1917 the Head of General Command felt obliged to issue an order to all commands stating that officers had to refrain from 'rides in official cars – cars or horse and carriage – in the company of ladies' because this had led to 'the most spiteful comments' in the past. 'Particularly in the rear-echelons everything that leads to such gossip has to be avoided in the interest of the image of the rear-echelon administration and rear-echelon formations.'[54] The likelihood is that some of these 'ladies' would have been nurses as the number of women army auxiliaries was still comparatively small then.

It is much more difficult to determine and discuss the gender image attributed to the women army auxiliaries, as their image remained rather ill-defined compared to the nurses throughout the war. There are two reasons for this. Firstly, they lacked visual presence, as all attempts to uniform them failed, when the War Office turned down the request arguing that there was a lack of cloth.[55] This had far-reaching consequences for their public perception as there were practically no identifiable images of them in the press. While the nurses' iconography played an important role in the way the public perceived them, the women army auxiliaries were lacking any visual presentation. Secondly, the employment of women army auxiliaries in the rear of the fighting armies had – in contrast to the case of the nurses – initially taken place without any public advertisement. The Women's Department of the War Office feared a massive job change by women into the better-paid auxiliary jobs that might cause disruption on the labour market, and so it was decided to desist from advertisement in the press.[56] The office of the General Quartermaster to whom women's auxiliary service was subordinated in the military hierarchy, too, warned against issuing slogans such as 'German women, go to the occupied territories!'[57] Hence women army auxiliaries and their work were noticed to a much lesser extent, and one looks in vain for reports about women army auxiliaries in many journals and newspapers which regularly featured nurses. 'A *certain increased public interest* concerning women's war work in the occupied territories and the creating of uncontrollable and often simply false *rumours* which come in its wake',[58] however, forced the War Office finally to address the public in 1918. It issued press releases which were reprinted in many newspapers, and which characterized the women army auxiliaries as follows: 'Not lust for adventure, at least not in the negative meaning of the word, drives these women into these surely austere and arduous positions. Besides the wish to serve their fatherland in difficult times, it was rather the wish to support the family at home which made them come to this decision.'[59]

The attempt of the Women's Department in the War Office to establish a well-administered and uniform women's service ran into trouble right from the start in the spring of 1917. As a result the effort to set up women's non-medical service with the army in the occupied territories was in Germany from the beginning a story of disputes over competence and power, and of conflicting interests. In the months following the decision to include women in the army auxiliary service, representatives of the military in the field, War Office staff and the Heads of Women Affairs in the local War Office Bureaux met on several occasions to discuss the conceptualization, implementation, and supervision of women's service, and these meetings became the scene of the confrontations surrounding the nation-wide mobilization of women for work in the occupied territories. Firstly, the service and the ladies running it were deplored in many parts of the army, which was in constant struggle with the Women's Department of the War Office.[60] The rear-echelon became the battleground for concepts of a gender-specific scope of action. Lüders also disagreed with her male colleagues in the War Office over many issues concerning the service as well as over the role of women in its conceptualization. The close liaison between the women's movement and women's auxiliary service was most counterproductive in this respect. The military only reluctantly accepted the members of the women's movement as a cooperating partner, condemning them wholesale as 'infertile', 'family-destroying' and 'Jewish-social-democratic'.[61] Marie-Elisabeth Lüders, worn down after months of struggle, resigned in December 1917. Eventually the military depended on the expertise and the networks of the women's movement to set as many men as possible free for the front. Even with Agnes von Harnack, however, the relationship did not remain without conflicts. Secondly, Lüders, Harnack and the War Office were locked in a power struggle with the military authorities in the field which wanted to employ women army auxiliaries without the interference of the authorities on the homefront. The result was an administrative chaos in which the service was caught up for most of its existence. These shortcomings stand out when the service is compared with its British counterpart.[62] Hierarchical structures were weak due to the administrative chaos at all levels of the German service, which made the military in the field ignore many of the decrees issued regarding the service. The women in charge of the service felt throughout the war that the situation in the occupied territories was out of control, in particular with regard to the auxiliaries' moral behaviour.[63]

The close association of women with the army in any capacity other than nursing carried negative connotations for contemporaries in almost all belligerent nations, and Germany was no exception.[64] Furthermore, women from the lower strata of society who led an independent life based on their high income were bound to be criticized in highly sexual terms. Not surprisingly, the reputation of women army auxiliaries was bad, especially compared to the Red Cross nurses. Unlike the nurses, their social background was one that did not allow them to serve the fatherland without being paid or only for pocket-money. The post of an army auxiliary was very attractive for women who had to earn a living. Women army auxiliaries were divided into three classes of income and received a comparatively high salary of 3–6.5 marks a day including board and lodging depending on the nature and the length of their employment.[65] In comparison, nurses and soldiers earned a disproportionately low salary of 70 pfennigs a day and 1 mark a day respectively.[66] Hence the patriotism of these unmarried and financially independent women, promoted by the War Office, was doubted in the press, which vilified them as young typists 'who were not burdened with worldly wisdom' and to whom Brussels lace was 'fairer than service in the orderly rooms'.[67] Women's auxiliary service not only allowed mostly young single women to take up jobs in the army formerly performed by soldiers. Compared to their brothers and fathers[68] in the trenches, they were also in a much better financial position to provide for the family.[69] This was conceived as an attack on the gender and social order and in the public sphere it was avenged with harsh criticism from the press. As in the case of female clerks on the homefront, this escape from traditional ties was expressed in eroticized ciphers according to which 'pecuniary, and other, namely sexual independence'[70] attracted women to join the service. This was also connected with the assumption that the material independence of this type of 'New Woman' went hand in hand with declining moral standards.

The importance of class in the appraisal of women's war service can also be illustrated by the following example. The members of the small circle of translators who were also part of the women's auxiliary service were largely from a cultured middle-class background (*Bildungsbürgertum*). The reporting on these 'fine, elegantly dressed ladies' who had gone to the rear-area 'to defend the fatherland' was decidedly different from the usual reporting on the service.[71] The War Office Bureaux tried desperately to counteract the 'danger' of moral misconduct by recruiting 'educated ladies'. The number of women from the higher social strata, however, remained small.

The flow of information between the rear-echelons and the home-front also played an important role in regard to the public perception of the auxiliaries. The list of reports about both sexual provocations on the part of the soldiers and erotic adventures of the women army auxiliaries is long. Observers blamed both 'the dear Officers' who treated the auxiliaries as 'female creatures to amuse themselves with'[72] as well as the 'behavior of a large number of auxiliaries'[73] – noone, however, could dispute that in a matter of months the reputation of these women was ruined.[74] The soldiers were held responsible for creating their bad reputation; they saw the arrival of the women army auxiliaries behind the fronts as a threat to the exclusiveness of male military life, and they also feared being posted closer to the front lines. Many soldiers also considered the auxiliaries simply as a measure to prolong the war. A female official of the Women's Department in Munich reported back from her 'official journey to study the housing situation of women army auxiliaries' in September 1917:

From time to time a hostile attitude of the soldiers towards the arriving women army auxiliaries can be detected. The auxiliaries were sometimes greeted with outright threats, the statement 'the war would be prolonged because of them' and also with the exclamation 'show your machine-gun'. The very visible black-white-red auxiliaries' badge leads to frequent harassment. This has been noticed in many different rear-echelons.[75]

The 'harassment by military personal' was soon so frequent that the War Office and the Quartermaster General were inundated with numerous complaints and suggestions. The problem seemed to have occurred most often in the rear-echelons behind the western front.[76] The women army auxiliaries also complained that they were treated differently by the soldiers compared to the nurses. One women army auxiliary wrote from northern France to the Women's Department in Stuttgart:

During our journey the first thing we realized was the doubtful reputation of the women army auxiliaries. The soldiers and officers spoke decently and in a nice manner with the nurses; there was no word to the auxiliaries. Among the soldiers there is a sense of gratefulness towards the nurses (which is something good); they may have experienced themselves in some field hospitals what a good deed the work of the nurses is and how much it is needed out here. The women army auxiliaries, on the other hand, are always looked upon with contempt and during the journey we were only looked at with the most disgusting expressions.[77]

The rumors and reports about the women army auxiliaries that were brought from the front to the home-front made a decisive impact. In March 1918 the Quartermaster General wrote:

The War Office (AZS) raised the issue of women army auxiliaries from respected families who wanted to step down from their contracts in the occupied territory because they were worried that the allegedly bad reputation of the auxiliaries in the rear-area might harm their and their relatives' reputation. This has been prompted by the comments of officers who have declared it incompatible with the position of an officer to have a sister working as an auxiliary in the rear-echelons. [. . .] Although in a few cases the moral conduct of the auxiliaries has not been flawless, this fact should not give rise to generalizations and the female auxiliary service should not be discredited as such. It is, however, necessary to make sure that appropriate supervision and ruthless measures immediately eliminate all those elements which tarnish the honor of the German woman abroad. [78]

The propaganda of the War Office, which had started late, could not change the negative sentiments towards the women army auxiliaries coming from the soldiers in the rear-echelons. After the end of the war Agnes von Harnack, who had been responsible for the recruitment of these women since December 1917, concluded in the BDF-publication *Die Frau*: 'One should not try to conceal it: the female auxiliary service was all in all no pleasant thing; its reputation was bad, its members were held in low esteem.' [79] Agnes von Harnack and other leading members of the BDF contributed after the war to the negative image of the women army auxiliaries. Harnack herself published one of the most scathing pieces of criticism with the above mentioned article. She stressed that the reasons for the bad reputation 'lay in the women army auxiliaries themselves' and one had 'not to be surprised if the common soldier in particular looked upon the women's auxiliary service with disgust, or often even with hate'. Her arguments rested on the 'sociological pattern' of the 'average woman army auxiliary'. According to Harnack this young, single, employed woman was uneducated, without an 'inner connection to her work', and only motivated by the 'quite exciting mixed company' at the office and her 'addiction to buying new clothes'. It comes as no surprise that the members of the bourgeois women's movement, who organized the mobilization of women army auxiliaries in the War Office and the local War Office Bureaux, had urged for communal dorms and welfare workers already at the planning stage of the service. [80] They obviously fostered the same concerns as expressed in conservative circles about possible sexual misconduct or even prostitution on the part of the women army auxiliaries. Alice Salomon wrote in her memoirs:

Grave responsibility came with sending out women to the occupied territories and to the lines of communications behind the front, where they should replace men. [. . .] We asked ourselves again and again whether we should be hand-maids in this business. In former times an army was openly accompanied by prostitutes. With our modern ideas of what a woman should be, of her dignity and worth, we could not overlook the danger entailed in sending out girls of different social background to supply the army.[81]

In the face of the women's service, which was 'so completely unrestricted and independent' in the immediate proximity of soldiers, ways had to be found to regain the loss of control over female conduct and female sexuality. In this context, the billeting of the women army auxiliaries in dormitories under the watchful guard of middle-class ladies was a favored measure. The women army auxiliaries as the embodiment of the New Woman – the young, financially independent clerk – aroused negative reception not only in the conservative press, but also among the bourgeois women running the BDF.

Women's War Service beyond the Homefront

The dichotomized and at the same time complementary image of soldier and nurse, which the Red Cross had propagated long before the war, became the gendered model of women's service beyond the homefront despite the criticism from certain circles of society. When the war broke out, the Red Cross used this parallelism of military service and nursing in order to recruit new members, drawing on the wars of the nineteenth century from which the Red Cross movement had sprung. The Patriotic Women's Associations of the Red Cross appealed to women in August 1914 to fulfill the wish of the 'country's mother', the Empress herself, 'that all those, whom fate has not granted the possibility to fight for the fatherland, may help to heal the wounds and relieve the suffering'.[82] This parallelism can also be found in both the self-perception of the nurses and in the wartime press.[83] For example, the poem 'Two Crosses of Honour' in the *Breslauer Generalanzeiger* paired the 'Iron Cross' with the 'Red Cross'.[84] In the novel *Vogesenwacht* by Anny Wothe – which was a war-time best-seller with a circulation of 95,000 volumes – a nurse even saves soldiers who are under fire.[85] This juxtaposing of *Feldgrau* – the colour of the soldiers' uniforms – and the Red Cross uniform, however, not only reflected the iconography of the war, but also the everyday life of many bourgeois and noble families. A banker from Heilbronn wrote to a business partner in June 1915: 'My son Hans [. . .] became a lance corporal two weeks ago [. . .] The two younger ones are drummers at the Youth

Defence (*Jugendwehr*), my daughter is nurse in a hospital and my wife is a chairwoman etc. with the Red Cross [. . .].'[86]

In the second half of the war there were repeated claims in the press that the nurses' war service could both have an effect beyond the war itself and be a stabilizing factor in society. Through this war service 'all the girls in nursing [. . .] proved and are still proving every day their excellent qualifications for becoming a wife and mother.' And that was a good thing, because the men returning from the front did not want 'clever and intelligent but homely and motherly women'.[87] A letter to the editor of the Kölnische Zeitung by a 'psychiatric nurse' backed this view by stressing that 'one could expect' that 'most of the nurses who have shown patriotism in the war will show this patriotism also in the future by marrying an invalid [. . .].'[88]

Even though it might have seemed obvious to compare the auxiliaries' service with the soldiers' service, as auxiliaries carried out jobs formerly done by soldiers, no such association can be found in the contemporary literature. The role of the 'heroine' and that of a figure complementary to the soldier was occupied by the Red Cross nurse, in whose shadow the auxiliaries stood throughout the war. It was mainly the auxiliaries' bad reputation which made it impossible for them to find a place beside the soldiers and the nurses in the tableau of the front community and rear-echelon community respectively. This negative image was closely related to the fact that, in contrast to the nurses, the auxiliaries' service transgressed traditional ideas of gender roles. If women could successfully take up the jobs of soldiers, for whom were the men fighting then?

An important feature that distinguished the auxiliaries from the nurses in the public discourse was the question of women army auxiliaries' assumed motivation. Their high income made it impossible for them to participate in the elevated common ideal of 'sacrifice for the fatherland'. The nurses' work, being conceptualized as the complementary service to men's military service, made the auxiliaries' service look more like a means of earning money than a national sacrifice, even where their patriotism was acknowledged in principle. The women army auxiliary also occupied a different geographic space with less positive connotations than the nurse. The hospitals as the domain of Volunteer Nursing were situated mainly in the rear rather than in the operation area, but in the propaganda and press coverage they seemed to be either in the proximity of the fighting line or completely detached from any geographical place as an 'island of humanity'. The women army auxiliaries, however, were usually employed and imagined in the rear-echelons (except for those who worked in the General Administrations). When their service was implemented in the summer of 1917 the rear-area had already experienced a 'fatal, because undifferentiated depreciation' - the brave trench-fighter and his daily fight for survival were contrasted with the cowardly quitter in the tranquil rear-echelons.[89] There can be no doubt that the arrival of the women army auxiliaries led to a further deterioration of the public image of the occupied territories, even though this aspect has so far been neglected in the study of the rear-echelons' reputations. Soldiers posted in the rear-echelons lost even more of their masculine and 'warrior' appeal now that they were working alongside women. In the booklet *Zur Psychologie der Etappe*, which was published in 1918, the author summed up the prevailing image as follows:

> In the general awareness and in the linguistic usage of the public, the rear-echelon is associated with disrespect or even contempt. [. . .] Talking about the rear-echelon one thinks mainly or even exclusively of a cozy life miles away from where the action is, a life of pleasure rather than work, a life of shameless enjoyment rather than a strict organization full of privation.[90]

The image of the auxiliaries was affected accordingly. They were perceived as taking over jobs of quitters and shirkers. Nurses, on the other hand, were juxtaposed with the soldiers coming from the battlefield. Agnes von Harnack recalled shortly after the war: 'Everyone knows the reasons [for the unpleasant state of women's auxiliary service] and names them now more openly than during the war: Rear-echelon is rear-echelon.' For Harnack the attempt to establish a women's auxiliary service with the army had failed. 'The whole chapter lies behind us as a war memory, an episode which will surely not repeat itself in this form. A war memory – albeit not one we like to think back to.'[91]

Conclusion

Women's auxiliary service in Germany did not change prewar ideals about women and war, which had juxtaposed women's caring nursing work and men's fighting at the front. In the public memory of the First World War there was a uniform male war experience – the trench-fighter who stands by his post in a 'storm of steel' somewhere in the no-man's land of the western front. The female war experience was diverse and played a subordinate role. The defeat of the army was soon explained by the theory that the army was stabbed in the back by the Left and by the homefront, which gave in while the army fought bravely at the front. As early as 1921 Colonel Bauer, a colleague of Lüders in the War Office, cursed the 'extended self-adulation, [. . .] the ridiculous gushing' about women's war work when it was 'women in particular who did not do as much as they could have done' to win the war.[92] Only the nurses who supposedly stood by the side of the soldiers seemed to have escaped the wrath of the humiliated military and public. Yet even their war experience paled next to that of the trench-fighter. It is telling that in Germany the only female heroine of the First World War is a Swede: the nurse Elsa Brandström became famous for tending German prisoners of war in Russia.[93] Only in the context of the preparation for the next war were the nurses' contributions to the war effort remembered and celebrated in the 1930s.[94] On the other hand, the experience of the women army auxiliaries was almost completely submerged after 1918 and aroused only limited interest under the Nazis.[95] In retrospect it is hard to believe that in First World War Germany there were almost as many women army auxiliaries as nurses working for the war effort in the occupied territories. The figure of the Red Cross nurse is simply too dominant in both literature and iconography during the war. The Red Cross nurses enjoyed a predominantly positive image, stylized as the counterpart to men's military service. The nurses' uniform allowed women to participate in war, to travel unchaperoned, to mix with men of different social classes and hence overcome temporarily prewar gender and class boundaries. At the same time the ideals associated with the nurses' uniform, such as motherliness and purity, created a sense of distance and protected their reputation and social position. The transgressing of gender boundaries was embedded in pseudo-family relations, corresponding to the social order.[96] In this way the inequality of the sexes was fostered during the war on the basis of the prewar gender order. Also, the close connection between the Red Cross and noble families, not at least the Emperor's family, 'ennobled' the work of the Red Cross and elevated it onto a national level, insulating it from much of the criticism it received. It is interesting to see that in Britain Queen Mary supported the case of the WAAC, which in 1918 changed its name to 'Queen Mary's Women's Army Auxiliary Corps', while in Germany it would have seemed quite impossible to bring the Empress into connection with the ill-regarded women army auxiliaries. The 'Empress' Army' was the Red Cross only. The task and role which was attributed to the Red Cross nurse before the war and which was fostered in an idealized image during the war complied largely with traditional ideas of women's role in philanthropic work, which had already before the war given middle-class and upper-class women the opportunity to care unpaid for members of the lower and lowest classes.

The women army auxiliaries, on the other hand, were of peripheral importance, and by 1919 they had become a 'war-memory' (Harnack) already. Their service was not appreciated, their high salary which enabled them to have an autonomous lifestyle was seen as a threat to the social order, their advance into military orderly rooms as an attack on the gender order. Agnes von Harnack's complaints about the auxiliaries' lack of 'intellectual interests', their insufficient education and their non-existing 'orderly and long-term job training' already prefigured criticisms of women's education in general and women clerks in particular which were voiced in the Weimar Republic.[97] Hence after the war the auxiliaries did not find a place in public memory with the soldiers and nurses in the tableau of those who 'did their duty' and 'sacrificed themselves'. They were soon forgotten. Excluded from the collective memory of the war, they disappeared from the public eye.

By 'casting one's gaze more broadly'[98] and including women in the picture, the home-made chaos and incompetence the German army displayed in the running of women's auxiliary service also add some correctives to a picture of the German army that has so far been based on 'strategy, tactics and the net body count'.[99] A comparison of the German and British auxiliary services shows that the idea that German military planning was superior in all respects to that of the British is not tenable. In regard to the mobilization of women as soldiers' replacements it was exactly the other way around.

Notes

I would like to thank Christa Hämmerle, Karen Hagemann, Janet Howarth, Stefanie Schüler-Springorum and Hans-Peter Ullmann for their comments on different versions of this article.

1. Petition by Anna Sauter, Fürth, to King Ludwig of Bavaria, 2 August 1915; Bayerisches Hauptstaatsarchiv/Kriegsarchiv Munich (=BayHStA/ KA), Files of the Ministry of War (= MKr) 13753.
2. The German word for women army auxiliaries is *Etappenhelferinnen*. When the advance of the German army came to a standstill in the autumn of 1914, the occupied territories were divided into numbered 'rear-echelons' (*Etappen*) named after the army occupying the area.

There were also the two General Administrations (*Generalgouverne-ments*) in Belgium and Poland, and, at a later stage of the war, military 'Safeguard-Administrations' in the Ukraine and Romania. The sep-arate spheres of front and rear-echelon had become quite static once the fronts were fixed, with a geographic distance of 10–15 km from the rear-echelons. The borders of the rear echelons were delineated in one direction by the front area and in the other by either the General Administrations or the homefront. Hermann Cron, *Geschichte des Deutschen Heeres im Weltkriege 1914–1918*, reprint of the 1937 edn (Osnabrück, 1990), 265–276.

3. Ursula von Gersdorff's *Frauen im Kriegsdienst 1914–45*, published in Stuttgart in 1969, is the only major study which includes original material on women army auxiliaries. Franz W. Seidler gives a short description in his *Frauen zu den Waffen? Marketenderinnen, Helferin-nen, Soldatinnen*, 2nd edn (Bonn, 1998). Women army auxiliaries are also briefly mentioned in Susanna Dammer, *Mütterlichkeit und Frauendienstpflicht: Versuch der Vergesellschaftung 'weiblicher Fähigkeiten' durch eine Dienstverpflichtung. Deutschland, 1890–1918* (Weinheim, 1987). The author, however, bases her findings mainly on printed sources and literature. Some authors also imply that there were no German women army auxiliaries in the First World War at all, such as Joyce Marlow, ed., *The Virago Book of Women and the Great War 1914–18* (London, 1998). Others get the story of the service wrong – most recently Martin v. Creveld, *Men, Women, and War* (Cassell, 2001), 126.

The only work published on German Red Cross nurses behind the frontlines in the First World War stems from studies in institutional history: Dieter Riesenberger, 'Im Dienst des Krieges – im Dienst des Friedens: Zur Geschichte der Krankenschwestern vom Roten Kreuz 1864–1918,' in *Die Medizin und der Erste Weltkrieg*, ed. Wolfgang Eckart and Christoph Gradmann (Pfaffenweiler, 1996), 23–43. Riesen-berger, however, discusses the First World War only briefly, focusing primarily on the organization of military nursing in the army and on the homefront. In 1994 Regina Schulte published her article 'Die Schwester des kranken Kriegers: Krankenpflege im Ersten Weltkrieg als Forschungsproblem,' *BIOS* 7/1 (1994): 83–100. (English edition: 'The Sick Warrior's Sister: Nursing during the First World War,' in *Gender Relations in German history: Power, Agency and Experience from the Sixteenth to the Twentieth Century*, ed. Lynn Abrams and Elizabeth Harvey (London, 1996), 121–141. For a discussion of the lit-erature on nurses and women army auxiliaries see Bianca Schönberger,

'Mobilising "Etappenhelferinnen" for Service with the Military: Gender Regimes in First World War Germany' (University of Oxford D.Phil. thesis, 2002), 8–14.

4. See articles in Karen Hagemann and R. Pröve, eds., *Landsknechte, Soldatenfrauen und Natonalkrieger: Militär, Krieg und Geschlechterordnung im historischen Wandel* (Frankfurt/New York, 1998); Regina Schulte, *Die verkehrte Welt des Krieges: Studien zu Geschlecht, Religion und Tod* (Frankfurt/New York). For the latest account of German-speaking studies on women and war see Christa Hämmerle, 'Von den Geschlechtern des Krieges und des Militärs: Forschungseinblicke und Bemerkungen zu einer neuen Debatte,' in *Was ist Militärgeschichte?* ed. Thomas Kühne und Benjamin Ziemann (Paderborn, 2000), 229–62.

5. Yvonne Klein, *Beyond the Homefront: Women's Autobiographical Writings of the Two World Wars* (New York, 1997); Margaret R. Higgonet, *Nurses at the Front: Writing the Wounds of the Great War* (Boston, 2001).

6. Diana Shaw, 'The Forgotten Army of Women: Queen Mary's Army Auxiliary Corps,' in *Facing Armageddon: The First World War Experienced*, ed. Hugh Cecil and Peter Liddle (London, 1996), 365–379.

7. Jenny M. Gould, 'Women's Military Service in First World War Britain,' in *Behind the Lines: Gender and the Two World Wars*, ed. Margaret R. Higonnet et al. (New Haven, 1987), 114–25; Anne Summers, *Angels and Citizens. British Women as Military Nurses, 1854–1914*, 2nd edn (London, 2000).

8. Janet K. Watson, 'Khaki Girls, VADs, and Tommy's Sister: Gender and Class in First World War Britain,' *International History Review* 19/1 (1997): 32–57; Henriette Donner, 'Under the Cross – Why V.A.D.s performed the Filthiest Task in the Dirtiest War: Red Cross Women Volunteers, 1914–1918,' *Journal of Social History* 30/3 (1997): 687–704.

9. Krisztina Robert, 'Gender, Class and Patriotism. Women's Paramilitary Units in First World War Britain,' *International History Review* 19/1(1997): 52–65; Susan R. Grayzel, '"The Outward and Visible Sign of her Patriotism": Women, Uniforms, and National Service during the First World War,' *Twentieth Century British History* 8/2 (1997): 145–164; Doron Lamm, "Emily Goes to War: Explaining the Recruitment to the Women's Army Auxiliary Corps in World War I," in *Borderlines: Gender and Identities in War and Peace 1870–1930*, ed. Billie Melman (New York/London), 377–97.

10. Elizabeth Crosthwait, '"The Girl Behind the Man Behind the Gun"': The Women's Army Auxiliary Corps, 1914–18', in *Our Work, Our Lives, Our Words*, ed. Leonore Davidoff and Belinda Westover (Totona, NJ, 1986), 161–81; Sandra S. Gilbert, 'A Soldier's Heart: Literary Men, Literary Women and the Great War', in Higonnet et al., *Behind the Lines*, 197–226; Sharon Ouditt, 'Nuns and Lovers. Voluntary Aid Detachment Nurses in the First World War', in her *Fighting Forces, Writing Women. Identity and Ideology in the First World War* (London, 1994), 7–46; Susan K. Kent, 'Love and Death. War and Gender in Britain, 1914–18', in *Authority, Identity and the Social History of the Great War*, ed. Frans Coetzee and Marilyn Shevin-Coetzee (Providence and Oxford 1995), 153–74. For a more general study of war and gender in First World War Britain and France see Susan R. Grayzel, *Women's Identities at War: Gender, Motherhood, and Politics in Britain and France during the First World War* (Chapel Hill and London, 1999).
11. Susan Zeiger, *In Uncle Sam's Service: Women Workers with the American Expeditionary Force, 1917–1919* (Cornell, 2000).
12. Hanna Hacker, 'Die Frau als Regimentsgeheimnis: Irritationen zwischen Front und Geschlecht im Ersten Weltkrieg', in *Soziale Konstruktionen: Militär und Geschlechterverhältnis*, ed. Christine Eifler and Ruth Seifert, (Münster, 1999), 135–154.
13. Margaret H. Darrow, *French Women and the Great War: War Stories from the Homefront* (New York, 2000).
14. All nursing organizations that wished to complement the military medical service in the First World War had to be affiliated with the Red Cross before sending their nurses to the rear-echelons and the General Administrations. During the First World War the total of more than 28,000 female nursing personnel who worked beyond the homefront was made up mainly of Red Cross nurses and nursing aides (19,800), religious sisters (6,000) and nurses of the Professional Organization of Nurses in Germany (2,500). Numbers from Elfriede von Pflugk-Harttung, *Frontschwestern: Ein deutsches Ehrenbuch*, 2nd edn (Berlin, 1936), 340 and Verband der Pflegeanstalten vom Roten Kreuz, *Geschäftsbericht des Verbandes deutscher Pflegeanstalten vom Roten Kreuz* (Stendal, 1919). Almost all nursing aides were trained by the Red Cross. To the embitterment of the professional nurses, these aides were referred to as 'sister', too, in their daily work, in contemporary literature and reports, and also in the military files. Therefore it is impossible to make a distinction between these two groups in my study. The contribution of the religious sisters

and the nurses of the Professional Organization to military nursing was acknowledged in the wartime discussions. Yet, the stereotype of the military nurses was the Red Cross sister (both professional and amateur), and therefore she is in the center of this study.

15. Jean H. Quataert, "'Damen der besten und besseren Stände'": "Vaterländische Frauenarbeit" in Krieg und Frieden,' in Hagemann/Pröve, *Landsknechte*, 247–275. See also her *Staging Philanthropy: Patriotic Women and the National Imagination in Dynastic Germany, 1813– 1916* (Ann Arbor, 2001).

16. On the 'mother's houses' see Riesenberger, *Dienste*. See also Andrea Süchting-Hänger, "'Gleichgroße mut'ge Helferinnen" in der weiblichen Gegenwelt: Der Vaterländische Frauenverein und die Politisierung konservativer Frauen 1890–1914,' in *Nation, Politik und Geschlecht*, ed. Ute Planert (Frankfurt/New York, 2000), 131–146.

17. See the tables in the annual reports of the Badenese Women's Association. Generallandesarchiv Karlsruhe (=GLA Karlsruhe) 443/15. On the Red Cross nurses before 1914 see Dieter Riesenberger, 'Zur Professionalisierung und Militarisierung der Schwestern vom Roten Kreuz vor dem Ersten Weltkrieg,' *Militärgeschichtliche Mitteilungen* 53/1 (1994): 49–72.

18. Jakob Vogel, 'Samariter und Schwestern: Geschlechterbilder und – beziehungen im Deutschen Roten Kreuz vor dem Ersten Weltkrieg,' Hagemann/Pröve, *Landsknechte*, 325–345.

19. Oberin Anna von Zimmermann, *Was heißt Schwester sein? Beiträge zur ethischen Berufserziehung*, 2nd edn (Leipzig, 1912), 15. This idea dates back to the Wars of Liberation (1813–15); see Karen Hagemann, 'Deutsche Heldinnen: Patriotisches Frauenhandeln in der Zeit der Antinapoleonischen Kriege,' in Planert, *Nation*, 86–112.

20. Friedrich von Criegern, *Das rothe Kreuz: Handbuch der freiwilligen Krankenpflege für die Kriegs- und vorbereitende Friedensthätigkeit* (Leipzig, 1883), appendix 1. The Medical Service in War Act was reworked and amended several times until 1914.

21. 'Die Kriegsvorbereitung der Vaterländischen Frauenvereine,' *Das Rote Kreuz* 1. Kriegsnummer (16 August 1914): 12.

22. Petition of Maria Sämmer to King Ludwig of Bavaria; Munich, 12 March 1915, in BayHStA/KA MKr 13753.

23. Bayerischer Frauenverein vom Roten Kreuz, *Bericht über die Tätigkeit während des ersten Kriegsjahres: 2 August 1914–31 July 1915* (Munich, 1915).

24. Report of a trip to study the housing situation of the auxiliaries, Munich, 3 September 1917; BayHStA/KA MKr 14384.

Bianca Schönberger

25. Ute Daniel, *Arbeiterfrauen in der Kriegsgesellschaft: Beruf, Familie und Politik im Ersten Weltkrieg* (Göttingen, 1989), table 18.
26. Letter by Anna Murr to King Ludwig of Bavaria; Munich, 16 June 1918; BayHStA/KA MK 10595.
27. Unlike the case of the women army auxiliaries, there is no statistical material available on the nurses' social background.
28. Women working in medical labs and x-ray technicians were informally included in the nursing staff, too.
29. Gerald D. Feldmann, *Army, Industry and Labor in Germany, 1914– 18*, 2nd edn (Providence/Oxford, 1992). On the administrative implementation of the law see Daniel, *Arbeiterfrauen*, 74–96.
30. Statistics of the Prussian Ministry of War, printed in Gersdorff, *Frauen*, 162. Most men who had been not drafted for military service were in the majority of cases working in what was classified as 'war industries' anyway, so the number of those who could replace soldiers was small. *Jahresbericht der Gewerbeaufsichtsbeamten und Bergbaubehörden*, vol. 2 (Berlin, 1914/18), 367.
31. Letter by the War Office, 27 April 1917. BayHStA/KA MKr 14383.
32. Marie Elisabeth Lüders, *Das unbekannte Heer: Frauen kämpfen für Deutschland 1914–1918* (Berlin, 1936), 216.
33. Sabine Hering, *Die Kriegsgewinnlerinnen: Praxis und Ideologie der deutschen Frauenbewegung im Ersten Weltkrieg* (Pfaffenweiler, 1990).
34. Alice Salomon, *Charakter ist Schicksal: Lebenserinnerungen*, ed. R. Baron and R. Landwehr (Weinheim/Basel, 1983), 158.
35. Order of the War Office, Berlin, 26 May 1917. BayHStA/KA Etappeninspektion 6, Bund 103.
36. Agnes v. Harnack, 'Etappen-Helferinnen: Ein Nachwort,' *Die Frau* 26/9 (1919): 273. Her statement also corresponds with the results of my evaluation of the data on the profession of 574 auxiliaries' fathers, which were recorded by the War Office Bureaux. Schönberger, *Mobilising 'Etappenhelferinnen'*.
37. BayHStA/KA Etappeninspektion 6, Bund 103.
38. Regine Deutsch, 'Weibliche Kriegsteilnehmer,' *Die Staatsbürgerin*, 14/4 (March 1916): 186. Red Cross nurses were not the only nurses endowed with this kind of heroism as titles such as Regine Barth, *Aus dem Heldenleben einer Diakonisse. Für das Vaterland gestorben in Brest-Litowsk am 22. Oktober 1915*, 2nd edn (Winnenden, 1915), show. For married women, however, family was expected to still have priority even at times of national emergency, and there were in fact very few mothers employed as nurses in the rear-echelons.

39. Dr. Amelungen, 'Schöne und gescheite Frauen oder häusliche und mütterliche Frauen,' *Kölnische Zeitung*, 13 May 1917, 2. Morgenausgabe.
40. Charlotte Gräfin Rittberg, "Helden," *Die Woche* 19/2 (13 January 1917): 69.
41. Hedwig Voss, *Im Dienste des Roten Kreuzes. Erlebnisse und Eindrücke aus dem Weltkrieg 1914* (Stuttgart 1915), 77.
42. *Die Woche* 16/47 (21 November 1914): 1915. See also: Paula Kaldewey, 'Im Kriegsdienst der Heimat: Dekorierte Frauen,' *Die Woche* 18/44 (28 October 1916): 1560–1566.
43. It is telling that many nurses who had found a post in a hospital on the homefront still kept applying for a job in the rear-echelons.
44. This can be seen from the numerous petitions sent to the Ministries of War and the Royal Houses.
45. Agnes von Harnack, 'Der Krieg und die Frauen,' in *Agnes von Zahn-Harnack: Schriften und Reden 1914 bis 1950*, ed. Agnes von Zahn-Harnack (Tübingen, 1964), 9.
46. Poem by Alice Kurs, published in *Deutsche Tageszeitung* in the autumn of 1914. Quoted in Hermann Hilger (ed.), *Krieg und Sieg nach Berichten von Zeitgenossen: Vol 1 – Das Rote Kreuz in Feld und Heimat* (Berlin/Leipzig, 1914), 20.
47. See Ute Planert, *Antifeminismus im Kaiserreich: Diskurs, soziale Formation und politische Mentalitäten* (Göttingen, 1998), 219–223.
48. 'Religiöser Rückblick auf das Erste Kriegsjahr,' *Historisch-Politische Blätter des katholischen Deutschland* 56 (1915): 360.
49. One could argue that the Red Cross, which was originally a Protestant organization, is being unfairly attacked here by the Catholic press which usually issued very positive reports on nursing by religious sisters. However, during the war Catholic and Protestant (as well as a small number of Jewish women) joined the Red Cross; thus a denominational explanation does not suffice. It is more likely that in this article the *Historisch-Politischen Blätter* simply drew on the current public discourse.
50. *Saarbrücker Volkszeitung*, 26 August 1914; quoted in Jutta Helmerichs, *Krankenpflege im Wandel (1890 bis 1933): Sozialwissenschaftliche Untersuchung zur Umgestaltung der Krankenpflege von einer christlichen Liebestätigkeit zum Beruf* (Göttingen, 1992), 123.
51. Quoted in Magnus Hirschfeld and Andreas Gaspar, eds, *Sittengeschichte des Ersten Weltkrieges*, 2nd extended edition (Hanau, 1965), 127.
52. Planert, *Antifeminismus*, 223.

53. Wolfgang Kruse, 'Krieg und Klassenheer. Zur Revolutionierung der deutschen Armee im Ersten Weltkrieg,' *Geschichte und Gesellschaft* 22 (1996): 530–561.

54. BayHStA/KA Etappeninspektion 6, Bund 103.

55. The Women's Departments were unhappy with the fact that the *Reichsbekleidungsstelle* had turned down their request for uniforms for the women army auxiliaries because of an apparent lack of material. Some even suspected a 'basic attitude' behind this decision. Lüders, *Das unbekannte Heer*, 224. The argument of the *Reichsbekleidungsstelle* could, however, not be dismissed completely. From October 1917 onwards, the green identification numbers on the helmet covers of the soldiers disappeared because of a shortage of green cloth. See Cron, *Geschichte*, 38.

56. The existing files of the local labor exchanges were used instead.

57. Minutes of the War Office, 28 April 1917, on the 'Experiences and new Principles for the Deployment of Persons under the Patriotic Service Act and other Civilians, including Women, in the Occupied Territories'; BayHStA/KA MKr 17309.

58. [Marie Elisabeth Lüders], 'Frauenarbeit in der Etappe und im besetzten Gebiet,' *Deutscher Tagesanzeiger*, 28 August 1918. Bundesarchiv Koblenz, Nachlaß 1151 – Marie Elisabeth Lüders (= Lüders Papers), 163. Emphasis as in the original.

59. *Württembergische Zeitung*, 28 August 1918.

60. Lüders, *Das unbekannte Heer*, 217.

61. Bauer, *Der große Krieg*, 137.

62. On a detailed comparison see Schönberger, *Mobilising 'Etappenhelferinnen'*.

63. Salomon's report about an official journey to the rear-echelons behind the western front, 12 January–2 February 1918; LP 164; minutes of the meeting of Heads of Women's Departments, 19 April 1918 ibid.

64. On Britain see Watson, *Khaki Girls*.

65. Order of the Rear-Echelon Inspectorate, 16.6.1917. BayHStA/KA Stellvertretendes Generalkommando II. Armeekorps, Bund 67. The salary varied from rear-echelon to rear-echelon; the ones paid in rear-echelon 6 were about average. The head of the Women's Department of the War Office Bureau Ludwigsburg stated in her weekly report on 28 August 1918: 'The girls work hard and they behave. They have made substantial savings of up to 800–1000 marks.' Ibid.

66. Cron, *Geschichte*, 39.

67. 'Deutsche Mädchen in Belgien,' *Kölnische Zeitung*, 3 June 1917 (2. Morgenausgabe). The name of the (female) author is not known.
68. Roughly 5/6 of the auxiliaries were single.
69. Ca. 40 per cent of all auxiliaries sent out by the War Office Bureau in Würzburg claimed to have relatives they needed to support. BayHStA/ KA Stellvertretendes Generalkommando II. Armeekorps, Bund 88.
70. This is how Max Bauer – an influential staff member of Ludendorff and a colleague of Lüders in the War Office – summed up the criticism. Max Bauer, *Der große Krieg in Feld und Heimat. Erinnerungen und Betrachtungen*, 2nd edn (Tübingen, 1921).
71. 'Dolmetscherinnen,' *Kölnische Zeitung*, 14 June 1917 (1. Morgenausgabe).
72. First draft of a report by the female consultant in rear-echelon 4. Bundesarchiv/Militärarchiv Freiburg, PH 5 II 468/84.
73. Report by Theodore Bross, War Office Bureau Kassel, 16 April 1918. Lüders Papers 162.
74. The number of auxiliaries sent home for indecent behavior was eventually very small. According to documents of the War Office Bureau Würzburg, only four of its 253 women army auxiliaries had to be dismissed for indecent behavior or VD. BayHStA/KA Stellvertretendes Generalkommando, Kriegsamtstelle II. Armeekorps, 83.
75. BayHStA/KA MKr 14384.
76. Letter from the Quartermaster General, 25 March 1918. GLA Karlsruhe, 456/EV146/Bund 83. See also Minutes of a meeting of the *Nationalausschuß für Frauenarbeit im Kriege*; BayHStA/KA MKr 14385.
77. Hauptstaatsarchiv Stuttgart, M 1/9 – 316, undated.
78. Letter from the Quartermaster General, 25 March 1918. Bundesarchiv/Militärarchiv Freiburg, PH 5 II 468/197.
79. Harnack, *Etappen-Helferinnen*, 270–5.
80. Minutes of the War Office, 28 April 1917, on the 'Experiences and new Principles for the Deployment of Persons under the Patriotic Service Act and other Civilians, including Women, in the Occupied Territories'; BayHStA/KA MKr 17309.
81. Salomon, *Charakter*, 158.
82. 'Die Kriegsvorbereitung der Vaterländischen Frauenvereine,' *Das Rote Kreuz* 1. Kriegsausgabe (16 August 1914): 12.
83. The lyrics of one 'Nurses' Wartime Song': 'Just like the brothers facing the enemy in the field / We are united as sisters for the Fatherland / [. . .]'. Hand-written lyrics, undated. Private collection of

Bianca Schönberger

Matron Leist, Schwesternschaft vom Roten Kreuz, Karlsruhe, file 1914–1915.

84. The poem is quoted in Hillger, *Krieg*, 3.

85. Anny Wothe, *Vogesenwacht. Kriegsroman aus der Gegenwart* (Reutlingen, 1915). See H.-O. Binder, 'Zum Opfern bereit. Kriegsliteratur von Frauen', in *Kriegserfahrungen: Studien zur Sozial- und Mentalitätengeschichte des Ersten Weltkriegs*, ed. Gerhard Hirschfeld, Gerd Krumeich, Dieter Langewiesche and Hans-Peter Ullmann (Tübingen, 1997), 107–28.

86. Quoted in Elke Koch, '"Jeder tut was er kann für's Vaterland": Frauen und Männer an der Heilbronner Heimatfront,' in Hirschfeld, Krumeich, Langewiesche and Ullmann, *Kriegserfahrungen*, 36–52, quote 42.

87. Amelungen, *Schöne*.

88. *Kölnische Zeitung* 19 February 1918 (1. Morgenausgabe).

89. Bernhard R. Kroener, 'Frontochsen und Etappenbullen: Zur Ideologisierung militärischer Organisationsstrukturen im Zweiten Weltkrieg,' in *Die Wehrmacht. Mythos und Realität*, ed. Rolf-Dieter Müller and Hans-Erich Volkmann (Munich, 1999), 372.

90. Herman Hefele, *Zur Psychologie der Etappe* (Jena, 1918), 4–5. See also the extremely critical assessment of life in the occupied territories in Heinrich Wandt, *Etappe Gent*, 2nd edn (Vienna/Berlin, 1926). With a circulation of more than 200,000 volumes it was one of the most popular and influential books of the postwar era.

91. Harnack, *Etappen-Helferinnen*, 270–3.

92. Bauer, *Krieg*, 137–55.

93. *Geschichte der Krankenpflege: Handbuch der Entstehung und Entwicklung der Krankenpflege von der Frühzeit zur Gegenwart* (Kulmbach, 1965), 296.

94. H. Mierisch, *Kamerad Schwester, 1914–1918* (Leipzig, 1934); S. v. Hoerner-Heintze, *Mädels im Kriegsdienst. Ein Stück Leben*, 3rd edn (Munich, 1935); K. Russner, *Schwesterndienst im Weltkriege. Feldpostbriefe und Tagebuchblätter* (Leipzig, 1936); M. Schickedanz, *Das Heimatheer der Frauen. Band 2- Frauenhilfe hinter der Front und hinter Stacheldraht* (Leipzig and Berlin, 1936); Pflugk-Harttung, *Frontschwestern*.

95. Only one auxiliary published an account of her war work. She could, however, not even find a publisher in 1932 for her little book and had to publish it at her own expense. Dorothea Hansen, *Frauen hinter der Flandernfront* (Kiel and Altona, 1932).

96. Schulte, *Schwester*, 96.

97. Harnack, *Etappen-Helferinnen*.
98. This is a reference to Roger Chickering, '"Casting their Gaze more broadly". Women's Patriotic Activism in Imperial Germany,' *Past and Present* 118 (1988): 156–185.
99. Niall Ferguson, *The Pity of War*, 282.

–4–

Homefront

Food, Politics and Women's Everyday
Life during the First World War
Belinda J. Davis

'The women', Police Officer Adolf Palm observed in pointedly categor-
ical fashion in the wake of the January 1918 mass strike in Berlin, 'took
part in an outstanding way in the strike [. . .] [as well as] in the demonstrations on the street'. In turn, he wrote, 'the strike [. . .] exercised a
certain pressure on the government'.[1] As this urgent police report to high-
level civilian and military officials suggests, consideration of the homefront, including the role specifically of women, is essential to understanding
political changes in Germany during the First World War, and the postwar
impact of these changes. Indeed, viewing the war from this perspective
provokes a number of revisions of our understanding to date of the war in
Germany. Evidence of the transformation of relations between government officials and the homefront population in the course of the war
demonstrates that the potential political outcomes of the war were broad
indeed, including moves toward participatory democracy, popular sovereignty, and an expanded notion of citizenship, as the range of participants
in the November 1918 revolution promoted to varying degrees. Insofar
as the war experience also engendered brutalization, an exclusive notion
of *Volksgemeinschaft*, and simultaneously deepened rifts within the
population, these characteristics were to a significant degree the result of
the homefront experience as well as that of the battle front. On the homefront, these paradoxical outcomes were largely a function of the crippling
wartime food shortages and officials' inability to remedy this crisis. These
shortages also transformed relations within the populace, rendering
relations of consumption central to wartime social organization and
lasting into the postwar period. A broad population of Germans came to
imagine women on the home front, as consumers, producers, and as
activists, as the 'protagonists' in the social and political conflict that
marked the era.

The 'history of everyday life' as well as feminist theory and method-
ologies are important tools to get at the politics of street-level activity on
the home front. These methods shed new light on the police and military
reports on popular morale or mood (*Stimmungsberichte*), taken 'in the
streets' and usually at the site of long queues for scarce food. These *Stimmungsberichte* provide a central source for this account, particularly those
concerning the capital city, Berlin, in which unrest was especially frequent.[2]
Looked at from day to day, alongside contemporary press, position
papers, political pamphlets, memoirs, and documents from throughout the
government hierarchy, these mood reports offer a fresh perspective on
relations between officials and the populace, as well as within the broader
public. Read against one another, these various sources permit us to detect
unofficial relations of power, and to examine the ways in which these
relations promoted or prohibited change. One finds that police reports
were contemporaneously a conduit of political information in unexpected
ways; they transmitted popular concerns and desiderata upward to the
highest-level officials in many respects as effectively as representatives of
the state communicated their will downward. Mood reports, the broad
press, and the 'street scene' (*Straßenbild*) itself influenced one another and
worked collectively to pressure officials to respond to popular concerns.

Food shortages in Germany were bound to play a significant role in
life on the wartime home front.[3] On the eve of war, Germany imported
about one-third of its food supplies, including ca. 40 per cent of its dietary
fats. Of the foods in which the country was self-sufficient, including rye
and pork, farmers required imported fertilizers and feed to sustain production. As early as a decade before the outbreak of war, Britain had warned
of imposing an embargo on food imports into Central Europe in the event
of hostilities. As such a possibility loomed, by 1911 the German government initiated planning for wartime food supplies coincident with stock-
piling raw materials for military needs. But if the latter progressed only
haltingly, the former ceased entirely by 1913: authorities preferred to rely
on the expectation, should hostilities break out, of a *Blitzkrieg*, a very
brief, successful war. These circumstances set the stage for the crisis of
homefront provisioning that began as early as fall 1914, and formed a
focal point of domestic politics for the four years of war.

For four decades, historians have argued the 'primacy of domestic
politics' in motivating German officials to prosecute a major war. That is,
perceived domestic problems, such as class conflict, the polarization of
politics, the rising strength of the Social Democratic Party (SPD), and the
shrill demands of radical nationalists, inspired officials to look to military
solutions.[4] Domestic politics remained central to authorities' decisions

throughout the war, in ways that have not to date been completely acknowledged. Fundamental to this decision-making was the issue of guaranteeing adequate food supplies to the civilian population. By fall 1914, bread and potato supplies dwindled; by late 1915 and for the duration of the war, insufficient basic foods and perceived unjust distribution thereof arose as the foremost issue of contention between the government and the civilian population, as well as the premier cleavage among civilians. Struggles over questions of food production and distribution – in which poorer urban women featured as the outstanding actors – helped to fundamentally transform relations between the German state and population. For, in the course of the war, the broad public came to view the government as responsible for serving the German people rather than vice versa, as had been the case. The Wilhelmine state's ultimate failure to meet this new obligation, specifically in the form of adequate provisioning, was a signal cause, alongside the military failure, for the collapse of that regime.

Focusing especially on morale reports as a chronicle of day-to-day experiences, this contribution seeks to demonstrate the significance of women practicing politics in the broadest sense for the domestic and even military policy of the German state, and how these politics contributed ultimately to the collapse of that state and the rise of its successors. This essay will first trace the new dynamic that developed between officials and the broader society, precipitated by the actions of poorer urban women. It then discusses how these actions may be constituted as political. Further, it will highlight a concomitant transformation of social relations, cutting across gender, class, and other cleavages. It speaks finally to the significance of these transformations for the aftermath of the war.

State and Society in War

As early as February 1915, Berlin Police Commissioner Traugott von Jagow warned civilian and military authorities that the 'economic war' (as Germans dubbed the British blockade and subsequent related hostile measures) increasingly overshadowed Germany's military successes in the minds of the public, particularly in the cities. 'Unpleasant scenes', he explained, 'are taking place more than ever in front of butcher shops [. . .]' He counseled, 'To intervene in the price of meat lies very much in the state's interest.'[5] These 'scenes' of crowds gathering for food riveted public attention even when no protest took place. Officer Paul Rhein of the Berlin political police described one such incident in Berlin in February 1915:

thousands of women and children gathered at the municipal market hall in Andreas Street to get a few pounds of potatoes. As the sale commenced, everyone stormed the market stands. The police [. . .] were powerless against the onslaught. A life-threatening press at the stands ensued [. . .] [W]omen who got away from the crowds with some ten pounds of potatoes were bathed in sweat, and dropped to their knees involuntarily before they could continue home.[6]

Such dramatic tableaux, replayed in newspapers and by word of mouth, captivated the public eye well outside the poorer segments of the population regularly engaging in this experience.

By October 1915 – still long before the devastating 'turnip winter' of 1916–17 – such scenes frequently culminated, especially in cities but also in smaller towns, in riots and protests against merchants, rural producers, and the government itself. 'It should certainly come as no surprise', Police Officer Ludwig commented in late 1915 during a moment of quiet, 'if enormous butter riots arise [again] very soon. [. . .] The bad humor among the people, especially the proletariat and also the lower middle class (*Mittelstand*), grows from day to day. The view is frequently voiced that the war will not be decided on the front, but rather through Germany's economic defeat.'[7]

This sentiment was astonishingly widespread; even the most conservative press took a stand, publicly at least, demanding government satisfaction of the needs specifically of poor urban consumers, even declaring identification with this population. The Evangelical *Reichsbote* chastised the imperial government in February 1915 for its reckless inattention to the food question, commenting, 'unfortunately we people cannot yet live entirely on air alone'.[8] The conservative *Deutscher Kurier* concurred in December 1915, 'One is asking not for words but for an asssurance of daily bread [. . .] To care for our infantrymen and young officers is to do only half the work [. . .] What use is it to us to defeat the outer enemy, when our people at home fall to the inner one [. . .]?'[9]

The press, police, and others drew government and public attention to those they characterized as 'those of lesser means' and above all 'women of lesser means' (*minderbemittelte Frauen*): the poorer consumers who waited in food queues and who protested throughout Germany, above all in its large cities. Special 'political police', in Berlin largely from the lower middle class, had been assigned as soon as war was declared to oversee this predominantly working-class population, to ward off potential unrest. But, as police and others characterized it, this unrest was well justified. Officer Gustav Gerhardt reported with notable sympathy:

it is impossible for the population of lesser means to continue for any length of time only approximately nourishing themselves. The populace maintains the most heartfelt desire that the ongoing manipulation of prices soon be ended once and for all, and that the government take energetic steps against it [. . .][10]

This population seemed to offer specific viable solutions to address the 'food question', solutions that were worth listening to – and following. Caught up in their own concerns regarding civilian and soldier morale, international prestige, and ambitious military plans, Prussian and imperial authorities for their part moved rapidly to respond to the demands of poor consumers, as translated through public media and inside reports. This response proved a marked contrast to the prewar habit of forcefully repressing protestors.

Government measures to combat the effects of 'economic war' won widespread popular approval for the state over and over again during the course of the war. This apparent responsiveness helps explain why the German revolution did not take place earlier than November 1918. But because these measures were consistently piecemeal, reactive, and contradictory, they were never adequate to subduing the food crisis for any length of time. In the end, officials' actions were far more effective in legitimating popular demands – and the populace's right to make demands – than in defending the state's right to rule. Urban Germans came to interpret officials' reactions as deferring leadership on the central domestic issue of food management to these poor women in the streets. They perceived official responsiveness moreover as affirmation of a new state responsibility to provide for the basic needs of the broad population, a standard German authorities found difficult to meet, all the more in wartime.[11] This outcome was certainly at odds with officials intent on prosecuting war as a means of quelling domestic discontent.

Thus these crowds in the street, composed primarily of poorer women – formally disenfranchised by virtue of both gender and economic position – helped spur a dynamic unlike prewar patterns. This dynamic in turn manifested new relations between state and society, including unprecedented levels of mass political influence and an expectation of government obligation to the broad populace, constituted as citizens in practice, if not in formal terms. Already by the rancorous riots of late 1915 this pattern emerged clearly. Beginning in early October of that year, shortages of dietary fats, particularly of butter and meat, brought Berliners, especially from the working and lower middle classes, into the streets to wait in long lines. The shortages resulted in a combination of real hunger, at least among the poorer populations, and a sense of deprivation for the greater public fostered by the absence of 'comfort' foods and customary patterns of consumption during this already difficult time. The shortages also communicated perceived inequities and injustices in distribution, as poorer consumers charged that producers withheld their products to drive up prices, and that merchants routed their goods to wealthier neighborhoods.

The long queues acted as tinder boxes for unrest, erupting one after the other as merchants raised their prices, declared themselves out of goods, and even insulted would-be customers, challenging their right to eat their fill – and to eat as proper Germans. Political police responded with a combination of fear for the violent crowds and commiseration in light of their own worsening economic situation. Officer Krupphausen reported in October 1915:

> After 25 minutes I entered Edison St. in Oberschöneweide [just outside Berlin] and found here too [. . .] a crowd of several thousand men and women, loudly howling and pushing the policemen aside. From there I learned from the sergeant on duty, whose head had been severely injured by the crowd, that the crowd had already stormed several butter shops because of the prices. In good time I could confirm for myself that several big show windows were shattered, shop doors destroyed, and entire stocks stolen. [. . .] I was asked to close off the street, as the present police and officers [. . .] were completely helpless against the crowd. [. . .] Various objects such as flower pots were thrown at us [. . .][12]

He and his colleagues concluded – despite the violence exercised against them – that 'relief [. . .] can only come in the form of a better and more equal distribution of all foods'.[13] These reports most often constituted 'women' and 'the women', as well as 'women of lesser means', categorically as the core population of these riots, whose actions were legitimated by their rational but frustrated quest for food. Police frequently contrasted such women with wayward adolescent boys and drunken men, whom they represented as gratuitously spurring violence.

Berlin Police Commissioner Jagow passed such ominous accounts on to the Prussian Interior Minister and other high civilian and military officials with the comment, 'unfortunately, one must reckon with the continuation of these attacks as long as these rising prices remain. I don't have to warn you of the importunate effects such events will have inter alia abroad.'[14] A would-be helpful civilian added his own apprehensive thoughts in a letter to the Prussian Interior Minister: 'Can the Minister not take the appropriate measures to push prices down forthwith? If it comes to revolts, the effect on the front will surely not be good.'[15] There is good evidence from 'letters of lament' (*Jammerbriefen*) that, despite censorship, the ill effects were already beginning. A woman from Saxony wrote her husband, a prisoner of war:

> The urgency is getting ever greater because we have nothing more [. . .] I'm so hungry all day long, it's as if I've been shot in the throat. Is this crap going to come to an end soon, or does one have to take up arms oneself to put at least the children out of their misery? I just can't take this misery anymore [. . .][16]

Authorities noted understatedly that such letters, frequent, steady, and expressing a desire for an immediate end to the war, were 'not without an effect on the men'.[17] Nervous officials, concerned to keep morale high both at home and on the front, as well as to protect the reputation of the German state abroad, responded positively, imposing a retail butter ceiling and rationing meat. Yet shortages returned within days, and the cycle began anew. In the succeeding months and years, authorities responded with ever more expansive systems and bureaucracies of food distribution, from the Price Monitoring Authority (*Preisprüfungsstelle*) to the War Food Office (*Kriegsernährungsamt*) to the State Distribution Office (*Staatsverteilungsstelle*). But they failed to adequately support these systems, leading to their rapid failure one after the other. Correspondingly, throughout the remainder of the war there were few extended periods of quiet in the streets. Such food-related upheaval was moreover closely related to the better-studied labor strikes of April 1917 and January 1918 (also reflecting heavy participation by women), as well as central to the revolution of November 1918.

Women and Wartime Politics

This activity was 'political', both as the broad public and officials received it, and, by mid-war certainly, in intent. It was political moreover both in content and in form. In early 1916 Commissioner Jagow cited to his superiors a Social Democratic newspaper claiming that Germans found 'extraparliamentary means' to be the strategy to most successfully elicit change. At this moment, he added, '"extraparliamentary means" mean[t] none other than demonstrations in the street'.[18] Earlier work on the political history of the war has characterized food-related unrest, carried out primarily by women, as 'economic' only and 'prepolitical', and thereby largely irrelevant to the history except as background.[19] To include this unrest in the political narrative of the war requires a broader definition of politics than has regularly been used among historians of this period.[20] Certainly scholars of the French revolution have for some time constituted women's street riots, including that over food shortages, as a part of the revolution's political history.[21] Such strategies came to constitute political protest no less in the twentieth century, despite some theorists' assertions that food riots represent a premodern, atavistic form.[22] Indeed, as hunger unrest continues around the world into the twenty-first century, there is still less reason to find such activity either premodern or essentially pre-political in form or content.

Many of the demands made by participants in eighteenth-century actions are similar to those in First World War-era Germany, reflecting for example an implicit notion of popular sovereignty, situating the nation in 'the people' rather than in the state. At the same time, the riots in the First World War do reflect the more 'modern' point in time in which they took place; demonstrators drew effectively on notions of civil rather than 'natural' rights to make demands on the government. Moreover, the German bourgeoisie on the whole, particularly in the cities, seemed to support the rioters, publicly at least, on the basis of the protestors' own contributions to and sacrifices for the nation. They called for the govern-ment to properly provide for the demonstrating 'patriots', compensating their efforts and enabling them to play their appropriate parts in the war effort. Demands for 'just distribution' may seem radical, but they were at this point not uncommon. As Officer Ludwig wrote, expressing public opinion of those in the streets:

> even good, faithful patriots have begun to turn into pessimists, and the thought is ever more compelling that Germany may fall as a consequence of its econ-omic defects. [. . .] [O]ne awaits relief, which can only come in the form of a better and more equal distribution of all foods.[23]

The middle class's initial support for these rioters may have stemmed from the perception that the latter were women pursuing their 'natural' right to feed their families, as opposed to the threatening, negative image they associated with factory workers, imagined as male, striking for higher wages. But in the course of the war the language used by all parties came to bespeak modern ideas of entitlement, born of citizens' contrib-utions and of a social contract with their government, rather than notions of 'noblesse oblige' and other ideas more prevalent still in the language of the eighteenth-century unrest and its reportage. These rights were based less on women's roles as wives or mothers of patriotic soldiers (*Soldaten-bräute* and *Heldenmütter*) and as mothers of future warriors of the nation than on a sense of their perceived more direct contributions to the war and to the nation, whether through munitions production or through their battle for justice in equitable food distribution for 'all Germans'.

The riots were thus also political in intent. At a certain level, questions of the distribution of basic necessary goods – such as 'why should the one who has the fatter wallet be able to feed himself differently and better than the greater mass of the population?' – can be said to be the most fundamentally political.[24] Beyond this, by early 1916, protestors in the streets combined their demands for officials to address the food crisis with calls for an immediate end to the war in which the state had invested its very legitimacy. 'The women's view of the war', police reported, was 'peace at any price'.[25] In turn, officials at every level made policy decisions – related to domestic and even military planning, from efforts to sabotage the blockade to negotiations for grain with Romania and, ultimately, Russia and Ukraine intended to placate protestors.

However, by early 1918, women protesting the food crisis were in the forefront of those claiming that the government had failed irrevocably in its responsibilities to the German people – responsibilities established in large part during the course of the war. Declaring the government was '*in control of nothing*', they rejected any government claims to authority, announcing they would move on their own to institute a 'bread peace'.[26] They shouted, 'Enough with the murder at the front, down with the war! We don't want to starve any longer!' and, in threatening fashion, 'When Wilhelm stands in the crosshairs, or stands in line for potatoes, then the war will end.' They thus rendered an equivalence between the experiences on the battle and home fronts. Women sent clear messages to the front, 'Finish up now with that ridiculous war, we're croaking of hunger!'[27] As authorities noted with concern and resignation, women wrote their husbands and sons on the front simply telling them to come home. Soldiers on the front, who had for four years demonstrated anger and disgust with the state in response to news of their families' homefront plight, began to respond to these demands.[28] This shift in popular estimation of the regime and its consequences was central to the government's effective implosion in November 1918.

Thus the riots clearly affected 'high politics', from early on in the war. Moreover poor women's activity was throughout the war increasingly directly connected with acts more explicitly recognized as political, in which women's role has been largely ignored. Such activity included not only factory-based strikes, the populations of which flowed from shop-floor to food queue (as well as simply individual departures from munitions jobs, despite government pressure). It also included countless 'deputations' and larger groups of women, both spontaneous and planned, marching into government offices at all levels and demanding to be heard. Factory worker Martha Balzer remembered that in February 1917:

> Despite the state of siege [imposed at the declaration of war on Prussia and elsewhere, prohibiting 'political' activity] we demonstrated with more than 500 women, heading toward the Britz [a suburb of Berlin] municipal office. The police were crushed to one side. Mayor Schmiedigen and the Bread Commission could not get away. The city council had to take its place. [. . .] As Schmiedigen [. . .] tried to insult me with the epithet 'representative of the people', many women responded, 'we are all representatives of the people.'[29]

By 1915, tales of such scenes regularly graced the press, despite censorship; by late in the war, these episodes were so commonplace they no longer garnered special notice but seemed rather an everyday part of the political landscape.

At the same time, protestors in the street, particularly women, often demonstrated a relatively cool response to strategies that historians typically treat as more formally political. Protesting women in the streets stood somewhat aloof from campaigns for franchise reform: they had become aware that officials acknowledged their opinions far more closely than any franchise would provide for. If, in spite of this, authorities were unable to address their concerns, then expanded franchise would hardly be the remedy, at least for the moment. Protesting poorer women also remained in the majority removed from radical left organizers' efforts to effect an imitation of the Russian revolution in 1917 (though these organizers themselves included many women). This was not a consequence of women's putative essential 'conservatism' or resistance to organization; nor does it indicate the fundamental meaninglessness of voting rights. Rather it demonstrates the importance of everyday life and experience in shaping political ideals and goals, and in determining the means and appropriate forms to reach those ends.[30] In 1917, poorer German women still maintained hope that the government would meet their needs, in light of officials' continued though inadequate efforts, which contrasted sharply with Russian civilians' experience of a completely unresponsive regime. It also demonstrates the fluidity of political forms and strategies. Paradoxical as it may seem, in 1916 and 1917, Hindenburg's effective military dictatorship appeared to many civilians at least initially as an answer to popular demand and as a sign of more responsive government.

The Transformation of Social Relations

Acknowledging the role of women on the home front during the war recasts not only the political history of the period and its aftermath, but also the history of wartime social relations. 'Class' relations in prewar Germany, and the enormous tensions they fomented, were defined through the relationship to production: factory laborer versus factory owner, etc. Parties, political lobbies, and a range of other organizations drew largely if not exclusively on class identification. In prewar Germany, the central cleavage fell between members of the upper classes, broadly conceived, and the working class, whose paradigmatic representative, the Social Democratic Party, was almost entirely shunned by the other parties, despite the SPD's majority victory in the 1912 national parliamentary elections. Relations based on ties to consumption as well as means of production grew in importance, however, in the years before the war, particularly as a result of new tariffs imposed to protect the competitiveness of German agriculture, causing rising prices on major foodstuffs in the cities.[31] Such new alliances, i.e. among urban consumers, simultaneously deepened other cleavages, for example, between urban and rural Germans, though these remained muted relative to wartime developments.

The wartime food crisis brought this consumption-based societal organization to the fore. Wartime propaganda promised that sufficient domestic food supplies existed despite the blockade, so Germans sought to identify the 'internal enemy' responsible for the shortages that arose almost immediately. Early on, consumers identified one another as at fault, 'stuffing their bellies' out of ignorance, greed, and insufficient patriotism. By 1915, however, urban consumers began to join together across class lines, rhetorically at least, to identify these 'internal enemies' in the form of the merchant, the distributor, and, especially, the agricultural producer, who they believed hoarded crucial supplies to drive up prices. Officer Schade wrote in 1916 of those in the cities seeking food, 'the bitterness grows each day against the rich, rural producers as well as against the businessmen. In general one regards these as the worst enemy, who don't possess the least glimmer of patriotism and love of one's fellow man.'[32]

This perceived common cause among urban consumers renders more complex the commonplace assertion (for which there is also good evidence) that relations between 'the working class' and 'the *Mittelstand*' were further poisoned as a result of the war. Indeed this effective unity across traditional class lines and even into the bourgeoisie caused by common suffering at some level was central to the ability of the poorest urban consumers to make their case to authorities with such potency. Policemen's own apparent sympathy in their reports for the largely working-class women they observed, contrasting sharply with prewar examples, offers powerful evidence for this case. Officer Kuhlmann averred in July 1917:

Discussion with completely reasonable women confirms that a portion of the population is now actually suffering from starvation. A number of persons who had to leave the market empty-handed exited the market in small groups headed for the city hall and demanded bread and potatoes there. With the indication from the civil servant that they should get bread where they have it to sell, a number of women now pushed down the Gürtel Street and from the shop of the baker Hans Schwarze [. . .], against the will of the clerk, they violently took 30 breads without paying. A riot arose over this, involving about 150 people, in which the shop's show window awning was damaged [. . .] This episode demonstrates that it is high time that efforts be made to bring in sufficient supplies of fruits and vegetables and distribute them to the broad masses of the population, whose patience is evidently exhausted.[33]

These policemen found their own most successful political strategies through such representation of food rioters. For their part, farmers naturally returned the charge of enmity, accusing city dwellers of an inability to give up lavish lifestyles and an insensibility to the burdens on the growers. To be sure, this also contributed to the breakdown of morale on the front as well as deterioration of the *Burgfrieden* at home; the conflict for officials was based on the legitimacy of farmers' concerns as well as those of urban consumers. But the public message, and the official response at all levels, overwhelmingly painted the hungry urban consumer as the protagonist in the war against the inner enemy, mirroring hostilities on the front against the foreign enemy. The urban consumer became in much of the public rhetoric synonymous with the 'good German', with whom one wished to identify.

And, notably, this 'good German' was most often portrayed, in police and other official reports as well as in public representations, as a woman, a 'woman of lesser means'. Those participating in food lines and food protests represented a mixture of men and women (as well as boys and girls), though, as the war raged on, the homefront was increasingly 'feminized' by the conscription of all available men. Certainly those commenting on the crowds in the streets were overwhelmingly men. And naturally all of these populations were 'consumers'; it was their common need for food and lack of access at some level that drew them together. Yet the broad public came to envision the poorer urban consumer, provisioner, and street-level activist as female, in a positive sense. Increasingly public rhetoric – in the press, public speeches, statements issued by a wide variety of organizations – represented the female consumer as the 'soldier on the home front', and even as the figure exemplifying and acting on behalf of the entire German population. Within the broader German public, men and women both seemed to identify with this active, leading female image. It is likely no coincidence that the figure of Germania, the female warrior representing Germany that emerged in the early nineteenth century, returned with a vengeance in penny postcards and other popular imagery in 1915, after a virtual absence of several decades in favor of masculine images.[34] This shift from images of women on the eve of war, as relatively passive, teary-eyed wives and mothers of soldiers who fought to protect their vulnerability, was striking. Combined moreover with the position of the 'woman of lesser means' as a lower-class urban dweller, this transformation in the image of the representative 'German' is all the more notable.

Although the image of the consumer might seem then to cast women in the roles of good wife and mother, these latter roles were not particularly valued among women in wartime. Women in the wartime streets did not seem connected to the public through their husbands or other male figures; their new greater prominence in public combined with the physical separation from men engendered this new conceptualization. Indeed, Germans overall demonstrated considerable resentment of special allowances and other benefits for *Kriegerfrauen*, claiming that such women were in no meaningful way connected to the sacrifices of their husbands.[35] Likewise, relatively few Germans continued to support prewar pronatalist efforts to raise declining birth rates and/or to produce new generations of soldiers for the fatherland. Pregnant women encountered great difficulty in exercising their right to go to the head of a food line, or to get extra rations of milk – until 1917, when officials withdrew these rights altogether, pressured by public opinion. A broad population of Germans who felt weakened and ill did not believe pregnant women were any more in need or deserving of rations taken at the former's expense. Indeed, childbearing seemed at worst a selfish act, hardly to be 'rewarded': creating new mouths to feed, even compromising a woman's ability to contribute more directly to the war effort – as through munitions labor. At the same time, while in the prewar era bourgeois men and women found little common cause with male factory laborers – the stereotypical worker – they seem to have been far more interested in women on the wartime shop floor, laboring for the nation. Once again, official policy, providing special advantages for these women, reflected an unacknowledged broad public opinion at that moment, as well as authorities' own interest in accelerating weapons production. These changes did not necessarily devolve into substantial political and social improvement specifically for 'real' women after the war; women were for example thrown out of factories unceremoniously as men returned from the front after the war.[36] It is true that the Weimar constitution fundamentally guarantees the same rights for men and women. The first women parliamentarians attempted thereby to insure that women would not be imagined after the war as limited to roles as wives and mothers.[37] But perhaps most significant, this image of the strong German woman in the streets, fighting for the German nation in an inner 'economic war', helped forge social relations – positive and negative – that long outlasted the war, as well as creating a new image of the German citizen that bore positive implications for *all* Germans.

Through their perceived unity as urban consumers (despite many actual conflicting interests), a broad swath of Germans, apparently represented by poorer women taking leadership in the street, voiced increasingly challenging demands on the government. Their calls for 'equitable' distribution implied a range of potentially radical political and economic reforms, including at various moments demands for complete equality of distribution. Bavarian Minister President (and future Chancellor) Georg von Hertling registered his concern for the 'socialist principles' city-dwellers seemed to desire – and which he perceived state-level authorities seemed determined to fulfill.[38] Commercial lobbies feared in 1916 and 1917 that the 'war socialism' they believed defined official policy would devolve into peacetime socialism. Yet poorer urban Germans were less convinced that such equitable distribution was in fact being instituted. By the end of 1917, they effectively offered an ultimatum to the central regime: either officials successfully provide for the needs of all Germans – an obligation officials themselves helped create – or these Germans would be unable to fulfill their own commitment, to support the war effort, or even to support the government itself.

Consequences of the War on the Homefront

By 1918, poor women in the streets lost hope that the existing government *could* fulfill these promises and newly created obligations. Gone now were the large-scale spontaneous demonstrations and calls to officials to respond with new measures to realize perceived agreed-upon goals. Remaining were rather small-scale desperate, hopeless, and increasingly violent interactions between buyers and sellers, as well as other acts of 'self-help' that signaled that the regime had to all effects already collapsed. These women, shaped by the experiences of the preceding four years, were thus as central to the German revolution of November 1918 as were the mutinous sailors and soldiers who poured into major German cities; indeed the unrest was closely related.

The turbulent war era, taken in its entirety, had brought to the foreground a range of political potentials for the postwar era that are not commonly recognized: republicanism, popular sovereignty, challenges to the political economy, guarantees of individuals' basic needs, and a basis for radical democracy were all products of the war that demanded a hearing during and made their mark on the successor Weimar era. The activities of women on the home front, and the representation of those women by the press, the police, and others, were central to these developments.

But the homefront experience of four years of unceasing tension over the most basic goods and the ultimate disintegration of civic life left its mark on the Weimar regime in far less appealing forms as well, forms that helped pave the way moreover for the National Socialist regime alongside the brutalizing experience of the battle front. Life in the streets proved an ambiguous lesson for 'direct democracy' played out in the streets, for example. One youth recounted a night in March 1919 in Lichtenberg, a working-class suburb of Berlin and site of almost constant wartime food-related unrest:

[The women] weren't supposed to go to their windows now: the 'pig butts' [policemen] would meet their just deserts [. . .]. But all at once the women were among us, swinging at [Officer] Dietz with carpet bags and market baskets. 'You scoundrel', they called, 'what are you looking for here, haven't you already guzzled enough blood from our husbands, sons and brothers?' [. . .] So genuine was the women's fury that we had to forcefully stop them [. . .] As the truck began to move [. . .], there was suddenly a great tumult. The sailors had the 'pig butt', the well-known criminal police commissar of all of Lichtenberg. At this moment the women could no longer be held back, because none of them had forgotten his threats to throw them into prison and shoot them. They boxed his ears with carpet beaters, scrub brushes and market baskets. His face was greenish yellow with fear, as his empty holster hung over his fat belly. Till the last he had willingly shot, wounding many workers and killing soldiers. The women beat him half dead [. . .][39]

In turn, the Weimar leadership did not hesitate to revert to traditional military authorities, drawing on the most violent police methods to put down challenges to the new government. Unfortunately, under the conditions of still greater scarcity and other circumstances that marked the Weimar Republic, it was ultimately the less attractive lessons of the war era that won out over those imagined by the framers of the Republican constitution, or by leaders of the Council Movement.

This everyday violence permeated social relations as well. The hatreds that developed or radically deepened through the experience of scarcity and perceived maldistribution survived throughout Weimar and into the National Socialist era. The homefront experience brought broad-based support to the notion of a *Volksgemeinschaft*, or community of the people, defining 'Germanness' by keeping whole groups out as well as bringing people together. Who was truly German based on wartime experience and perception? Scarcity divided Germans against one another, even as each group defended its own superior patriotism to those of perceived 'internal enemies'. Wartime public debates defining equitable food distribution concluded overall in 1917 the importance of properly supporting the working-class, majority female population that kept munitions and other factories running, as 'strong', 'hard-laboring' patriots working for all Germans. While salutary for the tens of thousands of poorer women who worked in these factories, both in terms of prestige and in sheer material terms, the ominous flip-side of this characterization was the identification of other populations as 'weak' – and as less worthy of properly feeding – including for example pregnant women. Supreme Army Commander Paul von Hindenburg and his military leadership happily lent support to this way of thinking, but the impulse came from a wide range of perspectives. While many protestors actively denounced the taxonomies of distribution that distinguished among the population based on one's societal 'value', the wartime scarcity fostered the diciest controversies over what constituted the most 'equitable' distribution of foodstuffs. The implicit identification of 'Germanness' as the quality constituting access to basic foods left an ominous legacy for the postwar regime.

Defining Germanness exclusively was also closely connected to a steep rise in anti-Semitism on the homefront in the second half of the war. It had become increasingly respectable to connect food profiteering and 'Jewishness', indeed as the latter came to be used as a synonym for the former, then speciously applied back against actual Jewish Germans. This new world view also promoted hatred toward ethnic Polish Germans, as for example word spread after the early 1918 'separate peace' that Poles received wheat from Russia and Ukraine that should have come to Germans. These animosities flourished unabated in the continuing crises of provisioning in the postwar era. Likewise, paranoid nationalism that distrusted all outside the country and eschewed transnational interdependence grew out of the experience of the 'economic war' as well as from the terms of military defeat.

The willingness of large populations during wartime to invest their trust from 1916 on in a military government and other leaders who promised 'total control' – a 'dictator of the pantry' – also lent its allure in the postwar period. Support for such political relations co-existed with the demand that any leader attend closely to the will of the people – however 'the people' and their 'will' were defined. The extreme wartime conditions offer a more compelling explanation for support for or acceptance of a dictatorship at the end of the Weimar period than do arguments concerning a national character, that is, some kind of essential German love for militaristic leadership and an innate deference to authority. If support for Adolf Hitler himself might be connected to a desire among Germans for a government that could transcend the political and economic chaos that had reigned since 1914, it is worth remembering moreover Hitler's own concern as he prepared for and entered war in the late 1930s to prevent a homefront experience like that of the First World War. The contradictory agenda of pursuing total war while attempting to maintain good domestic economic relations was a primary instigation for the brutal looting of occupied lands and exploitation of slave labor. Finally, if the horrors of the Nazi genocide can be traced in part to a need to overcome the experience of mass death and human suffering, this must be related to the violence of the homefront experience as well as to that, albeit very different, of the battlefront.[40]

Summary

Thus consideration of homefront life in the First World War, including both the experience and representation of German women, is central to understanding the political, social, and economic history of the war. Attention to wartime unrest must account not only for mass shop-floor strikes – including women's active role in these strikes – but also for four years of discontent over food played out in the streets. Poor urban women's role portrayed as consumers, and all the more as activists in the street who seemed to represent and lead the greater German people, lent these women new political power, which ultimately resulted in potentially positive political results for the populace as a whole.

A history of the war must attend generally to the entirety of the war period. A study of relations between state and society must focus not only on the dominating control of the 'military dictatorship' of the second half of the war, but must also fully treat officials' paradoxical efforts in the first two years of war, which helped transform Germans' understanding of their relationship with the state. The economic narrative cannot start – or end – with the horrors of the 1916–17 'turnip winter', but must likewise look to the entirety of the war (as well as before and beyond). It must take into account numerous facets: cultural as well as physical deprivations, the enormous political significance of food privisioning, the general transformation of class boundaries, and the new battles in defining German-ness in the distribution of scarce supplies. Finally, we are only beginning to understand the full effects of the war – 'positive' as well as 'negative' – in the decades to come. Attention to these effects must account for the experience of war on the homefront as well as on the battlefront, must look to both the more and less attractive of these effects in the years and decades to come, and must recognize the experience and roles of women as well as men in understanding them.

Notes

Special thanks to Elisabeth Meyer-Renschhausen and Karen Hagemann, most generous friends, engaged scholars, and Berlin activists.

1. Brandenburgisches Landeshauptarchiv, Provinz Brandenburg, Repositur 30, Berlin C Polizeipräsidium (hereafter BLHA PBB Polizei), Nr. 15851, 22 February 1918, Report Palm, 313.
2. Morale reports and military monthly reports have been regularly used by historians of the war, to be sure, but they have been most often used aggregately, rather than to mark day-by-day changes during the course of the war. Cf. Karl-Ludwig Ay, *Die Enstehung einer Revolution. Die Volksstimmung in Bayern während des Ersten Weltkrieges* (Berlin, 1968); Jürgen Kocka, *Klassengesellschaft im Krieg. Deutsche Sozialgeschichte 1914–1918* (Frankfurt a.M., 1988); Volker Ullrich, *Kriegsalltag: Hamburg im Ersten Weltkrieg* (Cologne, 1982); Ute Daniel, *Arbeiterfrauen in der Kriegsgesellschaft* (Göttingen, 1989). The last decades have seen a rapidly accelerating attention to the homefront; cf. as a small sampling in Germany additionally Gerald Feldman, *Army, Industry and Labor in Germany, 1914–1918* (Providence, RI, 1992[1966]); Wilhelm Deist, *Militär, Staat, und Gesellschaft: Studien*

zu Preußisch-Deutschen Militärgeschichte (Munich, 1991); Günther Mai, ed., *Arbeiterschaft in Deutschland, 1914–1918. Studien zu Arbeitskampf und Arbeitsmarkt im Ersten Weltkriege* (Düsseldorf, 1985); Benjamin Ziemann, *Front und Heimat: Ländliche Kriegserfahrungen im südlichen Bayern, 1914–1923* (Essen 1997); Gerhard Hirschfeld and Gerd Krumeich, eds., *Keiner fühlt sich hier als Mensch* (Essen, 1993); and pieces in Wolfgang Michalka, ed., *Der Erste Weltkrieg. Wirkung, Wahrnehmung, Analyse* (Munich, 1994). For comparative work, cf. Richard Wall and Jay Winter, eds., *The Upheaval of War: Family, Work, and Welfare in Europe, 1914–1918* (Cambridge, 1988); and Jay Winter and Jean-Louis Robert, eds., *Capital Cities at War: Paris, London, and Berlin, 1914–1919* (Cambridge 1997).

3. Cf. August Skalweit, *Der Deutsche Kriegsernährungswirtschaft* (Stuttgart, 1927); Archibald Bell, *A History of the Blockade and the Countries Associated with Her in the Great War* (London, 1937); Lothar Burchardt, *Friedenswirtschaft und Kriegsvorsorge* (Boppard am Rhein, 1968); C. Paul Vincent, *The Politics of Hunger* (Athens, 1985); Avner Offer, *The First World War: An Agrarian Interpretation* (Oxford, 1989); N. P. Howard, 'The Social and Political Consequences of the Allied Food Blockade of Germany, 1918–19,' *German History* 11 no. 2 (1993): 161–188.

4. Cf. the seminal statement in Fritz Fischer, *Germany's Aims in the First World War* (New York, 1967); and id., *War of Illusions: Germany's Policies from 1911 to 1914* (New York, 1975).

5. BLHA PBB Polizei, Nr. 15810, 15 May 1915, Report Jagow, 284.

6. Ibid, Nr. 15809, 17 February 1915 Report Rhein, 18.

7. Ibid, Nr. 15815, 6 December 1915, Report Ludwig, 128–129.

8. 'Zur Ernährungsfrage,' *Der Reichsbote*, 4 January 1916.

9. 'Die Teuerung und ihre Folgen,' *Der Deutsche Kurier*, 15 October 1915. The 'enemy at home' for this newspaper was the Social Democratic Party, but by this point in the war such a reference generally was more ambiguous than it had been before the war.

10. BLHA PBB Polizei, Nr. 15813, 3 September 1915, Report Gerhardt, 9.

11. Certainly work on modern wars in many national settings has in the last decades emphasized how fighting for one's nation, or even working in war factories, has led to postwar concessions from the state, especially to groups previously excluded for reasons of class, race, or gender. In the German setting, as early as the early nineteenth-century Wars of Liberation, members of the bourgeoisie claimed their sacrifices in the wars justified new rights; cf. Karen Hagemann,

Belinda J. Davis

Mannlicher Muth und Teutsche Ehre. Nation, Militär und Geschlecht in Preußen zur Zeit der Antinapoleonischen Kriege (Paderborn, 2001); on the First World War: Susan Pedersen, *Family, Dependence, and the Origins of the Welfare State* (Cambridge, 1993); Daniel, *Arbeiterfrauen.* See also Steven Lawson, *Black Ballots: Voting Rights in the South, 1944–1969* (Lanham, 1999).

12. BLHA PBB Polizei, Nr. 15813, 17 October 1915, Report Krupphausen, 67.
13. Ibid, Nr. 15815, 6 December 1915, Report Ludwig, 128–129.
14. Ibid, Nr. 15813, 16 October 1915, Report Jagow, 265.
15. Geheimes Staatsarchiv Preußischer Kulturbesitz, Rep. 77A, Io Nr. 1, 1, private letter to von Loebell, 13 October 1915.
16. Cited in Daniel, *Arbeiterfrauen*, 149–150.
17. Ibid. 150. There is extensive evidence of close communications between home and battle fronts, despite censorship, through correspondence, leaves of absence, news passed personally by other furloughed or garrisoned soldiers, etc. See besides Ute Daniel's work e.g. Bernd Ulrich and Benjamin Ziemann, eds., *Frontalltag im Ersten Weltkrieg. Wahn und Wirklichkeit. Quellen und Dokumente* (Frankfurt/M., 1997); Bernd Ulrich, 'Feldpostbriefe des Ersten Weltkrieges – Möglichkeit und Grenzen einer alltagsgeschichtlichen Quellen,' *Militärgeschichtliche Mitteilungen* 53 (1994): 73–84; Ziemann, *Front und Heimat.*
18. Jagow cites from 'Not kennt kein Gebot,' *Volksfreund Braunschweig,* 3 November 1915; he intimates his agreement in BLHA PBB Polizei, Nr. 15814, 5 November 1915, Report Jagow, 298.
19. Exceptions are recent aside from Ay, *Die Entstehung einer Revolution.* Cf. Gerald Feldman, *The Great Disorder: Politics, Economics, and Society in the German Inflation, 1914–1923* (New York, 1993); Martin Geyer, *Verkehrte Welt. Revolution, Inflation und Moderne. München 1914–1924* (Göttingen, 1998); Alf Lüdtke, 'Hunger, Essens-"Genuss" und Politik bei Fabrikarbeitern und Arbeiterfrauen. Beispiele aus dem rheinisch-westfälischen Industriegebiet, 1910–1940,' *SoWi* 14, no. 2 (1985): 118–125; Anne Roerkohl, *Hungerblockade und Heimatfront. Die kommunale Lebensmittelversorgung in Westfalen während des Ersten Weltkrieges* (Stuttgart, 1991); Robert Scholz, 'Ein Unruhiges Jahrzehnt,' in *Pöbelexzesse und Volkstumulte in Berlin,* ed. Martin Gailus (Berlin, 1984). Cf. also Klaus Tenfelde, 'La Riscoperta dell' "Autodifesa Collettiva": Protesta Sociale in Germania durante l'Inflazione del 1923,' *Annali dell' Istituto Storico Italo-Germanico* 11 (1983): 379–422.

20. On defining politics relative to gender, compare Karen Hagemann, *Frauenalltag und Männerpolitik. Alltagsleben und gesellschaftliches Handeln von Arbeiterfrauen in der Weimarer Republik* (Bonn, 1990).

21. Cf. as one example Harriet Applewhite and Darline Levy, eds., *Women and Politics in the Age of Democratic Revolution* (Ann Arbor, 1990).

22. Cf. most prominently Louise A. Tilly and Charles Tilly, eds., *Class Conflict and Collective Action* (Beverly Hills, 1981).

23. BLHA PBB Polizei, Nr. 15815, Report Ludwig, 6 December 1915, 128–129.

24. 'Aus Gross-Berlin. Keine Zwangsmässige Massenspeisung,' *Vorwärts*, 12 December 1916.

25. BLHA PBB Polizei, Nr. 15819, 19 July 1916, Report Görl, 4.

26. Ibid., Nr. 15822, 7 December 1917, Report Seeger, 48.

27. From *Beiträge zur Geschichte der deutschen Gewerkschaftsbewegung* 1, no. 2 (1918): 193; cited in Annemarie Lange, *Das Wilhelminische Berlin* (Berlin, 1967), 750–751. Cf. on frontline reception, Adolf Linke, 'Als Sozialdemokrat an der Ostfront,' in *1918. Erinnerungen von Veteranen der deutschen Gewerkschaftsbewegung an die Novemberrevolution*, ed. Werner Richter (Berlin, 1958), 347–78; Arthur Holitscher, *Lebensgeschichte eines Rebellen* (Potsdam 1928), vol. 2; Ziemann, *Front und Heimat*.

28. Cf. Bundesarchiv Lichterfelde, 15.01, Nr. 12476/1, 321, Treutler to Hertling, 12 August 1918.

29. Cited in Dieter Glatzer and Ruth Glatzer, eds., *Berliner Leben 1914–1918. Eine historische Reportage aus Erinnerungen und Berichten* (Berlin, 1983), 307

30. Cf. Hagemann, *Frauenalltag*; and Renate Bridenthal and Claudia Koonz, 'Beyond "Kinder, Küche, Kirche". Weimar Women in Politics and Work,' in *When Biology Became Destiny: Women in Weimar and Nazi Germany*, ed. Renate Bridenthal et al. (New York, 1984), 33–65.

31. Cf. recent work on consumerism, including Gert-Joachim Glaeßner et al., eds., *Arbeiterbewegung und Genossenschaften: Entstehung und Entwicklung der Konsumgenossenschaften in Deutschland am Beispiel Berlins* (Göttingen, 1989); and Christoph Nonn, *Verbraucherprotest und Parteiensystem im Wilhelminischen Deutschlands* (Düsseldorf, 1996). See recent comparative work: Victoria de Grazia, ed., *The Sex of Things. Gender and Consumption in Historical Perspective* (Berkeley, 1996); and Susan Strasser, et al., eds., *Getting and Spending: European and American Consumer Societies in the Twentieth Centuries* (Cambridge, 1998).

32. BLHA PBB Polizei Nr. 15820, Report Schade, 18 December 1916, 46. Certainly many merchants and farmers did engage in 'holding back' goods.

33. Ibid., Nr. 15821, Report Kuhlmann, 4 July 1917, 199. Those in the streets seeking food did not return the sympathy to the policemen who oversaw them.

34. Cf. e.g. postcards including the 1915 collection by Franz Stassen, Bildarchiv Preußischer Kulturbesitz, File 5796. Representations of Chancellor Otto von Bismarck were commonly used to represent a powerful German nation, militarily and otherwise, after its unification in 1871; great numbers of German homes contained small shrines to Bismarck. On the eve of war and in the first months of hostilities, the young officer leading his troops in heroic battle was a dominant image of the nation; compare for example the front pages of *Berliner Illustrirte Zeitung* early in the war. Images of General Paul von Hindenburg also represented the powerful warrior nation in the early-war period. By later in the war, insofar as a masculine figure was still used to represent Germany in popular settings, it was most often Michel, a humorous, bumbling character, at least in the so-called *Witzblätter*; insofar as papers like the *Berliner Illustrirte* continued to portray fighting men, the images were the rather less romantic and grimmer images of soldiers in the trenches. See Belinda Davis, 'Images of Gender and the Nation in Wilhelmine Germany,' forthcoming; compare Ute Frevert, *Mann und Weib, und Weib und Mann. Geschlechter-Differenzen in der Moderne* (Munich, 1995).

35. Cf. Belinda Davis, *Home Fires Burning: Food, Politics, and Everyday Life in World War I Berlin* (Chapel Hill, 2000), especially 24–47; Birthe Kundrus, *Kriegerfrauen, Familienpolitik und Geschlechterverhältnisse im Ersten und Zweiten Weltkrieg* (Hamburg, 1995); Daniel, *Arbeiterfrauen*.

36. Cf. Daniel, *Arbeiterfrauen*; Hagemann, *Frauenalltag*; and Julia Schneeringer, *Mobilizing Women for Politics: Gender and Propaganda in Weimar Germany, 1918–1932* (Chapel Hill, 2002).

37. Cf. Pedersen, *Family, Dependence*; Laura Lee Downs, *Manufacturing Inequality: Gender Division in the French and British Metalworking Industries, 1914–1939* (Ithaca, 1995); Susan Kingsley Kent, *Making Peace: The Reconstruction of Gender in Interwar Britain* (Princeton, 1993); Mary Louise Roberts, *Civilization without Sexes: Reconstructing Gender in Postwar France, 1917–1927* (Chicago, 1994); Françoise Thébaud, *La Femme au Temps de la Guerre de '14* (Paris, 1987); Pamela Haag, *Consent: Sexual Rights and the Transformation*

of American Liberalism (Ithaca, 1999); contrast in the Soviet Union, Elizabeth Wood, *The Baba and the Comrade: Gender and Politics in Revolutionary Russia* (Bloomington, 1997). Certainly there is considerable discussion of 'families' in the constitution, as well as in subsequent German legislation, though the regime's attitude toward 'families' was highly ambivalent in practice.

38. Cited in Feldman, *Army, Industry and Labor*, 104–105.
39. Franz Beiersdorf, 'Wir roten Matrosen haben bis zuletzt gekämpft,' in *1918: Erinnerungen*, ed. Richter, (Berlin, 1958), 312–317.
40. Cf. Ziemann, *Front und Heimat*, 9–18.

–5–

Enemy Images

Race and Gender Stereotypes in the Discussion on Colonial Troops. A Franco-German Comparison, 1914–1923

Christian Koller

In a survey conducted shortly after the Second World War involving about 150 French, Germans, English and Italians, in which the word 'negro' appeared among about twenty others in a word association test, nearly 60 percent of the participants associated 'Negro' with terms such as biological, sex, strong, athletic, powerful, boxer, Joe Louis, Jesse Owens, *tirailleur sénégalais*, wild, beast, devil and sin. The expression *tirailleur sénégalais* in turn evoked words like terrible, bloodthirsty, burly and strong.[1] The question about the origin of this image of the *tirailleur sénégalais* leads us back to the First World War and the early 1920s. In the First World War more than 600,000 non-white soldiers from the French and British colonies fought in the European theatre of war[2], among them 270,000 Maghrebins[3], 153,000 Indians[4] and 134,000 West Africans[5].

The previously unknown presence of a vast number of non-white men in Europe caused an intensive discussion about this phenomenon not only in the states employing such troops but also in Germany and in the neutral countries.[6] Yet, the discussion about colonial troops did not reach its climax until after the war, when France stationed colonial troops in its occupied zone west of the Rhine. Whereas the non-white soldiers had confronted Germans as equals during the war, now the colonial hierarchy was turned upside down, as non-white colonials routinely exercised power on former colonizers in the colonizers' own country. Although there were non-white soldiers in the Rhineland for the whole duration of the occupation (1918–30), the problem was only significant in Germany's discourse on foreign affairs from the French penetration into the demilitarized zone in April 1920 until the beginning of the occupation of the Ruhr area in January 1923.[7] During the war, German propaganda was aimed mainly at the neutral states of Europe and, until their entrance into the war, at the United States. After the war, Great Britain was to become another main target of this propaganda. Moreover, Germany itself was the intended target of propaganda during the period examined here. French counter-propaganda was likewise aimed at a domestic audience.

When addressing the discussion on colonial troops, I am referring to the European and North American debate on the employment of non-white troops from the colonies in Europe. My sources include press articles, propaganda treatises and political speeches. Thus, the producers of discourse are all members of the political, military, bureaucratic and cultural elites. I will concentrate on the discussion waged in France and Germany about African troops in French service. With regard to the Indian troops the situation was very different and will therefore not be discussed in this essay.[8] An analysis of this debate is bound to be largely concerned with the problem of racism. There is, on the one hand, Gisela Bock's suggestion that racism cannot be understood without understanding the dimensions of gender that contribute to its construction.[9] On the other hand, the debate about colonial troops in the French zone of occupation was mainly concerned with relations between non-white soldiers and German women. These two points make it clear that such an analysis cannot ignore the aspects of either gender or the body. A first glimpse at the evidence justifies this approach. In 1916, the correspondent of the *Neue Zürcher Zeitung* in France described the Indian soldiers as follows:

I admire their intelligent faces very much, whose nuances of color range from gold to bronze, whose wonderful beards embody the ideal of masculine beauty, whose coal-black eyes look so soulful and earnest. I can completely empathize with women's feelings of admiration towards these soldiers; it is more than pleasure taken in the exotic, it is an atavistic inclination towards genuine masculine beauty.[10]

On the other hand, in Klaus Mann's memoirs about the inter-war period, we find the following passage:

[. . .] I did not read the horror stories about the colored occupation troops' conduct without a certain creepy pleasure. One particular story that stuck in my mind concerned a Moroccan, who was not only said to have violated dozens of virgins and young boys but also – pinnacle of promiscuity! – a pretty horse [. . .] This absurd invention followed me for years [. . .] The shameless African's exorbitant potency worked on my fantasy.[11]

In the following discussion, I am going to proceed in three steps. Firstly, the basic development of *racial images* with reference to colonial troops will be analyzed and compared in both Germany and France. Secondly, I will focus on the *construction of masculinity* in several images of race, which will serve as a precursor to the third step of my analysis pertaining to *images of women* in discourses on the colonial troops. Finally, I will give a short overview of the debate on colonial troops in the Second World War. I thereby want to reinforce the thesis that the images of race and gender depended to a very high degree on shifting constellations. This might even lead to interchanges of French and German perspectives. However, this very exchangeability of perspectives makes it clear that those images, which seem so antagonistic, are rooted in common stereotypes. Gender research on nationalism has made the observation that in the construction of identities and alterities in emerging nation states, all the counter-images of the liberal-bourgeois and male subject were structured similarly – be it the image of women, that of colonized men, Jews, homosexuals or members of the lower classes.[12] The present study allows us to test this thesis with an example from the twentieth century. Moreover, we can observe which discourses engendered constellations in which conventional dichotomies of identity and alterity became obsolete.

Images of Race

Before the war and even during its outbreak, the image of the colonial soldier as a bloodthirsty savage was common all over Europe. In France, this image played an important role in the propaganda of colonial officer Charles Mangin, who favored building a strong *armée noire* for deployment on European battlefields from 1909 to 1912.[13] Germany, on the other hand, feared that national panic would result if, in the words of free-conservative General Liebert in a Reichstag debate on 1 November 1911, 'those black hordes were suddenly let loose from Belfort via Mulhouse into Southern Germany'.[14]

During the war, the image of African soldiers developed in a different way on both sides of the western front. In France beginning in 1915/16, officials propagated an image of infantile and devoted savages. This was done to counter German propaganda as well as subdue the French population's reservation about the African troops' presence in their native country. The image of colonial troops as bloodthirsty savages seems to have caused a latent popular opposition against stationing African troops at the Côte d'Azur. Lucie Cousturier, who had been acquainted with several wounded Senegalese soldiers in the military hospital at Fréjus during and after the war, wrote about the French population's feelings toward the Africans in her book *Des Inconnus chez moi* (1920):

> In April and May of 1916 we were very anxious about our future friends [. . .] There was simply no crime that one could put beyond them: [. . .] drunkenness, theft, rape, epidemics [. . .] 'What will become of us?' the farmers' wives moaned [. . .] 'We cannot let our little daughters go out alone any more because of those savages. We do not even risk going out alone ourselves any more [. . .] Imagine! If you were in the hands of those gorillas!'[15]

In Germany, on the other hand, representation had further developed along the lines of prewar imagery, even reaching the extremes of representing the African soldiers as beasts. In summer 1915, the German Foreign Office put a memorandum entitled 'Employment, contrary to International Law, of Colored Troops upon the European Theatre of War by England and France' into circulation, in which many atrocities were attributed to colonial soldiers, namely the poking out of eyes and the cutting off of ears, noses and heads of wounded and captured German soldiers. In chronicles of war, stories were to be found about the so-called *turcos*, North African soldiers, who 'after they had lost their weapons continued fighting scratching and biting like beasts', and about 'two-legged black beasts' approaching 'showing their teeth' until the 'Nordic calm' stopped the 'wave of half-humans with ape-shaped foreheads'.[16]

The colonial troops were designated with all sorts of expressions, which negated their quality as regular military forces, for example: 'a motley crew of colors and religions', 'devils', 'dehumanized wilderness', 'dead vermin of the wilderness', 'Africans jumping around in a devilish ecstasy', 'auxiliary rabble of all colors', and expressions such as: 'an exhibition of Africans', or 'an anthropological show of uncivilized or not enough civilized bands and hordes', 'black flood' or 'dark mud' or the catchphrase 'the black shame' that quickly attained common usage in the early 1920s.[17] Another image – diametrically opposed – was to be found in publications trying to justify the German practice of convincing Muslim POWs that they should enlist in the Ottoman army.[18]

During the occupation, German discourse altered the bloodthirsty beast into 'lusty colored murderers' who raped; the poster *Jumbo* became famous, showing an enormous black soldier wearing nothing but a helmet and pressing white women to his belly. Although the vast majority of the non-white occupation troops on the Rhine came from Morocco and

Algeria, people generally spoke of the 'black shame' and the 'black disgrace' in a propaganda campaign lasting more than two years and backed by all political parties with the exception of the extreme left wing. The colonial troops were often said to be stationed in the Rhineland as reward for services rendered during the war: 'The savages, having been abused as canon fodder, are now let loose on the "blondes", which they were promised for their own pleasure during the war!'[19] The few left-wing socialist and pacifist voices opposing the 'black shame' campaign went largely unheard. Yet, in spite of their anti-racist impetus, even their arguments betray a partial rooting in contemporary racial stereotypes.[20] So, the way that the Germans portrayed the colonial troops was very like how the Germans were portrayed by the propaganda of the Entente powers.[21]

In reaction to the German propaganda campaign, French officials backed the diffusion of a strongly paternalistic image of the *frères d'outre-mer* in the early 1920s, for instance through the publication of documents written by colonial soldiers[22] and through special monuments for colonial soldiers killed in the war. As an example of their dominating image in the early 1920s, I quote from General Mangin's book *Regard sur la France d'Afrique* published in 1924: 'Nothing permits us the thesis that the African race is inferior to the White as far as the intellect is concerned; at most we can say they are several stages behind.'[23] The French Left, having already opposed the deployment of West African troops in Europe before the war, resumed an attitude of fundamental opposition because they feared that African troops would be used to suppress social protests in France. They sometimes made use of racist images comparable to those of the German propaganda campaign.[24]

Images of Masculinity

The divergent but evidently interdependent development of racial images in Germany and France corresponded with an analogous construction of masculinity. The above-mentioned German Foreign Office memorandum from summer 1915 alleges that colonial soldiers had raped interned German women with *viehischen Lüsten* (bestial lust).[25] German satirical journals used to joke about the French *poilus* (footsoldiers) who risked their lives for the French revenge policy whereas Africans and Asians made themselves comfortable with their wives behind the front.[26] On the other hand, the infantile savages in the French wartime propaganda – often described as *grands enfants* – appear almost sexless. Yet, below the level of official propaganda, for instance in trench journals, images very similar to those of German propaganda can be found. A postcard depicting an African grasping a white French woman's breast with the outcry *Vive les Teutons* has to be seen in this context.[27] Thus, German propaganda on this topic seems to have reflected French *poilus'* fears.

The relentless allegations concerning sex crimes after the war were countered by the French with an image of the noble and beautiful savage, irresistibly attractive to white women. Georges Clemenceau, for instance, said in 1920: 'The *boches* are complaining that we sent them Blacks? But there's no *boche*, no Doctor of the University of Berlin or Munich, who was able to compete with the first Senegalese as far as beauty and grandeur are concerned.'[28] Colonial soldiers' alleged sexual attacks became the dominating topic in German propaganda. The *Deutsche Studentenschaft* wrote in an appeal in June 1920: 'The excessive sexual savageness of these Negroes, who stagger from rape to rape whips up resistance from the depths of our souls.'[29] In 1920, the Bavarian mint brought a medal into circulation which showed under the words 'The Black Shame' a phallus wearing a helmet to which a naked German woman was tied. The fact that this medal is alluded to in Jean Giraudoux's novel *Siegfried et le Limousin* shows it had a wide dissemination and received attention also in France.[30]

In this context, two points of discussion are of particular interest. Firstly, there are differences between official and semiofficial mainstream propaganda and the right-wing opposition's discourse as far as allegations of rape are concerned. The former was content with associating colonial soldiers with rapes committed on German women of all ages and only in a few cases made allegations concerning 'unnatural inclinations' – at the time signifying homosexuality and pedophilia[31] – whereas the latter continued to allege vampirism, sodomy, and similar practices and non-white troops were branded *entmenschte farbige Horden* (dehumanized colored hordes), *wollüstige farbige Mordbuben* (lusty colored murderers) with *tierischen Instinkten* (animal instincts), *farbige Sadisten* (colored sadists), *Halbtiere* (half-brutes), *schwarze Teufel* (black devils) with *sexueller Tierheit* (sexual bestiality), *vertierte Schwarze* (bestialized blacks), *schwarze Bestien* (black beasts), *Tiere in Menschengestalt* (beasts in human form), *schwarze Pest* (black plague) or *Raubtiere* (beasts of prey).[32] In a right-wing propaganda pamphlet entitled *Die schwarze Schmach. Frankreichs Schande* the following passage can be found: 'Victims of those colored monsters' unrestrained bestiality are found half-dead in meadows and ditches, their clothes torn to pieces, some of them with bites showing clearly how the beast has pounced upon his pitiable victim [. . .] The black soldier only follows his instincts [. . .]'[33] In the debate about French brothels in the occupied zone, right-wing politicians used to mention alleged homosexuality amongst North African soldiers: 'Soon, brothels with boys for the honorable Moroccans will be demanded, who [. . .] have dangerous pederast inclinations and are the most terrible savages anyway.'[34] In these discussions there were also allegations about the abduction of German girls to serve in brothels for African soldiers.[35]

Another point of controversy was the causes of these alleged sexual attacks. Mainstream propaganda linked them to the colonial soldiers' long sexual abstinence caused by war and occupation, and the African's allegedly stronger sexual drive.[36] The discourse of the right-wing opposition contained full-fledged conspiracy theories that the French colonial troop policy was a strategy to 'infect' the German people with the blood of 'inferior races'. Most of the propagandists charged that the French government were pulling the strings in this plan.[37] The above mentioned pamphlet *Die schwarze Schmach. Frankreichs Schande* claimed that the stationing of colonial troops in the Rhineland aimed to 'contaminate the German people and annihilate German sanity according to a plan devilishly reasoned, a plan that could not be more bestial that is dictated by an unrestrained desire for extermination and hatred.' The French hatred against the German people 'and everything of German character, German spirit, and German nature' was very old and had also caused the outbreak of the World War. The French people were very well aware of their national decline because of demographic developments; this fact increased French hatred against Germany and its solid population growth.[38] In addition, the National Socialists saw the Jews as being behind the stationing of non-white soldiers in the Rhineland. Adolf Hitler claimed in *Mein Kampf*: 'It was and still continues to be the Jews who bring the Negro to the Rhine with the clear aim to annihilate the detested white race by bastardization and to become its masters themselves.'[39] Common to all these patterns of interpretation was the idea – attributed to the physical constitution of the Africans – that the stationing of Africans in an area inhabited by the Whites is destined to result in a plethora of rapes.

Images of Women

If we recapitulate the images of race analyzed above and the constructions of masculinity connected with them, we become aware that these images were at the disposal of the respective propagandistic needs. Yet the common denominator in all these representations is a fundamental inferiority of Africans perceived by both French and German as well as a virility different from 'normal' white men – be it a special attraction for white women, an aggressive sexuality reaching to extremes of violence or even 'unnatural inclinations'. Interestingly, a comparable disposability is also evident in the images of women in the discussion about colonial troops. In French wartime propaganda, women only appear as nurses of wounded colonial soldiers. Sexual relations between the *grands enfants* and these selfless helpers seem unthinkable. German propaganda, on the other hand, alluded to the alleged attractiveness of the colonial soldiers to the obviously lustful and unfaithful French women, especially in cartoons[40] – an image of women also found in non-official French publications. After the war, these national perspectives were reversed as it was no longer French women who were confronted with colonial soldiers, but German women instead. German propaganda represented women most of the time as the victim, whereas now, French counter-propaganda attempted to represent the German 'Gretchens' as nymphomaniacs way-laying the innocent colonial soldiers anywhere they could.

On 19 May 1920, the German Constitutional Assembly passed an interpellation backed by all political parties, with the exception of the Independent Socialists, denouncing the 'abusive employment of colored people' and the fact 'that they routinely exercised power in cultivated German countries': 'Those savages are a horrible peril for German women and children. Their honor, bodies and lives are annihilated.'[41] The day after SPD representative Elisabeth Röhl spoke in a debate which was observed internationally in which she noted the 'special disparagement and degradation of German women, when a multicolored mixture of peoples are employed as occupational forces in the German Rhineland'.[42] On 23/24 June, the German Federation of Protestant Churches passed a resolution complaining:

> Oppressed by hunger and poverty [. . .] our people have to see with horror how its women and children are [. . .] dishonored and maltreated. No military discipline [. . .] is able to restrain these men's wild instincts devoid of any Christian education [. . .] Mouth and pen refuse to describe the atrocities exceeding all war horrors [. . .] Christendom all over the world, raise your voice against the atrocity of these ravages.[43]

When Adolf Hitler spoke of female workers having relationships with black Africans at an assembly of the *Deutschvölkische Schutz- und Trutzbund* at the end of May 1920, the journal *Der Sozialdemokrat* depicted this statement as defilement.[44] Yet, there were semi-official statements appealing to German women to arm themselves 'with the whole pride of German women's dignity and chastity' and not to forget, 'that in your hands, in the glance of your eyes, in your facial expressions, there lies Germany's honor, too'.[45] This quotation provokes some reflections about the semantics of national honor. The fact that the behavior of German women was linked to German national honor[46] indicates that individual and collective honor were linked – a linking that allows us to make inferences about images of women and images of the German nation.[47]

Dominant in this issue was the attitude that a white woman – German or French – dishonored herself by having sexual relationships with an African (although the later ubiquitous term *Rassenschande*, or racial disgrace, hardly appeared in this context). At the same time, these relationships also affected national honor, which in my opinion refers to the metaphor of the *Volkskörper* (the 'social body') which had to be kept 'clean' of foreign elements. In the above-mentioned parliamentary debate of 20 May 1920, Foreign Minister Adolf Köster spoke critically of the consequences of the French occupation policy which meant 'that the German *Volkskörper* was facing permanent annihilation on his western front'.[48] Here, the German nation appeared as a person with a vulnerable body[49] and an equally vulnerable honor. Ruth Seifert has posited that the female body is often employed as a symbol or a sign to represent the *Volkskörper* in Western societies: for instance Marianne, Bavaria, the Statue of Liberty or the fettered naked woman on Kurt Goetz's medal mentioned above. Through this symbolism, we see that violence against women is perceived as attacking the integrity of the group concerned. Thus, raping a national community's women can be perceived as symbolically raping the respective *Volkskörper* and dishonoring the nation.[50]

The slogans 'black shame' and 'black disgrace' had therefore a double meaning: on the one hand, France was ashamed for causing *Rassenschande* at the level of the *Volkskörper*. The socialist paper *Vorwärts* wrote in May 1920 that the British did not feel like sharing in the French *Negerschmach*, although, since the armistice, France did not have much honor to lose in the eyes of the democratic world anyway.[51] On the other hand, the 'black horror' was also a shame felt by Germany, whose *Volkskörper* was dishonored in two ways: both by the alleged sexual attacks on German women and by the fact that these attacks were committed by non-white men. Whereas the latter meaning of 'black shame' was largely directed inwards – the humiliation of 'national manliness'[52] was to be exploited in favor of the idea of revenge and sometimes also against the impotent Weimar Republic – the former was directed abroad, mainly at Great Britain and the United States.

Representative of images of women in the French discussion of the early 1920s is an article written by the Scandinavian author Karen Bramson, which appeared in several French newspapers and which proposed that German propaganda was fueled by the jealousy of German men: 'The German men hate the colored soldiers because women are much too interested in them. Men cry "rape" in order to purify their women in the eyes of the world. Yet, the truth is that in the evenings, German women queue up at the barracks awaiting the soldiers' nightly sorties [. . .]: These are the rapes!'[53] French newspapers matched the slogan 'black shame' with 'white shame' (*honte blanche*), referring to the several marriages and love affairs between German women and French colonial soldiers. Thus, on the French side, relationships between white women and Africans were also seen as dishonoring their women. Under the administration of the *Comité d'Assistance aux Troupes Noires*, marriage statistics, German women's love letters to colonial soldiers and photographs showing dark soldiers embracing blond *Gretchens* as well as allied military headquarters' inquiries about alleged rapes were disseminated. In July 1920, the French position was characterized by an image in the satirical journal *Le Rire* showing a jeweled pig trying to hand over a bunch of flowers to an African soldier. The image was subtitled: 'We wanted to guard an eagle and instead we have to protect ourselves from a swine.'[54]

From Nationality via Bestiality to Humanity

In the aftermath of the Franco-Belgian invasion of the Ruhr area in January 1923, the German propaganda campaign against the 'black shame' evidently decreased. Apparently, in the eyes of the Germans the French had discredited themselves so deeply before the international community that the topical debate on 'colonial troops' was no longer needed. Furthermore, after the Americans withdrew from their occupation zone, they gradually lost interest in the Rhineland question. But the colonial troops were not yet forgotten in Germany. When the French withdrew from the Rhineland in summer 1930, the Nazi journal *Der Stürmer* complained:

> The occupation troops have gone, but the occupation remains [. . .] 15,000 children are still in the German Rhineland! [. . .] 15,000 children with the blood of Mongols, Negroes and Jews. 15,000 bastards remain and [. . .] have become [. . .] poisoners of German blood. 15,000 bastards bring decay to what was German and therefore good. The people of antiquity perished because of this decay. If National Socialism was not destined to fight back and save the German people, any hope that the Rhineland would be free one day should be buried as a distant dream.[55]

After their assumption of power, the National Socialists did not wait long to fulfill these prophecies. On 13 April 1933, the registration of the 'mixed-breed' children in the Rhineland started. Three hundred and eighty five children were registered, but their total number was estimated to be 500 to 800.[56] Sterilization of these 'Rhineland bastards' was demanded.[57] For reasons of foreign policy, the Nazi regime hesitated to pass a corresponding law, but in the summer of 1937 illegal sterilization of the 'mixed-breed' children began. The exact number of victims is not known. Reiner Pommerin, who did a study of this sterilization program in the 1970s, suggests that all registered 'Rhineland bastards' were subject to sterilization.[58]

Colonial soldiers appeared sporadically in the Nazi propaganda of the 1930s. When the Rhineland was re-militarized in 1936, a medal was introduced bearing a map of the area and Nazi party emblems on one side and on the other a French Negro soldier attacking a German woman.[59] During the western campaign at the beginning of 1940, a similar propaganda initiative was planned. As early as on 7 January 1940, Alfred Rosenberg wrote in his diary that 'propaganda sheets should be dropped over the French frontline accusing Negroes of inhabiting their villages with their wives and daughters'.[60] On the 23 May, the section *Wehrmacht-propaganda* of the *Oberkommando der Wehrmacht* (OKW) passed an urgent directive that all propaganda channels should 'quickly take photographs showing particularly good-looking German soldiers with particularly bestial-looking Senegalese Negroes and other colored prisoners of war [. . .] Sharp racial contrasts are of special importance.'[61] Because of the western campaign's brevity, the propaganda in the spring of 1940 was not as intense as in the years 1914–1923. In the last months of war, German propaganda again represented French – as well as American[62] – soldiers as murderous and raping black men.[63]

Shortly after the German defeat, France withdrew most of its colonial units from Germany. Nevertheless, the topic 'colonial troops' again drew attention in the summer of 1945. In July, Stuttgart's chief of police Karl Weber published a report charging Moroccan occupation troops with 1,198 cases of rape and four cases of murder.[64] In postwar Germany, however, black GIs were seen in a much less negative light than French colonial troops. In the early Federal Republic, biracial children originating from the American occupation were used as examples, both internally and to the world, of what Germans had learned from the experience of Nazism and to show that they had broken with their racist past. When the first of these children began school in 1952, Germans marked the occasion, hoping to show that they had become good democrats.[65]

Conclusion

In trying to recapitulate stereotypes of race and gender associated with colonial troops from 1914 to 1923, we are confronted with the following situation. In Germany, throughout this period, colonial soldiers were represented as bloodthirsty, uncivilized and uncivilizable barbarians with unrestrained sexual drives. Images of women, on the other hand, varied according to the respective hierarchy: From 1914 to 1918, when mostly French women were confronted with African soldiers, German discourse represented them as unfaithful nymphomaniacs, whereas postwar German women were represented in the role of the victim.

In France, impressions of colonial soldiers were mainly reactions to German allegations. As a reaction to increased German propaganda, the bloodthirsty savages of the prewar period had become infantile during the war, and even mutated into noble savages after the war. French images of women developed as mirror images of those found in German discourses: good French women of the war years were very similar to women of the Rhineland in German postwar discourse, although they were not represented as victims but as caretakers of the colonial soldiers. On the other hand, immoral German women found in French postwar discourses were almost identical to French women in German war propaganda.

Despite the utterly contrary lines of argument, basic common structures can be delineated. Regarding the African soldiers, both sides held a similar consensus that the blacks were fundamentally different and inferior, which implies a common European racism. With regard to women, however, a boundary between 'good' women of moral integrity and 'bad' women who wanted to engage in sexual relationships with Africans existed in both France and Germany. This boundary between the good and the bad mirrored national boundaries. If the images of race or gender in one nation deviated from the dominant discourse of that nation, they coincided almost exactly with corresponding stereotypes in the other country.

Not only do we notice similarities between the images of race and of gender in both states, but also in the structure of the images of Africans and women, namely in the image of the 'superior' gender of the 'inferior' race and of the 'inferior' gender of the 'superior' race.[66] Both were divided into a 'good' and a 'bad' version. Whereas in one country Africans, as well as women, were represented in a subservient – or perhaps suffering – position determined by white men, they appeared in the other as symbols of the body and of sexuality. Both of these categories represented the antithesis of the white man, who embodied mind, reason and self-determination. 'Civilization', the shift from the 'bad' to the 'good' type of woman or African, was equivalent to the shift from an instinct-driven to a white male-dominated heteronomy. Sigrid Weigel's observation concerning Enlightenment literature that 'analogous concepts can be seen in discourses about the savage/the foreign and in discourses about woman/ womanliness which organize the dialectics of the self and the other from the perspective of the self with a view of the other' also has validity in the twentieth century.[67] Thus, alluding to Max Weber, we might say that the axiomatic basic structures of the white male view of the world pointed out the direction in which the dynamics of national interest moved discursive agency.[68] The discussion about colonial troops provides an instructive example of the discursive intertwining and the propagandistic utilization of racism, sexism and nationalism.

Notes

I am very grateful to Elizabeth Harvey, Sandra Mass, Bianca Schönberger, Rita Stöckli and Gerhard Hirschfeld for their valuable contributions as well as to Katja Seemann and Tobias Hug, who assisted me in translating the German manuscript.

1. Frantz Fanon, *Schwarze Haut, weisse Masken* (Frankfurt, 1980), 105.
2. See Gregory Martin, 'Koloniale Truppenkontingente im Ersten Weltkrieg,' in *Fremdeinsätze. Afrikaner und Asiaten in europäischen Kriegen, 1914–1945*, ed. Gerhard Höpp and Brigitte Reinwald (Berlin, 2000), 15–34.
3. See Gilbert Meynier, *L'Algérie révélée. La guerre de 1914–1918 et le premier quart du XXᵉ siècle* (Geneva, 1981).
4. See Jeffrey Greenhut, 'The Imperial Reserve. The Indian Corps on the Western Front, 1914–15,' *Journal of Imperial and Commonwealth History* 12 (1983): 54–73.
5. See Marc Michel, *L'appel à l'Afrique. Contributions et réactions à l'effort de guerre en A.O.F.* (Paris, 1982); Joe Harris Lunn, *Memoirs of the Maelstrom. A Senegalese Oral History of the First World War* (Portsmouth etc., 1999).
6. See Christian Koller, *'Ein buntes Völkergemisch auf dem Schlachtfeld'. Die Diskussion um die Verwendung von Kolonialtruppen in Europa im Ersten Weltkrieg*, MA Thesis (University of Zurich, 1995); idem, *'Halbtierische Völker Afrikas hatte der Gegner geschickt, als er*

Christian Koller

sich stellen sollte'. Der Einsatz afrikanischer Soldaten in Europa im 1. Weltkrieg (= BAB Working Paper no. 1) (Basel, 2000); Gregory Martin, 'German and French Perceptions of the French North and West African Contingents, 1910–1918,' *Militärgeschichtliche Mitteilungen* 56 (1997): 31–68; Eberhardt Kettlitz, *Das Bild vom französischen Kolonialsoldaten des I. Weltkrieges in Deutschland,* MA Thesis (University of Leipzig, 1996); Annabelle Melzer, 'The "Mise-en-Scène" of the "Tirailleur Sénégalais" on the Western Front, 1914–1920,' in *Borderlines. Genders and Identities in War and Peace 1870–1930,* ed. Billie Melman (New York/London, 1998), 213–244; Joe Harris Lunn, '"Les Races Guerrières". Racial Preconceptions in the French Military about West African Soldiers during the First World War,' *Journal of Contemporary History* 34 (1999): 517–536.

7. See Keith S. Nelson, 'Black Horror on the Rhine. Race as a Factor in Post-World War I Diplomacy,' *Journal of Modern History* 42 (1970): 606–627; Sally Marks, 'Black Watch on the Rhine. A Study in Propaganda, Prejudice and Prurience,' *European Studies Review* 13 (1983): 297–333; Gisela Lebzelter, 'Die "Schwarze Schmach". Vorurteile – Propaganda – Mythos,' *Geschichte und Gesellschaft* 11 (1985): 37–58; Hans-Jürgen Lüsebrink, 'Die marokkanischen Kolonialsoldaten (*Tirailleurs*) in Deutschland 1919–1923. Präsenz, Wahrnehmungsformen, Konflikte,' in *Die Sicht des Anderen. Das Marokkobild der Deutschen, das Deutschlandbild der Marokkaner,* ed. Herbert Popp (Passau, 1994), 53–64; Peter Martin, 'Die Kampagne gegen die "Schwarze Schmach" als Ausdruck konservativer Visionen vom Untergang des Abendlandes,' in *Fremde Erfahrungen. Asiaten und Afrikaner in Deutschland, Österreich und in der Schweiz bis 1945,* ed. Gerhard Höpp (Berlin, 1996), 211–224; Anja Schüler, *'The Horror on the Rhine'. Rape, Racism, and the International Women's League* (= John F. Kennedy-Institut für Nordamerikastudien Working Papers no 86) (Berlin, 1996). Including the whole period from 1914 to 1923: Christian Koller, *'Von Wilden aller Rassen niedergemetzelt'. Die Diskussion um die Verwendung von Kolonialtruppen in Europa zwischen Rassismus, Militär- und Kolonialpolitik (1914–1930)* (Stuttgart, 2001); János Riesz and Joachim Schultz, eds., *'Tirailleurs sénégalais'. Zur bildlichen und literarischen Darstellung afrikanischer Soldaten im Dienste Frankreichs* (Frankfurt, 1989); Sandra Mass, 'Das Trauma des weissen Mannes. Afrikanische Kolonialsoldaten in propagandistischen Texten, 1914–1923', *L'Homme* 12/1 (2001): 11–33.

8. See Koller, 'Von Wilden aller Rassen niedergemetzelt,' 103–134, 152–157, 160–165, 174–176, 178–186; Jeffrey Greenhut, 'Race, Sex and

War. The Impact of Race and Sex on Morale and Health Services on the Western Front, 1914,' *Military Affairs* 45 (1981): 71–74.

9. Gisela Bock, 'Geschichte, Frauengeschichte, Geschlechtergeschichte,' *Geschichte und Gesellschaft* 14 (1988): 364–391, 390.

10. Max Müller, *Frankreich im Kriege 1914–1916* (Zurich, 1916), 120.

11. Klaus Mann, *Der Wendepunkt. Ein Lebensbericht* (Memmingen, 1952), 87–88.

12. See Ute Planert, 'Vater Staat und Mutter Germania. Zur Politisierung des weiblichen Geschlechts im 19. und 20. Jahrhundert,' in *Nation, Politik und Geschlecht. Frauenbewegungen und Nationalismus in der Moderne* (Frankfurt/New York, 2000), 15–65, 21–25.

13. See Charles Mangin, 'Troupes noires,' *Revue de Paris* 16 (1909): 61–80 and 383–398; idem, 'Soldats Noirs en Europe,' *Questions Diplomatiques et Coloniales* 13 (1909): 449–460; idem, *La Force Noire*, 3rd edn (Paris, 1911); idem, 'Troupes noires,' *Revue de Paris* 18 (1911): 484–494; idem, 'De l'emploi des troupes noires,' *Revue Anthropologique* 21 (1911): 113–128.

14. *Verhandlungen des Reichstages*, vol. 268 (Berlin, 1911), 7792.

15. Lucie Cousturier, *Des Inconnus chez moi. Tirailleurs Sénégalais* (Paris, 1920), 12–13.

16. Anton Fendrich, 'Die Schlacht von Soissons,' in *Der Krieg. Illustrierte Chronik des Krieges 1914/15* (Stuttgart, 1915), 346–352, 348; idem, 'Die grossen Durchbruchsschlachten im Westen. I.,' in *Der Krieg. Illustrierte Chronik des Krieges 1914–1916* (Stuttgart, 1916), 77–84, 82–83.

17. Erwin Rosen, *England. Ein Britenspiegel*, 7th edn (Stuttgart, 1916), 96 and 98; Victor Valois, *Nieder mit England! Betrachtungen und Erwägungen* (Berlin, 1915), 7; Rudolf Borchardt, 'Der Krieg und die deutsche Selbsteinkehr,' in *Gesammelte Werke in Einzelbänden. Prosa V*, ed. Marie Luise Borchardt and Ulrich Ott (Stuttgart, 1979), 217–264, 243; *Ein Dutzend englischer Sünden wider das Völkerrecht. Tatsachen und Feststellungen* (n.p., 1916), 5; *Kriegschronik. Kriegstagebuch, Soldatenbriefe, Kriegsbilder* (Berlin, 1915), 48; *Illustrierte Geschichte des Weltkrieges*, vol. 5 (Stuttgart etc., 1916), 307; E.H. Baer, ed., *Der Völkerkrieg. Eine Chronik der Ereignisse seit dem 1. Juli 1914* (Stuttgart, 1914–18), vol. 3, 217 and vol. 10, 107.

18. See for example Gottfried Hagen, *Die Türkei im Ersten Weltkrieg. Flugblätter und Flugschriften in arabischer, persischer und osmanisch–türkischer Sprache aus einer Sammlung der Universitätsbibliothek Heidelberg* (Frankfurt, 1990).

19. Martin Hobohm, 'Die französische Schande im Rheinland,' *Deutsche Politik* 5 (1920): 242–249, 248.

20. See *Verhandlungen der verfassunggebenden Deutschen National-versammlung*, vol. 333 (Berlin, 1920), 5694–5697; *Freiheit*, 21.5.1920, 1–2; Maximilian Harden, 'Wehmutterhäublein,' *Zukunft* 109 (1920): 292–299; Lilli Jannasch, 'Schwarze Schmach – Weisse Schmach,' *Friedenswarte* 22 (1920): 273–274; eadem, *Schwarze Schmach und Schwarz-Weiss-Rote Schande* (Berlin, 1921); Fritz Naphtali, 'Kolonisation. Rassenwahn,' *Sozialistische Monatshefte* 55 (1920): 716–717.

21. See: Ruth Harris, 'The "Child of the Barbarian". Rape, Race, and Nationalism in France during the First World War', *Past and Present* 141 (1993): 170–206; John Horne, 'Les mains coupées. "Atrocités allemandes" et opinion française en 1914', *Guerres mondiales et conflits contemporains* 43/171 (1993): 29–45; Nicoletta F. Gullace, 'Sexual Violence and Family Honor. British Propaganda and International Law during the First World War', *American Historical Review* 102 (1997): 714–747.

22. See for example Bakary Diallo, *Force-Bonté* (Paris, 1926); Mohammed Ben Cherif, *Ahmed Ben Mostapha. Goumier*, ed. Ahmed Lanasri (Paris, 1997); also Christian Koller, 'Überkreuzende Frontlinien? Fremdrepräsentationen in afrikanischen, indischen und europäischen Selbstzeugnissen des Ersten Weltkrieges,' *War and Literature* 6 (2000): 33–57.

23. Charles Mangin, *Regards sur la France d'Afrique* (Paris, 1924), 175.

24. See *Humanité*, 21.2.1910, 1 and 22.2.1910, 2 resp. 31.10.1920, 1.

25. *Schweizerisches Bundesarchiv* E 2001(A)/733/54 *Völkerrechtswidrige Verwendung farbiger Truppen auf dem europäischen Kriegsschauplatz durch England und Frankreich* (Berlin, 1915), 2.

26. See for example *Simplicissimus*, 5.10.1915, 315.

27. Melzer, 'Mise-en-Scène,' 222–228. It is a play on words with the expressions *teutons* (Teutons, Germans) and *tétons* (boobs). On conflicts between French and colonial soldiers resp. workers see Philippa Levine, 'Battle Colors. Race, Sex, and Colonial Soldiery in World War I', *Journal of Women's History* 9/4 (1998): 104–130; Tyler Stovall, 'The Color Line behind the Lines. Racial Violence in France during the Great War', *American Historical Review* 103 (1998): 737–769.

28. See: Shelby Cullom Davis, *Reservoirs of Men. A History of the Black Troops of French West Africa* (Geneva, 1934), 167.

29. *Neue Preussische Zeitung*, 3.6.1920, 1–2.

30. Jean Giraudoux, *Siegfried et le Limousin* (Paris, 1922), 186.

31. See for example *Hauptstaatsarchiv Wiesbaden* 405/5583.

32. Joseph Lang, *Die schwarze Schmach. Frankreichs Schande* (Berlin, 1921), 4, 7, 10 and 12; Martin Hobohm, 'Die französische Schande

im Rheinland,' *Deutsche Politik* 5 (1920): 243 and 245; *Von Haus und Hof vertrieben. Bilder und Berichte zur Praxis der französischen Ausweisungen aus dem Rhein- und Ruhrgebiet* (Berlin, 1923), 16; Heinrich Distler, *Das deutsche Leid am Rhein. Ein Buch der Anklage gegen die Schandherrschaft des französischen Militarismus* (Minden, 1921), 13; *Neue Preussische Zeitung*, 15.10.1920, 1; *Völkischer Beobachter*, 1.2.1922, 2.

33. Lang, *Die schwarze Schmach*, 8 and 11.
34. Wilhelm F. von der Saar, *Der blaue Schrecken (la terreur bleue) und die schwarze Schmach*, 2nd edn (Stuttgart, 1921), 39.
35. See for example Lang, *Die schwarze Schmach*, 7.
36. See for example *Farbige Franzosen am Rhein. Ein Notschrei deutscher Frauen*, ed. Rheinische Frauenliga, 4th edn (Berlin, 1923), 57.
37. See for example Hans F. K. Günther, *Rassenkunde des deutschen Volkes*, 2nd edn (Munich, 1923), 121.
38. Lang, *Die schwarze Schmach*, 5–6.
39. Adolf Hitler, *Mein Kampf. Zwei Bände in einem Band*, 676–680th edn (Munich, 1941), 357. See also *Völkischer Beobachter*, 22.5.1920, 4 and 14.4.1921, 4–5.
40. See for example *Simplicissimus*, 5.10.1915, 315.
41. *Verhandlungen der verfassunggebenden Deutschen Nationalversammlung*, vol. 343 (Berlin, 1920), 304.
42. Ibid., vol. 333, 5691.
43. *Deutsche Allgemeine Zeitung*, 26.6.1920, 2.
44. Eberhard Jäckel and Alex Kuhn, eds., *Hitler. Sämtliche Aufzeichnungen 1905–1924* (Stuttgart, 1980), 136.
45. Ritter von Eberlein, *Schwarze am Rhein. Ein Weltproblem*, ed. Pfalzzentrale Heidelberg (Heidelberg, 1921), 147.
46. On national honor see: Max Weber, *Wirtschaft und Gesellschaft. Grundriss der verstehenden Soziologie*, ed. Johannes Winckelmann, 5th. edn (Tübingen, 1980), 520f.; Geoffrey Best, *Honour among Men and Nations. Transformations of an Idea* (Toronto, 1982); Christian Koller, *Die Ehre der Nation. Überlegungen zu einem Kernelement der politischen Kultur im 19. Jahrhundert* (unpubl. paper, 2002); Andreas Dörner, 'Die symbolische Politik der Ehre. Zur Konstruktion der nationalen Ehre in den Diskursen der Befreiungskriege,' in *Ehre. Archaische Momente in der Moderne*, ed. Ludgera Vogt and Arnold Zingerle (Frankfurt, 1994), 78–95; Friedrich Zunkel, 'Ehre, Reputation,' in *Geschichtliche Grundbegriffe*, vol. 2, ed. Otto Brunner et al. (Stuttgart, 1975), 1–63, 56–61; Beth Baron, 'The Construction of National Honour in Egypt,' *Gender & History* 5 (1993): 244–255.

47. See also Doris Kaufmann, 'Die Ehre des Vaterlandes und die Ehre der Frauen, oder: Der Kampf an der äusseren und inneren Front,' *Evangelische Theologie* 46 (1986): 277–292, 290–292. On the connection between individual and collective honor see Georg Simmel, *Soziologie. Untersuchungen über die Formen der Vergesellschaftung*, 3rd edn (Munich/Leipzig, 1923), 326.

48. *Verhandlungen der verfassunggebenden Deutschen Nationalversammlung*, vol. 333 (Berlin, 1920), 5692–5693.

49. For fundamental reflections thereupon see Theresa Wobbe, 'Die Schwelle des Körpers. Geschlecht und Rasse,' *Feministische Studien* 11 (1993): 110–116; eadem, 'Die Grenzen des Geschlechts. Konstruktionen von Gemeinschaft und Rassismus,' *Mitteilungen. Institut für Sozialforschung an der Johann Wolfgang Goethe-Universität Frankfurt am Main* 2 (1993), 98–108.

50. Ruth Seifert, 'Der weibliche Körper als Symbol und Zeichen. Geschlechtsspezifische Gewalt und die kulturelle Konstruktion des Krieges,' in *Gewalt im Krieg. Ausübung, Erfahrung und Verweigerung von Gewalt in Kriegen des 20. Jahrhunderts*, ed. Andreas Gestrich (Münster, 1996), 13–33. On body metaphors in political language see: Gerhard Dohrn-van Rossum, *Politischer Körper, Organismus, Organisation. Zur Geschichte naturaler Metaphorik und Begrifflichkeit in der politischen Sprache*, Ph.D. Diss. (University of Bielefeld, 1977).

51. *Vorwärts*, 27.5.1920, 2.

52. Seifert, 'Der weibliche Körper,' 27.

53. *Echo du Rhin*, 26.7.1920, 1–2.

54. See Eberlein, *Schwarze am Rhein*, 143.

55. *Stürmer*, July 1930, 2.

56. Reiner Pommerin, '*Sterilisierung der Rheinlandbastarde*'. *Das Schicksal einer farbigen deutschen Minderheit 1918–1937* (Düsseldorf, 1979), 72.

57. See for example Hein Schröder, 'Farbiges Blut in Deutschland,' *Volk und Rasse* 9 (1934): 153–155.

58. Pommerin, *Sterilisierung der Rheinlandbastarde*, 84.

59. Nelson, *Black Horror*, 626.

60. Hans-Günther Seraphim, ed., *Das politische Tagebuch Alfred Rosenbergs aus den Jahren 1934/35 und 1939/40* (Göttingen,1956), 96.

61. Willi A. Boelcke, ed., *Kriegspropaganda 1939–1941. Geheime Ministerkonferenzen im Reichspropagandaministerium* (Stuttgart, 1966), 130.

62. See *Völkischer Beobachter*, 22.3.1945, 1 and 14.4.1945, 1.

63. See James de Coquet, *Nous sommes les occupants* (Paris, 1945), 107.

64. See *New York Times*, 11.8.1945, 10, also Susan Brownmiller, *Against our Will. Man, Women and Rape* (Toronto, 1975), 73–74.

65. See Tina Campt et al., 'Blacks, Germans, and the Politics of Imperial Imagination, 1920–60,' in *The Imperialist Imagination: German Colonialism and its Legacy*, ed. Sara Friedrichsmeyer et al. (Ann Arbor, 1998), 205–229, 222–229. See also Johannes Kleinschmidt, 'Besatzer und Deutsche. Schwarze GIs nach 1945,' *Amerikastudien* 40 (1995): 646–665.

66. Terminology according to Frances Gouda, 'Das "unterlegene" Geschlecht der "überlegenen" Rasse. Kolonialgeschichte und Geschlechterverhältnisse,' in *Geschlechterverhältnisse im Wandel*, ed. Hannah Schissler (Frankfurt/New York, 1993), 185–203. See also Birgit Rommelspacher, 'Freund- und Selbstbilder in der Dominanzkultur,' in *Projektionen – Rassismus und Sexismus in der Visuellen Kultur*, ed. Annegret Friedrich (Marburg, 1997), 31–40.

67. Sigrid Weigel, 'Zum Verhältnis von "Wilden" und "Frauen" im Diskurs der Aufklärung,' in *Topographien der Geschlechter. Kulturgeschichtliche Studien zur Literatur* (Reinbek, 1990), 118–148, 121.

68. 'Interests (materiel and ideal), not ideas, determine human agency. But: "Conceptions of the world" constructed by "ideas" very often prepared the path in which the dynamics of interests moved agency.' (Max Weber, *Die Wirtschaftsethik der Weltreligionen. Konfuzianismus und Taoismus. Schriften 1915–1920*, ed. Helwig Schmidt-Glintzer (Tübingen, 1989), 101).

–6–

Gender Wars

The First World War and the
Construction of Gender Relations in
the Weimar Republic
Birthe Kundrus

What effect did the First World War have on relations between men and women? This question has long been a topic of interest and inquiry among historians of gender. Early research concluded that the war had served to promote women's emancipation by drawing women into paid employment, awarding public recognition to women's work, and granting women the franchise at war's end. Recently, however, historians have become more differentiated in their assessment of the war's effect.[1] The First World War, according to recent arguments, resulted not in a reformulation of the gender dichotomy, but rather in its cultural accentuation. Prevailing models of femininity, in fact, had proven themselves equal to the demands that wartime crisis had placed on women's flexibility. Although women's sphere of influence and scope for action expanded under conditions of war, any new opportunities that exceeded the 'true' female sphere were clearly bounded, limited to the duration of men's absence, and caused no permanent shift in power relations. Men attempted to recapture the war as the 'last exclusively male grand affair'.[2] Historians who have examined the experience of women in the First World War thus have concluded that, while women's participation did offer new scope for female agency, the war also resulted in new burdens and restrictions.

In a corollary interpretation, historians who have examined the experience of the 'stronger sex' in the First World War have put forth an image of a disoriented and unsettled generation of men.[3] Not only had German men been stripped of their role as provider and father, but wartime conditions and the defeat had called into question their status as soldiers and protectors of home and fatherland. Many men returned home not as heroes, but damaged in body and spirit. Confronted by the fear that women were the 'true victors of the war', upon their return men resisted all changes to the established gender order.

In contrast, recent research on letters from the front has demonstrated that the wartime experiences of men were in fact quite diverse and multi-faceted, varying along lines of class, region, religion, and generation.[4] This research thus has served to relativize a key trope of wartime, post-war, and historical discussion that stressed the experiential divide between of men at the front and women on the 'home-front'. In fact, by means of letter writing, front leaves and visits home, and the replacement of soldiers, men and women remained in fairly close contact throughout the war. Many contemporaries were well aware of the problem of how to bridge the differences between men's and women's experiences and perceptions.[5] In fact, often men's and women's perception of the war and of their own personal circumstances were quite similar. Also questionable is whether men's and women's hopes and expectations always remained fixed on the prospect of a return to the prewar world they had left behind.[6] As news and information flowed back and forth in the letters, men and women directed their attention not only to the past, but also to the present and the future, and especially to the prospect of reunion. Furthermore, the letters from the front also testify to a wide diversity in constructions of male identity. According to Benjamin Zieman, for example, drafted farmers were not fervent war supporters, nor did they seek confirmation of their male identity via their soldierly role. Instead, drafted farmers remained focused on civilian normality.[7] Finally, the rapid reintegration of those returning soldiers who appeared physically and mentally undamaged, if only outwardly, also played a role in tempering what was presumably a deeply rooted insecurity.

This article undertakes a further revision to the notion that the First World War resulted in a generation of insecure men or in a 'gender war'.[8] Focusing on the level of public discourse rather than individual experience, my central question is how different groups of men and women reflected upon their wartime experiences through the prism of developments in gender relations. I first demonstrate that, although the war was perceived as a turning point in relations between men and women, this transformation was understood not only as a crisis, but also as an opportunity. In the second part of my analysis, I examine the effect of this discourse by way of two examples: first within the realm of state policy and action, and second within the symbolic arena of public war memorialization.

The source materials for my argument are writings that might best be described as 'stock takings'. At the beginning of the war, and especially following the war's end in 1918, many authors conceived of their writings as 'capturing the spirit of the times', and they ventured to speculate on the effect of the war in spheres well beyond their area of authorial expertise. In these 'years without synthesis', in the words of Robert Musil, a widespread yearning for meaning triggered a proliferation of prognostic writings on topics relating to the psyche, sexuality, marriage, and social relations between men and women that were inspired and written from a variety of perspectives. Men and women of the educated middle classes, including writers, scientists and members of the women's movement, figured prominently as authors of these texts. My main concern is to delineate the scope and the limits of this discourse, leaving a more precise depiction of its phases of development, goals, and controversies as the topic of further research. This essay thus should be regarded as a starting point and as stimulus for further research, with the larger project remaining as yet unfinished.

Competitors or Comrades? Collective Constructions

Wilhelmine Germany had already been rent by a never-ending quarrel over the meaning of 'male' and 'female'. This debate became more pointed and more varied in its spectrum of opinion during the First World War and especially under the Weimar Republic. The growth of the media in turn played a key role in these developments. For many leading figures from the spheres of politics, the women's movement, the churches, the academy, literature and the media, the war was perceived as a turning point in gender relations; at the same time, the problem of gender was regarded as paradigmatic of the profound upheavals that followed the war.[9] The outbreak of war, with its dichotomization of the masculinized 'front' and the feminized 'homeland', at first seemed to result in unexpected clarity and reinforce bourgeois ideologies of gender. But this tranquility on the 'gender front' would be only of short duration. First of all, the total mobilization of modern warfare[10] demanded the participation of both sexes and thus necessitated a reformulation of outdated conceptions of men's and women's roles. A militarized conception of female duty thus found its expression in the apt coinage of the term 'homefront'. Politicians envisaged that women would provide for reinforcements on the 'battlefront' by assuming at least partial responsibility for the wartime economy in the food production as well as the armaments sector; women's reproductive services, in turn, were to staff future replenishments for the military. To a certain extent, women were also supposed to serve as proxies for men in the family and the larger realms of society. Furthermore, contrary to the imaginings of many at the time, especially among the educated middle classes, the war did not have its hoped-for cathartic effect: the renewal of an 'insecure masculinity' in the heroic battle of man against man. Two main reasons account for this failure of masculine regeneration: first, the older figure of the 'hero' no longer was adequate to the reality of modern mechanized warfare, and second, the war and the attendant absence of millions of men and husbands lasted much longer than anticipated. As a result, many authors interpreted the war as promoting the 'emancipation' of women and as detrimental to male dominance in straightforward fashion. *Vorwärts*, seizing on images of blood-drenched carnage on the battlefield, was quick to employ violent metaphors to refer to the 'battle of the sexes' over employment.[11] In 1918, Wilhelm Schwaner, publisher of the conservative and nationalistic *Volkserzieher*, proffered a similar summary: 'It is sad but true: during this most manly of times, during the war, it is women who rule "at home".'[12] While some observed these contested developments with concern, for others they were grounds for optimism.

The popular debate regarding the effect of the First World War on gender relations reclaimed the already overladen figure of the 'front soldier', now expanded to include his wife, as the key symbol for both crisis and opportunity. In these depictions, the typical soldier and his wife were young, urban residents, and members of the middle to lower classes. Both had survived the war whole in mind and body. The authenticity of the image of the supposedly typical 'front soldier's family' was repeatedly invoked in legitimation of post-war narratives in which the moment of the husband's return home from the front functioned as the key motif. Such narratives were founded on three linked premises. First, the war and especially the years of separation had resulted in a mutual estrangement of the soldier and his wife. This notion had its foundations in the traditional division between society and the military, which was in turn projected onto the family. In 1917, for example, the Social Democrat Paul Göhre, a theologian and co-founder of the National Social Union (*National-sozialer Verein*), who served as an officer in the war, authored an essay titled 'Front and Homeland' (*Front und Heimat*). Describing the reaction to the separation of the soldiers and the wives they had left behind, Göhre wrote: 'They [the married couple], when they see each other again, believe they are seeing a completely different person than the one whom they had left behind.'[13] The second premise was that women, forced to rely upon themselves, had through their employment acquired greater independence. In a 1919 issue of the magazine of the nationalistic and conservative League of Four-Leaf Clovers, a Bismarckian Tower of German Womanhood (*Kleeblattbund, ein Bismarck-Thurm der deutschen Frauen*), for example, Anna Brunnemann proclaimed the partial triumphal reversal of popular stereotypes of femininity:

> For the war, which has removed so many male workers from their trades and professions, has compelled the state to fill the gaps with women, and everywhere women have proven their worth. Indeed, today we can say that no woman has disappointed us in any of the positions that women have now occupied for the span of a generation. In all the profession and pursuits into which women have entered into competition with men, women have proven themselves their equals, if not their superiors. The average woman is decidedly more intelligent than the average man. She has stronger and better nerves, is quicker of mind, and is more adaptable.[14]

In 1917, the leader of the radical wing of the bourgeois women's movement, Minna Cauer, also noted with satisfaction an increased sense of self-worth among women. In her essay titled 'Some Observations Regarding the Effects of the War on the Female Psyche' (*Einige Betrachtungen über die Wirkungen des Krieges auf die Psyche der Frau*), which appeared in the journal *Die Frauenbewegung*, Cauer adopted an almost threatening tone: 'The men who have returned home are discovering a different sort of woman – more self-confident, more experienced, hardened, more independent, more difficult to control.' It was Cauer's hope that this would result not only in women achieving a more important status in civil society, but also in an intensification of pacifistic efforts.[15] Maria Lischnewska, a member of the executive board of the Union of Progressive Women's Associations (*Verband Fortschrittlicher Frauenvereine*) envisaged the future in even more euphoric terms. At the 1916 war convention of the Federation of German Women's Associations (*Bund Deutscher Frauenvereine*; *BDF*) in Weimar, Lischnewska proclaimed that women's war work was the 'greatest victory of the women's movement of the past 50 years', predicting that female university professors would soon appear alongside forewomen in the factories.[16] Although such social and political euphoria evaporated quickly within the women's movement, the belief in a new female autonomy remained. In 1928, the sex researcher Curt Moreck summarized in his book titled 'Contemporary Sexual Lifestyles' (*Geschlechtsleben der Gegenwart*): 'The war [. . .] shattered confidence in male superiority and led to disillusionment among women; now that women have assumed the work of men at home, they have become free and independent.'[17] In 1929, Robert Musil observed with a mixture of resignation and relief that: 'Woman has tired of serving as the ideal for man, who no longer has the strength sufficient to idealization, and she has taken upon herself to become her own ideal.'[18] Paul Göhre, by contrast, examining the disjunctures between life at the front and at home, arrived at a more negative estimation of these supposedly emancipatory impulses in his 1917 essay. During this modern war, women had abandoned the old rules of the gender game: 'While he fought to protect her, she became his economic rival at home.'[19] However, Göhre also predicted an increase in male self-confidence now that men had succeeded in breaking free of their dependence on women:

> Thus [. . .] the war has made men into men, made them harder, more resolute, more objective [. . .] than before. The war has also made men less dependent on women. Though before the war men often seemed completely at a loss without women's helping hand, for several years now men have lived at the front in a completely woman-free, entirely male society self-sufficient to all its needs and wishes. [. . .] The war has made men manly and independent of women. But the war has thrown women's development off its proper course. In addition to her previous burdens, the war has heaped upon her all the obligations that men had carried out at home prior to the war. Women stand at the lathe and at the ladder, they are conductors and tram drivers, coach and train drivers, they work in the mines as well as in the laboratory, day in and day out, on the day and the night shift. They represent themselves and their families, including their husbands, before the court and with government authorities, in writing and in person. [. . .] So she has become man and woman both. Her essential nature has been rent apart, divided, hurled from its unique equilibrium. [. . .] She has lost most of her previous sense of dependence on the man, his indispensability to her, his dominance over her. A hundred threads that bound her to him have thus been severed.[20]

This wartime crisis in marriage, it was believed, also confronted its observers – as the social and political elite – with a new set of responsibilities and new opportunities for exerting influence. Smoothing over discord, defusing tension, and struggling against the 'state of emergency' with a 'farsighted social policy' – this was what Josephine Levy Rathenau, for example, envisaged as the proper role of social-welfare 'women's projects' following the war.[21]

For contemporaries, the meaning of women's paid work was located not in its falsely assumed quantitative increase, or in an similarly factually incorrect transformation of structural conditions.[22] Rather, the key import of women's employment was located on the symbolic level. In the war years and after, it was the *possibility* of an economically, socially, politically and sexually independent woman that so strongly captured the imagination of contemporaries. Over the course of the postwar debate, this figure of the modern 'new woman', though it had existed since the turn of the century, was further negotiated and extended. Along with the loss of the hero soldier, women's new autonomy seemed to strike at the foundations of yet another cornerstone of masculinity – its domination over the feminine and over women.[23]

Such discursive scenarios served to marginalize the wartime experiences of many families and marriages, among them the war injured and widows, and the men who had either returned home early in the war, or who failed to return until long after the war's end. All the experiences that failed to fit into the dominant discursive framework were thus relegated to the fringes of the narrative. Although divorce rates rose until 1924, many women presumably directed their newly acquired competence toward maintaining the unity of the family, not least because so many had perceived the circumstances of war as a burden. This was true for women from all levels of society. In August 1918, for example, Dorothy von Moltke wrote to her parents in South Africa, describing her husband's leave from the front: 'It was a wonderful relief to lean upon the shoulder of a good man for a brief while, and to not be forced to carry the burden of the war alone, and I enjoyed his visit immensely.'[24] Debates on gender, therefore, were no exception to what historians regard as a perplexing disjuncture between public and individual perceptions of the war.[25] For the educated, bourgeois participants of the debate, such apparently realistic portrayals of intrafamilial difficulties served rather as a foil against which to measure their own social interests and their own (gendered) political fears and aspirations.

Finally, women's heightened self-confidence also served to trigger an emancipatory leap in the political arena, a prospect that inspired dread among organized anti-feminists. Anti-feminists had already imagined themselves engaged in a defensive battle prior to 1914. The war experience and its anticipated consequences served only to confirm their belief in the existence of a war between the sexes. In a treatise titled 'Psychological Reflections' (*Psychologische Betrachtungen*) on 'the life of the psyche during war', for example, the Viennese psychoanalyst Wilhelm Stekel invoked a state of *permanent* gender war:

An eternal battle rages between men and women in which there may be an occasional temporary truce, but never a lasting peace. This battle of the sexes seemingly has been suspended during the world war, since the two sexes supposedly have united in warding off a common enemy. In reality, women are taking advantage of the war to assume the status of men, and perhaps to occupy it permanently.[26]

In contrast, at least toward the end of the war, the women's movement was euphoric in its anticipation of transformation. Though they otherwise were very different in vision and belief, feminist leaders such as Gertrud Bäumer, the former head of the *BDF* and co-founder of the German Democratic Party, the national-conservative Anna Brunnemann, and the *völkisch* Margarete Pochhammer joined in sounding a similar note. In the 1919 essay mentioned above, Brunnemann summed up the situation as follows: 'There can be no doubt that the world war has occasioned a tremendous advance in the status of women. Indeed, history perhaps will judge the war to have been one of the most important stages on the path to the movement's achieving its final end.'[27] Only two years later, however, Brunnemann was to express her disillusionment following women's demobilization from the work force.[28] Similarly, in 1922, the '*völkisch* feminist' Pochhammer felt obligated to counter the military leadership's accusation that women had betrayed the military through their sexual demoralization, their pleasure-seeking and self-indulgence, and their ever-present discontent. In his memoirs, Colonel Max Bauer was among the first to promulgate this anti-feminist version of the 'stab in the back legend', claiming that the wartime women's movement had been 'sterile and the ruin of the family'.[29] In her review of Bauer's book, Pochhammer objected that while such an accusation might be leveled at the 'Jewish Social Democratic' women's movement and against a number of 'fanatics' among bourgeois feminists, the charge did not apply to the 'circles of nationalist women'. It was unfair for Bauer to extrapolate from the behavior of a few to level accusations at the entire German 'universe of women'. The 'representative German woman' had faithfully carried out her duty and so made it possible for the homefront to stay the course. For this reason, it was now incumbent that 'women's spirit and women's strength be encouraged to develop to its highest perfection'.[30] Neither positive nor negative attitudes toward the 'New Woman', therefore, correlate directly to any particular political outlook toward the prospect of Weimar democracy.

How then should or could German men react to women's proclaimed new independence according to the authors? Paul Göhre was among those who believed that the concurrent strengthening of masculinity in wartime had caused the relations between the sexes to become a 'field of rubble'. By contrast, other men believed that the 'stronger sex' could also profit from the new self-confidence of the 'weaker sex'. In the vision of these intellectuals, communists, sex reformers, women's rights advocates, and members of the youth movement, the relationship between men and women could henceforth be rendered in a mentally, culturally, socially and sexually more satisfactory fashion via the new model of companionable relations between the sexes.[31] In his 'Cultural and Moral History of the Modern Era' (*Kultur- und Sittengeschichte der Neuesten Zeit*), the sex researcher Curt Moreck detected similar impulses toward a renewal of relations between the sexes:

> In a spirit of camaraderie, she stepped to her man's side [. . .] and in a single instant she acquired a new status, perhaps henceforth and for all time. [. . .] Outwardly as well, women found enjoyment in the severity of style, the unfeminine gesture, which demonstrated her female self-worth and economic independence, underscored her camaraderie with men, and proclaimed her break with tradition. [. . .] Her very appearance signals a decided rejection of all male claims to dominance, which men, astonished and at first even vexed by the change in her appearance, made no claim to assert. [32]

But did this not entail the risk of a 'masculinization of women' and a 'feminization of men'? Intellectuals such as Thomas Mann remained serene at the prospect of a new 'unisex'. Mann approved of what he regarded as a newly de-eroticized and dispassionate relationship between the sexes. In 1925, Mann contributed a treatise titled 'Marriage in Transition' (*Die Ehe im Übergang*) to Hermann Kayserling's anthology of essays by leading Weimar intellectuals on the institution of marriage. According to Mann, these new conceptions of gender, which aimed at equivalence rather than strict equality, distinguished themselves in positive fashion from both the ambitions and aesthetics of the women's movement as well as from conservative morality:

> However, by and large an inescapable tendency toward equivalence and assimilation holds sway in all aspects of life, in education and employment, in the scope for action within sports and politics: no longer with an ambitious-emancipatory-competitive tone, but with an accent on matter-of-factness. Rather than women encountering any real resistance on the part of men, men are displaying a 'spirit of cooperation' that is more than mere show. By this I do not mean that men have been 'feminized'. Indeed, the word 'masculinization' is similarly inaccurate to describe women. Their practical, low-maintenance 'page-boy' style is full of feminine charm and has nothing in common with the tendentious coiffures of earlier suffragettes. But something has gone astray: a certain conception of Fity – gallant, cocky, raw, inflated, at once stupidly condescending and stupidly venerating; the atmosphere of the bourgeois dance hall, tense and silly, erotic, stiff, formal, foolish and risqué. This course of events, it should be noted, was preceded by a sort of mutual humanization that made such camaraderie possible. [. . .] There is something of the romantic fantasy of the androgynous in all this humane and harmonious camaraderie of the sexes.[33]

Collective perceptions both during and after the war, therefore, cannot simply be summarized within a grand narrative of a 'crisis in masculinity' that found its resolution in the misogynistic *Männerbund* ('association of men'), as Klaus Theweleit's reading of the *Freikorps* literature would suggest.[34] Theweleit is correct in noting that right-wing revolutionary authors associated with the *Freikorps* movement had proclaimed a retreat into male fellowship. For these male authors, the war experience constituted a moment in which men might come to terms with themselves and their masculinity. However, it was not only the wartime generation of men who identified with such notions; increasingly a younger generation of men also flocked to these radical factions. These new oaths of masculine regeneration, therefore, may more accurately be explained as a reaction to the multiple crises of the 1920s rather than as a disembodied return to the 'front experience'. In a similar reversal of Theweleit's argument that the *Freikorps* men had withdrawn from and armored themselves against the feminine, nature and the irrational, the literary scholar Franziska Meier recently has uncovered evidence of contradictory tendencies within the writings of Ernst Jünger. As Meier demonstrates, Jünger also had partaken of 'the spirit of male community' during the wartime 'battle of matériel'. During the 'storm of steel', for example, Jünger rejected the frontline presence of nurses, who were a disruptive influence in an exclusively male war zone, an attitude that Jünger shared with Remarque's heroes in *All Quiet on the Western Front*. Jünger had also not failed to note the waning of external and internal polarities between the sexes. Nonetheless, Jünger rejected the notion that these developments could or should be undone. Jünger neither blindly rejected female emancipation, nor did he advocate a clichéd image of housewife and mother. Instead, Jünger envisaged the emergence of a new and strong woman who would enter into partnership with men and serve to arouse and inspire men in mind and body.[35]

It is similarly misleading to reduce the National Socialist movement to the expression of an unequivocally retrograde and backward-looking male conspiracy. The National Socialists, in fact, also attempted to straddle the ideological gender divide. In the staging of their public appearances, the performance of a militarized male association – the 'men of action' – received highest priority. However, by 1928 there is evidence of a new discursive trope of a hierarchical 'camaraderie' between men and women. In 1926, for example, Hitler already had called for a special session on the women's question at the Weimar Reich Party Congress, employing a decidedly plebian and masculine inflection: 'We need German women (*Weiber*) who will assume their place at the side of men in our time of greatest need, who will shoulder their load alongside men, and help ensure the success of our grand work.'[36]

In place of disturbing transformation and disquieting multiplicity, the National Socialist movement promised to enforce an ordered reconciliation of the sexes.[37] The concept of 'camaraderie' was a clever tactical choice given that the notion could serve as a foil for the projection of a diverse range of lifestyles while at the same time remaining highly vague in its actual formulation. The notion of 'camaraderie', for example, permitted fantasies of equality without excluding the possibility of hierarchy. Furthermore, the essence of 'camaraderie' was founded not in personalities and individuals, but rather, as Martin Broszat has noted, in 'codes and duties.'[38] In its evocative objectification of relations between the sexes, the ideal of 'camaraderie' harmonized with lifestyles and attitudes that appealed to the younger postwar generation as well as to the *völkisch* conservatives and the Weimar political left.[39] Finally, the notion of 'camaraderie' borrowed from the repertoire of military language of the Great War to draw support from the already overladen mythical figure of the 'front soldier'. 'Camaraderie' contained the promise that the alienation of war and homefront, and of men and women, might yet be overcome in the achievement of a unity imbued with meaning and significance. This image of perfect complementarity was further facilitated by the tropes of sacrifice and duty in allegiance to National Socialism's key tenet: the as yet unrealized 'racially pure *Volk* community' (*Volksgemeinschaft*).

For some authors, the new 'camaraderie of the sexes' that followed the war was regarded as an opportunity rather than as a threat – for men as well as for women. The notion of a 'gender war' – that is, the extension of the war metaphor to the relation of the sexes, and the corollary implication that wartime injuries to the masculinity of front soldiers had transformed them into militant anti-feminists – thus must be approached with caution. Indeed, in capturing only one aspect of the debate, the concept of a 'gender war' serves to contribute to the marginalization of other, divergent contemporary explanations of the meaning of the First World War.

Drawing Boundaries

Despite the existence of voices that heralded the war as a promising turning point for gender relations, it is important to note that popular and political attitudes largely conceived of such transformations as a challenge, even an attack, on male power and male identity. First of all, as a heroic mythologization of the wartime experience took hold during the waning years of the Weimar Republic, a climate of opinion developed that increasingly favored a 'call to clarity' in relations between the sexes.[40] However, these calls for a regeneration of masculinity were not simply a response to wartime injuries to male identity. Rather, such yearnings were also a response to more recent dilemmas facing men and women, including the challenge posed by complex newer models of gender, whose appeal was directed mainly at the postwar generation. Finally, the influence and effectiveness of these political calls to order also testify to the dilemma of a democracy where economic survival appeared increasingly precarious, and where social and individual yearnings for meaning and significance remained largely unfulfilled.

Furthermore, popular understandings of the wartime experience remained accompanied and contained by 'a complex symbolic system that gave economic, social, and cultural priority to soldiers at the front'.[41] This preferential treatment is evidenced in wartime social policy as well as later symbolic memorializations of the war. Thus, for example, war memorials and ceremonial addresses largely excluded mention of women and failed to honor women's wartime contributions.[42] Yet another example documenting women's marginalization was the occasion of a minor theatrical scandal that took place in 1929, at a moment when war memorializations had become more prominent and politically-laden than ever before. Written by the author Ilse Langner, the anti-war drama 'Frau Emma Fights in the Hinterlands' (*Frau Emma kämpft im Hinterland*) premiered at the Unter den Linden Theater in Berlin.[43] According to her critics, Langner had committed her first crime in electing to vividly portray women's hardships and the female struggle for survival rather awarding center-stage to the wartime experiences of men. Even more problematic was Langner's harsh and uncompromising criticism of the male sex, whose 'lust for war' had contributed to the war's duration.[44] Male critical reaction was overwhelmingly negative. Although he praised the play's antimilitarism, Alfred Kerr, for example, objected to Langner's implication that the soldiers' service on the battlefield was 'mere pudding' (*ein Quark*) when compared to the 'torments' of women: 'What an exaggeration. Let us be serious! I am a women's attorney, but this is quite simply an exaggeration.'[45] Kerr, a progressive theater critic, thus was vehement in his protest against what he regarded as an attempt to belittle the services of soldiers on the battlefield. In the *Frankfurter Zeitung*, Ernst Heilborn went even further, arguing that women in the hinterland had fought for 'total amorality'. The *Berliner Lokalanzeiger* theater reviewer concurred, adding: 'Is this to be the new female sex with whom we now must reckon?

Thanks but no thanks, Frau Langner! Thank goodness this is merely a fantasy.'[46] The commemoration of a heroic soldier and the invocation of a glorious past thus continued to take center-stage in the popular culture of war memorialization. Especially during the waning years of the Weimar Republic, there was little resonance or scope for literary and dramatic portrayals of the wartime experiences of women, particularly when they gave evidence of pacifistic, anti-soldier, or feminist leanings.

Finally, irrespective of party affiliation, the wartime and Weimar political leadership expressed little or no enthusiasm for this new 'female independence' and 'camaraderie of the sexes'. Political leaders and policy-makers instead remained steadfast in their allegiance to a hierarchy of gender. Politicians, for example, loudly lamented the welfare service's supposed 'gap in control' (*Kontrollücke*), which was believed to have allowed war wives to lead lives devoid of all moral restraint in the absence of male supervision. The reigning political reality is further evidenced by the demobilization policies that favored former soldiers in the employment market, the 'dual-earners' campaign directed against employed married women, and the inadequate pension support for war widows.[47] However, characterizing these policies and initiatives under the rubric of a 'the reconstruction of gender relations' or a 'return to the *status quo ante*' falls short of an adequate explanation.[48] Neither the actual policies nor the preceding popular debates on questions of gender ultimately envisaged a return to the prewar world and way of life. Rather, these discourses aimed at a reformulation of male dominance within a transformed set of social and political conditions. The National Socialist movement, in particular, was successful in promoting a distinctly youthful and anti-bourgeois image to set itself apart from the 'old-fashioned types'. Within their image and projected ideology, the National Socialists thus aimed not to abandon but to modify bourgeois expectations for the gender order. This new order was not conceived of as a exclusive 'male community of warriors', but rather made a limited concession to the new figure of the 'modern woman'. Such concessions were necessary given that the Nazi movement's central goal and principle – the attainment of a 'racially pure *Volk* community' – would require the participation of both men and women.

Conclusion

In the judgment of its contemporaries, the First World War's effect on men cannot be reduced to a single common denominator, but rather varied significantly according to social and cultural milieu. What appeared unequivocal was the collective perception that the war had served to expand the possibilities for female action and enhance women's sense of self-worth. However, such transformations were not universally regarded as a declaration of war on men and masculinity, but as an opportunity to reformulate the relationship between the sexes along more 'humane' lines. In political and symbolic representations, this call for renewal was interpreted as a challenge to regenerate male hegemony. The National Socialist 'youth movement' proved itself exceptionally flexible in the fashioning of its image. Within this debate, many of its participants claimed with considerable success to have documented the wartime experiences of soldiers and their wives. While continuing to invoke older images of gender, these representations simultaneously contributed to their radicalization. The crisis in masculinity and its mirror image of an autonomous femininity had already become the topic of intense debate by the end of the nineteenth century. However, during and after the First World War, such debates for the first time seemed to pave the way for new models of gender to become lived reality for large segments of the population. The question of precisely which groups of men experienced the First World War as a crisis in masculinity, and how this crisis in turn affected male subjectivity, awaits further analysis from within the framework of a history of mentalities. Contrary to contemporary perceptions, there is considerable evidence that the First World War did not constitute a turning point in gender relations and identity. The daily realities of life under Weimar appear to have been more influential in shaping postwar discourse than suppositions of a male identity destabilized by war. Given the perceived uncertainty of the times, anything new, including new models of gender, was likely to be regarded as yet another burden, by women as well as by men. What remains a fascinating topic for further investigation is why and how men and women under Weimar conceived of their present-day experiences within the prism of their memories and their understanding of the war.

Notes

1. See Ute Daniel, *Arbeiterfrauen in der Kriegsgesellschaft. Beruf, Familie und Politik im Ersten Weltkrieg* (Göttingen, 1989), Engl.: *The War from Within. German Working-class Women and the First World War* (Oxford 1997); Elisabeth Domansky, 'Der Erste Weltkrieg,' in

Bürgerliche Gesellschaft in Deutschland. Historische Einblicke, Fragen, Perspektiven, ed. Lutz Niethammer et al. (Frankfurt am Main, 1990), 285–319; Christa Hämmerle, 'Von den Geschlechtern der Kriege und des Militärs. Forschungseinblicke und Bemerkungen zu einer neuen Debatte,' in *Was ist Militärgeschichte,* ed. Thomas Kühne and Benjamin Ziemann (Paderborn, 2000), 229–262, see specifically 252–257; Susanne Rouette, 'Nach dem Krieg: Zurück zur normalen Hierarchie der Geschlechter,' in *Geschlechterhierarchie und Arbeitsteilung. Zur Geschichte ungleicher Erwerbschancen von Männern und Frauen,* ed. Karin Hausen (Göttingen, 1993), 167–190; for a discussion of the situation in other countries, where coping with the 'gender disorder' was on the agenda as well, see Françoise Thébaud, 'The Great War and the Triumph of Sexual Division,' in *A History of Women: Towards a Cultural Identity in the Twentieth Century,* ed. idem (Cambridge, MA, 1994), 21–75.

2. Ute Planert, *Antifeminismus im Kaiserreich. Diskurs, soziale Formation und politische Mentalität* (Göttingen, 1998), 223.

3. See, for example, Katharina von Ankum, 'Introduction,' in idem, *Women in the Metropolis: Gender and Modernity in Weimar Culture* (Berkeley, 1997), 1–11, see specifically 6; Herrad-Ulrike Bussemer, 'Der Frauen Männerstärke. Geschlechterverhältnisse im Krieg,' in *Der Tod als Maschinist. Der industrialisierte Krieg 1914–1918,* eds. Rolf Spiker and Bernd Ulrich (Bramsche, 1998), 190–201, see specifically 200–201; Domansky, 'Der Erste Weltkrieg,' 313; Annette Dorgerloh, 'Sie wollen wohl Ideale klauen [. . .]?' Präfigurationen zu den Bildprägungen der "Neuen Frau",' in *Die Neue Frau. Herausforderung für die Bildmedien der Zwanziger Jahre,* ed. Katharina Sykora et al. (Marburg, 1993), 25–50, see specifically 25; John C. Fout, 'Sexual Politics in Wilhelmine Germany: The Male Gender Crisis, Moral Purity, and Homophobia,' in *Forbidden History. The State, Society, and the Regulation of Sexuality in Modern Europe* (Chicago, 1992), 259–292. A contradictory and questionable analysis is that of George L. Mosse, *Das Bild des Mannes. Zur Konstruktion der modernen Männlichkeit* (Frankfurt am Main, 1997), 107–201; Joachim Radkau, *Das Zeitalter der Nervosität. Deutschland zwischen Bismarck und Hitler* (Munich and Vienna, 1998), 389–416. For a more general examination, see Jürgen Reulecke, 'Das Jahr 1902 und die Ursprünge der Männerbund-Ideologie in Deutschland,' in *Männerbande, Männerbünde. Zur Rolle des Mannes im Kulturvergleich,* vol. 1, ed. Gisela Völger and Karin von Welck (Cologne, 1990), 3–20; Nicolaus Sombart, *Wilhelm II. Sündenbock und Herr der Mitte* (Berlin, 1996), 66–75.

4. Richard Bessel, *Germany after the First World War* (Oxford, 1993); Richard Bessel, 'Kriegserfahrungen und Kriegserinnerungen. Nachwirkungen des Ersten Weltkrieges auf das politische und soziale Leben der Weimarer Republik,' in *Kriegsbegeisterung und mentale Kriegsvorbereitung. Interdisziplinäre Studien*, ed. Marcel van der Linden and Gottfried Mergner (Berlin, 1991), 125–140; Richard Bessel, 'Die Heimkehr der Soldaten: Das Bild der Frontsoldaten in der Öffentlichkeit der Weimarer Republik,' in *Keiner fühlt sich hier mehr als Mensch. Erlebnis und Wirkung des Ersten Weltkriegs*, ed. Gerhard Hirschfeld, Gerd Krumeich and Irina Renz (Essen, 1993), 221–240; Christine Brocks and Benjamin Ziemann, '"Vom Soldatenleben hätte ich gerade genug." Der Erste Weltkrieg in der Feldpost von Soldaten,' in *Die letzten Tage der Menschheit. Bilder des Ersten Weltkrieges*, ed. Rainer Roher (Berlin, 1994), 109–120; Christa Hämmerle, '"[. . .] wirf ihnen alles hin und schau, daß du fort kommst." Die Feldpost eines Paares in der Geschlechter(un)ordnung des Ersten Weltkriegs,' *Historische Anthropologie* 6:3 (1998): 431–458; Bernd Hüppauf, ed., *Ansichten vom Krieg. Vergleichende Studien zum Ersten Weltkrieg in Literatur und Gesellschaft* (Königstein, 1984); Inge Marßolek, 'Liebe und Politik im Ersten Weltkrieg. Der Briefwechsel Helene und Wilhelm Kaisen,' in *Geschichte und Emanzipation. Festschrift für Reinhard Rürup*, ed. Michael Grüttner et al. (Frankfurt am Main, 1999), 137–159; Bernd Ulrich and Benjamin Ziemann, eds., *Frontalltag im Ersten Weltkrieg. Wahn und Wirklichkeit, Quellen und Dokumente* (Frankfurt am Main, 1994), 16–19; Benjamin Ziemann, *Front und Heimat. Ländliche Kriegserfahrungen im südlichen Bayern* (Essen, 1997).

5. This is also a theme in battlefield newspapers. See Anne Lipp, 'Heimatwahrnehmung und soldatisches "Kriegserlebnis",' in *Kriegserfahrungen. Studien zur Sozial- und Mentalitätsgeschichte des Ersten Weltkriegs*, ed. Gerhard Hirschfeld, Gerd Krumeich, Dieter Langewiesche and Hans-Peter Ullmann (Essen, 1997), 225–242.

6. See also Aribert Reimannn, 'Die heile Welt im Stahlgewitter: Deutsche und englische Feldpost aus dem Ersten Weltkrieg,' in Hirschfeld et al., *Kriegserfahrungen*, 129–145, see specifically 143.

7. This is evident, for example, in the following statement in a soldier's letter to his wife written in January 1918: 'One is only half of a person here. The other [half] is always at home. In a way, one is always ready to break things off here and [so] only absorbs half of everything because the soul is already on its way home. Hopefully, this intolerable double life will soon come to an end.' Cited in Ziemann, *Front und Heimat*, 238. A farmer also aptly described his two identities as a

man in a letter to his wife in which he explained in detail her tasks on the farm, upon which he suddenly realized: 'Why am I always writing to you about work, it has just occurred to me that I am a soldier.' Nevertheless, his thoughts returned to his farm and family. Letter 29 March 1917, cited in Ulrich and Ziemann, *Frontalltag*, 189.

8. Michael Geyer, 'Gewalt und Gewalterfahrung im 20. Jahrhundert. Der Erste Weltkrieg,' in Spiker and Ulrich, *Der Tod*, 241–257, see specifically 254; Elisabeth Domansky, 'Militarization and Reproduction in World War I Germany,' in *Society, Culture, and the State in Germany, 1870–1930*, ed. Geoff Eley (Ann Arbor, 1996), 426–454. A comparison with the allied powers would be instructive in explaining the meaning of victory or defeat in regard to the thesis about the 'generation of insecure men'. See Joanna Bourke, *Dismembering the Male: Men's Bodies, Britain and the Great War* (Chicago, 1996). In this work, Bourke finds no evidence for the rise of a militant masculinity.

9. See, for example, the articles which first appeared in 1929 in: F. M. Huebner, ed., *Die Frau von morgen wie wir sie wünschen* (1929; reprint, with a foreword by Silvia Bovenshen, Frankfurt am Main, 1990).

10. See also Michael Geyer, 'Krieg als Gesellschaftspolitik. Anmerkungen zu neueren Arbeiten über das Dritte Reich im Zweiten Weltkrieg,' *Archiv für Sozialgeschichte 26* (1986): 557–601, see specifically 558.

11. *Vorwärts*, 24 February 1916.

12. *Volkserzieher* 22 (1918): 142.

13. Paul Göhre, *Front und Heimat. Religiöses, Politisches, Sexuelles aus dem Schützengraben* (Jena, 1917), 27. Regarding the theme of alienation, see Regina Schulte, *Die verkehrte Welt des Krieges. Studien zu Geschlecht, Religion, Tod* (Frankfurt am Main, 1998), 15–34.

14. Anna Brunnemann, *Bismarck Jahrbuch für Deutsche Frauen* (1919), 99–100.

15. Minna Cauer, 'Einige Betrachtungen über die Wirkungen des Krieges auf die Psyche der Frau,' *Die Frauenbewegung* 23:15/16 (1917): 49.

16. See *Deutscher Frauenbund* (Bundeszeitschrift) 8:4 (1916): 4.

17. Curt Moreck, *Kultur- und Sittengeschichte der Neuesten Zeit. Geschlechtsleben und Erotik in der Gesellschaft der Gegenwart* (Dresden, 1928), 234–235.

18. Robert Musil, in Huebner, *Die Frau von morgen*, 91–92.

19. Göhre, *Front und Heimat*, 29.

20. Ibid., 28–29.

21. Josephine Levy-Rathenau, 'Frauengedanken zur sozialen Übergangsfürsorge,' *Zeitschrift für das Armenwesen* 19:1/3 (1918): 21–23, see specifically 23.
22. See the standard work by Daniel, *Arbeiterfrauen.*
23. See Planert, *Antifeminismus*, 279.
24. There is no sense of crisis in the rest of the letter. She continues, perhaps somewhat too cheerfully: 'He [her husband] looks splendid, and, like many of us, the war seems to have done him morally a lot of good. At least I am much more energetic and independent than earlier, which is only natural when one has Creisau, the family, etc. to carry on one's shoulders.' Dorothy von Moltke, *Ein Leben in Deutschland. Briefe aus Kreisau und Berlin 1907–1934*, ed. Beate Ruhm von Oppen (Munich, 1999), 55. It must also be pointed out that the number of marriages after the war was very high, and that there are almost no qualitative studies examining the reasons for divorce. See Bessel, *Germany,* 228–233.
25. See Hüppauf, *Ansichten vom Krieg.* Regarding collective memory after wartime, see Jay Winter and Emmanuel Sivan, eds., *War and Remembrance in the Twentieth Century* (Cambridge, 1999).
26. Wilhelm Stekel, *Unser Seelenleben im Kriege. Psychologische Betrachtungen eines Nervenarztes* (Berlin, 1916), 65–66. Regarding the antifeminists, see Planert, *Antifeminismus.*
27. Brunnemann, *Bismarck Jahrbuch,* 99–100; for an overview, compare Gertrud Bäumer, 'Frauenleben und Frauenarbeit,' in *Der Weltkrieg in seiner Einwirkung auf das deutsche Volk,* ed. Max Schwarte (Leipzig, 1918), 311–330.
28. See Karin Bruns, 'Machteffekte in Frauentexten. Nationalistische Periodika (1895–1915),' in *Weiblichkeit in geschichtlicher Perspektive. Fallstudien und Reflexionen zu Grundproblemen der historischen Frauenforschung*, ed. Ursula A. J. Becher and Jörn Rüsen (Frankfurt am Main, 1988), 309–338. Regarding the 'backlash', see also Stefana Lefko, '"Truly Womanly" and "Truly German". Women's Rights and National Identity in *Die Frau*,' in *Gender and Germanness. Cultural Productions of Nation*, ed. Patricia Herminghouse and Magda Mueller (Providence and Oxford, 1997), 129–144.
29. Max Bauer, *Der große Krieg in Feld und Heimat. Erinnerungen und Betrachtungen* (Tübingen, 1921), 53. The political left also pronounced an accusation of guilt, claiming that aristocratic and upper middle class women, in a fit of national enthusiasm, threw their sons to the jaws of the death machine. See, for example, Kurt Tucholsky, 'Der Krieg und die deutsche Frau,' in *Gesammelte Werke,* vol. 5 (Reinbek, 1975): 267–269.

30. Margarete Pochhammer, 'Die deutschen Frauen während des Krieges,' in *Die Deutsche Frau* 16:11 (1922): 171.
31. See, for example, Ilse Reicke, *Das junge Mädchen. Ein Buch der Lebensgestaltung* (first edition, 1925; Berlin, 1928): especially 39; Huebner, *Die Frau von morgen.* On the discourse of marriage, see also Anja E. Bagel-Bohlan and Michael Salewski, eds., *'Sexualmoral' und Zeitgeist im 19. und 20. Jahrhundert* (Opladen, 1990); Atina Grossmann, 'Die "Neue Frau" und die Rationalisierung der Sexualität in der Weimarer Republik,' in *Die Politik des Begehrens. Sexualität, Pornographie und neuer Puritanismus in den USA*, ed. Ann Snitow et al. (Berlin, 1985), 38–62; Cornelie Usborne, *Frauenkörper – Volkskörper. Geburtenkontrolle und Bevölkerungspolitik in der Weimarer Republik* (Münster, 1994); regarding the Communist Party of Germany (KPD), see Eric D. Weitz, *Creating German Communism, 1890–1990. From Popular Protest to Socialist State* (Princeton, 1997), 188–220. The term 'camaraderie' (*Kameradschaft*) resonated not only among men and between the sexes, but also in the conservative spectrum of the women's movement. Thus, members of the 'League of Queen Luise' (*Bund Königin Luise*), founded in 1923, addressed one another as 'comrades' (*Kameradinnen*) as they deliberately imitated the supposed comradely relationships of the front soldiers. Charlotte von Hadeln, ed., *Deutsche Frauen – Deutsche Treue 1914–1933. Ein Ehrenbuch der deutschen Frau* (Berlin, 1935), 319.
32. Moreck, *Kultur- und Sittengeschichte*, 236.
33. Thomas Mann, 'Die Ehe im Übergang,' in *Das Ehe-Buch. Eine neue Sinngebung im Zusammenklang der Stimmen führender Zeitgenossen*, ed. Hermann Keyserling (Celle, 1925), 212–226, see specifically 214–215. Edlef Köppen, *Heeresbericht* (reprint, Reinbek, 1979), 149–150. By contrast, in his successful anti-war novel, Köppen appeased fears of masculinization by eroticizing the encounter between men and women:

> Couldn't it happen to you, Reisiger, that the eyes of the young woman, who appeared in a threadbare pair of men's pants with a coal basket on her bent shoulders, that these eyes would suddenly throw off a gleam? That the mouth, black with dust, would suddenly lift into a soft curve? [. . .] That out of the breast, panting, mounds would appear? That nothing would be a lie anymore, that no war could violate a woman into a man.

34. Klaus Theweleit, *Männerphantasien*, vols. 1 and 2 (Frankfurt am Main, 1977/78). Theweleit's analysis unfortunately has been subject

to both a reduction and an over-generalization to those aspects of his argument that emphasize crisis, which in part can be explained by the wide reception of his work. The same holds true for Magnus Hirschfeld, ed., *Sittengeschichte des Ersten Weltkrieges* (Hanau, 1966).

35. See Franziska Meier, *Emanzipation als Herausforderung. Rechtsrevolutionäre Schriftsteller zwischen Bisexualität und Androgynie* (Vienna, 1998), 195–273. Regarding the negative attitude towards nurses, see, for example, Stekel, *Unser Seelenleben*, 123. For a general overview, see Regina Schulte, 'Die Schwester des kranken Kriegers. Verwundetenpflege im Ersten Weltkrieg,' in idem, 95–116.

36. Cited in Hans-Jürgen Arendt, Sabine Hering and Leonie Wagner, *Nationalsozialistische Frauenpolitik vor 1933. Dokumentation* (Frankfurt am Main, 1995), 108.

37. See Siegfried Kaltenecker, 'Weil aber die vergessenste Fremde unser Körper ist. Über Männer-Körper-Repräsentationen und Faschismus,' in *The Body of Gender: Körper/Geschlechter/Identitäten*, ed. Marie-Luise Angerer (Vienna, 1995), 91–109; Planert, *Antifeminismus*, 293–294. See also Inge Marßolek, '"Ich möchte Dich zu gern mal in Uniform sehen." Geschlechterkonstruktionen in Feldpostbriefen,' *WerkstattGeschichte* 8:22 (1999): 41–61, see specifically 45–47.

38. Martin Broszat, 'Einleitung,' in *Kommandant in Auschwitz. Autobiographische Aufzeichnungen des Rudolf Höß*, ed. idem (Munich, 1987), 21.

39. Regarding objectivity, see the comments by Ulrich Herbert, *Best. Biographische Studien über Radikalismus, Weltanschauung und Vernunft 1903–1989* (Bonn, 1996), 522.

40. For an overview, see Ute Frevert, *Frauen-Geschichte. Zwischen Bürgerlicher Verbesserung und Neuer Weiblichkeit* (Frankfurt am Main, 1986), 185–195.

41. Thébaud, 'The Great War,' 43.

42. See Birthe Kundrus, *Kriegerfrauen. Familienpolitik und Geschlechterverhältnisse im Ersten und Zweiten Weltkrieg* (Hamburg, 1995), 398–400. For an overview discussion of memorializations of the First World War, see Benjamin Ziemann, 'Die Erinnerung an den Ersten Weltkrieg in den Milieukulturen der Weimarer Republik,' in *Kriegserlebnis und Legendenbildung. Das Bild des 'modernen' Krieges in Literatur, Theater, Photographie und Film*, ed. Thomas F. Schneider (Osnabrück, 1999), 249–270, see specifically 259–261.

43. Ilse Langner, *Frau Emma kämpft im Hinterland. Chronik in drei Akten* (reprint, Darmstadt, 1979). For another critical portrayal, see Clara Viebig, 'Töchter der Hekuba,' in idem, *Das rote Meer. Roman*

(Berlin, 1920). See also Agnès Cardinal, 'Women on the Other Side,' in *Women and World War 1. The Written Response*, ed. Dorothy Goldman (London, 1993), 31–50; Inge Stephan, 'Weiblicher Heroismus: Zu zwei Dramen von Ilse Langner,' in *Frauenliteratur ohne Tradition? Neun Autorinnenporträts*, ed. Inge Stephan, Regula Venske and Sigrid Weigel (Frankfurt am Main, 1987), 159–189. See Hans-Otto Binder, 'Zum Opfern bereit: Kriegsliteratur von Frauen,' in Hirschfeld et al., 107–128; Catherine O'Brien, *Women's Fictional Responses to the First World War. A Comparative Study of Selected Texts by French and German Writers* (New York, 1997).

44. Langner, *Frau Emma*, 48.

45. Cited in Ilse Langner, *Mein Thema und mein Echo. Darstellung und Würdigung*, ed. Ernst Johann (Darmstadt, 1979), 10.

46. Cited in Anne Stürzer, *Dramatikerinnen und Zeitstücke. Ein vergessenes Kapitel der Theatergeschichte von der Weimarer Republik bis zur Nachkriegszeit* (Stuttgart, 1993), 48.

47. See Richard Bessel, '"Eine nicht allzugroße Beunruhigung des Arbeitsmarktes." Frauenarbeit und Demobilmachung in Deutschland nach dem Ersten Weltk'ieg,' *Geschichte und Gesellschaft* 9 (1983): 211–229; Susanne Rouette, *Sozialpolitik als Geschlechterpolitik. Die Regulierung der Frauenarbeit nach dem Ersten Weltkrieg* (Frankfurt am Main, 1993). On the social services provided by the German government to war widows, see Karin Hausen, 'Die Sorge der Nation für ihre "Kriegsopfer". Ein Bereich der Geschlechterpolitik während der Weimarer Republik,' in *Von der Arbeiterbewegung zum modernen Sozialstaat. Festschrift für Gerhard A. Ritter zum 65. Geburtstag*, ed. Jürgen Kocka et al. (Munich, 1994), 719–739; Karin Hausen, 'The German Nation's Obligations to the Heroes' Widows of World War I,' in *Behind the Lines. Gender and the Two World Wars*, ed. Margaret R. Higonnet, Jane Jenson, Sonya Michel and Margaret Collins Weitz (New Haven, 1987), 126–140; Robert Weldon Whalen, *Bitter Wounds. German Victims of the Great War (1914–1939)* (New York, 1984).

48. See, for example, Rouette, *Sozialpolitik als Geschlechterpolitik*, 175.

–7–

Body Damage

War Disability and Constructions of Masculinity in Weimar Germany

Sabine Kienitz

Politicians and military officers hoped the First World War would become something of a 'fountain of youth' for the German nation. There was a sense that it would radically renew a society that individualism had rendered sickly and decrepit. The war was to toughen up and regenerate a manhood described as effeminate, insecure and nervous; it would recover under the healthy influence of fresh air and male camaraderie.[1] The frequently used metaphor of the war as a 'steel bath' (*Stahlbad*)[2] connoted its therapeutic effect, which together with military drill would discipline and transform the man softened by civilian society into a soldier hard as metal. Even during the war, physicians and psychologists asserted the sure success of this 'cure for the nerves', and artists such as Fritz Erler translated it into new body images with public appeal: his 1917 poster for war bonds stylized the steel-blue-eyed warrior of Verdun in a steel helmet as the ideal of the *Neuer Mensch*.[3] As a smoothly functioning part of a modern war machine, de-individualized, mask-like in his lack of emotion and at the same time highly aggressive, the new soldier seemed the ideal incarnation of the mythically transfigured modern heroic man.[4]

This typification of the militant man as an unfeeling and resolute battle machine was reflected most strikingly in the contemporary writings of Ernst Jünger. Because of the expressive power of his portrayal and the interpretive competence ascribed him by German historians and literary scholars due to his war experience as commander of a fighting patrol, Jünger has been elevated to a sort of spokesman on questions of 'masculinity in modern times'.[5] At the very least, his literary-autobiographical sketches from the 1920s dominate the historical view of men in modernity and seem to have achieved acceptance in the scholarly reception and deciphering of male stereotypes thought of as hegemonic after the First

World War. Again and again, Jünger exegetes have used his texts to trans-
mute his body-oriented images of 'masculinity' into authentic depictions
of the man formed by the First World War; this is especially the case in
those interpretations that anticipate fascism. In this way, the historian
George L. Mosse arrives at the conclusion that the experience of the First
World War, having followed a fundamental crisis phase at the turn of the
twentieth century, led to a reconstitution of aggressive masculinity. And
he cites Ernst Jünger as proof for his thesis that after the Great War 'what
was regarded as true manliness gained a new dimension of brutality' in
Germany.[6] But beware: the overly simplified thesis of the 'survival of the
masculinity of the warrior'[7] *after* the war and of the brutalization of men
by the war is a one-sided reflection of the point of view of those survivors
who, like Ernst Jünger, could reinterpret the war, in spite of defeat, as
confirmation of their life philosophy. Thus, it reproduces and uncritically
perpetuates the construct of the time, i.e. the 'steely nature' (*Stahlnatur*)
of masculinity shaped by the military. The claim to authenticity is attributed to the author Ernst Jünger because he is a self-reflective and eloquent
eyewitness of the war. A critical reading, however, that takes into consideration the constructed and compensatory character of such texts is hardly
undertaken, and alternative or deviant constructions of masculinity as a
result of the war seem not to occur. Mosse does lay out a range of variously configured types of masculinity and also analyzes forms of a male
'anti-type', against which the stereotype of the virile man had to assert
itself. But beyond that, in his fixation on Jünger, Mosse loses sight of the
traumatizing experiences and consequences of the war and with it the possible function of such a militant male image. The question is, specifically,
which destructive war experiences and which fears and inner conflicts
had to be covered up, reshaped and reconfigured (in the sense of a dialectical process) by the counter-image of a 'warrior' and its attributes?[8]

In the heroization of the man as 'war machine', a profound confrontation with the devastating consequences of industrialized mass war and
the experience of physical and psychic demolition has historically been
tabooed and negated. These experiences were visibly and invisibly inscribed on the memories and bodies of millions of soldiers from all the
countries participating in the war and transformed the male body into a
site of the collective memory of destructive military power never before
experienced in Europe. With these consequences of the war in mind,
constructions of masculinity and their postwar interpretations cannot be
reduced to the Jüngerian image of the militant warrior and worker-soldier
alone. Before coming to the conclusion that a collective remasculinization
took place *through* the war as a form of positive crisis management – a

dubious thesis at that, as it in fact legitimizes war activity in historical retrospect as a therapeutic means of restabilizing the balance of a symbolic order of gender gone awry – one should investigate the possible effects of the war much more comprehensively from the perspective of the actors and victims.[9] In this way, the cultural consequences of the threat to bodily self-certainties and the resulting fragility of masculinity constructs themselves become the object of analysis. The inquiry is directed toward the male body of the soldier, which stood at the convergence of the threats of war technology; its psychic and physical destruction – that is to say, the perception, processing and remembrance of it, particularly with regard to contemporary constructions of masculinity – has only begun to be studied.[10] Rather than conceiving of the war as a means of collective remasculinization, the thesis would be that it was just those effects of industrialized mass war that called traditional conceptions of masculinity into question and thus launched a new set of collective modes of experience and hermeneutic models as well as a transformation of models of manhood.

Support for this thesis can be found on different levels. A discourse analysis by the literary scholar Ulrike Baureithel examines cultural critiques by literati and publicists whose attempt in the 1920s and early 1930s to describe the current state of a social order thrown into disarray by the war utilized categorizations connotive of gender. In so doing, they reverted to forms of cultural critique from as early as the nineteenth century based on metaphors of the conflict between the genders. Intellectual Weimar journalism thus constituted a discourse on society and gender that can itself be 'conceived of as an indication for the increasing insecurity of traditional cultural patterns of order'.[11] Baureithel sees in the formulation of blame the work of a 'stranded male generation', speaking in defamatory undertones of an 'effeminization' of society and indeed diagnosing their own condition as a 'collective neurosis of modern men'. Accordingly, Baureithel reads the 'male pathos' of the cult of masculinity in the literature of the *Neue Sachlichkeit* movement not as a sign of a reestablishment of manhood but rather as a compensation for the loss of meaning of male existence caused by the war and at the same time a concealment of men's lack of orientation in the face of the demands of modern society.[12]

The cultural studies scholar Gabriele Mentges also argues against the simplistic stereotype of a brutalized masculinity as a result of the First World War. She examines the phenomenon of new male habits which had obviously arisen during the war, and which had already distanced itself to a large extent from warlike military models. These habits offered not hegemonic but instead strongly distinctive, exclusive forms of masculinity, which were staged through the presentation of the body. Thus, Mentges develops the thesis that, with the modernization and mechanization of war, a new, male-coded casualness or 'coolness' arose simultaneously as a counter-scheme to the Prussian military ideal and indeed was already picked up on by contemporaries as a kind of model.[13] Evidence for her thesis are new textiles and materials produced especially for war use and the clothes developed from them as well as correspondingly innovative fashions and changed postures of the body. The protagonists of this new, positive form of male casualness are, according to Mentges, the elite troops that arose during the war known as the *Aviatiker*, i.e. the pilot heroes such as Manfred von Richthofen and Oswald Boelcke,[14] who promoted these male body images and popularized them in a media-friendly manner. It could be seen as an irony of history that, according to Mentges's research, it was none other than the machine-man Ernst Jünger who was fascinated by these 'dandies' of the air and their casual masculinity,[15] which had so little in common with his own notion of a soldierly, masculine *Stahlnatur*.[16]

This reinterpretation, which also meant a restabilization, of military masculinity was reserved, however, for a small male elite. More far-reaching was the experience of a radical war-related challenge to masculinity through threatened and real dismemberment of the body, which connoted maleness.[17] This had been experienced by a much larger group of soldiers in the First World War, either personally or by the example of their co-combatants.[18] In this article, I will discuss this point in two steps: The first step will present the conceptual frame for a methodological understanding of the nexus of body and masculinity, that is, those theoretical premises that are important for naming different forms of bodily dismemberment and their cultural processing as a part of constructions of masculinity. In a second step I will discuss the technical reconstruction and the staging of masculinity conceived as normative in the Weimar Republic through a study of the issue of labor and physical capacity, both of which connoted manhood. My main source is literature from war disability welfare organizations (*Kriegsbeschädigtenfürsorge*) of the time, whose perspective presents a 'success story' which must be read against the grain with attention to its constructed character.

Masculinity/ies: On the Nexus of Gender and the Body

Under the influence of current deconstructivist theories, the question of the connection between war disability and constructions of masculinity creates methodological difficulties, since those theories tend to view the body as singularly discursive. At one time, the category 'sex' was considered the basis for statements made about the cultural construct known as 'gender'; biological classification of historical subjects made possible by the body represented the ground upon which the interpretation of culturally shaped forms of behavior and expression took place. But with the conceptualization of 'sex' as a *part* of 'gender', the body began to slip from its seemingly secure place in the system of coordinates established by the symbolic order of the sexes.[19] But this does not render the issue of historical bodies being defined and formed by gender obsolete; on the contrary: if the point is not only to work out theories on constructions of masculinity far from an empirical basis, but also to grasp historically existing forms of lived manhood and theorize from there, then methodological approaches are needed both for interrogating those historically produced certainties about the ostensibly biological essentialism of the body and for finding new ways of approaching historical constructions of gender identities.[20] This is not an attempt to re-biologize the body itself nor to naturalize bodily experience in its historically asserted authenticity. Rather, the example of the experience of bodily dismemberment in war will be used to historicize the process of the cultural construction of masculinity/ies via the body understood to be male.

Thus, before proceeding further, it is necessary to clarify the question of the meaning of the body, the experience of having a body and being a body for male identity construction; that is, how gender and gender identity is constituted in the web of ascriptions by the self and the other. This is particularly necessary in light of the observation that sex cannot be reduced to the body in and of itself, for as Ute Frevert summarizes the argumentation of the anti-essentialist and deconstructivist approach: 'Manhood and masculinity do not adhere primarily to the body', but instead represent 'cultural constructs [. . .] which are greatly differentiated socially as well as being varied temporally and spacially.'[21] The historian John Tosh also considers the definition of masculinity as a normative stereotype or as a scheme of process-defined cultural attributes to be inadequate and instead speaks of masculinity/ies as formulations of social and psychic identities which must be historically contextualized.[22] However, he also largely avoids theorizing on how much the body itself – in its materiality and thus outside discourse – is a part of this cultural system of meaning and plays into these areas and therefore must be considered a fundamental prerequisite of efficacious cultural practice.

Even if the body does not produce and present gender from within itself, it does represent a key medium of social communication through which the objectivity of the symbolic order of the sexes is constructed.[23] Thus, gender and the body represent an inextricable interconnection, which can be analyzed particularly well within the framework of a theory of human action, namely by inquiring as to processes and rules according to which genderedness is acquired, lived, construed and reproduced in each historical context. The materiality of the body has a highly symbolic quality, through which among other things gender, gender difference and gender identity are constructed in social action.[24] The levels of discourse and concrete social practice interrelate constantly: thus the body becomes the site in which the culturally anchored 'system of knowledge of the duality of gender' and, with it, discourse on gender difference appears to be materially inscribed. The concept of 'performing masculinity'[25] developed by ethnomethodology makes clear why such significance is allotted to the self-presentation and self-perception of gender and its interactive confirmation, known as 'doing gender', through the medium of a sexually marked body in the context of a social construction of reality. For it is in fact the perception of the body, dealings with it as the 'constant reiteration of cultural conventions on the body and through the body'[26] and culturally mediated interpretations of bodily experiences that must be understood as the essential elements of a cultural construction of masculinity/ies, for they are the very precondition of a successful socialization process within the symbolic system of the gender order. That is why Helmuth Plessner anchored the possibility of identity construction in precisely the question of whether embodiment can be transcended, i.e. in the ability of an individual to perceive his or her own body as socially mediated and culturally interpreted, and thus attribute meanings themselves in action to his or her own body, even from a historical perspective.[27]

The body in its physically apprehensible materiality must be brought into the analysis of each historical construction of masculinity/ies, not simply as symbolic metaphor nor as a passive surface of discursively attributed interpretations and reinterpretations,[28] but rather both as an active part itself in social processes of negotiation and as their product.[29] But how does one reconstruct the emergence of masculinity/ies, when more than just the sedimentation of textualized attributions, discourses and imaginations are at issue? How are masculinity/ies as material embodiments of gender as a cultural practice, of value systems and meanings constructed, and how exactly does the process which we try to denote with the term 'embodying masculinity' work?[30]

War Disability: On the Collapse of Masculine Body Images

A look at the war-wounded can help us understand this. In the First World War, the large numbers of those who suffered as a result of war activity were men of all social classes, each with correspondingly differently formed body images, who survived the war with psychic damage, chronic organic diseases and, in part, hideous physical mutilation.[31] With their massive impairments, the approximately 2.7 million war-disabled in Germany had lost more than just the use of their bodies: men of very different occupations – civil servants, office workers, craftsmen, intellectuals, factory workers, farmers – were robbed of the security of culturally transmitted bodily certainties by the war. This security was part of their masculine identity as expressed in class-specific male self-conceptions. Losing it meant losing that very scope of action in which their identity was grounded, which was closely tied to a specific soundness and capability of the body they not only took for granted, but also experienced and construed as male: not only the ability to do hard physical labor, the habitus and practice of intellectual productivity, mobility and independence in their everyday lives, but also the entitlement to those forms of authority enacted directly via the body. Furthermore, war-disabled veterans saw themselves as disadvantaged in their dealings with and their attractiveness to the opposite sex.[32] All these things were bodily practices that had been inscribed in specific ways into a habitus identified as male in Wilhelmine society and for whose realization the tension between the objectivity of 'having a body' and the bodily experience of 'being a body' was a fundamental precondition. Within this context, various processes of deconstruction can be described, which on the one hand must be understood as ascriptions of a symbolic nature, but which first and foremost took effect via the maimed body no longer considered masculine and which had consequences for concrete everyday interaction. The physical traumatization of the war went along with an experience of marginalization, with the lack of recognition not only of achievements, but also of demands and needs.

The injury of their bodies not only called into question the conceptualization of conduct understood as masculine, but also obviously set in motion the reinterpretation of ascriptions by others, which can be described as processes of infantilization and feminization. War-disabled ex-servicemen, depending on their level of disability, were reduced to the cultural developmental stage, and thus also the social status, of children, since their physical impairment meant they had to relearn such key cultural techniques as writing, reading or speaking and had to be reinstructed in the routines of daily life on the basis of their changed physical condition. Furthermore, as war heroes, they experienced less of the admiration they had expected from those around them and more of the pity they dreaded. They became the object of care for middle-class women looking for an opportunity to prove their willingness for patriotic duty and living out vicariously through work with the war-wounded their social commitment to the wounded and beaten *Vaterland*.

Reorientation and classification in the symbolic order of the sexes took place for the war-disabled through their crippled bodies: the war disability welfare organized by the private sector directed them, for example, toward activities with connotations that did not correspond with their self-image as men, or in fact seemed to damage it further. This process began as early as convalescence in the military hospitals, where men crippled by the war went to 'dexterity class', where they were instructed by women in so-called 'women's handicrafts' such as crochet, knitting and macramé in order to be prepared for their future occupations.[33] Male contemporaries observed this symbolic form of feminization with concern and complained about the fact that grown men lost their independence in the care of women and were 'softened' by such work, which had 'something delicate, playful, unmasculine'[34] about it. The Red Cross, one of the bourgeois organizations offering war disability welfare, attempted to stop the trend toward the feminine handicrafts, at first in words only, then in action: dilettantish work with female needlecraft and ornamentation was discredited as not manly enough and was soon complemented by the introduction of occupationally relevant activities, which eventually replaced them completely. Work with a saw and drill was praised as a 'strengthening remedy'[35] and was considered appropriate physical therapy for a man. Not the female handicrafts teacher but the male craftsman was to physically train the disabled man and prepare him for his return to daily life and occupation.

The connection between a construction of identity understood as masculine and a material corporeality on which this identity is based – that is to say, the necessary reconstitution of it – only became tangible once the self-evidence of a way of life connoting masculinity was threatened or in fact negated, i.e. in the fragmentation of the real body. And it was not until millions of male combatants experienced physical mutilation that fundamental changes became necessary in a lifestyle that had been perceived and construed only implicitly as masculine as well as in attitudes considered manly. The physical and psychic injury of the war acted as a form of decorporealization, which via the negation of the body also threatened the performance and thus the bodily experience of an identity identified as masculine.

John Tosh's notion of the basic instability of historically varying compositional elements of masculinity is clearly seen in the moment of destruction, when the body, through which gender identity is to be constructed, is no longer available in the self-evident way it was before and this was not just an individual problem, but had to be managed collectively. The constructed nature of masculinity becomes tangible only *ex negativo*, namely in a situation in which seemingly firm certainties break apart, and it becomes a topic of social discourse because of the obvious need for reconstructive measures. For the people of the time, however, not the necessity of a reconstruction of gender-specific identity was at stake, but rather the possibility of regaining and taking for granted a non-threatening normality disguised as what was generally considered the social norm.

Social dealings with the war-disabled was, however, self-contradictory: the fragmented and maimed body was apparently not appropriate for symbolic amplification in post-war society and thus offered those affected no concrete basis on which to develop a positive masculine identity as 'war heroes'. Whereas from the perspective of the war-wounded of all political orientations the presentation of their bodies became the most important moral argument in the fight for their rights as victims of war, in the face of national defeat no one wanted to see the maimed bodies as proof of willingness to sacrifice, courage and bravery nor to recognize the financial commitments that were demanded as obligatory. Showing one's wounds, the publicly visible presentation of suffering was regarded in the postwar years as lachrymose, unmasculine and reprehensible; it was no longer appropriate in a modern society and was morally discredited by representatives of state-run and privately owned welfare institutions. 'Germany,' according to the nationally charged creed of the self-appointed "cripple psychologist" Hans Würtz, 'does not wish to see war-disabled ex-soldiers begging in the streets of the city or on the highways!'[36] The notion of a publicly visible *belle blessure*, the cultural amplification of the wound as a demonstration of manly heroism, seemed to be annulled to a large extent in the Weimar Republic. The civilian population reacted primarily with repulsion and exclusion to the great number of affected individuals, the monstrosity of their injuries and the public debate over economic entitlements for the multitude of amputees, blinded, ill and psychically shattered 'war quiverers' (*'Kriegszitterern'*). The opportunity for symbolic recognition remained reserved for those war-disabled who were willing to adapt, to make invisible the destruction of their bodies and thus to follow the appeal made as early as 1915 by the orthopedic surgeon Konrad Biesalski, '[to] melt into the mass of the people as if nothing had happened [. . .]'.[37]

The spectrum of possibilities of suitable social interaction with the bodies of ex-soldiers maimed in combat was wide. It ranged from the morally dictated hiding of the wounds, which forced the men to deny their physical state, all the way to the purposeful presentation of the body as the bearer of elaborate technical prostheses. This strategy of public presentation of the invalid as proof of national inventiveness was pursued primarily by those specialists involved professionally with war injuries and who were able to construct their own social significance through them. Thus, the destroyed, sickly bodies of these men became a central object of public discussion in postwar society. The emphasis, however, was on the determination, analysis and management of their *lack* of proper physical function, a debate dominated by the expertise of the interpretive elites from the medical and, above all, the commercial/ technical field. The socially institutionalized interest in the war disabled was focused exclusively on the externally visible state of their bodies and the possibility of their technical reconstruction. The reform of the state benefits law (*Reichsversorgungsgesetz*) of May 1920 revised the pension claims of the war-disabled; they were no longer calculated according to the military rank of the individual but exclusively according to the physical ability remaining to him. This new system of assessment[38] measured the war injury on each part of the body with seeming exactness according to percentages and excluded for the most part individual interpretations of the impairment. According to the law, the war wounded had a right to therapeutic measures, social welfare and an economic compensation of their occupational disadvantages in the form of a war pension. The criteria for this entitlement had been defined by the legislature according to a sophisticated scale of physical impairment, which was interpreted not by the affected themselves, but exclusively by experts, mostly the evaluating physicians. The interpretive scheme of the administrative authorities became definitive and stood between the subjectively experienced traumas and their official recognition while remaining for the most part inscrutable for the affected individuals themselves.[39] On behalf of the state, physicians and surgeons, psychologists and orthopedists, technicians and engineers seized the bodies and psyches of the war-disabled and subjected them to evaluation as well as a variety of reconstructive procedures which in part were still of an experimental character. The categorization of the impairment reduced the affected individuals in their social existence to the body which had become dysfunctional and was perceived as deficient, which as such had to be discarded or 'repaired' like a work piece and thus, through operative techniques, adapted to the demands of a modern industrial production process.

On the one hand, the heads of the military hospitals as well as the organizers of state-supported workshops in the hospitals argued in favor of total control over the bodies of the war-disabled, which included military drill and was almost tantamount to expropriation and deprivation of their adult autonomy.[40] On the other hand, the affected were declared responsible for their own bodies in the sense of self-discipline. They were completely on their own when expected to fulfill the main task assigned to them, i.e. in spite of all their physical disabilities to function successfully as the breadwinner and head of a family and to reintegrate as a 'useful' part of society. This process was coupled with the insight of national economists that, in view of the growing number of war-disabled, the growing burdens of the war and – after the war – the reparation demands of the victorious powers, the war pensions would enormously burden the government's budget. As mitigation, therefore, the war-disabled should make the transition 'from needy cripples to taxpayers'[41] as quickly as possible and legitimate the reduction of their pensions through the work capacity they had attained. The ritual talk of 'willpower winning out' placed all individual responsibility for the body on the disabled themselves. They were to overcome their physical damage through an act of willpower also conceived of as masculine.[42] Thus, along with their devaluation as men, the war-disabled had to deal with demands that related to traditional and normative conceptions of masculinity, the focal point being the aspect of labor and work ability.

Remasculinization, or the Triumph of Technology

The most striking characteristic of the official war disability welfare agencies, which existed in all the German *Länder* and some of which were also entrusted with counseling and finding employment for the war-disabled, is the assertion of the unchanged ability of the war-wounded to work. In cooperation with technicians and engineers who worked in the private industrial sector and/or for the decentralized 'Evaluation Offices for Prostheses' (*Prüfstellen für Ersatzglieder*), physicians and agency representatives collaborated on the development of a hermeneutic model of the war-wounded body nevertheless capable of work, a body which, with the proper prosthetic equipment, could be employed in all areas of trade and industry. This discourse of overcoming and normalization was reflected in the media, in text as well as in visual images. Many popular magazines such as *Gartenlaube* or the popular-technical magazine *Die Umschau*, but also many publications and treatises for technical, medical or rehabilitation specialists even during the war but particularly in the early 1920s, published series of photographs depicting war-disabled ex-servicemen at work in occupational settings.[43] The areas of gainful employment represented are extremely varied and present the war-disabled as highly productive craftsmen or capable agricultural workers, industrial workers at machines or office workers, that is to say, doing a job declared each time to be perfectly normal. These photographs, static and repeatedly of the same set-up, seemed to communicate a certain message: the disabled male bodies depicted and staged here are presented, in the most varied ways possible, as capable of work and therefore of competition, and they suggest through these pictures a norm of behavior required by the culture amounting to discipline through work and encompassing instructions on how one could apply one's own capabilities in a useful manner.[44] This recontextualization of the war-disabled through representation in the workplace also withheld from them the sense of themselves they preferred, namely as 'victims of the war', and provided the opportunity to celebrate them as 'heroes of the workplace'. The invisibility of the disabled in the public realm, where they were denied pity and sympathy, could be compensated for by a deliberate staging of them in the partially public working world, where power over interpretive attributions lay in the hands of specialists and could no longer be controlled by the affected persons themselves.

By asserting that the body can be completely reconstructed particularly for the requirements of modern industrial forms of production, the photographs also offer a reconciliatory and glossed-over interpretation of the war. The pictures suggest a stability of social circumstances and provide reassurance that in the years between 1914 and 1918, in the end, nothing really grave had happened which could have disordered society at all. After their stay in sick bay, the victims of the war, according to this message, returned to their jobs and could successfully take up their rightful place as capable 'men' in society. The war-disabled were able to 'hold their own' again in daily life as providers for the family and thus proved themselves to be capable of integration.

These photographs of the war-disabled at their 'rightful' jobs point to yet another meaning, however: at issue was also the maintenance of the traditional order of the sexes and thus the attempt to reduce the rise in employment among women caused by the war and perceived as threatening, and thus to exclude women from many areas of employment, not only symbolically but also in reality. The photos mark the gender coding of those varieties of occupations in which the disabled are presented and emphasize the priority given claims by male ex-servicemen to occupational reintegration in technically qualified and better paid areas of work.[45] The conclusion comes full circle: the photographs show war-disabled veterans seemingly 'frozen' in the culturally coded enactment of work. Work capacity is thus asserted as a masculine norm and is pasted on these bodies, as in a montage: the depiction of the ability to work and the asserted claim that they can work, is at the same time transferred into a gender-coded and habitual practice, which itself points to the reconstructed gender identity of the actors.[46]

This observation becomes particularly important against the backdrop of the concurrent, extensive demobilization measures taking place after the war, with which women were to be excluded from just these occupations.[47] The notion that labor and work ability is gender-coded is also confirmed by the portrayal of women in the context of organized 'cripple care': in their publications, such as the *Zeitschrift für Krüppelfürsorge*, it was common to show physically disabled women and girls only at sewing machines and with knitting needles. The pictorial representation of female rehabilitation was therefore always shown in private spaces and contexts, never at a workplace with machinery. Relatively seldom do the publications show pictures of women maimed in accidents or those congenitally disabled, who – like their male counterparts – would have been equipped with highly technical prostheses. The female body was mostly only stabilized externally, with braces and simple devices. The photos and texts suggest that the intensive technical outfitting of the body and implantation of technology *into* the body was reserved for men only, because it was for them only that the enactment of labor and the staging of work ability was coupled with the technical enhancement of the body necessary to achieve it.

Therefore, let us turn briefly to the process by which masculinity and technology are linked and melded in the mechanized (technically enhanced) body. The notion that the implantation of technology could also have served as an aesthetic overlay for the physical abnormality could be considered a side-effect. It seems more important to me that through the mechanization of the body, a manipulation took place that must be interpreted as a symbolic remasculinization. For the reintegration of the war-disabled into the labor market, which was proclaimed to be male, could obviously not be declared a question of the will alone, but was also presented as a victory of technology over the dysfunctionality of the maimed body: thus, a male body is presented that is a part of the machine or indeed had become a machine, that was forced into wrought iron corsets and had to be formed according to the ideal of a working machine and 'reinvented'. The technical reconstruction of the male body had been an unrealized project of the eighteenth century,[48] and it seemed after the First World War that the scientific breakthrough had finally been achieved: now the real human body was a central object of the engineering sciences. The perfect imitation, the 'Sunday hand',[49] externally as realistic a reproduction of the human hand as possible, purely aesthetic but not suitable for work purposes, was not in demand, but rather the technical hand as a sign of usefulness: it was considered an effective technical instrument which not only covered up but also overcame the incapacities of the maimed body.

In modern technology, in technological development, new opportunities were seen for overcoming dismemberment and mortality, i.e. that fundamental instability of the human body which humans were only to be able to cope with using appropriate 'prostheses'. Linked to this notion were the fantasies and expectations of progress-oriented thinking, which could be demonstrated in a positive manner on the male body. At the same time the excrescence of omnipotent notions of feasibility became manifest, against which Sigmund Freud had warned in his 1930 essay *Civilization and its Discontents*. For the prosthesis as a technological masterpiece could also take over humans, occupy them and degrade them to the level of a generator, to nothing but a source of energy for the prosthesis itself.[50] Against the backdrop of variously formed body images, it becomes clear that competing body-experts from the areas of surgery and orthopedics propagated the technological equipping of the body on the one hand and on the other brought to bear arguments against any use of prostheses at all.[51] Technology-euphoria stood side by side with technology-critique, and parallel to an aggrandizement of technical devices, the specialists also promoted the simple wooden leg and archaic-looking 'work claw' as well. The shaping of the technically equipped disabled ex-combatant 'according to the model of the functional context of machines' can thus be understood as a precursor to the 'fascist path to modernity',[52] as Peter Sloterdijk has remarked. But the existence of the war-disabled man also led to a contemplation of the cost–benefit analysis of technology and to an exaltation of the prosthesis-free body, understood as somehow 'natural'.

Conclusion

The postwar discourse on war disability, technology and labor confirms the thesis of the war as a key location for the production of knowledge:

the medical and scientific discourse on war-disabled male bodies that began during the war proved to be productive; through it, body images defined as male and, furthermore, a consciousness of the male body was created, that is to say, an understanding of the demands this specific body and those who had it were required to fulfill.[53] In this case, knowledge was produced through the connection of masculinity and the body, understood to be 'biological'. In the process of measuring and optimizing work procedures, as in a Taylorian style of labor organization, norms of male work capacity were established and standardized. Technical engineers were engaged to tackle, among other things, problems with the economics of employing war-disabled men, which were linked to the question of how much of a body a man required for which level of work ability, and in what condition the male body had to be in order to be able to fulfill each different occupational demand.[54] Here new body norms were being established, which can also be read as statements about the male body from the perspective of modernity.[55]

In closing, I would like to point out the dialectic nature of the historical process of equipping the body with technology: the prosthesis was considered the technical instrument with which the war-disabled man could be reintegrated into the working world, which was imagined to be masculine. It was considered a sign of technical progress and was to reconfirm the man maimed in the war as a man who fulfilled modern industrial demands and labored at a machine. At the same time, it was the prosthesis itself as a part of technical innovation that dissolved masculinity in its traditional values and forms, for broad mechanization and differentiation of industrial labor routines reduced the body to individual functions. Complex procedures were divided up into effort-saving individual subroutines, whose execution, based on the technical conditions and the demands on physical strength, was no longer bound to a certain sex. Those war-disabled who were transferred to jobs that were considered appropriate to their remaining physical capabilities experienced work that they themselves perceived and devalued as 'women's work'. They protested against this because it did not correspond to their self-perception as 'men' and their expectations of their own physical competence, which they defined as male.[56] Their complaints about the monotony of the labor processes they defined as 'female' were for a time, shortly after the war, successful: they were transferred to jobs which, according to their wishes, were defined by the use of physical strength. It was already becoming clear, however, that the new methods of industrial production would bring more competition with female workers and that in the future, work at the machine would no longer be classifiable according to gender. Thus, war-disabled men became agents and at the same time victims of the mechanization of the 1920s: the promise of masculinization through the mechanization of the body led, on the contrary, to its dissolution – at least in the labor process.

Notes

Translated by Monique Scheer

1. See Joachim Radkau, *Das Zeitalter der Nervosität. Deutschland zwischen Bismarck und Hitler* (Munich/Vienna, 1998); Martin Lengwiler, 'Jenseits der "Schule der Männlichkeit". Hysterie in der deutschen Armee vor dem Ersten Weltkrieg,' in *Landsknechte, Soldatenfrauen und Nationalkrieger. Militär, Krieg und Geschlechterordnung im historischen Wandel*, ed. Karen Hagemann and Ralf Pröve (Frankfurt a.M./New York, 1998), 145–167; see also the classic by Klaus Theweleit, *Männerkörper. Zur Psychoanalyse des weißen Terrors, Männerphantasien*, vol. 2 (Munich, 1995).
2. See Bernd Ulrich, 'Krieg und Nerven – Skizzierung einer Beziehung,' in *Geschichte und Psychologie. Annäherungsversuche*, ed. Bedrich Loewenstein (Pfaffenweiler, 1992), 163–192.
3. Typification of images of soldiers at the level of popular media between 1870/71 and 1914/18 is dealt with by Jürgen Reulecke, 'Vom Kämpfer zum Krieger. Zur Visualisierung des Männerbildes während des Ersten Weltkrieges,' in *Medien, Kommunikation, Geschichte*, ed. Siegfried Quandt (Giessen, 1993), 158–175; he emphasizes more strongly, however, the advertising nature of such pictures, 173.
4. See the reconstruction of the myth of Verdun and the corresponding male images in Bernd Hüppauf, 'Schlachtenmythen und die Konstruktion des "Neuen Menschen",' in *Keiner fühlt sich hier mehr als Mensch [. . .] Erlebnis und Wirkung des Ersten Weltkriegs*, ed. Gerhard Hirschfeld, Gerd Krumeich and Irina Renz (Essen, 1993), 43–84; 62ff., 67.
5. See also Anja Seiffert, 'Männer – Soldaten – Krieger. Zur Männlichkeitskonstruktion im Frühwerk Ernst Jüngers,' *Widersprüche* 15 (1995): 129–143. In this study, she also assumes that, for the people of that time, the war had become 'a medium of renewal par excellence,

especially for the renewal of insecure manhood', 130. On Jünger as an 'apologist of the frenzied warrior' see also Eva Horn, 'Die Mobil-machung der Körper,' *Transit. Europäische Revue* 16 (1998/99): 92–107; 99.

6. George L. Mosse, *The Image of Man. The Creation of Modern Masc-ulinity* (Oxford, New York, 1996), 110ff. Mosse's approach remains fundamentally debatable regarding the extent to which his recon-struction of male stereotypes and his attempt to construct a fixed image of masculinity over many centuries is a worthwhile enterprise.

7. See Ernst Hanisch, 'Die Rückkehr des Kriegers. Männlichkeitsbilder und Remilitarisierung im Österreich der Zwischenkriegszeit,' *Transit. Europäische Revue* 16 (1998/99): 108–124; 110.

8. See also Jens Schmidt, *'Sich hart machen, wenn es gilt': Männlich-keitskonzeptionen in Illustrierten der Weimarer Republik* (Münster, 2000), which explores Weimar German conceptualizations and various representations of masculinity in three illustrated periodicals ranging on the political spectrum from the left (*Arbeiter-Illustrierte Zeitung*) to bourgeois and liberal (*Berliner Illustrierte Zeitung*) to national/conservative (*Deutsche Illustrierte*).

9. See Thomas Kühne, 'Männergeschichte als Geschlechtergeschichte,' in *Männergeschichte – Geschlechtergeschichte. Männlichkeit im Wandel der Moderne*, ed. Thomas Kühne (Frankfurt a.M./New York, 1996), 7–30; 18ff. For a classic social history of the German war victims and their political self-organization see Robert W. Whalen, *Bitter Wounds: German Victims of the Great War, 1914 – 1939* (Ithaca/New York, 1984). On the representation of the disabled veteran and the evolution of public policy towards war victims in different societ-ies (Europe, Russia, United States and Canada) throughout differing centuries of war experience see the volume *Disabled Veterans in History*, ed. David A. Gerber (Ann Arbor, 2000).

10. See for example Paul Lerner, '"Ein Sieg deutschen Willens": Wille und Gemeinschaft in der deutschen Kriegspsychiatrie,' in *Die Medizin und der Erste Weltkrieg*, ed. Wolfgang U. Eckart and Christoph Gradmann (Pfaffenweiler, 1996), 85–108; Elisabeth Malleier, 'Formen männlicher Hysterie. Die Kriegsneurosen im Ersten Weltkrieg,' in *Körper–Geschlecht–Geschichte: Historische und aktuelle Debatten in der Medizin,* ed. Elisabeth Mixa et al. (Innsbruck/Vienna, 1996), 147–163; Georg Hofer, 'Nerven-Korrekturen. Ärzte, Soldaten und die "Kriegsneurosen" im Ersten Weltkrieg,' *zeitgeschichte* 4 (2000): 249–268. For the British war experience in the First World War and the symbolic reconstruction of the wounded soldier's masculinity see

Sabine Kienitz

Seth Koven, 'Remembering and Dismemberment: Crippled Children, Wounded Soldiers, and the Great War in Great Britain,' *American Historical Review* 99 (1994): 1167–1202. On the experience of destruction of the male body in the First World War and the consequences for the social and medical reconstructing of masculinity in Great Britain see Joanna Bourke, *Dismembering the Male. Men's Bodies, Britain and the Great War* (London, 1996). [11]See on this point also the article by Birthe Kundrus in this volume.

12. See Ulrike Baureithel, '"Kollektivneurose moderner Männer". Die Neue Sachlichkeit als Symptom des männlichen Identitätsverlusts – sozialpsychologische Aspekte einer literarischen Strömung,' *Germanica* 9 (1991): 123–143, 127–129; id., 'Masken der Virilität. Kulturtheoretische Strategien zur Überwindung des männlichen Identitätsverlustes im ersten Drittel des 20. Jahrhunderts,' *Die Philosophin* 8 (1993): 24–35.

13. Gabriele Mentges, 'Cold, Coldness, Coolness: Remarks on the Relationship of Dress, Body and Technology,' *Fashion Theory* 4 (2000): 27–48.

14. See also the article by Stefanie Schüler-Springorum in this volume.

15. See Mentges, *Coolness*, 29f. On the connection of modern aesthetics and images of modern heroes see also Modris Eksteins, *Tanz über Gräben. Die Geburt der Moderne und der Erste Weltkrieg* (Hamburg, 1990), 395–405.

16. See Alexander Meschnig, 'Die Stahlnatur. Vom Gesicht zur Maske,' *Medium Gesicht. Die faciale Gesellschaft, Ästhetik und Kommunikation* 25 (1996): 89–96.

17. On the normative construction of traditional military masculinity in the nineteenth and twentieth centuries see Ute Frevert, 'Das Militär als "Schule der Männlichkeit". Erwartungen, Angebote, Erfahrungen im 19. Jahrhundert,' in *Militär und Gesellschaft*, ed. Ute Frevert (Stuttgart, 1997), 145–173; Sabina Brändli, 'Von "schneidigen Offizieren" und "Militärcrinolinen": Aspekte symbolischer Männlichkeit am Beispiel preußischer und schweizerischer Uniformen des 19. Jahrhunderts,' in id., 201–228; Marianne Rychner and Kathrin Däniker, 'Unter "Männern". Geschlechtliche Zuschreibungen in der Schweizer Armee zwischen 1870 und 1914,' in *weiblich – männlich. Geschlechterverhältnisse in der Schweiz: Rechtsprechung, Diskurs, Praktiken*, ed. Rudolf Jaun and Brigitte Studer (Zurich, 1995), 159–170.

18. The description of the experience of injury and the physical dismemberment of comrades is one of the key scenes in many autobiographical texts by German combatants in the First World War with

which they could express their disillusionment and skepticism of the purposes of war.

19. See the critique in Kathleen Canning, 'Feminist History after the Linguistic Turn: Historicising Discourse and Experience,' *Signs* 19 (1994): 368–404; id., 'The Body as Method? Reflections on the Place of the Body in Gender History,' *Gender & History* 11 (1999): 499–513.

20. On a gender history that demands a denaturalization of the male body, see Eve Rosenhaft, 'Zwei Geschlechter – eine Geschichte? Frauengeschichte, Männergeschichte, Geschlechtergeschichte und ihre Folgen für die Geschichtswahrnehmung,' in *Was sind Frauen? Was sind Männer? Geschlechterkonstruktionen im historischen Wandel*, ed. Christiane Eifert et al. (Frankfurt a.M., 1996), 257–274.

21. See Ute Frevert, 'Männergeschichte oder die Suche nach dem "ersten" Geschlecht,' in *Was ist Gesellschaftsgeschichte? Positionen, Themen, Analysen*, ed. Manfred Hettling et al. (Munich, 1991), 31–43, 42.

22. See John Tosh, 'Was soll die Geschichtswissenschaft mit Männlichkeit anfangen? Betrachtungen zum 19. Jahrhundert in Großbritannien,' in *Kultur & Geschichte. Neue Einblicke in eine alte Beziehung*, ed. Christoph Conrad and Martina Kessel (Stuttgart, 1998), 160–206; 180, 196.

23. See, for example, Aleida Assmann, 'Externalisierung, Internalisierung und Kulturelles Gedächtnis,' in *Die Objektivität der Ordnungen und ihre kommunikative Konstruktion*, ed. Walter M. Sprondel (Frankfurt a.M., 1994), 422–435.

24. Sabina Brändli emphasizes in particular the significance of 'textile armor', the uniform, and its effects on posture, which can be used to produce the illusion of a collective masculinization in the military. See Brändli, 'Von "schneidigen Offizieren",' 222, 227.

25. See Gesa Lindemann, 'Wider die Verdrängung des Leibes aus der Geschlechtskonstruktion,' *Feministische Studien* 11(1993): 44–54; id., 'Zeichentheoretische Überlegungen zum Verhältnis von Körper und Leib,' in *Identität, Leiblichkeit, Normativität: Neue Horizonte anthropologischen Denkens*, ed. Annette Barkhaus (Frankfurt a.M., 1996), 146–175; Stefan Hirschauer, *Die soziale Konstruktion der Transsexualität. Über die Medizin und den Geschlechtswechsel* (Frankfurt a.M., 1993).

26. Judith Butler, cited in Petra Küchler, *Zur Konstruktion von Weiblichkeit: Erklärungsansätze zur Geschlechterdifferenz im Licht der Auseinandersetzung um die Kategorie Geschlecht* (Pfaffenweiler, 1997), 68 (n. 1).

27. See Hermann Ulrich Asemissen, 'Helmuth Plessner: Die exzentrische Position des Menschen,' in *Grundprobleme der großen Philosophen*, ed. Josef Speck (Göttingen, 1973), 146–180; 173–175.

28. On the problem of the significance of the body for the social construction of reality, see Stefan Hirschauer, 'Wie sind Frauen, wie sind Männer?,' in *Was sind Frauen? Was sind Männer? Geschlechterkonstruktionen im historischen Wandel*, ed. Christiane Eifert et al. (Frankfurt a.M., 1996) 240–256; 249.

29. See Robert W. Connell, *Masculinities. Knowledge, Power and Social Change* (Berkeley/Los Angeles, 1995), 50ff.

30. See ibid., 61.

31. See the following essays in Claudia Schmölders and Sander Gilman, eds., *Gesichter der Weimarer Republik. Eine physiognomische Kulturgeschichte* (Cologne, 2000): Michael Hagner, 'Verwundete Gesichter, verletzte Gehirne. Zur Deformation des Kopfes im Ersten Weltkrieg,' 78–95; Sander L. Gilman, 'Das Gesicht wahren. Zur ästhetischen Chirurgie,' 96–112; Maria Tatar, 'Entstellung im Vollzug. Das Gesicht des Krieges in der Malerei,' 113–130. For France see Sophie Delaporte, *Les gueules cassées. Les blessés de la face de la Grande Guerre* (Paris, 1996).

32. See Sabine Kienitz, 'Die Kastrierten des Krieges. Körperbilder und Männlichkeitskonstruktionen im und nach dem Ersten Weltkrieg,' *Zeitschrift für Volkskunde* 95 (1999): 63–82.

33. See the report on the 'Handfertigkeitsunterricht in den Lazaretten des württembergischen Landesvereins vom Roten Kreuz' Hauptstaatsarchiv Stuttgart M 1/8, Bü 83, fasz. 214; and the monthly reports in the *Mitteilungen des Roten Kreuzes*.

34. 'Ziele der Verwundetenfürsorge,' *Die Hilfe* 27, 6 July 1916, in Bundesarchiv Berlin R 8034 II–2323 Reichslandbund-Pressearchiv: Kriegsbeschädigtenfürsorge in Deutschland, Oktober 1915–Juni 1917.

35. Heinrich Zwiesele, *Ein Gang durch die Lazarettwerkstätten der Abt. XXIb 'württembergisches Rotes Kreuz'* (Stuttgart, 1917), 32.

36. Hans Würtz, 'Dein Wille!,' in *Unsern Kriegsbeschädigten* (Potsdam, n.d.), 7. Würtz was employed as 'educational director' (*Erziehungsdirektor*) at the Oskar-Helene-Heim for Crippled Children in Berlin, where a ward for the rehabilitation of war-disabled servicemen was made available from 1914 on.

37. See Konrad Biesalski, ed., *Kriegskrüppelfürsorge. Ein Aufklärungswort zum Troste und zur Mahnung* (Leipzig/Hamburg, 1915), 34. Biesalski was the director of the Oskar-Helene-Heim and played a key role in organized war disability welfare in Germany; see also

Klaus-Dieter Thomann, 'Der "Krüppel": Entstehen und Verschwinden eines Kampfbegriffs,' *Medizinhistorisches Journal* 27 (1992): 221–271.

38. See Michael Geyer, 'Ein Vorbote des Wohlfahrtsstaates. Die Kriegsopferversorgung in Frankreich, Deutschland und Großbritannien nach dem Ersten Weltkrieg,' *Geschichte und Gesellschaft* 9 (1983): 230–277.

39. See Rainer Gensch, 'Der Körper als Werkzeug – der Körper als Werkstück: Die Professionalisierung der Beziehungen von Körper und Arbeit,' in *Der Mensch und sein Körper. Von der Antike bis heute,* ed. Artur E. Imhof (Munich, 1983), 243–262, 257f.

40. See the many reports in *Vorwärts* in the year 1920/21 on dealings with inmates of a military hospital in Berlin who attempted to evade this self-contained system of 'safekeeping'. Whoever refused to cooperate with the educational system could expect to be excluded from all therapeutic measures they were legally entitled to. Military drill was deemed necessary to discipline the war-disabled in the sick bay workshops in order to keep them from drifting off into idleness, which was seen as socially detrimental.

41. Josef Rey, 'Grenzgebiete ärztlicher Kunst,' *Zeitschrift für Krüppelfürsorge* 16 (1923): 40–42; 42.

42. On willpower and its connotation as masculine see Mosse, *Image*, 100. On the construction of the will in the psychiatry debate see also Lerner, '"Sieg deutschen Willens".' On the propagandistic term of the 'iron will to work' as a challenging moral concept in the German Weimar Republic see Deborah Cohen, *The War Come Home. Disabled Veterans in Britain and Germany, 1914–1939* (Berkeley/Los Angeles/London, 2001).

43. Parallel to the propagandizing use of photos, films and demonstrations in the context of exhibitions on war disability welfare there was an intensive debate over virtuoso 'prosthesis artists', presented as ideals, as well as over the photographs, whose value as evidence was doubted, since it said nothing about the competitive and concrete work ability of the prosthesis wearers. See for example the article 'Filmzauber,' *Der Kriegsbeschädigte* 7, 16 February 1918.

44. See Martina Kessel, 'Balance der Gefühle. Langeweile im 19. Jahrhundert,' *Historische Anthropologie* 4 (1996): 234–255; 238, 243.

45. On labor market policy see also Karin Hausen, 'Die Sorge der Nation für ihre "Kriegsopfer". Ein Bereich der Geschlechterpolitik während der Weimarer Republik,' in *Von der Arbeiterbewegung zum modernen Sozialstaat,* ed. Jürgen Kocka (Munich, 1994), 719–739; 722ff;

Gunter Mai, 'Arbeitsmarktregulierung oder Sozialpolitik?' in *Die Anpassung an die Inflation*, ed. Gerald D. Feldman et al., Veröffentlichungen der Historischen Kommission zu Berlin, vol. 67 (Berlin/ New York, 1986), 202–236.

46. On the ritualized enactment of labor see Christoph Wulf, 'Geste und Ritual der Arbeit,' in *KörperDenken. Aufgaben der Historischen Anthropologie*, ed. Fritjof Hager (Berlin, 1996), 153–163.

47. On the restructuring of the labor market and the hierarchical organization of the right to gainful employment, see Susanne Rouette, *Sozialpolitik als Geschlechterpolitik. Die Regulierung der Frauenarbeit nach dem Ersten Weltkrieg* (Frankfurt a.M./New York, 1993), 251ff.

48. See for example Horst Bredekamp, *Antikensehnsucht und Maschinenglauben. Die Geschichte der Kunstkammer und die Zukunft der Kunstgeschichte* (Berlin, 2000).

49. See the historical presentation by Lieselotte Kugler, '"Arbeitshand" oder "Sonntagshand"? Zur Frage der technischen Wiederherstellung durch künstliche Glieder,' in *'Als der Krieg über uns gekommen war. . .', Die Saarregion und der Erste Weltkrieg* (Saarbrücken, 1993), 239–247.

50. See also Marie-Anne Berr, *Technik und Körper* (Berlin, 1990).

51. See the pioneering work of the surgeon Hermann Krukenberg, *Über plastische Umwertung von Armamputationsstümpfen* (Stuttgart, 1917).

52. See Peter Sloterdijk, *Kritik der zynischen Vernunft*, vol. 1 (Frankfurt a.M., 1983) 791–814; quote from 805.

53. On the historical context and development of a science of labor that dealt with the questions of how far workers could be burdened, see Anson Rabinbach, *The Human Motor: Energy, Fatigue, and the Origins of Modernity* (Berkeley/Los Angeles, 1992); Philipp Sarasin, 'Die Rationalisierung des Körpers. Über "Scientific Management" und "biologische Rationalisierung",' in *Obsessionen. Beherrschende Gedanken im wissenschaftlichen Zeitalter*, ed. Michael Jeismann (Frankfurt a.M., 1995), 78–115.

54. See for example Oberingenieur Beckmann, 'Amputierte und Schwerverletzte in der Industrie,' in *Ersatzglieder und Arbeitshilfen für Kriegsbeschädigte und Unfallverletzte*, ed. Moritz Borchardt et al. (Berlin, 1919), 995–1011; Felix Krais, *Die Verwendungsmöglichkeiten der Kriegsbeschädigten in der Industrie, in Gewerbe, Handel, Handwerk* (Stuttgart, 1916).

55. See Andrea Bührmann, 'Die Normalisierung der Geschlechter in Geschlechterdispositiven,' in *Das Geschlecht der Moderne. Genealogie und Archäologie der Geschlechterdifferenz*, ed. Hannelore Bublitz (Frankfurt a.M./New York, 1998), 71–94; 83f.
56. See Hans Fritz Ziegler, *Die Leistungen kriegsverletzter Industriearbeiter und Vorschläge zur Kriegsbeschädigtenfürsorge* (Düsseldorf, 1919), 120ff.

–8–

Flying and Killing

Military Masculinity in German Pilot Literature, 1914–1939

Stefanie Schüler-Springorum

When during the Kosovo War German pilots flew combat missions for the first time since 1945, the local popular press celebrated its fresh, still anonymous 'heroes'. The journalists immediately placed them in the 'ancestral line of German combat pilots', thus drawing an unbroken line of tradition from the First World War to the skies over Belgrade.[1] The image of the combat pilot as a masculine ideal and role model, as the incarnation of the technically skilled fighter, or as a member of a select elite still fascinates broad circles to this very day, and not only in times of war. One look at the catalogues of specialized publishers and used book dealers, or at films, comics and computer games will verify this.[2] However, this essay does not deal with the longevity of this phenomenon, but rather with its genesis and development in Germany between the First and Second World Wars. This period saw the publication of innumerable texts belonging to different genres that generally fall under the category of 'pilot literature'. In addition to novels, this literature consists of biographies, biographical notes, and autobiographies, as well as anthologies of newspaper articles, letters, and diary excerpts published partly by the pilots and their relatives and partly by journalists and authors for a predominantly middle-class public.[3] In these texts, the line between fiction and non-fiction is not as clear as the character of the respective publication might suggest. The novels suggest authenticity through the use of the first person and other stylistic devices. However, letters and diaries were not only subject to censorship and conventions of self-representation but in addition were often revised by relatives prior to publication. Therefore, they clearly are of limited quality as a historical source, at least as far as the reconstruction of the immediate war experience is concerned.[4] If, however, the focus is on the mechanisms underlying the original construction of the image of 'the pilot' persisting until today and on how flying and air warfare were popularized from 1914 to 1939, then pilot literature as a category in its own right deserves detailed analysis. The fact that this literature as well as the cult surrounding the World War Aces met with a considerable response, at least from the male part of the German population, is verified by the extraordinarily high print runs of the most well-known books, sometimes soaring to several hundred thousand during the First World War. Manfred von Richthofen's autobiography *Der Rote Kampfflieger* (The Red Combat Pilot) alone sold over half a million copies by 1920. In 1933 a new edition of 700,000 copies was released. Ernst Udet, Richthofen's 'squadron comrade', at this time published the first edition of his second autobiography, printing 350,000 copies. Of the six best-selling German war books, three dealt with the pilot milieu, a remarkable finding given the secondary role that the air force played from a military point of view during the First World War.[5]

As for historical research, only Peter Fritzsche has dealt with the enthusiasm for flying between the two World Wars and its significance for the development of German nationalism, but without paying too much attention to the gender-specific aspects of this phenomenon.[6] The male and female historians who dealt with the relationship between war experience and masculinity during the First World War mostly focused on the 'simple front-line soldier' and not the pilot, who was almost always an officer. This was due in great part to the relatively minor role of the air force mentioned above.[7] The emphasis of this study does not lie on the war experiences of these pilots neglected thus far by research, but rather on discovering what images portraying flying and mainly aerial combat arise in popular literature. Moreover, I wish to explore what, possibly contradictory, masculinity constructs are presented and in what way gender relationships – between men and between men and women – are portrayed or undergo transformation. The construction of the pilot hero over the course of time is the center of my analysis. For this purpose, I shall examine pilot literature in the chronological order of publication to identify transformations, shifts in emphasis, and new interpretations.

The Dream of Flying, 1914–1916

All peaceful and warlike fantasies about aviation during the pre-war period mainly concentrated on the Zeppelin,[8] while aeroplanes and their crews initially only played a minor role in the perception of war in Germany. Nevertheless the fascination with the new technology continued and soon a number of books and anthologies on air warfare were published. In the first two war years, these works were predominantly written by journalists and some by the pilots themselves. The works reflect the fact that this kind of literature constituted an absolute novelty for the authors, who are looking for ways to adequately describe 'aerial warfare in its horrific beauty'.[9] Thus, they first feel obliged to present their readers with a detailed description of this strange means of transportation and its war potential. Depending on the authors' political perspective, they associate the new weapon either with hope for a glorious victory or a longing for peace. Several authors, for example, stated with a sense of relief that their own aviation was able to compete with that of other nations despite the well-known 'German plumpness'. Others, such as the editor of the *Jahrbuch der Luftfahrt* (Year Book of Aviation), were already a step further in their considerations: 'Through aircraft the horrible effects [of war] reach monstrous proportions, and peace among people is bound to follow this exaggerated form of armament and warfare.'[10]

In the early anthologies, such general explanations were followed by brief or extensive accounts, mostly taken from newspapers or letters from soldiers on the front. Here, extensive coverage is given to the horrors of aerial warfare for those on the ground and to their fears. Time and again the consequences of bombardments, by friends or foes, are described in drastic terms. Despite an occasionally triumphant tone, the descriptions of the horrors prevail. A German soldier who observed a French attack on a city occupied by the German army is quoted in the following words: 'A young lady was soaked in her own blood. Her right thigh and abdomen were torn to pieces. I almost began to sob. In such moments even the roughest man would go soft.'[11]

The demise of the pilots themselves is described in these books in no less vivid terms. They go to their death 'torn to pieces, burned, killed by bullets, and blown apart by bombs and grenades'.[12] But since aeroplanes were primarily used for relatively safe reconnaissance missions during the first two years of war, such accounts are infrequent. In the rare event that combat actually took place in the air, the reporter preferred to describe events from a ground perspective: 'In the streets life was paralyzed. Troops, infantry, artillery, cavalry, everyone (even some women in their petticoats) stood in the streets immobilized, staring up at the sky in turmoil.' This soldier's description of an air duel on the western front appeared in the *Magdeburger Central-Anzeiger* in 1915.[13] The true 'aviatic adventures' occurred on the ground. Such promising headlines as 'Flying Adventure over Enemy Territory' or 'A Small Daring Escapade' announce exciting stories about crafty, yet generally anonymous pilots who defend themselves against hostile peasants after an emergency landing and cunningly save themselves behind their own lines.[14] One of the most popular pilot books of the First World War, Erich Killinger's *Die Aben-teuer des Ostseefliegers* (The Adventures of the Baltic Sea Pilot), follows this pattern when describing the odyssey of the first-person narrator on his way home to Russia via the United States, after having crashed on a reconnaissance mission in the Baltic region.[15]

By contrast, the dangers confronted in the air only consisted of storm, snow and darkness. If these do not crop up, the pilots have time to intoxicate themselves on the 'magic of flying never before experienced', and on the 'gruesomely exalted feeling' they sensed at the unfamiliar sight of battlefields, or at the sight of 'God's beautiful nature'.[16] The war takes on a new, less threatening dimension from this perspective, as we see in the following account by an English pilot: 'Everything looks so queer and peculiar because one can see the story on both sides of the battlefield, while those down below in most cases cannot even see what they are shooting at.'[17]

Moreover, it is striking that particularly the authors of the few lengthy autobiographical pilot accounts written during the first two years of war refrain from any kind of emotive portrayals. Flying is first and foremost 'beautiful' and 'not so difficult that it could not be learned'. It has little to do with war. The worst that can happen is that a flight through inclement weather might cause stomach upset. And should a pilot be forced to return to the infantry 'due to heart trouble', he does not take it as a personal defeat or failure, but simply feels he has had an enriching experience.[18]

The Knights of the Air, 1916–1918

All of these characteristics, the ground perspective, the depiction of the horrors of war, the sobriety and anonymity of the protagonists, disappear from pilot literature as of 1916. The initial reason for this is of a technical nature. Due to the use of new, one-seater planes, aerial warfare underwent a fundamental transformation during the course of 1915. Until then the planes had been flown by two pilots who occasionally shot at the enemy with pistols or dropped bombs. However, their primary concern was to stay out of the enemy's way, in the air as on the ground. The new planes were equipped with machine guns operated by the pilot himself which made real 'man to man' air combat possible.[19] Thus, the pilot hero was born, characterized above all by his individuality and the distinctiveness of his actions in the theater of war. Although the heyday of German aerial warfare essentially only lasted a few years and the period of actual 'pilot against pilot' fighting was even shorter (see below), a mass following developed around 'aces' like Max Immelmann, Oswald Boelcke, and Manfred von Richthofen within a very short time and with media attention reminiscent of modern film stars.[20] As a result of this, the anthologies so popular at the beginning ceased to appear, replaced by almost sacral (auto)biographies, correspondence, and diaries focusing on the personalities and actions of individual pilots.

In their portrayals, the authors drew on familiar models. They made an effort to illuminate the extraordinary qualities, the particular talent of the respective hero, placing him within the context of the classical middle-class biography, with his talents evident in early childhood and his budding interest developing in adolescence. In line with this pattern, almost all of the future 'aces' began to show a technical interest at a very early age. They often were excellent sportsmen with a preference for everything that took them 'to high places': Boelcke's father reports that his son had been an enthusiastic mountain climber from an early age. Erwin Böhme traces his own talent for flying back to ski-jumping practiced in his youth. A rumor had it that Max Immelmann had a key experience as a four-year-old during a summer vacation in the Alps and later was a friend of all physical activity. Even his name Immelmann (= bee man) was viewed as an indication of his future means of locomotion. While the technically inclined boy at first concentrated his passion on motorcycling, he later studied mechanical engineering before turning to aviation. Heinrich Gontermann, according to his grandfather, had inherited 'a disposition for everything industrial'. And Ernst Udet, who began the war as a cyclist, writes in his autobiography that his childhood revolved around model aeroplanes, ski-jumping, and gliding. Even when such biographical details were missing due to the scarcity of information, an apprenticeship as a roofer working at dizzying heights was used to make a future career as a pilot plausible.[21] All of the future flying heroes were mediocre pupils at school, which, according to Immelmann's biographer, proved that 'bad students often become men of great importance in life.'[22]

Only the last point is reflected in Manfred von Richthofen's autobiography, in which he relates having developed an interest neither in technology nor in flying. His account begins in 1917 when as an officer cadet in the cavalry he was admitted to the army. Instead of talking about his childhood, he includes a lengthy description of his various horses, and only in a later edition did his younger brother add some details about his family origin and tradition.[23] While other 'great pilots' allegedly enjoyed the speed and freedom of movement in the new element (Immelmann

thought it was almost as beautiful as driving a car, only without policemen) or brooded on 'a peculiar combination of feelings' evoked by flying,
Richthofen simply stated that flying was a 'damned thrill'.[24] For him, the
aristocrat, his war activities as a pilot were part of a clearly different
tradition: that of hunting. 'There is nothing more wonderful for a young
cavalry officer than to go hunting in the air.'[25] As the cult surrounding
Richthofen only reached its climax later, statements about his personality
or even his looks by his contemporaries are rare. His 'conqueror', the
Canadian Roy Brown, is said to have been in shock at the sight of the
'small, fragile' body of the dead pilot whose 'blond child-like hair soft as
silk [. . .] fell from his high wide forehead'. Richthofen's squadron
comrade Erwin Böhme described him as 'someone free of conceit, aristocratic but at the same time an absolutely natural person'. This judgement,
at least from a contemporary point of view, is somewhat surprising
considering the burning ambition that pervades Richthofen's autobiography, which is only thinly veiled by an artificial self-irony.[26] Most likely,
it soon became important to stress the 'modesty' of the pilot due to the
extensive use of the boastful pilot lingo. Ultimately the quality of modesty
is attributed to every hero without exception.[27] Indeed this tendency does
not seem completely arbitrary, at least with regard to those pilots who
wrote personal accounts. The wartime accounts and diaries of Immelmann, Boelcke, and Gontermann are in fact partly written in a sober,
sometimes even boring style. They repeatedly and explicitly opposed the
glorifying, 'invented, exaggerated, and false' reports in the press as well
as the commercialization of their military success by their own families.
Yet, in neither endeavor were they particularly successful.[28] On the other
hand, a discrepancy between the public figure and the private person
emerged when journalists remarked with some surprise that the 'great
Immelmann' did not at all seem like a '"hero" with a stern, energetic face'
but in reality was 'an amiable young man' and a 'reserved soldier with
large, calm eyes'.[29] Boelcke, too, won over domestic and foreign corres-
pondents with his 'soft voice', his 'charming nature', and 'grayish blue
eyes whose friendly expression eased the work of the interviewer'. In
addition, the members of his squadron commended and admired the
'maturity and serenity' of the 25-year-old who, according to his biggest
competitor Immelmann, was an 'extremely calm and level-headed person
with sensible opinions'.[30] Only the description by Boelcke's father cor-
roborates the hero cliché. He wanted his son to be remembered as a
'staunch man of action'. This ran contrary to the portrayal by Heinrich
Gontermann's grandfather, who relentlessly praised the 'tender and sensitive nature' of his grandson killed in action.[31] He also recalled that his

grandson preferred milk to alcohol, did not smoke, and went to bed early. These were qualities he shared with Max Immelmann, who was in addition a vegetarian, which caused him quite a few problems while he was a soldier.[32] Considering that a similarly ascetic behavior was also attributed to Boelcke and above all to Richthofen, the question arises as to what sources fed the common picture of the luxurious lifestyle of the pilots. All reports published during the war gave more or less detailed accounts of the lavish living conditions of the squadrons. They were accommodated on estates, in 'quaint, small villas', and little palaces. They always looked elegant and well groomed, overcoming their boredom, frequent during their leisure time, with a game of tennis or an outing to a lake. The pilots also enjoyed a certain freedom of movement through the motorcars generously put at their disposal, as well as through the aeroplanes themselves that were used from time to time for 'cheeky flying escapades', i.e. private visits that surely did not fail to impress. In view of the contrast to life in the trenches, it is hardly surprising that the rumor of a 'life in laziness and luxury' led by the pilots spread quickly, a lifestyle that did not at all conform to the one attributed to individual protagonists.[33]

Both the exuberant and ascetic qualities seem to substantiate a certain egocentricity of the pilots, additionally fuelled by numerous stories about their superstitious customs and rituals. However, this notion was ultimately based on the image of the single fighter, the individualist as reflected in the early personal accounts that were all 'ego documents' in the true sense of the word. The protagonists time and again write almost exclusively about their own actions and thoughts; relationships with other squadron members or even in the group as a whole rarely occur. The authors do occasionally mention that they flew with a few 'gentlemen', yet these are rarely referred to by name (mostly in the event of death). According to the autobiographies, close relationships between men only seem to have existed among reconnaissance pilots who flew in pairs. They called their relationship a 'pilot marriage' and addressed each other with standardized nicknames. 'Franz' was the observer and 'Emil' the pilot. It is always stressed how important a good relationship was for a harmonious 'pilot marriage'. There are also negative examples: for instance when Manfred von Richthofen's early 'marriage' was strained because he and his 'Emil' accused each other of bad flying and shooting. Often, brothers liked to take on these duties as partners because they could be sure, as Boelcke put it, that 'one could rely on the other as he would rely on himself'.[34] Only Ernst Udet and Heinrich Gontermann write about relationships with other men that were not tied to a certain function. It was the latter who emphasized time and again how important 'his best friend'

Hans Hermann von Budde was to him, 'whose picture is always in front of me'. 'Hopefully we shall always remain friends,' he wrote shortly after they had met. After bringing him into his squadron, he noted: 'A lovely friendship between men is something ever so beautiful.'[35]

Relationships with women are discussed even more rarely, which does not mean that they did not exist. Immelmann complained about the '30 to 40 letters and postcards per day' received from 'certainly very [. . .] sensitive young ladies' who presented him with 'rosaries, crosses, and other talismans'. 'Should I really wear this leaf?' he asked his mother shortly before his death. 'If I did that with every good-luck flower and every four-leaf clover, I would constantly be carrying a small vegetable garden around with me.'[36] Gontermann referred to the subject of love in a letter to a 'motherly friend' in a more serious, albeit remote, manner. According to him, love was 'the lodestar illuminating the path leading to everything that is good'. Actual love relationships, if they existed, did not seem to conform to the image of the 'pilot hero' at this time. The 'deliciously tender and yet so masculine letters' of the combat pilot Erwin Böhme 'to a young girl who was to become his sweetheart and bride' were withheld from the interested public until 1930.[37]

The only women always present in the books published between 1916 and 1918 are the mothers of the pilots, whose sole purpose is to be the passive recipients of their sons' accounts and letters. Immelmann, like many other pilots, endeavored 'to at least let mother partake of all the beauty he experienced through his long accounts'.[38] He frequently sent letters home, as did Boelcke, Gontermann and the Richthofen brothers. Immelmann, who grew up without a father, seems to have had a particularly close relationship with his mother with whom he enjoyed appearing in public. 'Soon a sense of community was established between Max and Mother, who could not have wished for anything better', his brother recalled later. 'Mother had to take part in everything Max did!'[39]

In view of the fact that the original recipients were close relatives, it is hardly surprising that in most of these published personal accounts, particularly in letters, the pilots only rarely wrote about their own mortal fears. While Boelcke sought to reassure himself and his parents by pointing out his 'vast experience' and 'other technical skills in flying and shooting', Gontermann emphasized time and again that he was really being 'very, very careful'. Immelmann, in contrast, joked: 'A crash from an altitude of 500 meters takes ten seconds, so you have time enough to sing "Heil dir im Siegerkranz" [Hail to you in the victor's laurel] or to exclaim "Long live his Majesty"'. Udet also tried to be humorous, although he often mentioned his anxiety, while Richthofen apparently had to conquer his weaker self only once when flying alone for the first time.[40] Yet death is indirectly present in their writing, for instance when the pilots write about squadron comrades screaming at night or the 'nervous shocks' suffered by other pilots. At the same time it is remarkable that the German pilots almost always met their deaths 'unconquered', namely through an accident or by 'treacherous fate', and allegedly remained physically unscathed (with the exception of a 'clean shot to the heart or the head'). This, however, was simply impossible in a crash from an altitude of 4,000 meters.[41] Only Gontermann, a man of faith, explicitly reflected upon his own proximity to death in his letters and diaries and also shared these thoughts with others, if Udet's recollections are to be believed:

> You have the feeling, though, as if you were standing next to the thread on which your life hangs, with a pair of scissors in your hand. One tremble of your hand and the thread is cut that otherwise would have held. That is how you have your life in your hands up there. A wonderful feeling for the courageous, but a diabolical one for the anxious. My body is in my hands, my soul in the hands of God![42]

Nevertheless, such philosophical reflections are the exception in these accounts. The emphasis lies on the pilot's own actions and in this case on the air battles described again and again. Since a three-dimensional, rapidly occurring event is very difficult to put into words, many authors – besides presenting rather sober technical explanations – tend to resort to familiar metaphors taken from the world of animals and hunting. They 'go hunting', hoping for good fortune. 'Here on the Somme we are in a real pilot's Eldorado', Boelcke wrote to a friend in 1916. 'In reasonably good weather the sky is full of Englishmen, although there are a lot less now.'[43] But despite poetical paraphrasing, the emphasis lay on the killing of the enemy, a fact perceived differently by the various pilots. After his first air battle, Udet was expressly happy that they had not hit one another and that it was possible to fly home 'contentedly'. Shortly thereafter, however, following his first 'victory', he could have 'shouted out with pride and joy'.[44] Others such as Hans Joachim Buddecke or Heinrich Gontermann tried to force their adversaries to the ground without killing them. Yet if the adversary did end up going down, the victor regularly justified himself before his parents by stating: 'I hoped he would land smoothly [. . .] one always regrets this, but I had to do it, he simply defended himself too well.' For him war ultimately was a 'cruel occupation' and the sight of his dead adversaries made a deep impression on him every time. Buddecke, on the other hand, expressly avoided looking at his victims so as not to burden himself with 'impressions that would stay with him his whole life'.[45] Such scruples seem to have been completely unknown to other pilots. Manfred von Richthofen, who strove to become the best combat pilot from the start, remembered first and foremost 'the lovely times' when he had 'great fun' and always went on his sorties in the 'best of moods'. Besides his pronounced cheerfulness, from time to time he patronizingly expressed 'human compassion' for his defeated adversary, characterizing himself as relatively moderate compared to his brother Lothar who was occasionally seized by a real killing frenzy:

> When I have shot down an Englishman, my hunting passion is satisfied for the next quarter of an hour. That means I am not capable of shooting down two Englishmen in immediate succession. When one of them goes down, I sense an absolute feeling of satisfaction. [. . .] With my brother things were different [. . .] All he did was turn his machine gun away from the first target, point it at the second, and continue shooting immediately.[46]

Even if the scruples were of differing nature or at least articulated differently, the texts make it clear that all the pilots sooner or later came under the spell of this supposed 'sportsmanship'; they competed to bring down the most planes and remembered their victories in sporting terms ('my first Englishman', 'the first double'). Since decorations were awarded according to the number of victories, a veritable competition arose, with 'objectively' measurable competitive criteria, unlike other forms of warfare. This ultimately led to the practice – as Boelcke reports – of shooting down obviously defenseless or already defeated adversaries in an attempt to set planes ablaze, if possible while they were still in the air.[47] This sort of behavior in numerous pilots, as well as the introduction of combat squadrons operating on the offensive, and the unscrupulous treatment of inexperienced squadron members obliged to give cover to the 'aces' who sought to shoot down as many planes as possible were actions that all strongly contradicted the myth of the 'chivalry' of air combat.[48] Chivalrous behavior would have included 'one on one' combat between equally armed opponents and meant turning away from an enemy obviously incapable of fighting. Moreover, it would have implied that the pilots show respect for the enemy's dead, and last but not least demanded courteous treatment of the defeated enemy whom officers liked to invite to their own casino, if he was in an appropriate condition.

Examples of such chivalrous behavior can be found in abundance in the accounts, letters, and diaries.[49] They connect the different characters and narrative styles, thus forming the core of the early image of the pilot hero. This image only rudimentarily reflected reality even at the time of its genesis, which, however, did nothing to harm its astounding resilience over the decades to come.

The Soldier Pilot Hero, 1929–1933

In the years of the Weimar Republic, combat pilots continued to be described as 'the last knights' in aerial warfare literature. Initially this hardly differed from the works written during the war. Thus anthologies containing war accounts continued to be published. Some were written in a matter-of-fact, informative style while others were emotive and nationalistic. Occasionally, some transported the old pacifist message of aviation as a means of creating an understanding between peoples.[50] However, the number of publications indicate that the interest in aerial warfare seems to have diminished during the 1920s, despite the impressively orchestrated 'return home' of Manfred von Richthofen's body in 1929 and the enthusiasm for aviation that reached Germany after the first successful transatlantic flights. It was only against the background of the boom in war literature beginning in 1929 that the pilots were once again dealt with, starting with an anthology of hero biographies edited by Ernst Jünger and shortly thereafter in actual front-line aviation novels.[51]

At this stage a transformation takes place among the protagonists that is evidently connected with changes in the description of their characters. In Jünger's anthology, for instance, 'the big triple star in the German pilot sky' (Immelmann–Boelcke–Richthofen) is still glorified, but a pilot is added in the person of Rudolf Berthold who had hardly been taken notice of during the First World War. At the same time, the figure of Max Immelmann receives less and less attention, and only an author from the United States had written a biography of Richthofen by 1933. During the Weimar Republic, Oswald Boelcke remains by far the most popular and 'folksy' pilot hero of the Germans, to whom numerous monographs were dedicated.[52] All of the pilots undergo a more or less strong process of 'nationalization', and are cast as 'shining patriotic figures'. This was hardly surprising in view of the general tendencies in the war literature during the late 1920s. Immelmann did not have much to offer in this respect, as his accounts were devoid of patriotic emotiveness, which was evidently one of the reasons why he slowly disappeared from the public eye. In contrast, Rudolf Berthold provided a completely different surface for projections and was a more suitable object for instrumentalization in terms of party politics, as he had led a Free Corps in the Baltic Region after the war and was slain in Harburg during the Kapp Coup.[53]

The formative childhood experiences are still emphasized, but in a nationalistic fashion and transferred directly into the German landscape. Thus Berthold, son of a forester, breathed in the 'unwavering love for the German Fatherland' along with 'the scent of the German forest'. Meanwhile Boelcke's origins in the 'German heartland', Thuringia and Havelland, and his 'good old simple ways' instilled in him in his 'genuinely German parental home' laid the foundation for his later career. In the case of Richthofen, 'a Silesian Junker of best stock' and 'military soldier' by birth, his talent was self-explanatory. And also Erwin Böhme turned into 'a real man [. . .] of the truly German kind, tall as a tree and at the same time deeply emotional'.[54] The use of the adjective 'German' as the dominant trait blurred the character differences that had been clearly emphasized during the First World War:

> Truly German through and through, pious at heart without ever mentioning a word about it, an immaculate character, devoted to duty until his death, cheerful and a joyous spirit for life, firm and strong, plain and honest, aware of his strength and value and yet modest, friendly towards everyone and yet full of dignity.[55]

All pilot heroes were stereotypically characterized in this or a similar manner during the late period of the Weimar Republic. Rudolf Berthold was the only exception. His biographer portrayed him as 'wild and passionate', with a 'fiery soul' that 'incessantly ignited and emitted sparks'. From his appearance alone his 'big, dark, fiery eyes' distinguished him from others. As for his character, a 'burning demon in his soul' drove him to fight and kill.[56] Even Richthofen is now able to gain more from his actions than mere hunting pleasure – if we are to believe his biographers in the Weimar period. When the enemy appeared directly in front of him, 'he turned pale, was overcome by a strong, passionate shudder, a passion that was not free of a dark anxiety that bold men use to face the moment of deadly decision.'[57] At the end of the 1920s, an alleged or real demonic and passionate pleasure for killing was no longer discredited, nor did it have to be camouflaged behind amusing hunting scenes, and at least in some cases it provided the hero with an even stronger aura.

The war novels popular from 1929 do not describe any kind of middle-class family background, nor is there reference to the formation of the character of the often anonymous protagonists. Instead the reader is dropped into the midst of action and is immediately sent to the front, as it were, where an authenticity-generating first-person narrator relates his experiences within a small community of fighters. The novels *Die Jagd-staffel – unsere Heimat* (The Fighter Squadron – Our Home) by Rudolf

Stark and *Fliegerschule 4* (Pilot School 4) by Richard Euringer are both set in a pilot environment and contain all the structural and linguistic characteristics of the classical 'anti-democratic front-line novel', either describing the inner monologue of the main protagonist in an austere masculine style or in lyrical hymn-like passages.[58] Despite the titles that suggest the existence of a community and despite the camaraderie pledged time and again, friendships between men are portrayed in a peculiarly lacklustre manner in both books, with the exception of pilot 'marriages' through which 'the same kind of blood flows'. Yet even in such a relationship the first-person narrator 'yearns [. . .] to be alone' right from the outset and decides to leave his 'Franz' and join a fighter squadron.[59] The privileged lifestyle of the squadron pilots, only superficially referred to in the books published during the war, is now painted in vivid colors. The pilot hero as a soldier definitively rids himself of the ascetic ideal depicted in the early pilot biographies and approaches the ideal of the 'front-line soldier'. In addition, a new image of the enemy appears: the incapable military bureaucracy on which a 'pilot trick' must be played in order to guarantee an adequate supply of goods – mainly alcohol.[60] Now stories of 'wild parties' are told that are justified and excused by the unusual tension and the permanent proximity to death to which the young men are exposed, as well as by their 'natural zest for life': 'We are still alive, today our life of 20 years is still our own but tomorrow, tomorrow perhaps no longer' is what a few Austrian pilots tell the uncomprehending local commander in the story *Nahaufklärung* (Close Reconnaissance) published in 1930.[61] In contrast to the classical front-line novel, the protagonists of the fighter-pilot novels have permanent contact with the area behind the lines. This not only adds an important ingredient to their knowledge about the ups and downs of war, it also widens their opportunities for pleasure: 'We pilots sleep in silk bedding, dine in palaces, drink champagne. Certainly this does not happen on a daily basis. But every day the life behind the lines embraces us with soft arms. It doesn't even necessarily have to be the arms of a little French girl.'[62]

Whether they were French women or 'little Flemish girls' with whom so 'many lovely hours' were spent,[63] sexual contacts with women at home or in the occupied countries suddenly appear in abundance. Even heroes previously described in asexual terms such as Boelcke or the Richthofen brothers now explicitly become objects of feminine desire: 'What a stunning guy, so young and handsome [. . .] and he dances like a young god', we are told with regard to Boelcke. Excerpts from his letters alluding to a certain 'Miss Ninette', among others, are now published.[64] But while the stories of Lothar von Richthofen's Don Juan behavior or his brother

Manfred's 'moving dedication' to only 'one woman whom he did not want to make a widow' were evidently rumors from the same source, 'authentic' documents of quite a conventional pilot's love were published in 1930 in the form of Erwin Böhme's letters to his fiancée.[65]

The sexualization of the pilot hero in the texts published in the late 1920s and the early 1930s are accompanied by the disappearance of the mother and the previously close contact with home. The family is replaced by frivolous and uncomprehending, yet always anonymous, sweethearts back home with whom the protagonists are looking for a brief ecstatic encounter. This relationship is immediately projected onto the partners: 'They should die and live like princes', we are told about the pilots in Euringer's novel, 'and they are loved by women uninhibitedly, women who in the madness of their disintegrated households, broken marriages, shattered nerves, and broken pride only want to kiss, forget and lose themselves in fainting.'[66]

According to another classical theme in war novels, these women personify 'home', quickly provoking an open conflict with the front. What they supposedly like about war is the erotic effect of uniforms. They are more or less immoral and not choosy. One women for instance lets her lover know that if he could not come personally, he should at least send her 'a blond [. . .] boy from [his crew] in his place'. The fact that this kind of feminine sexuality represents a threat requires no further explanation, and so these women remain childless and 'unredeemed' as a punishment, so to speak.[67] However, more important than their sad destiny is their effect on those men who come to see them during leave hoping for some meaning and understanding, and whom they bitterly disappoint. One of the women talks about 'your stupid squadron' and another about her most ardent wish to leave Germany – the country for which he was just risking his life – and to head for southern scenery with 'more southernly people'. The message of these pilot novels was that the gulf between home and front made an understanding between men and women impossible. It is not surprising that under these circumstances the pilots who were not understood and suffered from solitude soon 'only [had] one desire, to get back to the front'.[68]

From there, i.e. from the front, no more amusing little combat pilot stories or passionate killing frenzies are told, instead scenes are depicted bearing an often depressive atmosphere in which the protagonists face their own death: 'We laugh and sing and our mouths tell fantastic stories. Our heart asks in fear, what is going to happen to all of you? Who will I see again? Who will be the next one to go?'[69] Part of this is that the pilots no longer 'die beautifully'. Their death is described time and again in drastic tones. 'The casualties in air accidents, the pilots killed in training, smashed to death in collisions, torn to pieces by grenades, shot down in flames, or crushed after emergency landings behind enemy lines' constantly accompany those still alive. And the living withdraw more and more from any form of civilian life.[70] The 'endless solitude' of the fighter pilots finally becomes the dominating theme of pilot literature in the Weimar Republic. In the end, the heroes are left as hopelessly depressed men, devoid of human relationships and orientation: 'There is no way back. We have lost our home. We are now being seized by a country foreign to us. We are being absorbed by a life foreign to us. [. . .] Home, our home is dead. Our home was our squadron.'[71]

Flying as a Communal Masculine Experience, 1933–1939

From 1933 depression and alienation disappear from pilot literature. At the same time, the authors attempt to turn this individual war activity not only into a communal affair of the pilots but one involving a whole people.[72] Surprisingly, in this process the nobleman Manfred von Richthofen is cast as the fascist pilot hero par excellence, while the much more popular Boelcke withdraws into the background. As to the reason, one can only speculate. Perhaps the Boelcke family was opposed to an instrumentalization of their son by the National Socialists. In view of their previous behavior, however, this does not seem probable. On the other hand, it is clear that the von Richthofen family actively took part in the cult now developing around Manfred. In this spirit, his mother established a Richthofen Museum in her Silesian home town filled with 'hunting trophies', i.e. remnants of planes shot down by her son. On the anniversary of his death, which became known as 'airforce day' after 1935, she gave radio addresses. Furthermore, she published a heavily revised *Kriegstagebuch* (War Diary); while the youngest brother Bolko had already published a new edition of *Der Rote Kampfflieger* back in 1933.[73] Richthofen's success was generated by the 'fresh and amusing' character of his memoirs that, in contrast to Boelcke's, were devoid of any moralistic, pensive intellectual tone. His success could also be attributed to his close proximity to Göring who in 1918 had taken over the squadron after Richthofen's death. In addition, his figure made it possible to link the 'old' aristocracy, with its allegedly natural leadership qualities, and the new hero of the people, as was often done in the first years of the National Socialist regime. In contrast, Max Immelmann's family was 'inconsolable [. . .] about apparently having been forgotten by the German people'.

Against the background of the newly aroused interest in flying, they tried in vain in 1934 to draw public attention to their most prominent family member through a new edition of his wartime letters. However, the conflicts of the vegetarian and teetotal cadet coupled with his close and emotional relationship with his mother, in short Max Immelmann's 'soft core', were no longer in demand at a time when soldierly masculinity prevailed. This contrasted with the biography of the 'boisterous Franconian' Rudolf Berthold that was published roughly at the same time. A few years later the history of aerial warfare was rewritten to the complete disadvantage of Immelmann, with the first German war hero being transformed into the pupil of the 'great master' Boelcke in Walter Zuerl's extensive biographical anthology *Pour-le-Mérite*.[74] The pilots represented in this work were, to differing degrees of intensity, all exemplary virile heroes. The words used for their characterization clearly describe what was understood by masculinity in the Germany of the 1930s: 'daring' and 'unscrupulous' were the two most frequently used adjectives that appeared in various combinations. Under these circumstances, it is hardly surprising that the only quality that could be underscored in such a cautious and scrupulous pilot as Gontermann was his sense of duty.[75]

Yet the time of the individualists belonged to the past. Instead, the authors now tended to write the history of the the First World War pilots as a squadron history. Albeit not always successful,[76] this opened the path for recasting the pilot's experiences as a group experience. Thus, the National-Socialist air fighter's community was born in which a small group of closely connected men played the leading roles. An impressive example of this 'communalization' of the combat pilots was Thor Goote's novel . . . *rangehen ist alles!* (Go for it!) published in 1938 that centers around Manfred von Richthofen's 'circle of young pilot comrades'. The book is exciting to read and contains numerous dialogues and thoughts paraphrasing previously published letters and diaries. The plot deals with friendships between men, at first between Richthofen and Böhme and then between the latter and Boelcke (up to his crash caused unintentionally by Böhme), and finally describes the friendship between the brothers Lothar and Manfred von Richthofen. Goote presents a picture of a sworn community of men of the most different characters and origins who had an 'aura of exclusiveness' solely due to their duties in war and not because they led a luxurious lifestyle. The relationships between the squadron members are highly emotional despite their use of a concise, matter-of-fact, 'masculine' manner of speaking. Manfred von Richthofen, for instance, in a lengthy passage mourns the death of his comrade Kurt Wolff killed in a crash, describing in elegiac prose how much he misses 'his voice, his laugh' before pulling 'the mask of imperturbability' over his face again.[77] As the leader of the squadron, it is his task to keep positive and negative feelings, a constant topic in the book, under control. Here as in other texts from the 1930s, the death of the pilot is rarely glossed over and the killing of the enemy is not reinterpreted as an 'amusing hunting scene'. Instead, aerial warfare is a hard business that has to be carried out 'for the men in the trenches'.[78] The nerves might sometimes be strained, but they can be conquered. Anxiety no longer leads to a state of depressive alienation, but is overcome in the group. Following an air battle, for instance, the pilots all talk with each other, 'without listening properly and without being able to wait for the end of their own story, laughed a lot although they had just escaped death, laughed again and again [. . .] In the bottom of their hearts something seemed to be in turmoil and yet was suppressed with iron self-discipline.'[79]

'Self-discipline', 'camaraderie', 'fulfillment of duty', and 'unconditional willpower' were the main elements of the National Socialist pilot image that now developed into a group image. However, the quite unheroic memoirs of individualists like Ernst Udet, who even in the past was more an artistic than a fighter pilot, were still very popular with the public. This popularity was not dampened even when the new *Generalluftzeugmeister* tried to adopt a more serious tone, integrating the required slogans into the description of his experiences.[80] In the end, all of these were stories about 'the father's deeds'[81] with an explicit educational function which, however, had little to do with the reality of male youth in Nazi Germany. Young people had discovered another passion: gliding.

Back in the 1920s an enormous boom in gliding had taken place. This phenomenon could partially be explained by the restrictions imposed on motorized aviation by the Versailles peace treaty. Gradually gliding fell into the nationalist current.[82] Only after 1933 was it upgraded to a modern leisure activity, supposedly open to everyone. A countless number of anthologies, non-fiction literature, as well as fiction, all containing a foreword written by Göring himself, acquainted the male *Jung-Volk* with the subject. In these books one sentence was repeated over and over again: 'Every true German boy wants to become a pilot.' Especially the anthologies reflect a shift in emphasis between the generations. While the First World War combat pilots are integrated into an 'ancestral gallery' beginning with Leonardo da Vinci, the editors of the 1930s start the heroic period with the onset of gliding in the 1920s, when the 'wings of the German eagle were cut', but 'the youth side by side with the old flying front-line soldiers fought for the continued existence of German aviation and performed such a wonderful job'.[83] The shoulder-to-shoulder stance with the First World War pilots also occurs in exciting novels that competed every year for the award of the 'best pilot book of German youth'. In these stories, typically a group of boys clustered around a main protagonist of simple background experiences the beginnings of gliding before 1914. They subsequently fight and fall in the First World War; the survivors pass their knowledge on to the younger generation, whose yearnings are at last fulfilled in National Socialist Germany. The focus on gliding makes it possible to cast the latter as a 'youth movement of fliers' that leads an ascetic and hard, yet nature-loving life in the mountains. This lifestyle stands in opposition to 'human rights and human dignity, to dancing and corruption' in the valleys and towns where one had to fight against the lack of understanding from parents and teachers, i.e. against the entire middle-class world.[84] In this way, a link could be established between the joint effort demanded in gliding, where everyone contributes to the greater endeavor according to his abilities, with the military ideal of the single fighter still useful as a source of identification. 'To become a pilot means becoming a personality; to be a pilot means being a leader'[85] was the second part of the National-Socialist aviation message.

This ideologically loaded means of locomotion is now explicitly defined as a 'masculine task' where women are no longer an ornament or a dangerous temptation, but rather are assigned a clear function: as mothers supporting their sons – as exemplified so impressively by Kunigunde von Richthofen. To promote this ideology, they or future mothers are even permitted to accompany the pilots in the air from time to time: '[. . .] for there cannot be enough young Germans who promote flying. [. . .] The girl of today is the mother of tomorrow. One day her son will approach her with his wish to become a pilot. If the mother knows from her own experience how majestic and beautiful flying is, she will let her son go with a calm heart.'[86]

In the novels for adolescents published during the National Socialist period we only find understanding mothers, occasionally sisters, if they include women figures at all, but no potential or real brides anymore. Sometimes they include allusions that the pilot might have good chances with the opposite sex, the implicit message being however that actual relationships are more of a hindrance to the hero's career.[87]

In view of these hermetic and continually repeated gender-specific roles, the existence of highly successful female pilots in the 'Third Reich' may seem surprising at first glance, as is the fact that their experiences were published in anthologies or in the form of novels. The pilot Elly Beinhorn, for example, wrote a highly amusing story about the career of a female pilot cadet in which she makes fun of masculine vanities, the 'demigod' combat pilots and the whole dramatic pilot myth. For her flying is 'sooo beautiful', easy to learn and ultimately a 'global pursuit'. Her fictitious heroine, Miss Rosalind von Ebersbach, routinely demonstrates her superiority over the performance of her male counterparts, refuses all of their approaches, and only has one aim, to become an 'Africa pilot'.[88] Beinhorn's example, as well as the publication of other women's accounts, make two facts clear: Even if it only hovered in the shadows, the dream of flying as a means of achieving peace and understanding between peoples, as frequently articulated at the beginning of the First World War, still existed after twenty years of intensive literary and (auto)biographic militarization, albeit as a phenomenon that could only be expressed by women in the 'Third Reich'.[89] In the meantime, the image of the masculine, militaristic pilot hero was so firmly established that a few 'token women' could not endanger it.

Conclusion

The close connection between flying and military culture was due in part to the coinciding phenomena of technological development and the First World War, and above all to the possibility of remaining an individual fighter with individual victories and an individual death, at least for a short time during the modern mass war. Parallel to this, the image of the pilot as a cosmopolitan air acrobat or adventurer in the international family of pilots still existed during the Weimar Republic, the most prominent example being Ernst Udet. Only towards the end of the 1920s was the pilot seized by the spirit of 'soldierly nationalism' as cultivated by Ernst Jünger. This movement did take notice of women, albeit only in a sexualized and hostile fashion. In the 'Third Reich' the last remnants of individuality with regard to the image of the pilot were finally leveled and exaggerated into a militaristic and masculine image, while at the same time gliding made this image accessible to all male adolescents.

Despite Elly Beinhorn and her female counterparts, only half of the Germans belonged to 'the nation of fliers', which however did nothing to damage the effectiveness of this phrase coined by Göring. Flying carried a clear masculine and ultimately military connotation. If we read the works on pilot literature in chronological order, it becomes clear that the construction of the pilot hero tended to be an open-end process – as opposed to Peter Fritzsche's interpretation – and that the image of the pilot so firmly established nowadays as a masculine ideal was much more heterogeneous in the beginning and had to be re-created for each generation.[90]

I would like to argue that this fact in particular accounted for the enormous attraction of the image, since at the beginning 'the pilot' was an option for all men, from the experienced roofer to the baron obsessed with hunting, from the good-natured Catholic to the aggressive macho. The 'knight of the air' was a role model with which everyone could identify. This figure connected the old values and behavioural codes with the sophisticated command of the most modern technology. At the same time, he was conceded a certain tendency for dandy-like, playful, and excessive behavior.[91] The stability of this model and its popularity may have significantly contributed to the fact that after 1945 the airforce succeeded so effectively in casting itself as an apolitical institution, hovering – in the true sense of the word –over the realities of National Socialist politics.[92]

Notes

Translated by Nicholas Yantian

1. *BZ*, 26 March 1999, 1–3.
2. See the analysis of Burkhard Fuhs, 'Fliegende Helden. Die Kultur der Gewalt am Beispiel von Kampfpiloten und ihren Maschinen,' in *Gewalt in der Kultur. Vorträge des 29. Deutschen Volkskundekongresses*, ed. Rolf W. Brednich and Walter Hartinger (Passau, 1994), 705–720; as well as the impressively illustrated catalogue by Dominick Pisano, ed., *Legend, Memory and the Great War in the Air* (Washington, 1992). Ten years ago, Manfred von Richthofen's autobiographical notes from 1917 were reedited: Manfred von Richthofen, *Der rote Kampfflieger. Die persönlichen Aufzeichnungen des Roten Barons* (Hamburg, 1990).
3. See Karl Köhler, *Bibliographie zur Luftkriegsgeschichte* (Frankfurt a.M., 1966); Edward L. Homze, *German Military Aviation. A Guide to the Literature* (New York, 1984); Peter Fritzsche, *A Nation of Fliers. German Aviation and the Popular Imagination* (Cambridge, 1992), 100.
4. This did not go unnoticed even in 1940, when the South African psychologist Paul Skawran examined hundreds of pilots' books, nevertheless taking them at face value for a psychological study: Paul Skawran, *Psychologie des Jagdfliegers. Berühmte Flieger des Weltkrieges* (Berlin, 1940), 40.

5. See Manfred von Richthofen, *Der rote Kampfflieger*, ed. Bolko Freiherr von Richthofen (Berlin, 1933); Ernst Udet, *Mein Fliegerleben* (Berlin, 1935); for the number of copies see Fritzsche, *Nation of Fliers*, 235, fn. 42; On the German Air Force in the First World War see John Morrow, *German Air Power in World War I* (Nebraska, 1982).

6. Fritzsche, *Nation of Fliers*.

7. The only exception being René Schilling, who dealt with Richthofen in the context of his research on the construction of the war hero in Germany: René Schilling, *Heroische Männlichkeit. Die Konstruktion des Kriegshelden in Deutschland zwischen 1813 und 1945 am Beispiel der Rezeptionsgeschichte Körners, Friesens, Richthofens und Weddigens* (Paderborn, 2002); see also Gerhard Hirschfeld and Gerd Krumeich, ed., *'Keiner fühlt sich hier mehr als Mensch[. . .]' Erlebnis und Wirkung des Ersten Weltkriegs* (Frankfurt a.M., 1996); Gerhard Hirschfeld et al., ed., *Kriegserfahrungen: Studien zur Sozial- und Mentalitätsgeschichte des Ersten Weltkrieges* (Essen, 1997); Christa Hämmerle, '". . . wirf ihnen alles hin und schau, daß du fort kommst." Die Feldpost eines Paares in der Geschlechter(un)ordnung des Ersten Weltkriegs,' *Historische Anthropologie* 6 (1998): 431–458; and Christa Hämmerle, 'Von den Geschlechtern der Kriege und des Militärs. Forschungseinblicke und Bemerkungen zu einer neuen Debatte,' in *Was ist Militärgeschichte?* ed. Thomas Kühne and Benjamin Ziemann (Paderborn, 2000), 229–262.

8. See Fritzsche, *Nation of Fliers*, 35–43; for Great Britain: Michael Paris, 'The Rise of the Airmen: The Origins of Air Force Elitism, c. 1890–1918,' *Journal of Contemporary History* 28 (1993): 123–141.

9. Announcement of the book *Die fliegenden Pioniere* by Friedrich Otte, in Hanns Floerke and Georg Gärtner, ed., *Deutschland in der Luft voran! Fliegerbriefe aus Feindesland* (Munich, 1915), 197.

10. *Der Luftkrieg 1914–1915. Unter Verwendung von Feldpostbriefen und Berichten von Augenzeugen, dargestellt von einem Flugtechniker* (Leipzig, 1915), 9.

11. Floerke and Gärtner, *Deutschland*, 117.

12. *Der Luftkrieg*, 270, on bombardments and fear see: ibid. 210–214; Floerke and Gärtner, *Deutschland*, 11–21, 88–102, 110–112; Hans Lüdersdorf, *Die Kunst des Kriegsfluges* (Berlin/Leipzig, 1916), 100–129; Emil Ferdinand Malkowsky, ed., *Vom Heldenkampf der deutschen Flieger. Ein Ruhmesbuch der deutschen Tapferkeit* (Berlin, 1916), 101.

13. Malkowsky, *Heldenkampf*, 44; see also *Der Luftkrieg*, 271f.; Floerke and Gärtner, *Deutschland*, 60, 73.

14. See in general the table of contents of the aviation literature quoted here, and, as examples: Floerke and Gärtner, *Deutschland*, 39, 54, 64f., 67, 161; Lüdersdorff, *Kunst*, 186; *Der Luftkrieg*, 243f.

15. Erich Killinger, *Die Abenteuer des Ostseefliegers* (Berlin, 1917). During the war, 340,000 copies were sold, see Fritzsche, *Nation of Fliers*, 235, fn. 42.

16. Otto Lehmann, *Überm Feind* (Berlin, 1916), 3; *Der Luftkrieg*, 42, see also ibid. 261–268.

17. Floerke and Gärtner, *Deutschland*, 74.

18. Lehmann, *Überm Feind*, 13, 115–117, 125f.; equally sober: Rudolf Requadt, *Im Kriegsflugzeug* (Berlin, 1916).

19. See Floerke and Gärtner, *Deutschland*, 78f.; Hans Joachim Buddecke, *El Schahin. Der Jagdfalke. Aus meinem Fliegerleben* (Berlin, 1918), 45; and Fritzsche, *Nation of Fliers*, 66–70.

20. Frizsche, *Nation of Fliers*, 74–82.

21. See the paternal introduction in Hauptmann Bölckes (sic!) *Feldberichte. Mit einer Einleitung von der Hand des Vaters* (Gotha, 1917), 5–16; and: Rudolf Oskar Gottschalk, *Boelcke, Deutschlands Fliegerheld. Schilderung seines Lebensweges und seiner Heldentaten im Luftkampf* (Leipzig, 1916); Wilhelm Kranzler, ed., *Bezwinger der Luft im Weltkrieg. Siegreiche Fliegerkämpfe und Luftschifffahrten unserer großen Helden* (Berlin, 1916), 38; Leonhard Müller, *Fliegerleutnant Heinrich Gontermann* (Barmen, 1918), 6; Ernst Eichler, ed., *Kreuz wider Kokarde. Jagdflüge des Leutnants Ernst Udet* (Berlin, 1918), 11–16; Walter Zuerl, ed., *Pour-le-Mérite-Flieger. Heldentaten und Erlebnisse unserer Kriegsflieger* (Munich, 1938), 8, 15f., 22: on the roofer-pilots Max von Müller, Fritz Rumey und Julius Buckler.

22. Kranzler, *Bezwinger*, 6; see also the analysis of Skawran, *Psychologie des Jagdfliegers*, 79–85.

23. Quoted from the 1933 edition: Richthofen, *Kampfflieger*, 9–24, 68; also Skawran, *Psychologie des Jagdfliegers*, 59.

24. Max Immelmann, *Meine Kampfflüge. Selbsterlebt und selbsterzählt* (Berlin, 1916), 13; similiar Buddecke, *El Shahin*, 24f.; in contrast the pensive assessment of Erwin Böhme, *Briefe eines deutschen Kampffliegers an ein junges Mädchen* (Leipzig, 1930), 15; similiar: Müller, *Gontermann*, 54; Richthofen, *Kampfflieger*, 63.

25. Ibid. 102. His lesser passion for flying and his great enthusiasm for hunting is corrobated by his contemporaries, see Böhme, *Briefe*, 112.

26. Report Roy Brown, quoted in Richthofen, *Kampfflieger*, 249; Böhme, *Briefe*, 101.

27. Floerke and Gärtner, *Deutschland*, 70; on pilot lingo and modesty see Malkowksy, *Heldenkampf*, 22 (on Immelmann); Kranzler, *Bezwinger*, 154f. (on Boelcke); Böhme, *Briefe*, 52; Müller, *Gontermann*, 114.

28. Max Immelmann in a letter to the editor, 6.6.1916, reprinted in Malkowsky, *Heldenkampf*, 18; see also Immelmann, *Kampfflüge*, 65, 82–87; Boelcke to his parents, 16.7.1915, in *Bölckes Feldberichte*, 40f.; Müller, *Gontermann*, 84, 90.

29. See the newspaper covering in *BZ am Abend* and *Berliner Tageblatt*, quoted by Malkowsky, *Heldenkampf*, 27, 22.

30. Kranzler, *Bezwinger*, 155; New York journalist Herbert Swope on Boelcke, quoted by Anton Lübke, *Hauptmann Boelcke. Ein Gedenkblatt für den ruhmbedeckten Heldenflieger* (Warendorf, 1917), 16, 19; Böhme, *Briefe,* 64; Immelmann, *Kampfflüge*, 43.

31. Boelcke's father quoted by Malkowsky, *Heldenkampf*, 43; Müller, *Gontermann*, 104.

32. Ibid. 115; Immelmann, *Kampfflüge*, 14ff.; see also: Malkowsky, *Heldenkampf*, 32; Kranzler, *Bezwinger*, 38.

33. See Immelmann, *Kampfflüge*, 24f., 39; *Bölckes Feldberichte*, 23; Müller, *Gontermann*, 70, 90; Eichler, *Kreuz*, 22, 58; Lübke, *Hauptmann Boelcke*, 18; Richthofen, *Kampfflieger*, 249; Böhme, *Briefe*, 21, 23, 28–30; Felix A. Theilhaber, *Jüdische Flieger im Kriege. Ein Blatt der Erinnerung* (Berlin, 1919), 68.

34. Boelcke himself started flying together with his brother Wilhelm in 1915, see Lehmann, *Überm Feind*, 42; *Bölckes Feldberichte*, 16; Richthofen, *Kampfflieger*, 77; whose squadron later on would be joint by his brother Lothar: Richthofen, *Kampfflieger*, 182f. For more examples see Skawran, *Psychologie des Jagdfliegers*, 33–37.

35. Müller, *Gontermann*, 55f., 95; Eichler, *Kreuz*, 62f. Another exceptional friendship seems to have existed between Erwin Böhme and Oswald Boelcke, although this is only reported by others, for example by Richthofen, *Kampfflieger*, 111. Boelcke himself tends to write in a rather impersonal style about the 'gentlemen' of his squadron, see *Bölckes Feldberichte*, 122, 172.

36. Immelmann, *Kampfflüge*, 97, 127.

37. Müller, *Gontermann*, 106, 111; Böhme, *Briefe* (quote taken from the advertising of the book in Johannes Werner, ed., *Boelcke, der Mensch, der Flieger, der Führer der deutschen Jagdfliegerei* (Leipzig, 1932)).

38. See the letters to mothers or parents in: Immelmann, *Kampfflüge*; *Bölckes Feldberichte*; Müller, *Gontermann*; and: Kunigunde von Richthofen, *Mein Kriegstagebuch. Die Erinnerungen der Mutter des roten Kampffliegers* (Berlin, 1937). Quote taken from the foreword of

his brother Franz Immelmann, in: Franz Immelmann, *'Der Adler von Lille'. Eines Fliegers Werdegang und Erfüllung* (Leipzig, 1934), 6.

39. Immelmann, *'Der Adler von Lille'*, 30; see also the report in *BZ am Mittag* about an aviation festival in Leipzig in November 1915, quoted by Malkowsky, *Heldenkampf*, 27.

40. Bölckes *Feldberichte*, 123; Müller, *Gontermann*, 108; Immelmann, *Kampfflüge*, 12; Eichler, *Kreuz*, 36, 62f., 68, 78; Richthofen, *Kampfflieger*, 81.

41. In early reports on Immelmann's death, for example, one can find the remark that he could only be identified by his medals. Only in 1930 was it possible to say openly that his body was 'crushed beyond recognition', see Arthur Pfleger, *Franz im Feuer. Vier Jahre Flugzeugbeobachter* (Regensburg, 1930), 64; also Buddecke, *El Shahin*, 124; *Bölckes Feldberichte*, 84; Lübcke, *Hauptmann Boelcke*, 57 (quote); Richthofen, *Kampfflieger*, 249; Müller, *Gontermann*, 117.

42. Müller, *Gontermann*, 70, 64 (quote); see also Udet, *Fliegerleben*, 61f.; Buddecke, *El Shahin*, 52f., 58, 67.

43. *Bölckes Feldberichte*, 76; Richthofen, *Kampfflieger*, 137; Boelcke quoted by Lübke, *Hauptmann Boelcke*, 50.

44. Eichler, *Kreuz*, 37f.

45. Buddecke, *El Shahin*, 48f.; Müller, *Gontermann*, 88, 83, see also ibid. 82, 107; Gontermann's 'considerate' way of fighting is confirmed by Udet, *Fliegerleben*, 48f.

46. Richthofen, *Kampfflieger*, 118, 108, 151, 115, 120, 186; on Lothar von Richthofen see Skawran, *Psychologie des Jagdfliegers*, 97–99; and Richthofen, *Kriegstagebuch*, 82–89.

47. *Bölckes Feldberichte*, 64, 75; see also Malkowsky, *Heldenkampf*, 46–48, 50–52; Immelmann, *Kampfflüge*, 107; Müller, *Gontermann*, 81; and the discussion between Böhme and his fiancée, who was taken aback by the practice of numbering the shot-down enemies, Böhme, *Briefe*, 61–67. On the intentional, and in some cases obsessional, burning of enemies, see *Bölckes Feldberichte* (1917), 121; Udet on Richthofen, quoted in: Otto Winter and Hans Georg Schulze, *Das Fliegerbuch der deutschen Jugend* (Reutlingen, 1933), 20; Fritzsche, *Nation of Fliers*, 93f.

48. After the introduction of fighter squadron tactics by Boelcke in the course of 1916, the famous duels disappeared gradually from the skies. Now, pilots rushed to defend each other or used members of their own squadron as protection, see for example Paul Bäumer's report about his first weeks as a fighter pilot: 'Voß shot down, while my machine only gave him the feeling of additional power, and

served as gun shield, as lightning conductor, so to speak. He was at the offensive, and I, a poor little greenhorn, had to back him and protect him from surprises', in: Zuerl, *Pour-le-Mérite-Flieger*, 33; see also: Fritzsche, *Nation of Fliers*, 82–101.

49. See Lübke, *Hauptmann Boelcke*, 16–18, 38; Kranzler, *Bezwinger*, 36f.; Malkowsky, *Heldenkampf*, 35, 45; Floerke and Gärtner, *Deutschland*, 59; Lüdersdorff, *Kunst*; 37; Buddecke, *El Shahin*, 49; Bölckes *Feldberichte*, 112; Immelmann, *Kampfflüge*, 33, 63, 99; Eichler, *Kreuz*, 67f.; Richthofen, *Kampfflieger*, 106, 114–117.

50. See Richard Wilhelm, *Zwischen Himmel und Erde. Von Luftfahrtzeugen, von ihrer Erfindung, ihrer Entwicklung und Verwendung. Ein Buch für die Jugend und das Volk* (Charlottenburg, 1920); Georg Gellert, *Flieger- und Luftschiffkämpfe im Weltkriege* (Berlin, 1920); Georg Paul Neumann, *In der Luft unbesiegt* (Munich, 1923); Ernst Schäfer, *Pour le Mérite. Flieger im Feuer* (Berlin, 1931).

51. For the popularity of flying in the 1920s, the boom in war literature and its historical interpretation see Modris Eksteins, *The Rites of Spring. The Great War and the Birth of the Modern Age* (London 1989), 242–267, 276–299; as well as Karl Prümm, 'Das Erbe der Front. Der antidemokratische Kriegsroman der Weimarer Republik und seine nationalsozialistische Fortsetzung,' in *Die deutsche Literatur im Dritten Reich, Themen – Traditionen – Wirkungen*, ed. Horst Danker and Karl Prümm (Stuttgart, 1976), 138–164; Waltraud Amberger, *Männer, Krieger, Abenteurer. Der Entwurf des 'soldatischen Mannes' in Kriegsromanen über den Ersten und Zweiten Weltkrieg* (Frankfurt a.M., 1984); Köhler, *Bibliographie*; Homze, *German Military Aviation*; Ernst Jünger, ed., *Die Unvergessenen* (Berlin/Leipzig 1928). Four pilots are to be found among the forty-four 'heroes' portrayed in this book. See also Pfleger, *Franz im Feuer; Richard Euringer, Fliegerschule 4. Buch der Mannschaft* (Hamburg, 1929); Rudolf Stark, *Die Jagdstaffel unsere Heimat. Ein Fliegertagebuch aus dem letzten Kriegsjahr* (Leipzig, 1932). On Richthofen's funeral see Schilling, *Heroische Männlichkeit*, 288–308.

52. See Neumann, *In der Luft*, 8; Floyd Gibbons, *The Red Knight of Germany. The Story of Baron von Richthofen* (Garden City, 1927); Walter Zuerl, *Fliegerhelden* (Reutlingen, 1939), 5 (triple star); Werner, *Boelcke, der Mensch*, 5 (quote); see also Fritzsche, *Nation of Fliers*, 82.

53. Werner, *Boelcke, der Mensch*, 218 (shining figures); Georg Schröder, 'Max Immelmann,' in *Die Unvergessenen*, ed. Ernst Jünger (Berlin/Leipzig, 1928), 169–173; Erich Balle, 'Rudolf Berthold,' ibid. 15–23; in general: Prümm, *Erbe der Front*.

Stefanie Schüler-Springorum

54. Prümm, *Erbe der Front*, 16; Werner, *Boelcke, der Mensch*, 7; Friedrich Georg Jünger, 'Manfred von Richthofen,' in *Die Unvergessenen*, ed. Ernst Jünger (Berlin/Leipzig, 1928), 279–286, 279, 282; Böhme, *Briefe*, 5.
55. Werner, *Boelcke, der Mensch*, 219; see also the remarks of the editor of Böhme's letters, Johannes Werner: Böhme, *Briefe*, 5–8; Schröder, 'Immelmann'; Jünger, 'Richthofen'; and Otfried Fuchs, 'Oswald Boelcke,' in *Die Unvergessenen*, 24–28.
56. Balle, 'Berthold', 15–19; on Berthold see also Klaus Theweleit, *Männerphantasien, vol. 1: Frauen, Fluten, Körper, Geschichte* (Frankfurt a.M., 1978), 40–42, 48f.
57. Jünger, 'Richthofen', 281–283.
58. Prümm, *Erbe der Front*.
59. Stark, *Jagdstaffel*, 8; see also Euringer, *Fliegerschule*, 25; Pfleger, *Franz im Feuer*, 32f.
60. See Prümm, *Erbe der Front*, 151, Stark, *Jagdstaffel*, 38, 54ff., 65–68; Pfleger, *Franz im Feuer*, 50; Euringer, *Fliegerschule*, 17–21; Werner, *Boelcke, der Mensch*, 82; Fritz Baur, *Wir Flieger! 1914–1918. Der Krieg im Fliegerlichtbild* (Vienna, 1930), 59.
61. Baur, *Wir Flieger*, 60; Skawran, *Psychologie des Jagdfliegers*, 181 (parties); see also Schäfer, *Pour le Mérite*, 11.
62. Euringer, *Fliegerschule*, 18.
63. Stark, *Jagdstaffel*, 39.
64. Fuchs, "Boelcke", 25; Werner, *Boelcke, der Mensch*, 6, 35, 117.
65. Böhme, *Briefe*. The Richthofen brothers' love life is first dwelt on in Gibbon's rather fictitious biography and quoted from there on, often without mentioning the source, see Gibbons, *Red Knight*, 2, 276; Skawran, *Psychologie des Jagdfliegers*, S. 69, 98; in comparison to their mother's assessment: Richthofen, *Kriegstagebuch*, 142.
66. Euringer, *Fliegerschule*, 20.
67. Ibid. 287, 55f. (quote), 50–52, 65–69, 74–92, 288 (quote); see also Stark, *Jagdstaffel*, 71–76; on the gender-specific dichotomy of 'home' and 'front' see Karen Hagemann's introduction to this volume.
68. Stark, *Jagdstaffel*, 76f.; Euringer, *Fliegerschule*, 73f.; see also Theweleit, *Männerphantasien*, 66–71; Prümm, *Erbe der Front*, 151f.
69. Stark, *Jagdstaffel*, 47. This depressive mood seems to have been rather typical for the last months of the war, see Werner, *Boelcke, der Mensch*, 204f.; Baur, *Wir Flieger*, 36; Pfleger, *Franz im Feuer*, 66, 72f.; Böhme, *Briefe*, 89f., 112, 127.
70. Euringer, *Fliegerschule*, 103, 85; see also Stark, *Jagdstaffel*, 43; Pfleger, *Franz im Feuer*, 82, 98; Interestingly enough, the most brutal

and detailed description of a pilot's death was given by an Austrian author: Baur, *Wir Flieger*, 84f.

71. Stark, *Jagdstaffel*, 57, 164.

72. See Fritzsche, *Nation of Fliers*, 185–219.

73. See René Schilling, 'Die "Helden der Wehrmacht" – Konstruktion und Rezeption,' in *Die Wehrmacht. Mythos und Realität*, ed. Rolf-Dieter Müller and Hans-Erich Volkmann (Munich, 1999), 550–572, 551, fn. 6; foreword and epilogue to Richthofen, *Kampfflieger*; Zuerl, *Pour-le-Mérite-Flieger*, 320, 337, 366f.; Karl Theodor Haanen, *Flieger vor die Front! Ruf und Befehl an die deutsche Jugend* (Berlin, 1936), 169. For his biography published in 1932, the editor Johannes Werner had enjoyed the full support of the Boelcke family, which even put the ace's adolescent letters at his disposal, see Werner, *Boelcke, der Mensch*.

74. Franz Immelmann, Foreword and Introduction, in *Der Adler von Lille*, ed. Franz Immelmann (Leipzig, 1934), 5–33, 6 (quote); Ludwig F. Gengler, *Kampfflieger Rudolf Berthold* (Berlin, 1934); Zuerl, *Pour-le-Mérite-Flieger*, 53, 224; see also: *Deutsche Jugend fliege . . .*, ed. Deutscher Luftsportverband (Frankfurt a.M., 1939); Willi Stiasny, *Deutsche Jugend fliege* (Berlin, 1936), 147–160; Schulze, *Flieger-buch*, 17–34.

75. See Zuerl, *Pour-le-Mérite-Flieger*, 196 (on Gontermann); similar: Hanns Möller, *Kampf und Sieg eines Jagdgeschwaders* (Berlin, 1939).

76. Despite the title ('Combat and Victory of a Fighter Squadron,' ibid.), Möller's book, for example, is really about the personality and heroic deeds of the squadron's three commanders.

77. Goote, Thor, '. . . rangehen ist Alles!' *Roman um geschichtliches Geschehen* (Berlin, 1938), 112f. (quote), 63, 111–15, 189–95, 140–43; very similiar: Möller, *Kampf*,

78. Goote, *. . . rangehen ist Alles!* 43 (quote), 143–147; Zuerl, *Pour-le-Mérite-Flieger*, 13, 84, 310, 360, 438, 442, 466; Möller, *Kampf*, 13, 23; 74, 88; Karl Steinig, *Von Dädalus bis Udet. Die Geschichte der Luftfahrt für die deutsche Jugend* (Langensalza/Berlin, 1935), 108, 361–363.

79. Goote, *. . . rangehen ist Alles!* 74 (quote), 26–29, 43f.

80. See Udet, *Fliegerleben*.

81. Zuerl, *Pour-le-Mérite-Flieger*, foreword; see also *Deutsche Jugend fliege* (1939), foreword.

82. Fritzsche, *Nation of Fliers*, 103–131.

83. Steinig, *Dädalus bis Udet*, 116; Fritz Stamer, *Deutscher Segelflug. Vater-ländische Tat und fliegerische Jugendbewegung* (Leipzig, 1937), 7;

see also: Schulze, *Fliegerbuch*; Fritz Brand, ed., *Deutsche Jugend, fliege! Vom Segelflug und seiner geschichtlicher Entwicklung* (Münster, 1936).

84. Stamer, *Segelflug*, 1, 12, 17; see also Fritz Stamer, *Jungen werden Flieger* (Stuttgart, 1937); Wilhelm Güldenpfennig, *Wir fliegen für Deutschland. Erlebnis und Technik des Fliegens* (Berlin, 1936); Haanen, *Flieger*; *Verwegene Burschen fliegen! Von Pimpfen, Jungfliegern und ihrem fröhlichen Weg in die Luftwaffe* (Berlin, 1936).

85. Brand, *Deutsche Jugend*, 10.

86. Stamer, *Jungen*, 184; Fried Lange, *Ritter von Schleich. Jagdflieger im Weltkrieg und im Dritten Reich* (Düsseldorf, 1939), 194; Richthofen, *Kriegstagebuch*.

87. Stamer, *Segelflug*, 25, 53; Udet, *Fliegerleben*, 2, 88, 93, 96; Stamer, *Jungen*, 53, 63; *Verwegene Burschen*, 25, 37; Goote, . . . *rangehen ist Alles!* 107–9, 136f., 153–160; Richthofen, *Kriegstagebuch*, 40, 43, 113.

88. Elly Beinhorn, *Grünspecht wird ein Flieger. Der Werdegang eines Flugschülers* (Leipzig, 1935), 7, 107, 60, 55.

89 See Schulze, *Fliegerbuch*, 166–69; the only exception to this rule being again Udet, who even in the 'Third Reich' does not stop praising the internationality of the 'great family of fliers', see Udet, *Fliegerleben*.

90. In order to corroborate his hypothesis on the construction and the war experience of the First World War aces, Peter Fritzsche (*Nation of Fliers*, 59–101) makes rather free use of sources and documents stemming from various decades, without distinguishing between novels, biographies and ego-documents. In my view, this material has to be analyzed carefully with regard to its chronological 'order of appearance' and its specific function. Only in this perspective, as I have tried to show, does the process of construction of the hero image and its historical variations become visible.

91. On the specific appeal of dandy-like masculinity see the contribution of Sabine Kienitz to this volume.

92. The most famous example being Carl Zuckmayer's *Des Teufels General* (The General of the Devil), not by chance one of the most successful stage plays and movies in postwar Germany.

Comradeship

Gender Confusion and Gender Order
in the German Military, 1918–1945

Thomas Kühne

'In every man's heart stirs from time to time a fine, womanly feeling: an admittedly quickly suppressed and never openly acknowledged desire to give love and to receive love.' This desire was acknowledged quite openly by a former wartime-volunteer in his wartime-memoirs published in 1919. High expectations for the community experience in the military, raised by contemporary youth-culture, bourgeois poetry and the propaganda of the authoritarian state, led him to join the colors as a student. The expectations, however, for the security of comradeship, which the bourgeois-national cult of the dead had raised since the nineteenth century in the song of the 'good comrade' ('Ich hatt' einen Kameraden'), were soon betrayed. 'Comrades' of the working class made life a living hell for the war-willing, bourgeois recruit. They didn't join the army voluntarily, but had been 'pulled' into the war. Only rarely did the author experience manifestations of 'what was called "comradeship" out there'.

For him (and others) comradeship meant a canon of ritualistic and altruistic acts carried out without respect of the person, from the equal sharing of private food-rations and cigarettes to the selfless rescue of injured comrades from the battle-zone. The bearers of such an idealized solidarity could only be men, yet at the same time their solidarity also formed a counterweight to the world of 'men'. Comradeship did not appear as a factor related to military strength. Rather, it was the opposite of outward aggression as much as of the violence that governed the 'community of soldiers' inwardly. Comradeship was explicitly encoded as feminine; it was 'personal warmth and the language of mutual consent and warmheartedness', in short: the 'warmth which lies within the woman'.

Although the author complained that his model of comradeship found only little manifestation in reality, he did not doubt the ideal itself. For him comradeship ranged 'far above' all other familiar social forms such as friendship. Also in other respects the author did not lose faith in his wartime experience. The drastic description of the rather rough and brutal manners among soldiers did not, in his case, result in one of the pacifistic and anti-militaristic condemnations of war and Prussian militarism which the bourgeois and in particular socialist left tediously engaged in after 1918 – from Kurt Tucholsky to Erich Maria Remarque. Equally, the author of the statement quoted at the beginning of this article was neither Hans Blüher, nor Magnus Hirschfeld or another advocate of the homoeroticism inherent to the male youth-movement or of male homosexuality. Rather, our author was one of the most prominent and productive representatives of the extremely nationalistic and war-glorifying circle during the Weimar Republic: Franz Schauwecker. In 1919 he created a vision of the *Todesrachen* (death jaws) of war and the soldier's life with all its attendant cruelties, destruction and degradation to effectively emphasize the suffering of his inner being, his education and self-education from a boy who was cared for to a 'real' man and soldier. He highly valued the harsh 'educational methods' of his comrades, for he 'understood' them as a first test of his male identity as warrior. The 'conquering of his weaker self' on the battlefield and the negation of the 'survival instinct' served him as the last proof in this respect. It was this that mattered to him. The pride of the former mother's boy was founded precisely on the fact that he had finally passed the test innumerable times and had soon been promoted to second lieutenant.[1]

Schauwecker's wartime memoirs of 1919 thus illustrate the contemporary ideal of martial masculinity with an inclination toward violence and death. It was this masculinity that recent literary, cultural, military and gender history have expounded on the basis of German nationalistic war and autobiographical literature associated with soldierly 'nationalism', 'conservative revolution' and National Socialism.[2] The greatest impact was effected by Klaus Theweleit's psychoanalytically based picture of the male volunteer-corps fighters' 'male fantasies'.[3] Theweleit and in particular his disciples frequently extrapolated these 'fantasies' and projected them directly onto male National-Socialistic society. From that point they were often depicted as an almost anthropological quality attributed to 'the' man in general. Theweleit's 'male fantasies' are dominated by a martial ideal of the soldier, by gender dichotomies and by the apotheosis of 'decision' and warlike violence. All 'fluid', 'soft', tender and 'womanly' emotions, implicitly or – as in Schauwecker's writings – explicitly ascribed to 'the' woman, have to be kept under control by a 'dam' or the iron 'body-shield' that dominates everything, or they have to be killed. The desire to kill and destroy, excessive symbolic and actually practiced violence, also and especially against women, is regarded the basis of the male sense of community. From the volunteer-corps fighters it is only a short way to the protagonists of the National Socialists' politics of extermination and their 'moralily of extermination', which has been assumed not only for Himmler's SS-men but also for the lower ranks of the Wehrmacht.[4] Indeed, according to a critical observer of feminist studies of the military – considered prejudiced because of its view from outside – historians from that discipline often regard male bonding of warriors and soldiers as diabolical, presenting it as a 'threatening horde' and interpreting male 'comradeship' as 'solidarity against women, against whom they had to protect themselves'.[5] It is, of course, not the point of this essay to dismiss the fact that these images and findings can help to establish central psychological structures and cultural concepts that had a devastating effect during the Nazi war. It is also beyond question that in every culture the institution of male bonding fulfilled an important role regarding carrying out and maintaining male supremacy and that, together with military initiation, a society dominated by male bonding has been (and still is) practiced.[6] It is also quite obvious that what Franz Schauwecker wrote about the 'womanly element' in men in 1919 says little about the relationship between real women and men. He was not concerned with the integration of women into the military bonds of men or to enhance the social status of women. In fact, he was not concerned with real women at all but with male imaginations. These actually helped him to express certain (male) emotional processes and problems and helped him to cope with them symbolically. 'The' woman referred only to images and myths of women. According to the literary and psychoanalytical foundations laid out by Silvia Bovenschen and Christa Rohde-Dachser, representations of femininity can be understood as 'containers'. Similar to art in general, but also to dreams and neuroses, they take up everything that has been ignored, suppressed or frowned upon by male self-definition, namely 'fears, wishes, longings and desires', in order 'to preserve it and to find it time and again.' Utopian dreams and fantasies related to aspects of identity, reconciliation and fusion, as well as to aggression, necrophilia and destruction are projected onto femininity as something that is seen as absolutely 'different', unfamiliar and not-understood.

It is the ambivalence of longings connected to desires and fears, the juxtaposition and fusion of idealized and demonized figures that essentially mark the imagined femininity of men. It alternately appears in the form of a Madonna and a witch, of innocence and a seductress, of a loving mother and a *femme fatale*, of purification and corruption. In the eyes of members of the volunteer-corps, it was the mean-spirited, dangerous 'red' women, the amazons and 'gunwomen' on the one hand and the noble, 'motherly' and 'white' women represented by nurses on the other. Recent gender research on military discourse and the mental household of soldiers from different regions and times has emphasized the pejorative and aggressive dimension of such constructs of femininity.[7] The defeated enemy, unfit and unwilling for battle – no matter whether this was the actual case or just supposed – was (and is) being looked at as 'effeminate'. A significant part of certain rituals of initiation and degradation was (and is) that recruits had (and have) to carry out feminine-connoted acts. Thereby, they were (and are) reduced to their mere body and thus to the status of an object which is usually reserved for women. Not least do 'women', i.e. male representations of women in the sexist discourses of the entertainment industry, serve to enhance masculinity symbolically. In the context of binary gender codes, femininity as it is imagined by men demarcates a distance from 'actual', 'true' and at least 'hegemonic' masculinity. The latter is defined through bodily strength, preparedness to take risks, emotional hardness and undoubted heterosexuality. But the importance of imagined femininity for military discourses on masculinities during the century of total wars is thoroughly underestimated, if it is only seen as a counterpart of 'true' masculinity. Imagined femininity, in particular within the symbolic order of the military, is nurtured by its ambivalence. Again, reference can be made to the representative of nationalist war memory quoted at the beginning: Schauwecker dissociated his understanding of 'womanly' comradeship from 'male' violence, yet according to his psychology the real man should integrate both.

In the following discussion, I undertake to show briefly that Schauwecker's outline of masculinity was of paradigmatic significance for the self-perception of soldiers during the Second World War and thus for the symbolic order of the Nazi war. It is my thesis that constructs of femininity, designed by men and connected to a notion of 'comradeship' that was of mythical dimension, served to smooth over symbolic contradictions, social differences and emotional tensions which existed in a world of war dominated by men.[8] Thereby, constructs of femininity made this world tolerable for both men and women and ultimately helped to stabilize it. Attention will be given to the tension between the 'hard' and heterosexual ideal of masculinity on the one hand and the practiced, sometimes 'soft' and sublime homosexual being of a man on the other, i.e. to the contrast between the symbolic and the psychological order. Light will be shed on two contrasting norms, namely a propensity to violence versus altruistic, brotherly love, and finally on the socially determined conflict between the sexes.[9]

These meanings of comradeship can be established by looking at diaries and letters written from the battlefield during the Second World War. In the following discussion, a wide spectrum of examples will be analyzed that span from a soldier who upheld a critical attitude toward the NS-regime and the war to a 'perpetrator' engaged in murdering Jews. My approach is based on the sociology of knowledge and the history of experience, which assigns great significance to those social and cultural patterns that leave their mark on war-experiences and the soldiers' ability to verbally come to terms with them.[10] For this reason, I will begin with an outline of the 'myth of comradeship' as a central element of those symbolic traditions which ultimately shaped the cultural order of the Nazi war.

The Myth of Comradeship After 1918

The way in which the participants in the Nazi war understood their actions, feelings and experiences and the way they put them into words was perhaps not determined by but in any case influenced by the symbolic order of war which collective, 'public' memory since 1918 had developed through manifold media: through the cult of fallen soldiers, through the publications of veteran organizations, through war-novels which became best-sellers, and through innumerable individual memoirs. Collective memory of the First World War was of an explicitly mythical nature. The myth of comradeship was not only based on accounts of the First World War but also on those that belonged to the misty past: Christian tradition, in particular the New Testament, the *Nibelungenlied*, and especially the song of the 'good comrade' written by Ludwig Uhland during the Wars of Liberation. All these texts give an account of the 'love' that existed among men in dangerous worlds where death was omnipresent. Assigning similar experiences during the First World War a sacral consecration, they call for a renewal of such experiences in the war to come. The myth of war in general and that of comradeship in particular depended upon this pragmatic impetus that aimed at constant renewal and repetition.

Schauwecker's 1919 description of the conflict-laden social interaction among soldiers corresponds to the findings of recent historical research on the military society during the First World War.[11] After 1918, in contrast, the national memory of the First World War rather stressed the inner unity of the front society against the background of the so-called *Dolchstoßlegende* (the myth of the stab in the back of the German army). It did not leave any room for more dissonant tones, as great veteran and military organizations claimed the opposite from the very beginning, and Schauwecker's later writings also paint a different picture. What he called an exception in 1919, he soon regarded as a general rule.[12] Doubt was not permitted regarding the ubiquity of a comradeship of front-line soldiers that encompassed all military ranks and social classes. The community of front soldiers (*Frontgemeinschaft*), as it was remembered in the 1920s and 1930s, was marked by an 'equal' sharing of the 'loving gifts' from home. In a similar way, there supposedly existed a general willingness to listen to the worries and emotional distresses of one's comrades, as well as a general preparedness to come to the comrades' rescue even at the risk of one's own life. Collective war memory did not conceal the fact that not every soldier was able to practice this sort of extensive altruism, which supposedly went without saying. Yet it presented the community of soldiers as a purifying, socializing institution in which 'egoistic' patterns of civil society were usually worn off without major problems. Out of bad men collective war memory made good ones.[13]

The myth of altruistic comradeship formed the starting-point of a discursive consensus that united the two competing camps of collective war memory which existed since 1918, the socialist-pacifist and bourgeois-nationalist camp. Although leftist war memory disavowed the legend of a rank-encompassing comradeship between officer and man,[14] the *Reichs-banner* in particular, the paramilitary movement of veterans from the social-democratic part of the working class, 'constructively' contributed to the myth of comradeship. Around 1930, leftist war novels brought this contribution to an end. Thereby, a picture of comradeship emerged that unveiled subversive tendencies and that was directed against military authority, against the idea of war as a crime against humanity and toward the survival of the ordinary soldier. Instead of the officer, the comrade from 'the other side of the trench', i.e. the military enemy, was made a member of the community.[15] Leftist war memory thus fitted comradeship into socialist tradition. Yet what marked both leftist and rightist memory was the apotheosis of a community that consisted exclusively of men. 'Feminine' gestures and rituals of affection, of empathy and devotion, as idealized by Schauwecker in 1919, served in both cases as the bond of this community.

This imagined world of comradeship amalgamated completely different social practices to a morally elevated, abstract unity, for part of comradeship was not only the inebriated conviviality at night or the liberal sharing of cigarettes and cake, but also the actualization of the Gospel according to St. John (15,13 and 3,16) which emphasizes the sacrifice of one's life for a friend or brother as an expression of the greatest 'love'.[16] In the ideal of comradeship, exceptional acts referring to sacred examples and norms, and ostensibly trivial rituals of everyday life merged.[17] Most characteristically, this world of comradeship camouflages military violence. Collective memory of the First World War did not conceal the horrors of matériel battles and positional warfare, yet it aestheticized them and apologized for them. Since 1930 war-novels in particular glorified the collective frenzy of fighting which the individual soldier could not escape from. The soldier didn't fight against his enemy but for his comrades. War memory also made no secret of the fact that social interaction in the military was 'rough', as it was based on violence, not only outward but also inward, with degradation, intrigues and brutality especially against loners and outsiders being a daily phenomenon even within the same rank. The topos of comradeship in collective war memory after 1918, however, was reserved for the altruistic and 'loving', non-aggressive side of military social cohesion. The active participation of soldiers in the violence of war and in the practice of killing was rhetorically concealed by using anonymous pronouns such as 'we' or 'they'. Only 'defensive' violence used for the protection of living comrades or for the revenge of those killed in action was assigned a natural place in the sacrosanct world of comradeship.[18]

Ideals of Comradeship and Preparation for War

This accentuating of comradeship was not a matter of course. Official military education, less concerned with the moral, emotional and social overcoming of past wars than with the psychological preparation for future wars, emphasized the function of comradeship as a factor of fighting strength much more than veteran organizations, the cult of the dead or war-fiction. Thereby, official military education anticipated the findings of military sociology that analyzed the pressure for conformity existing within face-to-face-groups of the army.[19] This pressure not only secured the soldiers' mutual support in need but also urged them to pull themselves together as 'men' and to join the battle. When in the 1930s the next war was actually being prepared and finally begun, propagators of the National-Socialist *Volksgemeinschaft* and its military increasingly cared about whether soldiers would be able 'to make the right decision when being torn between feelings of comradeship and soldierly duty'.[20] Therefore, considerable efforts were made to accentuate the aggressive side of comradeship more strongly, to take the term out of its 'soft' context and to adapt it to the 'hard' military ideal of masculinity. The polemical criticism was made that since 1918 the term had been 'idealized and sentimentalized into a moral and humanitarian dimension' and that it would primarily cause 'warm feelings of well-being' but would not teach 'decision-making and action'.[21] By contrast, comradeship was now to be understood as 'the concentration of energies' of the army, as a factor of military strength and discipline. The charismatic military leader served as the driving force in this sort of comradeship.[22] In the context of NS-propaganda, comradeship was presented as a synonym for *Gefolgschaft*, the body of followers.[23]

Apart from such dissociation the term kept its 'soft' meaning in the military discourse of the Third Reich as well.[24] Even the hierarchical understanding of comradeship could quite simply be perceived as 'soft'. Indeed, the effect of the myth of comradeship relied precisely on its semantic polyvalence. It assigned a meaning to the juxtaposition and fusion of 'hard' ideals of masculinity and 'soft', 'womanly' connoted feelings and social practices. Military and youth 'pedagogues' of the NS-system were well aware of the socially integrative and socio-psychological significance of comradeship. Comradeship was thought of as an 'indispensable binder' which apart from discipline and obedience was the primary factor that kept an army together. 'Without "*Mannszucht*" the army would degenerate to an unrestrained troop, without comradeship the life of a soldier would be equal to an unbearable existence.'[25] Comradeship thus counterbalanced repression, drill and discipline. Neither the terror of the draconian disciplinary machinery alone, nor the embedding of heroic virtues like courage and bravery guaranteed military fighting strength. The Nazi '*Wehrmacht* was an army of draftees, in which – despite all stereotyping of warlike masculinity as a common substrate – all kinds of people' and not only 'a band of soldiers like Theweleit's volunteer-corps Rambos' were under arms.[26] Comradeship, therefore, was supposed to give the soldiers 'a feeling of security and thus of being at home' that included also the 'weak' who would gain 'support' from the 'strong'.[27]

'Soft' and 'womanly' comradeship, however, was not restricted to those draftees who did not fulfill the martial-fearless ideal of masculinity upheld by volunteer-corps-fighters, 'political soldiers' of the SS, fighter pilots and other military elite units. When Schauwecker in 1919 localized a 'fine, womanly feeling' of comradeship 'in every man's heart', he anticipated a wide range of meanings which this feeling was to encompass in the psychological and cultural household of completely different types of soldiers. 'Comradeship' served as a pattern of interpretation for warlike violence that was shared both by members of Himmler's services, who murdered Jews, women and children, and by the conscripted draftees of other ranks of the mass army who heard of those crimes often only through rumors. Comradeship kept the fickle and ostensibly contradictory psychological needs, emotional moods and forms of social behavior together that marked individuals of different social and cultural backgrounds and different emotional states and that characterized every army.

Comradeship as a Community of Sufferance

Out of the spectrum of different soldiers to be looked at in the following, the poet and pastor Siegbert Stehmann will be considered first. He was one of those soldiers who interpreted their actions during the National Socialist war against the background of comradeship. As a member of the *Bekennende Kirche* (Confessional Church), he was an opponent of both the NS-regime and the Nazi war. Drafted at the age of twenty-eight, only a few days after his marriage in 1940, he served in the Wehrmacht as a private first class, in particular in northern Europe and Russia. In January 1945 he was killed in action in Poland. Siegbert Stehmann was very critical towards the Nazi propaganda of comradeship. In the letters to his wife he chastised the 'naked egoism' he was daily confronted with in his comrades of equal and higher rank, as well as their 'cynicism and inner brutality' 'which deeply hurt me'. The 'horrible, nihilistic existence, the thoughtless egoistic cheerfulness' that was 'regarded as particularly soldierly' was to him an atrocity. From early on he felt threatened by the scheming nature of military group culture. After a denunciation in 1944, he was court-martialed.

However, Stehmann also found comrades who long secured his physical, psychological and 'mental' survival. Entire barrack rooms or individual 'close comrades' provided him with an opportunity for 'quiet talks' and made it possible to discuss 'personal' and 'most intimate things'. The 'love of the comrades' comforted him and provided him with a 'good coat'. Stehmann made use of the myth of comradeship by presenting himself as a pastor in imitation of Christ and by imagining himself after early Christian examples as a preceptor of a community of sufferance in the midst of 'unbelievers'. To the latter belonged convinced Nazis as much as sadistic and bullying superiors and comrades boasting about their sexual adventures with women. The 'loyal comradeship' in which he regarded himself as integrated did not overcome the 'loneliness', yet it made it, and thus the war in general as much as the dominant, 'hard' masculinity, endurable.[28]

Thomas Kühne

Comradeship and the Ideal of Conformity

Jochen Klepper, the second example to be considered here, like Stehmann, was a poet and Protestant. Unlike Stehmann, however, Klepper remained committed to old Prussian military ideals. In addition, he was married to a Jewish woman. For this reason he was dismissed from the Wehrmacht in 1941, after having served as a private on the eastern front for about a year. Another year later he and his wife were driven to commit suicide. Klepper also noticed the violence among the privates as well as the officers' 'uncomradely' behavior. Yet for him both were of only secondary importance. Rather, his diary documents an almost unbridled desire for an actualization of the myth of comradeship. In Klepper's eyes comradeship neutralized warlike violence, troublesome group culture and not least the generally widespread anti-Semitism. Comradeship kept an affectionate and altruistic male community together that also allowed for physical closeness. He emphatically wrote: 'I will not forget those nights during the war that I spent at the camp with my comrades.'

Klepper's belief in the myth of comradeship was never put in question by the experience of daily tensions, intrigues and cruelties. He interpreted them as a test of masculinity. At the end of his short time in the military he satisfactorily came to the conclusion that he had passed this test: 'How do order and horrible confusion oppose each other in my life. Yet by now I have also experienced something new and positive, namely that I fit in with other men.' For Klepper, whom the Nazis had made an outsider, being a man meant to adapt himself socially. It did not mean to belong to those soldiers who in his eyes had made themselves outsiders through 'uncomradely', 'egoistic' behavior, by refusing to adapt to the social machinery of the military.[29]

The sort of group culture which a man had to adapt to could be defined differently. In one case the altruistic norm might have been in the foreground, in the other and surely more frequently the brutality of the military initiation rite, the degradation during basic training and the rough, inebriated and smutty conviviality. In any case it was the subjection to fate, from the arbitrary line-up of the barrack room community to the outcome of the baptism of fire that was important. The norm of violence is of course only indirectly purveyed by the ego-documents that have come down to us, like letters, diaries and memoirs. In these forms of media that were directed to civil society, soldiers preferred to articulate their own 'peacefulness' and the violence of the 'others', which a particular soldier was subjected to and had to react to if necessary.[30]

Comradeship and Motherly Security

Unlike Stehmann or Klepper, Peter Pfaff was drafted in 1943 directly from school. Yet like the other two, Pfaff interpreted his time in the military against the background of Christian norms with which he had grown up, and he kept a clear distance towards Nazism. Like the other two, he was critical of the troublesome group-culture in the military and his comrades' boasting about their womanizing. Unlike Stehmann and more determined than Klepper, however, in line with Schauwecker Pfaff took all deprivations and degradations as a test of military masculinity which he strove for from his time in the labor service (*Reichsarbeitsdienst*) till his death on the eastern front in October 1944. In line with contemporary dominant images, his ideal of masculinity was about 'fighting', 'toughness' and 'inner discipline', about proving oneself 'in the heaviest storm', submissiveness to fate, and conformity. For him, not to be branded as an outsider was most important.

Directly connected to this ideal of masculinity were certain emotions and social acts which Pfaff categorized as 'unmanly', yet did not dismiss. As much as he welcomed that 'fate treats me more coldly than motherly security' and as much as he yearned to be on the front and dismissed pre-military 'ideas of freedom', he held on to the desire of 'being sheltered' just as much. This desire was fulfilled through the 'helping, divine hand', as much as through earthly persons and customs. An aunt of his served him as 'a poor ash pan, whom I love so much and with whom I am allowed' – at least in the letter – 'to sob without being unmanly'. A similar function was fulfilled by the frequently melancholic collection of songs through which the soldier could 'express his homesickness' 'without losing his manly dignity'. Only at the beginning of his time in the military when still on fatigue duty did he raise the question: 'Would I have to be ashamed of myself if I needed help, searched for warmth in order to be able to live?' Yet even then he was sure that 'love', no matter in which form, did not conflict at all with being a man and male identity. For him it was the prerequisite, the 'barracks' – the symbol of 'hard' soldierly life, the metaphor for the ideal of masculinity to 'live' *per se*.[31]

Here 'love' stood for both motherly and fatherly love, in the second place also for the love of God, and not least for love among men for which the term 'comradeship' was used in military discourse. Although subjects and objects of this 'love' might have been very different, they always had the function that Pfaff was quite conscious of: to make warlike violence, the repressive sides of military group culture, and the toughness of the contemporary ideal of masculinity bearable. In Pfaff's eyes, therefore, the love of God, the security in the family and affectionate comradeship were interchangeable. To the soldier all meant being at 'home' – in the unfamiliar and rough environment of the military and of the horrors of warlike violence. They all appeared in a 'sacral' context, like the 'desire for affection with which God has befitted us and to which we are entitled' and that distinguished them from unsoldierly, i.e. unmanly sentimentality. Sentimentality presented something that could get out of control and become independent. By contrast, everything that was seen as 'womanly in man' as well as everything that was connected to it in contemporary discourse, especially comradeship, was kept under control and did not serve to question manly 'discipline' but made it flexible. In this context, imagined femininity served as the fundamental pillar of being a man. By categorizing emotions that conflicted with the ideal of masculinity as womanly (motherly, divine), a man was able to accommodate them in his psychological household. 'Being at home' in the 'barrack-room-community' and 'being fond of each other' amongst men helped, according to Pfaff, 'to bear' the 'hardship' of 'male living', the 'greatest strains and most terrible injustice'. The personification of manly love was the military leader, into whose role Pfaff – after the unspoken examples of Walter Flex and Ernst Wurche that were constantly present to members of the bourgeoisie – slowly grew.[32]

For this reason, motherly love, family and the military bond of men were not competitive, but rather complementary fields of existence and feeling.[33] Like innumerable other soldiers in their letters home, Pfaff expressed this inner connection by calling his mother his 'comrade' and the military his 'family'.[34] Although this family was a construct, it was not a mere virtual one. Soldiers constructed 'their' family through their daily conviviality, through the idyllic decoration of a bunker according to their living room at home with flowers and pictures of their real families, and finally through the mutual help and care in different situations. These constructions represented exceptions, 'islands' in an 'ocean' saturated with violence.[35] Imagined womanly elements in man, however, were socially reproduced to the extent that the rational understanding of comradeship ('if I help you, you will help me') was dominated by a libidinous and affectionate kind of being fond of each other.[36] This did not mean genital, 'practiced' homosexuality, but what was called 'homoerotic' feeling, which was firmly dissociated from the kind of detested, 'manifest' homosexuality in the contemporary discourse of the Youth Movement, which was marked by the suppression of sexuality.[37] In the language of 'comradeship', love among men could be discussed even more openly, as this military cardinal virtue was even more apt to suppress every doubt regarding the asexual nature of that kind of love that was a characteristic of male bonding.

Comradeship and Family

The construction of the community of comradeship as a 'family' – with the head of the troops as 'Dad' and the sergeant as the 'mother' of the company or with another distribution of roles – was a central basis for the symbolic order of war. It provided, first, a very flexible and at the same time universally familiar, discursive foundation for hierarchical military social structures as well as for relationships between equals (father/child, brother/brother). At the same time, the metaphor of the family reduced the 'ambivalence of feelings'[38] that is characteristic of both kinds of social relationships in the military (as in any organization) to a 'natural' formula that could not be further questioned. The family was sacrosanct and also the juxtaposition of hatred and love, altruism and aggression, subordination and security that exists in the family as in every 'community'.[39]

Secondly, the interpretative pattern of comradeship connected to the family metaphor functioned as a communicative code which made the barriers of communication and understanding between women and men, between the family at home and the warlike bond of men on the front appear permeable. As a reaction to the crisis in the order of the sexes in the aftermath of the First World War,[40] the concept of comradeship between the sexes found considerable resonance even before the onset of the Third Reich – both in the socialist and in the bourgeois-nationalistic milieu.[41] After 1933 the idea of comradeship between the sexes was elevated to the rank of a state ideology. This ideology removed the woman from her traditional private, domestic context and made her publicly visible as the comrade of man. The woman was no longer to play the domestic counterpart to the role of the man in civil or warlike 'work', but to actively support him in this role as a 'junior partner' without estranging herself from her 'original' role as a woman. The reason why this split was successfully accomplished was not least a consequence of the sex-specific spheres of socialization provided by the *Bund Deutscher Mädel* and the *Reichsarbeitsdienst*, in which women were able (and required) to perform and experience 'comradeship' among each other. Not only memoirs but also contemporary self-testimonials prove that especially girls and women from the bourgeois milieu were fascinated by the participation in such an organized 'experience of comradeship'.[42]

Letters between soldiers and their wives, girlfriends or mothers, however, also document how the tender, emphatic, and altruistic 'feminine' dimension of soldierly comradeship enabled the discursive participation of real women in this male world of warlike violence to exist. Hilde Wieschenberg hoped that her husband Franz, a carpenter from Benrath in the Rhineland who fought in the east as a private, would be assigned a post in the back lines of his front division. He himself long rejected this idea on the grounds that it was not compatible with his view of himself as a 'man' and 'comrade'. On the front, Wieschenberg had quickly integrated himself into the libidinous world of soldierly comradeship, which he used as an argument against his wife's wishes. He regularly told his wife about the comradely solidarity in his unit, which he did not want to give up. His wife was fully receptive to this argument: 'I am happy that you are in the company of dear comrades. Such a profound comradeship formed in the field must be something special.' She urged him: 'You comrades should take every opportunity to get closer to each other.' At the same time she and her husband increasingly referred to their marriage in the language of comradeship. He spoke of her 'great comradeship' to him, and she regularly called him 'my comrade for life'.[43] Like the Wieschenbergs, many other couples and families bridged the gap between the warfront and the 'home-front' in the Total War. The sense of comradeship as a feminine element in man thus reached far beyond the military world of men. However, comradeship always remained a concept shaped and dominated by masculinity. As a comrade to her husband, the woman presented a counterpole to the ordinary housewife. Yet she remained a creation of the man, a product of the sort of femininity imagined by men, no matter how much women identified with it.

The fascination of the experience of comradeship in the *Bund Deutscher Mädel* or in the *Reichsarbeitsdienst* thrived on the consciousness of being able to participate in the mysteries of a community experience that had been exclusively masculine before. Thus, it also reproduced the subtle camouflage of violence which the myth of comradeship achieved. Lore Walb, a 22-year old student and daughter of a dealer of agricultural machines who had entered the NSDAP in 1931, remembered the death of Werner Mölders in November 1941: 'Hermann [a friend of Lore's] told me of his [Mölders's] great spirit of comradeship and community during his flights. Through the aircraft's radio equipment he had given his pilots firing instructions. The boys had liked him a lot.'[44] These three sentences articulate the relationship of comradeship to warlike violence, and it would hardly be possible to express it more clearly. The firing instructions mentioned in the middle sentence are rhetorically framed and marginalized in their content by the conjuration of 'great' comradeship in the first and by the almost family-like, caring father–son relationship and the sons' love of their fathers mentioned in the third sentence.

Comradeship and the Murder of Jews

Siegbert Stehmann and Jochen Klepper may serve here as representatives of one end of the spectrum of soldiers who organized their war experience and masculine identity during the National Socialist war on the basis of the myth of comradeship. On the other side of the spectrum stood the 21-year old Austrian Felix Landau. He had entered the NSDAP in 1931 and was involved in the Dollfuß-affair, when he was almost shot. Having been taken into custody, he joined the Gestapo after the annexation of Austria. From 1940 on, Landau worked as a member of the *Sicherheitsdienst* (Security Service) in occupied Poland, was decorated with the *Blutorden* (Blood Medal) of the NSDAP, and during July and August 1941, together with a task force, he took part in the shooting of Jews in the area of Lemberg. His diary entries during this time constantly revolve around three themes: firstly, around his longing for his extramarital beloved who caused him worry because she did not want to separate from her fiancé; secondly, around the atmosphere among the comrades and his relationship to them; and finally around the murders, which he described without any scruples.[45]

In Landau's emotional economy, all three themes were closely connected to each other. Rather indifferently he described his 'work', even if he had some uneasy feeling from time to time:

> Falling in for execution. Well, why not play the executioner and subsequently the gravedigger? Isn't that strange: you like fighting and then you have to shoot helpless people down. Twenty-three were to be shot, among them the women I have mentioned before. [. . .] What is also strange is that I don't feel anything – not a stirring of human pity, nothing. That's how it is, and then everything is finished. My heart beats only quietly,

namely when he remembered his own fear of being shot after the assassination of Dollfuß. Yet back then he had quickly pushed away the fear of becoming 'soft'; actually he had not allowed himself to have it at all, and he did the same when shooting the Jews. Inside, however, he was in a state of inner turmoil. 'At night, while I lay in bed, I was overcome by an unrestrained desire, a desire for quiet, peace and love.' Eroticism and aggression were closely connected. The longing for the insecure beloved around whom his 'sensual', 'soft' and peaceful thoughts had once revolved eventually turned into anger because of his frustration caused by the separation: 'I am in the mood for killing everything.' Between the daily and barbaric violence and the unsatisfied longing for 'the woman' comrades and comradeship acted as mediators, and in the course of time they became increasingly better. At first, the nights among the inebriated comrades offered only limited distraction. 'My thoughts are too often with my Trude.' Yet eventually living among comrades became more intensive. Contributing to this development was not least the experience of violence from the 'others': 'Comrades' of the Wehrmacht were 'beaten up beastly' so that their own violence now appeared to be completely beyond a shadow of a doubt. At the same time, his own comrades provided 'comfortable' moments. Finally he recognized his superior, who was divorced and boasted about the letters from his 'girlfriend', as the ideal comrade after he had promised Felix his 'support' in bringing his beloved over. The comradely ritual of sharing one's supplies sealed the pact: 'Dolte offered me wine and cigarettes and thus we sat together like old comrades. [. . .] Finally, after a long time, my mood was cheery again.'

Male comradeship and male bonding did not compete with the 'love' which the real or imagined beloved was to give. Both complemented each other. Both, comradeship and the love of a woman, 'neutralized' and blurred the own brutal violence. They provided 'quiet, peace and love' in the midst of barbarity. 'Today my comrades and I have had our Jewish maid grill us chicken [. . .]. It was all very nice but right and left there were empty seats. I looked at both chairs and said to my comrades that only our girlfriends were missing.' This complementary relationship between the libidinous bond to comrades and that to women was not an exceptional phenomenon in the SS but corresponded to the norm propagated in different words by Himmler. The SS was not only to be a bond of men, but also a 'kinship group' (*Sippengemeinschaft*). This ideal did not apply to the protection of extramarital affairs but to the biological role of reproduction that was assigned to the family. Decisive in our context is the role which the bourgeois family as much as the extramarital affair had in the emotional economy of those people responsible for murdering the Jews. Both the family and the affair offered emotional and moral relief from the 'hard', murderous 'work' and thus made this work in certain respects possible. Among 'beloved friends' the operators of the killing machines experienced and cultivated 'softness, love and care'[46] and assured themselves of their 'humanity' in a quite bourgeois sense. Both the emotional and the moral function of this softness were closely connected, for paradoxically enough the apologists of the 'war of extermination' held to the settings of bourgeois morality despite all polemics against the morality of Christian pity. This can be proved not least by Himmler's speech in Posen on the 'respectability' of the mass-murderers.[47] Simultaneously, due to the spatial proximity to their work, the families of SS-men – wives, now and then also children – were frequently integrated into the barbaric community kept together through the 'bond of blood'.[47] Moreover, in the same way in which women were integrated into the aggressive side of male bonding, the comradeship of men served as a replacement of or as a supplement to the real family. As the latter, comradeship provided a space where men cultivated 'softness, love and care' among themselves and thus created an empathy that was frowned upon as soon as the limits of internal morality were transcended.[48]

Conclusion

Imagined 'femininity' in men and comradeship as a symbol of order did not only have an excluding function, but also an integrating one. They did not question the hierarchical order of the sexes, but stabilized it. They made possible, firstly, the communication about the tense relationship between heterosexual norm and sublimed homosexuality (in the Freudian sense) possible and thus secured both the individual and the biographical identity of men. The concept of comradeship balanced the complicated and tense relationship between the 'hard' ideal of masculinity and the 'soft' elements of being a man. Secondly, comradeship served as a symbolic hinge between violence and harmony, between war and peace. It vaulted the conflict between group-internal repression and affection as much as the conflict between warlike (even barbaric) violence and the civil norm of non-violence to which life before and after the war was obliged. The warlike, regular and barbaric violence was radicalized and totalized from Germany between 1939 and 1945 to an extent that had been impossible to imagine before; it was supported by the 'soft' relief provided by male comradeship and bonding as well as by the bourgeois idyll of the family or by extramarital affairs. Imagined femininity, conceived of as camaraderie, presented thirdly a cipher which during the war established a symbolic connection between home and the front, between the real family and the real military society of male bonding that largely excluded women.

Thomas Kühne

Notes

Translated by Rainer Gruhlich.

1. Franz Schauwecker *Im Todesrachen. Die deutsche Seele im Weltkriege* (Halle a.S., 1919), 4, 16–20, 22, 68, 100f., 216, 307, 359–365.
2. For recent research compare Thomas Kühne, 'Der nationalsozialistische Vernichtungskrieg im kulturellen Kontinuum des 20. Jahrhunderts. Forschungsprobleme und Forschungstendenzen der Gesellschaftsgeschichte des Zweiten Weltkriegs. Zweiter Teil,' *Archiv für Sozialgeschichte* 40 (2000): 440–486, especially 442–451.
3. Klaus Theweleit, *Männerphantasien*, 2 vols. (Frankfurt a.M., 1977/ 78), tr. as *Male Fantasies: Women, Floods, Bodies, History* (Cambridge, 1987). For a critical assessment compare Richard J. Evans, 'Geschichte, Psychologie und die Geschlechterbeziehungen in der Vergangenheit,' *Geschichte und Gesellschaft* 7 (1981): 590–613, 602; Walter Erhart and Britta Herrmann, 'Der erforschte Mann?' in *Wann ist der Mann ein Mann? Zur Geschichte der Männlichkeit*, ed. id. (Stuttgart/Weimar, 1997), 3–31, 7–12.
4. Hannes Heer and Klaus Naumann, eds, *Vernichtungskrieg. Verbrechen der Wehrmacht 1941–1944* (Hamburg, 1995), 30.
5. Ruth Seifert, 'Feministische Theorie und Militärsoziologie,' *Das Argument*, no. 190 (1991): 861–873, 862.
6. Michael Meuser, 'Mann,' in *Vom Menschen. Handbuch Historische Anthropologie*, ed. Christoph Wulf (Weinheim/Basel, 1997), 389–397, 389.
7. See, for example, the inspiring studies of Susan Jeffords, *The Remasculinization of America: Gender and the Vietnam War* (Bloomington/ Indianapolis, 1989); Frank J. Barrett, 'Die Konstruktion hegemonialer Männlichkeit in Organisationen: Das Beispiel der US-Marine,' and Kathrin Däniker, 'Die Truppe – ein Weib? Geschlechtliche Zuschreibungen in der Armee um die Jahrhundertwende,' both in *Soziale Konstruktionen Militär und Geschlechterverhältnis*, ed. Christine Eifler and Ruth Seifert (Münster, 1999), 71–91 and 110–134; the best critical review of this and other research is Christa Hämmerle, 'Von den Geschlechtern der Kriege und des Militärs. Forschungseinblicke und Bemerkungen zu einer neuen Debatte,' in *Was ist Militärgeschichte?* ed. Thomas Kühne and Benjamin Ziemann (Paderborn etc., 2000), 229–262.
8. Thomas Kühne, 'Männergeschichte als Geschlechtergeschichte,' in *Männergeschichte – Geschlechtergeschichte. Männlichkeit im Wandel*

der Moderne, ed. Thomas Kühne (Frankfurt am Main/New York, 1996), 7–30, 23. Compare John Tosh, 'Why Should Historians do with Masculinities? Reflections on Nineteenth-Century Britain', *History Workshop* 38 (1994), 179–202. Robert W. Connell, *Masculinities* (Berkeley 1995).

9. For more details see my forthcoming book on Hitler's soldiers and the myth of comradeship, 1918–2000.

10. Peter L. Berger and Thomas Luckmann, *The Social Construction of Reality. A Treatise in the Sociology of Knowledge* (New York, 1966); compare Lloyd B. Lewis, *The Tainted War: Culture and Identity in Vietnam War Narratives* (Westport, Conn. 1985). For anthropological research in myths and ritual see esp.Victor W. Turner, 'Myth and Symbol', in *International Encyclopedia of the Social Sciences*, ed. David L. Sills, vol. 10 (New York, 1968), 576–581; id., *From Ritual to Theatre. The Human Seriousness of Play* (New York, 1982). Compare Thomas Kühne, 'Zwischen Männerbund und Volksgemeinschaft: Hitlers Soldaten und der Mythos der Kameradschaft,' *Archiv für Sozialgeschichte* 38 (1998): 165–189, esp. 170–175.

11. Benjamin Ziemann, *Front und Heimat. Ländliche Kriegserfahrungen im südlichen Bayern 1914–1923* (Essen, 1997), 55–289.

12. Compare Eric J. Leed, *No Man's Land. Combat and Identity in World War I* (Cambridge, 1979), 82–94.

13. Compare Ann P. Linder, *Princes of the Trenches. Narrating the German Experience of the First World War* (Columbia, SC, 1996), 74–85.

14. Benjamin Ziemann, 'Republikanische Kriegserinnerung in einer polarisierten Öffentlichkeit. Das Reichsbanner Schwarz-Rot-Gold als Veteranenverband der sozialistischen Arbeiterschaft,' *Historische Zeitschrift* 267 (1998): 357–398.

15. Most influential: Erich Maria Remarque, *Im Westen nichts Neues. Roman* [first published in 1929, tr. as: *All Quiet on the Western Front*, London, 1929]. *Mit Materialien und einem Nachwort von Tilman Westphalen* (Cologne, 1987), cf. 46ff. for ‚subversive' comradeship, cf. 195ff. for comradeship with the enemy.

16. German war memories often cited Gospel passages such these, for example Theodor Bartram, *Der Frontsoldat. Ein deutsches Kultur- und Lebensideal* (Berlin, 1934), 21 (first published in 1919); more general: Volker G. Probst, *Bilder vom Tode. Eine Studie zum deutschen Kriegerdenkmal in der Weimarer Republik am Beispiel des Pieta-Motives und seiner profanierten Varianten* (Hamburg, 1986), 46ff.

17. Hans-Georg Soeffner, *Auslegung des Alltags – Der Alltag der Auslegung. Zur wissenssoziologischen Konzeption einer sozialwissenschaftlichen Hermeneutik* (Frankfurt am Main, 1989), 176ff.

18. In the left- and right-wing war narratives there are innumerable examples. For the linguistic traditions cf. Hugo Aust, 'Das "wir" und das "töten". Anmerkungen zur sprachlichen Gestaltung des Krieges in Theodor Fontanes Kriegsbüchern,' *Wirkendes Wort* 41 (1991): 199–211.

19. Samuel Stouffer et al., *The American Soldier: Studies in the Social Psychology in World War II*, 2 vols. (Princeton, 1949); more recent research is summarized in Reuven Gal and A. David Mangelsdorff, eds., *Handbook of Military Psychology* (Chichester etc., 1991), 449–558 (Individual and Group Behavior). An early German voice: Hanns Eggert Willibald von der Lühe, ed., *Militair-Conversations-Lexicon*, 8 vols. (Leipzig, 1831–41), vol. IV (1834), 141–143. Most influential on German discussions after 1945 was Edward A. Shils/Morris Janowitz, 'Cohesion and Disintegration in the Wehrmacht in World War II', *The Public Opinion Quarterly* 12 (1948): 280–315, see esp. ibid. 284, 286.

20. Otto Paust, ed., *Kameradschaft ist stärker als der Tod* (Berlin, 1943), 75.

21. Albrecht Erich Günther, 'Kameradschaftslehre,' *Deutsches Volkstum* 16 (1934): 11–15, 13.

22. Hermann Göring talking to '1,000 Pilots' in 1936, Hermann Göring, 'Kameradschaft, Pflichterfüllung und Opferbereitschaft,' in idem, *Reden und Aufsätze* (Munich, 1938), 226–244, 227.

23. Thomas Kühne, '"Kameradschaft – das Beste im Leben des Mannes". Die deutschen Soldaten des Zweiten Weltkrieges in erfahrungs- und geschlechtergeschichtlicher Perspektive,' *Geschichte und Gesellschaft* 22 (1996): 504–529, 511.

24. See, for example, P.C. Ettighoffer, ed., *'Wo bist du Kamerad?' Der Frontsoldat im Reichssender Köln* (Essen, 1938).

25. Wilhelm Reibert, *Der Dienstunterricht im Reichsheer. Ein Handbuch für den deutschen Soldaten*, 6th edm (Berlin, 1934), 96.

26. Michael Geyer, 'Das Stigma der Gewalt und das Problem der nationalen Identität in Deutschland,' in *Von der Aufgabe der Freiheit. Politische Verantwortung und bürgerliche Gesellschaft im 19. und 20. Jahrhundert*, ed. Christian Jansen, Lutz Niethammer and Bernd Weisbrod (Berlin, 1995), 673–698, 690.

27. Erich Weniger, *Wehrmachterziehung und Kriegserfahrung* (Berlin,

1938), 118.

28. Siegbert Stehmann, *Die Bitternis verschweigen wir. Feldpostbriefe 1940–1945* (Hannover, 1992), 19, 26, 42, 49, 55, 70, 73f., 86, 89, 126.

29. Jochen Klepper, *Überwindung. Tagebücher und Aufzeichnungen aus dem Kriege* (Stuttgart, 1958), 131, 211. Cf. Kühne, *Männerbund*, 176–185.

30. Thomas Kühne, 'Der nationalsozialistische Vernichtungskrieg und die "ganz normalen" Deutschen. Forschungsprobleme und Forschungstendenzen der Gesellschaftsgeschichte des Zweiten Weltkriegs,' Erster Teil, *Archiv für Sozialgeschichte* 39 (1999): 580–662, 643–649.

31. Peter Pfaff, *Die Briefe des Peter Pfaff 1943–1944*, ed. Hans Graf v. Lehndorff (3rd edn, Munich, 1988), 17, 35, 41, 46, 48, 52, 58, 60, 69, 75f., 113, 116, 121, 131, 135f., 138.

32. Ibid. 45, 70, 127.

33. Compare, on the basis of other war letters, Martin Humburg, *Das Gesicht des Krieges. Feldpostbriefe von Wehrmachtsoldaten aus der Sowjetunion 1941–1944* (Opladen, 1998), 173ff.; Klara Löffler, *Aufgehoben: Soldatenbriefe aus dem Zweiten Weltkrieg. Eine Studie zur subjektiven Wirklichkeit des Krieges* (Bamberg, 1992); and the illuminating case studies by Inge Marszolek, '"Ich möchte Dich zu gern mal in Uniform sehen." Geschlechterkonstruktionen in Feldpostbriefen,' and Ulrike Jureit, 'Zwischen Ehe und Männerbund. Emotionale und sexuelle Beziehungsmuster im Zweiten Weltkrieg,' *WerkstattGeschichte* 22 (1999): 41–59 and 61–73.

34. Pfaff, *Die Briefe*, 57 (the mother as comrade) and 97f. (military as family).

35. Ibid. 57, speaking of the real family, the 'Heimat' and the friends.

36. Ibid., 18, for the quotations. The whole letter series can be understood as an illustration of this process.

37. Compare Ulfried Geuter, *Homosexualität in der deutschen Jugendbewegung. Jungenfreundschaft und Sexualität im Diskurs von Jugendbewegung, Psychoanalyse und Jugendpsychologie am Beginn des 20. Jahrhunderts* (Frankfurt a.M., 1994).

38. Sigmund Freud, 'Massenpsychologie und Ich-Analyse' [1921], in idem, Studienausgabe, 10 vols. (Frankfurt a.M., 1974), vol. X, 61–134, 95, citing Schopenhauer's famous parable on freezing porcupines.

39. Compare Francesca Rigotti, *Die Macht und ihre Metaphern. Über die sprachlichen Bilder der Politik* (Frankfurt am Main/New York, 1994), 77–114.

40. Compare the contributions of Birthe Kundrus and Sabine Kienitz to

this volume.

41. Irmgard Klönne, *'Ich spring in diesem Ringe'. Mädchen u. Frauen in der deutschen Jugendbewegung* (Pfaffenweiler, 1990), esp. 258–273; and Karen Hagemann, *Frauenalltag und Männerpolitik. Alltagsleben und gesellschaftliches Handeln von Arbeiterfrauen in der Weimarer Republik* (Bonn, 1990), 325–331. There are some differences between socialist and bourgeois conceptions of gender comradeship, which cannot be dealt with here.

42. Sigrid Bremer, *Muckefuck und Kameradschaft. Mädchenzeit im Dritten Reich. Von der Kinderlandverschickung 1940 bis zum Studium 1946* (Frankfurt am Main, 1988). Cf. for further literature Kühne, 'Vernichtungskrieg II,' 463.

43. For the Wieschenberg letters see Kempowski-Archiv Nartum, no. 3386.

44. Lore Walb, *Ich, die Alte – ich, die Junge. Konfrontation mit meinen Tagebüchern 1933–1945* (Berlin, 1997, paperback edn 1998), 234.

45. Ernst Klee, Willi Dressen and Volker Rieß, eds., *'Schöne Zeiten.' Judenmord aus der Sicht der Täter und Gaffer* (Frankfurt a.M., 1988), see 88 and 262f. for the biography, 88–104 for the following quotations.

46. Gudrun Schwarz, *Eine Frau an seiner Seite. Ehefrauen in the 'SS-Sippengemeinschaft'* (Hamburg, 1997), 105.

47. Ibid. 104, 190ff. Christopher R. Browning, *Ordinary Men: Reserve Police Batalion 101 and the Final Solution in Poland* (New York, 1992), ch. 14; Daniel Jonah Goldhagen, *Hitlers Willing Executioners: Ordinary Men and the Holocaust* (London 1996), ch. 7 (the Wohlaufs).

48. Kühne, 'Kameradschaft,' 519–521.

–10–

Rape

The Military Trials of Sexual Crimes Committed by Soldiers in the Wehrmacht, 1939–1944

Birgit Beck

In March 2000 several former Serbian militia leaders were brought before the International Criminal Tribunal for the former Yugoslavia, accused of crimes against humanity, serious violation of the Geneva Convention, and breaches of the laws and customs of war. In what became known as the 'Foca Trial', an international tribunal treated rape and enforced prostitution as war crimes in their own right for the first time in the history of international law, punishing by law the mass rapes during the civil war in former Yugoslavia. During the trial, the cases of enforced prostitution and sexual assault in the Bosnian town of Foca were condemned as an essential component of the policy of ethnic cleansing and therefore defined as a 'war strategy'.[1] Until now, this term has mainly been used in historical and sociological research as a general term to refer to most rapes committed during war, without closer examination of political and social factors and above all of military aims.[2] Furthermore, most work on this subject is predominantly based on the analysis of the physical and above all psychological experiences and the severe consequences rape has had for the women involved. The question of whether rape during war can be considered a component of warfare and therefore has been and still is used as a strategic tactic cannot, however, be satisfactorily answered with this method of approach, nor if the situation is considered from this point of view. In order to find clear proof, it is necessary to examine the question of whether sexual violence was ordered by the military leadership, whether silent toleration constituted giving the soldiers permission to commit such acts, or whether there were any attempts to prevent such crimes by prohibiting and punishing them.

Until now, sexual crime during the Second World War has not been examined in any great detail within this context. While the mass rape of both eastern and western European women by soldiers from the Red Army at the end of the war in 1945 is anchored in the public consciousness and has been the subject of several studies,[3] rape committed by members of the Wehrmacht and the SS is a subject as yet largely untouched in the history of crime during the Second World War.[4] Even in works which deal mainly with the numerous atrocities perpetrated by the army or the SS, there are at most hints in footnotes and brief mentions in subordinate clauses that sexual crime was prevalent. Despite – or indeed rather because of – the scarcity of research on this subject, the view predominates that German soldiers systematically committed rape in order to spread terror and that the criminals could be certain of 'not being punished'.[5] An examination of Wehrmacht court verdicts from the time of the Second World War, however, reveals a very different picture. The verdicts do not only contradict the theory that such crimes went unpunished, they also give the impression that the army dealt with such crimes in a very different way, depending on whether they were committed on the western or eastern front. Furthermore, extensive records detailing the sentencing reveal much about the attitude of the military towards soldiers' sexuality and yield a characterization of the female victims that is marked by specifically National Socialist ideology. Some of these results will be presented in the following essay.[6] Before an examination of the legal sentences in detail, however, some introductory remarks on the crime of rape are necessary to elucidate the legal situation in the Third Reich.

The Crime of Rape under Military Law

Under §§ 1–3 of Military Law, members of the Wehrmacht were to be tried according to the German Criminal Code (*Deutsches Strafgesetzbuch*) for misdemeanors which were not classified as military offences.[7] 'Crimes and offences against moral conduct' were to be punished with prison sentences (*Gefängnis*) or, in severe cases, with up to ten years of *Zuchthaus*,[8] according to §§ 176 to 178 of the German Criminal Code. A person could be charged if they: 'use force in order to commit immoral acts on a female person or coerce that person to immoral acts by threatening her health or life [. . .]' or if they 'coerce a woman by using force or threats [. . .] to intercourse out of wedlock or impose extramarital intercourse upon a woman [. . .].'[9]

Beginning in 1941 such offences could be punished with the death sentence, if 'this is necessary for the protection of the national community or if the need for just atonement exists'.[10] But when this passage was included in the German Criminal Code, it was meant mainly for the criminal prosecution of sexual crimes committed against German women. Since women who lived in the countries occupied by the Wehrmacht did not belong to the 'Aryan' national community, they stood outside German law, and rapes committed against such women did not fulfill the definition of a criminal offence that was punishable by the death sentence.[11] It is often argued that in individual cases the Wehrmacht did actually punish rape with the death sentence, but this is mainly true in cases that were combined with other criminal offences such as pillage, so that the sentence reflected a combination of both offences.[12] In some cases the perpetrator was sentenced under the 'Decree against Violent Criminals' of 1939. This decree allowed for the death sentence for crimes that were committed under force of arms.[13]

The basis for wartime jurisdiction was the 'Decree on Wartime Criminal Proceedings' (*Kriegsstrafverfahrensordnung*) of 1938, which was brought into force before the war started. This decree laid down certain rules, such as the composition of the court or the procedure for drawing up a sentence and its content. It was above all to ensure swift proceedings in times of war.[14] In general each military unit had its own military court, which was usually presided over by three judges. One of them had to be a military lawyer, the other two soldiers functioned as lay judges. All verdicts made by this court had to be given in writing to the superior in charge; in the army this was usually the commanding officer of a division. It was his confirmation that brought a sentence into force. Usually the accused in military court proceedings were in a rather weak position. For instance, they only had the right to a defense lawyer if the crime they were accused of was punishable by death.[15] In all other cases, the soldier could merely give his version of the details of the crime and make a personal statement at the end of the trial. This meant that he had hardly any influence on the trial. However, both his private and military conduct up to this time were considered so that any possible previous criminal record could be taken into account and the accused could be classified as a certain 'perpetrator type'.[16] The assessment of the military conduct of the accused as well as the crime he was being tried for played a considerable role in determining the type of sentence he was given. A convicted soldier might be sent to a military prison at the front (*Feldstrafgefangenenlager*), probationary divisions (*Bewährungsbataillone*) or military prisons (*Wehrmachtgefängnisse*) back in Germany. As the war dragged on, however, and the German Wehrmacht found itself in a rather precarious situation, the army's constant need for human resources played a role in determining sentences. More and more soldiers were given the dubious opportunity to serve their sentence by taking part in the often very dangerous operations of the so-called probationary divisions.[17]

Court Verdicts on Rape: The Sources

More than 17 million men[18] served in the German Wehrmacht during the Second World War, but we do not know how many of them were ever caught in the wheels of military jurisdiction. Projections as well as a number of estimates claim that the military courts dealt with two to three million cases; of these, only about 44,000 cases dealt with by army military courts (*Heeresgerichte*) are still to be found in the Federal Archives in Kornelimünster/Aachen.[19] A specific search for files containing verdicts on sexual crimes is further complicated by the fact that only some of these records are filed according to the type of crime the particular case dealt with, and thus access to court proceedings against perpetrators of sexual crimes is limited. The military criminal statistics of the years 1939 to 1944 show that around one third of the crimes that took place in this period of time were classified as 'civil' offences, such as rape. The majority of offences was classified as military crimes and offences.[20] This fact, however, is only an indicator of the number of court proceedings regarding such offences, and it does not give us any idea about the numbers in which these crimes occurred. Furthermore, one should be aware that the estimated number of unreported cases of sexual assaults is much higher than in times of peace, so that here we are only dealing with the tip of the iceberg. It is worth noting, though, that the statistics show that prosecution of so-called 'crimes against morality' within the army peaked after the attack on France and then dropped considerably after a short period of time. The vast majority of soldiers, however, served on the eastern front, and the war against the Soviet Union was characterized by more criminal behavior from the outset – especially with regard to the treatment of the civilian population. This is a clear indication that criminal prosecution in the East was handled more leniently for a number of reasons.[21]

So just how reliable are the court verdicts if we take the above-mentioned details into consideration? It is obvious that the court files can only shed partial light on the complex problem of the rapes committed by German soldiers during the Second World War. Using these files, we can neither determine the overall scale on which sexual violence occurred, nor can we find any information on the experiences of women who were raped, since the offences are described merely from the point of view of the courts martial. The court verdicts are, however, a legitimate and very useful source if we are interested in learning more about the circumstances under which the assaults occurred or how the court martials dealt with such acts of violence. The files show how differently the courts martial interpreted existing law at the western and eastern fronts either against or in favor of the accused. The reasons given for the particular sentences also yield exemplary insight into the military's view of the soldiers' sexuality. Furthermore, the way the offences, the accused soldiers and the raped women are described in these court files shows just how much the judges were guided by National Socialist and therefore 'racist' ideology.

The findings of this essay are based on cases from the western and the eastern fronts between 1939 and 1944.[22] Most of the cases dealt with occurred behind the lines in France, Poland and Russia or while the troops remained stationed in an area at the front for a certain period of time. Therefore the military courts at the front (*Feldkriegsgerichte*) had to deal with a very wide range of different cases of rape. There are reports of rapes which occurred in combination with offences such as pillage, absence without leave or unlawful use of weapons. In such cases, individual perpetrators as well as groups of soldiers who had committed gang rape had to appear in court. There are also cases of attempted rape which were prevented because the victim was able to defend herself or because other soldiers stepped in. According to the testimonies of perpetrators and witnesses, the excessive consumption of alcohol also played a big role. However, such statements should be treated with caution, especially if the statement was made by the perpetrator himself, since acknowledging that the crime was committed under the influence of alcohol could lead to a verdict of diminished responsibility, thus resulting in greatly reduced punishment. Therefore the reference to inebriation was used in some cases in order to increase the chance of a more lenient sentence.

As is the case in other wars as well, there is no unified profile of either perpetrators or victims. Soldiers of all age groups and different marital status, some with and some without a criminal record (*Disziplinarstrafen*), appeared before the judges. The girls and women who were subjected to sexual violence also represented various age groups. Among them were single women as well as married women and mothers. While in France the women themselves often reported the assault to the local police and an account was then handed to the relevant local administrations of the Wehrmacht for further proceedings, in Poland and Russia such assaults were often brought to court after reports by other soldiers or the military police. Although on both fronts victims' testimonies were considered important when gathering evidence, there are – for reasons that will be looked at later – by far more instances of witnesses' reports to be found in files from the western front. In the following paragraphs, this essay will deal with the particular manner in which jurisdiction was practiced at the western and eastern fronts respectively.

The 'Reputation' of the Wehrmacht

On 4 June 1940 the military court of Division 251 of the German infantry in Lille sentenced a gunner to four years' prison (*Zuchthaus*) and stripped him of his honor as a soldier on the grounds that he had committed rape. The soldier had forced sexual intercourse on a French woman, a mother of two daughters, in the presence of her husband and had been found guilty on the evidence of reports by the woman and her family. When pronouncing the sentence, the judges gave several reasons for their decision, but they stressed in particular the fact that through his offence the accused had: 'severely damaged the reputation of the Wehrmacht in enemy country. Considering that several such cases of rape have occurred recently, a prolonged prison sentence also has to be imposed as a warning to other soldiers.'[23] A similar reason was given for the severe sentence in another case. In 1943 the martial court of the 29th Motorized Infantry Division sentenced a married lance-corporal to eighteen months in prison for 'attempted rape' and stripped him of his rank. He had knocked a 36-year-old French woman off her bicycle and tried to rape her in the ditch at the side of the road. Only because the victim was able to resist did this attempt at rape remain unsuccessful. The verdict reads: 'By his conduct the accused severely damaged the reputation of the Wehrmacht and the trust of the French population in it.'[24] The judges' opinion in both cases is typical for the proceedings in France, where the courts-martials' worries about the possible negative influence such acts might have on the relationship with the civilian population were of prime importance in determining the severity of the sentence. The rather vague term 'reputation of the Wehrmacht' and the worry that sexual crimes might considerably damage this reputation, can be found in most of the court files. Since the troops were usually stationed in one place for some time in occupied France, the courts feared that such assaults might further fuel the already hostile public opinion and make the forced coexistence with the occupation army even more problematic. German administration boards in occupied France soon realized that despite their massive propaganda attempts, the public attitude had become more and more anti-German.[25] In the first case cited above, prevention of other sexual offences also seems to have been a significant factor. The reference to other recent attacks on women was without doubt meant to stress their intention to deter other soldiers from committing such assaults; accordingly, the sentence was made known in the convicted soldier's unit. As was the case with other criminal offences, such as theft of military post, which were often punished much more severely, it is questionable if the goal of deterrence was actually achieved. In this context it would be interesting to find out from soldiers' letters and wartime memoirs just how much the military courts managed to influence the conduct of the soldiers.

Although military interests were considered far more important than the actual sexual assaults in determining the prosecution and assessment of such offences, the courts martial also took the victims' reports into account when reconstructing the actual course of the assault. Like such proceedings in times of peace, the judges' assessment of the female victims, particularly in regard to their outward appearance and their moral conduct, played an important role. In France, especially, a raped woman had to be able to convince the court that she had not 'caused' the assault herself through – from a male point of view – 'provocative' behavior or by going out with the soldier in question. Just how much the outward appearance of a woman could influence the judge is shown in a trial at the military court of the 159th Reserves Division in November 1942. The relevant court martial had a positive impression of the French witness because 'her dress, behavior and appearance were plain [. . .] and she showed no signs of hatred towards the rapist'. As a result, the judges deemed her trustworthy and she was not even sworn in.[26] Considerable effort was put into gathering evidence of the victims' moral conduct. In one case the warrant officer from the military police in charge of the case had managed to find out through extensive investigation in the local community that the woman was held in high regard by her neighbors. Furthermore, her testimony could not be doubted, since according to the report, she had suffered a number of injuries in the assault that had to be treated by a French doctor.[27] It was in particular young, single women or married women without children whose husbands had been taken prisoner by the Germans or who were serving at the front who were quickly suspected of having an immoral lifestyle and of having 'provoked' the rape by their 'thoughtless' behavior or even of having falsely accused an innocent German soldier. However, once the courts martial at the western front were convinced that an 'innocent' or defenseless victim had been assaulted and, in addition, the accused had a criminal record or a poor report on his conduct in the army, they often sentenced sexual criminals to long imprisonment that included dismissal from the army and therefore loss of pay (*Zuchthaus*).

Women's 'Sexual Honor'

The basis for prosecution of sexual crimes at the eastern front differed considerably from that at the western front. The rules of international law and military jurisdiction were ignored from the beginning. In accordance with the infamous 'Barbarossa decree on military jurisdiction at the eastern front' of 13 May 1941, all crimes and criminal offences committed by German soldiers on Soviet civilians were not to be punished unless a punishment by court martial was necessary to maintain military discipline (*Manneszucht*) or to safeguard troops. The edict defined such situations as 'serious deeds caused by a lack of sexual restraint or a criminal disposition or deeds which indicate a danger that discipline among the troops might break down altogether [. . .]'.[28] Since the 'lack of sexual restraint' was not further specified, it remained unclear whether this meant repeated sexual assaults or rapes conducted with particular brutality and thus left room for individual interpretation. It was mainly up to the disciplinary officer whether he regarded an offence as severe enough to call for court proceedings. According to Omer Bartov, crimes against the civilian population were rarely punished, on the one hand because of the commanders' underlying sympathy with such deeds, and, on the other hand, 'because they constituted a convenient safety valve for venting the men's anger and frustration caused by the rigid discipline demanded from the men and by the increasingly heavy cost and hopelessness of the war.'[29] Therefore, at first a far smaller number of crimes against civilians were brought before the court martials than at the western front. Sexual crimes in this ideologically justified war of conquest and extermination[30] were mainly brought to trial if they were regarded as a serious danger to discipline among the troops. While some soldiers and officers who reported a crime surely must have done so out of respect for both the rules of decency and the law, the most common reason for reporting such crimes was the worry that they might undermine military discipline.[31] In accordance with the nature of this war, criminal prosecution at the eastern front was less motivated by the fear of a negative influence on the Wehrmacht's reputation than by worries about the troops' cohesion and fitness for action. Although on both fronts military interests were without a doubt the main concern of the courts martial, it is obvious that at the eastern front sexual crimes were often punished with more lenient sentences than in France. The court verdicts clearly show that National Socialist and racist patterns of thought had an immense influence on the verdicts.

In 1941 the military court of the 7th Panzer Division sentenced a lance-corporal to eight months in prison for 'coercion to commit a sexual offense' because the judges in the case expressed an extremely low opinion of the victim, a Russian woman, and thus judged the case accordingly. This is especially obvious in the judge's opinion, which will be quoted here in full, since it serves as an example of the ideological attitude of a considerable number of courts martial:

> The accused must be punished under § 176 clause 1 of the Criminal Code of the German Reich for the crime of sexual assault. The court martial has, however, refrained from imposing a prison sentence (*Zuchthaus*) on account of mitigating circumstances, also taking into consideration the fact that the accused is in other respects a decent soldier who has confessed to his crime and who has fulfilled his duty in action both here and at the Western Front to complete satisfaction. A further extenuating factor which must be taken into consideration is the fact that the severe punishment set out in § 176 of the Criminal Code is justified by the German conception of the sexual honor of German women, but that such severe punishment cannot be applied when – as is the case here – the injured party belongs to a people for which the concept of women's sexual honor has more or less entirely vanished. The decisive factor for the punishment was first and foremost the serious violation of discipline which the accused, by committing this crime, is guilty of, as well as the serious damage to the reputation of the German Wehrmacht which is the result of his crime.[32]

This assessment shows again that the decisive factor for the sentence was, in addition to the positive assessment of the soldier's general conduct, fear for the reputation of the Wehrmacht and the concern about military order and discipline. It is worth having a closer look at the term 'sexual honor', which has a different definition for German women than for Russian women, and which was denied the Russian victim. First and foremost, 'sexual honor' meant women's sexual integrity, which was characterized as premarital chastity and sexual fidelity in marriage.[33] However, in National Socialist law the term came to mean much more than this, as can be seen from trials of illegal sexual intercourse between Germans and members of 'foreign races'. In these cases, sexual relationships between Polish or Russian slave workers and German women were judged '"anti-German" behavior', because not only did such relationships damage the honor of the woman in question, but they were also seen as an attack on the German people.[34] The 'Aryan' woman was seen as the 'guardian of the race' whose duty it was to keep the 'national body' pure.[35] The National Socialist concept of the Russian people as an 'inferior race', on the other hand, did not allow for a similar high regard and symbolic function for Russian women. Another verdict used the same racist language, although in this case the punishment was much more severe for the following reasons:

> The accused's offence had to be punished severely. The reason for this was not so much to protect the sexual honor of the injured Russian woman, but the fact that the accused has seriously damaged the interest of the German Wehrmacht. [. . .] Through this offence, the accused contributed to risking the process of pacification in a region that is of considerable importance due to its proximity to the front. The damage done to the reputation of the German Wehrmacht among the local population, as well as to interests which are essential to the war effort, calls for severe punishment.[36]

In April 1942 the gunner referred to in this passage was sentenced to four years' imprisonment (*Zuchthaus*) and dismissal from the army. Using serious threats, he had repeatedly raped a Russian woman on two consecutive evenings. As the quote above shows, the punishment had less to do with the offence as such than with its dangerous influence on the Wehrmacht's military interests in an occupied country. Of utmost importance was the fear that increasing occurrences of rape and other assaults might increase the population's support for the partisan movement.[37] In order to prevent further assaults, in this case the accused was given what has to be considered a relatively severe sentence for a crime committed at the eastern front.[38] The explicit emphasis on military interests shows clearly that rape was not used as a strategy of warfare, but should rather be prevented. However, the fact that rape was not consistently and harshly prosecuted, depended on factors which shall be discussed later.

In order to establish the details of an assault, witnesses, sometimes even including the victims themselves, were questioned at the eastern front, too. While witness accounts are often attached to the court files from France, women's testimonies can be found for very few cases that occurred in the East. In many cases it was not even possible to question the witnesses, since the front moved continually, and thus the military courts often were not situated in the vicinity of the scene of the crime. On the other hand, the women's fear of testifying to representatives of the occupying army was surely an important factor. The real reason for the non-existence of such reports, however, was probably that the body of evidence could not depend on witnesses who were considered an 'inferior race' and who were thus denied credibility. The balance of power between men and women, occupiers and civilians, as well as 'Aryans' and 'inferior people' was not only evident in the crime itself but was manifested once again in the trial.

A more detailed evaluation of the court opinions shows that on both fronts prosecution of rape was less about the violent relationship between the sexes than about safeguarding order among the troops and guaranteeing military discipline – the two core values of the German Wehrmacht. 'Military discipline' (*Manneszucht*) reflects the communal spirit among the troops and was seen as the 'prerequisite for the functioning of order and obedience, the highest law of military life and the most important requirement for the strike power'[39] of the Wehrmacht. Thus, sexual criminals on both the western and the eastern fronts were treated differently according to the differences in the conduct of war and were given diverse punishment in accordance with military interests and prerequisites. Particularly in the East, the Wehrmacht leaders found themselves in an almost irreconcilable conflict, on the one hand waging a war of extermination, using all means 'without limitation, also against women and children',[40] and at the same time making sure that discipline among the soldiers was never endangered by this.[41] It is therefore typical for jurisdiction in the East that some courts martial endeavored to show some understanding for the soldiers accused of rape and to ascribe their behavior to the difficult circumstances at the eastern front. The so-called 'sexual predicament' of soldiers played a considerable role here and was taken into account when a sentence was given.

The Wehrmacht and Sexuality

The fact that fighting in a war meant that soldiers had little opportunity for the apparently necessary act of sexual intercourse was considered by some court-martial judges to constitute extenuating circumstances when it came to sentencing sexual crimes. They pointed out that at the eastern front, soldiers were not allowed an extended leave, and could not, therefore, see their wives or girlfriends. Such banal explanations are fairly common in judicial opinions, indicating that those in the military accepted that there was a male need for regular satisfaction of the sexual urge. This point of view on the part of the judges was supported by a statement written by the commander-in-chief of the army in July 1940 which discussed, above all, the contact with the civilian population in occupied France and which stressed that since German soldiers stayed in the occupied territories for longer and longer periods of time, 'serious consideration must be taken of the *sexual* question in all circumstances and with all its consequences'. According to the statement, the soldiers had to serve at the front under circumstances which might lead to the 'occurrence of sexual tensions and urges now and then',[42] something which had to be taken into consideration. A general prohibition of sexual contact between soldiers and women from the occupied countries was considered undesirable, as it was feared that this would on the one hand lead to higher occurrences of rape, and on the other it could lead to an increase in homosexual relationships. In order to prevent both of these, it was deemed that the Wehrmacht should establish more brothels which could be regulated by the medical services. It is not particularly surprising, then, that judges refer to these sexual 'urges' during trials of rapists, and employed this argument to reduce the sentence. The fear of an increase in sexual crimes expressed in these documents is, however, further proof of the fact that for the reasons mentioned above, rape was not tolerated by the military leadership and it certainly was not used as a strategic tactic.

As in the jurisdiction of the Wehrmacht, cases of rape were also tried and sentenced within the SS. A decree from the SS Court Main Office (*Hauptamt SS-Gericht*) on the subject of rape committed by members of the Waffen SS or the police states that 'punishments for rape should always take the particular circumstances into consideration [. . .] under which these men serve'. The lack of opportunity for sexual intercourse as well as excessive alcohol consumption were considered extenuating circumstances, which meant that 'straying *once* from the path of moral decency' should not be punished as severely as it would 'under normal circumstances'.[43] The idea of masculinity which was propagated by the military and was clearly defined as heterosexual, as well as the simultaneous legitimization and stylization of violence, threw a less reprehensible light on rape, especially if it was committed against women from an 'inferior race'.[44] Within the Wehrmacht and the SS, then, sexual crimes, especially those committed on the eastern front, were regarded by many judges simply as 'minor errors', as consequences of a 'sexual state of emergency' caused by war, and therefore it was not only accepted that such crimes were hard for soldiers to avoid, but they were also seen as excusable in view of the victim's ethnic origin. Similar views of sexual violence can be found elsewhere, one example being the system of military brothels, which gives us further insight into the Wehrmacht leadership's attitude toward the sexuality of its soldiers.

Enforced Prostitution: The Sanctioning of Sexual Violence

Shortly after taking over power, the National Socialist leadership tried to remove prostitution from the streets and consequently out of the sight of the 'Aryan' community. Women who continued working publicly in this trade or who were suspected of working as prostitutes were in danger of being categorized as 'asocial' or 'mentally deficient'. This could mean being sent to a concentration camp or compulsory sterilization.[45]

Military prostitution, on the other hand, was not regarded in such a negative light.[46] Indeed, the matter was given much consideration well before the outbreak of the Second World War. The Wehrmacht leaders considered it necessary to set up brothels in order to prevent the spread of sexually transmitted diseases as well as occurrences of homosexual relationships within the army. A significant reason for dealing so early with the prevention of syphilis and gonorrhea was the fact that so many soldiers in the First World War suffered from sexually transmitted diseases and were therefore confined to the sick bay and were not fit for active duty.[47] It was the view of military leaders that soldiers in occupied territories should only satisfy their sexual urges if there was some form of medical regulation. This meant that their sexual activity was subject to military control with absolutely no regard for 'bourgeois' notions of morality. The result was that some 500 Wehrmacht brothels had been set up on both the western and the eastern fronts by 1942. In the occupied parts of France, many brothels were used which were already in existence, and the women who worked there were very quickly put through a strict inspection by the German medical services. New studies have shown that women from internment camps were sometimes forced to become prostitutes in Wehrmacht brothels. As Insa Meinen has pointed out, both German and French sources show that the military's function was that of a 'pimp'.[48] On the eastern front, on the other hand, entirely new military brothels were established, and here, too, some women were forced to work as prostitutes. Russian women, for example, were forced to choose between work in a Wehrmacht brothel or work as a slave laborer in the German Reich. Jewish women and girls from concentration camps, too, were sent to brothels especially set up for convicts and prison guards, or to Wehrmacht or SS brothels.[49] There is not yet sufficient research to indicate how many women were forced into prostitution. It is obvious, however, that all women who were held against their will and forced into prostitution were subject to an institutionalized and therefore sanctioned form of sexual violence.[50]

Conclusion

Court records from trials of rape committed by soldiers give a somewhat contradictory impression. On the one hand we can see that a hard line was taken by the military when it came to sexual crimes in France, partly for reasons of discipline, but above all because they feared for the reputation of the Wehrmacht; as a result, long prison (*Zuchthaus*) sentences were not uncommon. At the eastern front, on the other hand, we can see the effects of the criminal nature of the war in the Soviet Union also in the types of sentence given. Only a small number of cases of rape were reported and sexual crimes were only harshly punished in cases where military matters and interests seemed to be clearly threatened or in cases where the cohesion of the troops might suffer. What we can also see in the court records are unambiguously National Socialist and racist ways of thinking about 'non-Aryan' women. The victims only played a small role in the court cases at both fronts and could expect little in the way of understanding or sympathy from the judges. What is particularly striking in the East is the clemency with which the rapists were often treated, especially the consideration for the apparent 'sexual needs' of the soldiers. This meant that, unlike at the Western Front, the criminals were often given more lenient prison sentences for similar crimes (*Gefängnis* rather than *Zuchthaus*). While we should also bear in mind that as a result of the increasing war losses, prison sentences were measured against the best possible deployment of soldiers, still the attitude of the judges on the eastern front stands in sharp contrast to the extremely harsh treatment of other, far less serious crimes, such as the theft of luxury foodstuffs and tobacco. Crimes like these, which were said to undermine military morale, could be punished with execution, since the difficult circumstances were not accepted as an excuse because of the importance of the troop's fitness for military action.[51]

In conclusion it can be said that there is no evidence in the records which have been examined that rape was used as a 'war strategy', that is, as a means used by the military leadership to humiliate the enemy civilian population. The leniency of prison sentences at the eastern front, however, as well as the institution of military prostitution, which women were also forced into under the threat of violence, show clearly that sexual violence was treated in very different ways. Depending on the benefit or harm done to the Wehrmacht and on the individual attitude of the military judge, sexual violence might be severely punished, excused, or trivialized and – in the case of enforced prostitution – even sanctioned and promoted as an institution. Further research is needed on this topic, including a consideration of the women's experiences, before the manifold facets and the complexity of sexual violence in the Second World War can be examined thoroughly. The analysis of court records is a first step in this direction.

Notes

Special thanks to Bianca Barth and Ruth Wishart, Berlin, for their translation work.

1. The Prosecutor of the Tribunal against Dragan Gagovic, Gojko Jankovic, Janko Janjic, Radomir Kovac, Zoran Vukovic, Dragan Zelenovic, Dragoljub Kunarac, Radovan Stankovic. Indictment, The Hague 2000, available from http://www.un.org/icty/indictment. INTERNET, and *Tages-Anzeiger* (Zurich), 23 February 2001, 3.
2. Susan Brownmiller, *Against our Will. Men, Women and Rape*, 5th ed. (London, 1991), 15, 64, 139.
3. Helke Sander and Barbara Johr, eds., *Befreier und Befreite. Krieg, Vergewaltigungen, Kinder* (Frankfurt/Main, 1995); Andrea Petö, 'Stimmen des Schweigens. Erinnerungen an Vergewaltigungen in den Hauptstädten des "ersten Opfers" (Wien) und des "letzten Verbündeten" Hitlers (Budapest) 1945,' *Zeitschrift für Geschichtswissenschaft* 47 (1999): 892–913.
4. Birgit Beck, 'Sexuelle Gewalt und Krieg. Geschlecht, Rasse und der nationalsozialistische Vernichtungsfeldzug gegen die Sowjetunion, 1941–1945,' in *Geschlecht hat Methode. Ansätze und Perspektiven in der Frauen- und Geschlechtergeschichte. Beiträge der 9. Schweizerischen Historikerinnentagung 1998*, ed. Veronika Aegerter et al. (Zurich, 1999), 223–234, here 224–226; Birthe Kundrus, 'Nur die halbe Geschichte. Frauen im Umfeld der Wehrmacht zwischen 1939 und 1945 – Ein Forschungsbericht,' in *Die Wehrmacht. Mythos und Realität*, ed. Rolf-Dieter Müller and Hans-Erich Volkmann (Munich 1999), 719–735, especially 735.
5. Brownmiller, *Against our Will*, 53; Sander and Johr, *Befreier*, 70. As we will see, the opposite position can also be found: the Wehrmacht punished rape severely on principle, sometimes even with the death sentence.
6. The findings are part of a doctoral thesis on this subject.

Birgit Beck

7. *Strafrecht der deutschen Wehrmacht.* Militärstrafgesetzbuch, Kriegs-
sonderstrafrechtsverordnung, Kriegsstrafverfahrensordnung, Wehr-
machtdisziplinarstrafordnung, Beschwerdeordnung, Sondergerichts-
barkeit für Angehörige der SS und Polizeiverbände, Reichsstraf-
gesetzbuch und zahlreiche andere Bestimmungen. Textausgabe mit
Verweisungen und Sachverzeichnis, 7th rev. ed. (Munich, 1944), 1,
§ 3.
8. *Zuchthaus* meant an imprisonment that included dismissal from the
army and loss of pay. It was therefore more severe than a normal
prison sentence.
9. Strafrecht, 103, §§ 176–177.
10. Ibid. 103, § 1 des 'Gesetzes zur Aenderung des RStGB'.
11. Diemut Majer, *'Fremdvölkische' im Dritten Reich. Ein Beitrag zur
nationalsozialistischen Rechtssetzung und Rechtspraxis in Verwalt-
ung und Justiz unter besonderer Berücksichtigung der eingeglied-
erten Ostgebiete und des Generalgouvernements,* 2nd ed. (Boppard/
Rhine, 1993), 126.
12. Omer Bartov, *Hitler's Army. Soldiers, Nazis, and War in the Third
Reich* (New York, 1991), 68. See also Wolfgang Petter, 'Militärische
Massengesellschaft und Entprofessionalisierung des Offiziers,' in
Wehrmacht, ed. Müller and Volkmann, 359–370, here 369–370, n. 49.
13. Hans Frank, ed., *Das Kriegsstrafrecht. 2 Teile, Teil 1: Das allgemeine
Kriegsstrafrecht,* erläutert von Wenzel von Gleispach (Stuttgart,
1941), appendix, 68: 'Verordnung gegen Gewaltverbrecher vom
5.12.1939'.
14. Lothar Walmrath, *'Iustitia et disciplina'. Strafgerichtsbarkeit in der
deutschen Kriegsmarine 1939–1945* (Frankfurt/Main, 1998), 178–
179.
15. As Messerschmidt emphasizes, despite this regulation a defending
lawyer was not always brought in. Manfred Messerschmidt and Fritz
Wüllner, eds., *Die Wehrmachtjustiz im Dienste des Nationalsozialismus. Zerstörung einer Legende* (Baden-Baden, 1987), 41.
16. Ibid. 40–41, and Walmrath, *'Iustitia',* 182, 429–444.
17. Rudolf Absolon, *Die Wehrmacht im Dritten Reich, vol. 6, 19. Dezember 1941 bis 9. Mai 1945* (Boppard/Rhine, 1995), 572–575.
18. Rüdiger Overmans, *Deutsche militärische Verluste im Zweiten Welt-
rieg* (Munich, 1999), 215. If the members of the Waffen SS are also
included, the total figure is 18.2 million.
19. Messerschmidt and Wüllner, *Wehrmachtjustiz,* 49–50; Walmrath,
'Iustitia', 45. It is difficult to come to any definite conclusion about
the numbers of soldiers accused based on the court records, since in

some cases more than one soldier may have been on trial for a joint crime.

20. Otto Hennicke, 'Auszüge aus der Wehrmachtkriminalstatistik,' *Zeitschrift für Militärgeschichte* 5 (1966): 438–456, here 449.

21. Overmans, *Verluste*, 296; and Hennicke, "Auszüge", 454. The increasing number of recruits to the Wehrmacht must be taken into consideration here. As a result there is a discrepancy between the absolute and relative figures per 100,000 soldiers. Homosexual misdemeanours, which were also considered 'crimes against morality', are not included here.

22. Bundesarchiv/Zentralnachweisstelle Aachen-Kornelimünster (hereafter BA-ZNS), Record S from the former Military Archive at Potsdam.

23. BA-ZNS, S 226, 'Gericht der 251. Inf. Division, Feldurteil vom 4. Juni 1940', 13–14.

24. BA-ZNS, S 274, 'Gericht der 29. Inf.Division (mot.), Feldurteil vom 13. Mai 1943,' 8.

25. Hans Umbreit, 'Auf dem Weg zur Kontinentalherrschaft,' in *Das Deutsche Reich und der Zweite Weltkrieg*, ed. Militärgeschichtliches Forschungsamt, 7 vols. (Stuttgart, 1979–2001), vol. 5/1, *Organisation und Mobilisierung des deutschen Machtbereichs*, ed. Bernhard Kroener, Rolf-Dieter Müller and Hans Umbreit, 3–345, especially 196–198, 307.

26. BA-ZNS, S 251, 'Gericht der 159. Res.Division, Feldurteil vom 16. November 1942,' 36.

27. BA-ZNS, S 274, 'Gericht der 29. Inf.Division (mot.), Feldurteil vom 13. Mai 1943, Bericht vom 30.4.1943', 1.

28. *Der Prozess gegen die Hauptkriegsverbrecher vor dem Internationalen Militärgerichtshof Nürnberg vom 14. November 1945 – 1. Oktober 1946*. Amtlicher Text in deutscher Sprache, 42 vols. (Nuremberg, 1947–1949), vol. 34, 249–255, document 050–C, 'Erlass über die Ausübung der Kriegsgerichtsbarkeit im Gebiet Barbarossa und über besondere Massnahmen der Truppe,' 13.5.1941.

29. Bartov, *Hitler's Army*, 61, see also 71–72.

30. See two examples of the comprehensive literature on this topic: Jürgen Förster, 'Das Unternehmen "Barbarossa" als Eroberungs- und Vernichtungskrieg,' in *Das Deutsche Reich und der Zweite Weltkrieg, vol. 4, Der Angriff auf die Sowjetunion*, ed. Horst Boog et al., 413–447; and Christian Gerlach, *Kalkulierte Morde. Die deutsche Wirtschafts- und Vernichtungspolitik in Weißrußland 1941 bis 1944* (Hamburg, 1999).

31. Bartov, *Hitler's Army*, 70.
32. BA-ZNS, S 269, 'Gericht der 7. Panz.Division, Feldurteil vom 19. August 1941', 22–23.
33. For the historical development of the term see Ute Frevert, *'Mann und Weib, und Weib und Mann'. Geschlechter-Differenzen in der Moderne* (Munich, 1995), 187–212.
34. Majer, *'Fremdvölkische'*, 607.
35. Cited in Gisela Bock, *Zwangssterilisation im Nationalsozialismus. Studien zur Rassenpolitik und Frauenpolitik* (Opladen, 1986), 121, 116–40; Gabriele Czarnowski, *Das kontrollierte Paar. Ehe- und Sexualpolitik im Nationalsozialismus* (Weinheim, 1991), 205, 210–215.
36. BA-ZNS, S 334, 'Gericht der 339. Inf.Division, Feldurteil vom 28. April 1942,' 25.
37. For the contradictory treatment of the civilian population with regard to the partisans see Timm C. Richter, 'Die Wehrmacht und der Partisanenkrieg in den besetzten Gebieten der Sowjetunion,' in *Wehrmacht*, ed. Müller and Volkmann, 837–857, especially 853–854.
38. BA-ZNS, S 334, 'Gericht der 339. Inf.Division, Feldurteil vom 28. April 1942,' 19.
39. Franz W. Seidler, *Die Militärgerichtsbarkeit der deutschen Wehrmacht 1939–1945. Rechtsprechung und Strafvollzug* (Munich, 1991), 28.
40. Norbert Müller, ed., *Deutsche Besatzungspolitik in der UdSSR 1941–1944. Dokumente* (Cologne, 1980), 139–140, document 53: 'Anweisung des Chefs des OKW, Wilhelm Keitel, 16.12.1942,' 140. Wolfgang Petter points out that this passage does not call for rape to be committed, but that some soldiers, however, took this as an excuse for such acts of violence. See Petter, 'Massengesellschaft,' 370, n. 50.
41. Manfred Messerschmidt, *Die Wehrmacht im NS-Staat. Zeit der Indoktrination* (Hamburg, 1969), 409–16, 421–422.
42. Bundesarchiv/Militärarchiv Freiburg, RH 53–7/v. 233a/167, 'Anlage 1 zu ObdH, 6.9.1941 ('Betr. Selbstzucht'), ObdH, GenQu, GenStdH, 31.7.1940'. The italics are spaced out in the original text.
43. Sander and Johr, *Befreier*, 68, illustration 15: 'Erlaß-Sammlung des Hauptamtes SS-Gericht vom 15.12.1940.' The italics are bold print in the original text.
44. Ruth Seifert, *Frauen, Männer und Militär (II): Vier Thesen zur Männlichkeit (in) der Armee*, Sowi-Arbeitspapier Nr. 61 (Munich, 1992), 9–10.

45. Bock, *Zwangssterilisation*, 417–419; Gaby Zürn, "'Von der Herbert-straße nach Auschwitz'," in *Opfer und Täterinnen. Frauenbiographien des Nationalsozialismus*, ed. Angelika Ebbinghaus (Frankfurt a.m. 1996), 124–136.

46. The emphasis on heterosexuality in the military can be seen on the one hand in the prohibition of homosexual relationships, and, on the other hand, in the establishment of brothels which are an institutionalized part of the army. See Ruth Seifert, 'Militär und Geschlechterverhältnisse. Entwicklungslinien einer ambivalenten Debatte,' in *Soziale Konstruktionen – Militär und Geschlechterverhältnis*, ed. Ruth Seifert and Christine Eifler (Münster, 1999), 44–70, here 53–54.

47. See Franz W. Seidler, *Prostitution. Homosexualität. Selbstverstümmelung. Probleme der deutschen Sanitätsführung 1939–1945* (Neckargemünd, 1977); Lutz Sauerteig, *Krankheit, Sexualität, Gesellschaft. Geschlechtskrankheiten und Gesundheitspolitik in Deutschland im 19. und frühen 20. Jahrhundert* (Stuttgart, 1999), 416–419.

48. Insa Meinen, 'Wehrmacht und Prostitution – Zur Reglementierung der Geschlechterbeziehungen durch die deutsche Militärverwaltung im besetzten Frankreich 1940–1944,' *1999. Zeitschrift für Sozialgeschichte des 20. und 21. Jahrhunderts* 14, no. 2 (1999): 35–55, here 45.

49. Janet Anschütz, Kerstin Meier and Sanja Obajdin, "'. . . dieses leere Gefühl und die Blicke der anderen . . .' Sexuelle Gewalt gegen Frauen,' in *Frauen in Konzentrationslagern. Bergen-Belsen, Ravensbrück*, ed. Claus Füllberg-Stolberg et al. (Bremen, 1994), 123–133.

50. This phenomenon is not exclusive to the German Wehrmacht. The system of 'comfort women' introduced by the Japanese Army during the Second World War can be mentioned in this context; it is estimated that 80,000 to 100,000 women were abused to provide for the sexual needs of the troops, partly under severe use of force. Yuki Tanaka, *Hidden Horrors. Japanese War Crimes in World War II* (Boulder, Col., 1996), 99; and George Hicks, *The Comfort Women. Japan's Brutal Regime of Enforced Prostitution in the Second World War* (New York, 1995).

51. Messerschmidt and Wüllner, *Wehrmachtjustiz*, 169–78. See also Walmrath, *'Iustitia'*, 471–484.

–11–

Remembering and Repressing
German Women's Recollections of the 'Ethnic Struggle' in Occupied Poland during the Second World War
Elizabeth Harvey

Following the Nazi conquest of Poland, the territories annexed and occupied by the Reich became a laboratory for Himmler's policies of racial restructuring.[1] In the course of the drive to build a racial 'New Order' in Poland, German women from the 'old Reich'[2] were recruited to undertake tasks for the occupation regime ranging from clerical work to political organizing. Among them were several thousand women deployed as teachers and advisers to 'ethnic Germans' (*'Volksdeutsche'*).[3] Their tasks of caring, supervising and assisting were carried out within a context of an 'ethnic struggle' (*'Volkstumskampf'*) waged against the non-German population of Poland. Drawing on interviews with some of those involved, this essay explores how women viewed their involvement in implementing Germanization policies and what they made, at the time and later, of their experiences in wartime Poland.

Gender Roles and Racial Hierarchies: Perspectives on German Women's Work in Occupied Poland

One context within which German women's work in occupied Poland can be interpreted is that of the Nazi regime's wartime mobilization of women. Manpower shortages on the home front brought increasing pressures on women to undertake paid employment and various forms of 'service'; it also brought a growing emphasis in regime propaganda on the notion of women as comrades in a national struggle for German victory.[4]

The model of female comradeship within the wartime 'national community' did not erase polarized notions of gender. On the contrary, wartime propaganda projected an image of the front soldier as the supreme embodiment of masculinity and of the nation; meanwhile, women continued to be identified with the caring functions associated with reproduction.[5] Nevertheless, some erosion of gender boundaries took place as women shifted into areas of production formerly dominated by men and were recruited as military auxiliaries serving at home and abroad.[6] The war work undertaken by the regime's organizations for girls and women drew those with a taste for activism into positions where they could exercise public authority.[7] Such opportunities could mean, particularly for middle-class educated women, the fulfillment of professional ambitions, but they also widened the scope for female involvement and complicity in the policies and actions of the regime.[8]

Recruitment for tasks in occupied Poland thus constituted one aspect of the wartime career patterns for young, generally well-educated middle-class women. Such opportunities expanded within the 'old Reich' as well, but occupied Poland promised even greater freedom of action and the chance of responsibility. Such prospects went hand in hand with the privileges granted to 'Reich Germans' within the racial hierarchy imposed in Poland by the Nazi occupiers: this assigned to 'Reich Germans' ('*Reichsdeutsche*') a status superior to all other ethnic categories, ranging from the ethnic Germans to the Poles and the Jews.[9] Women's responses to these opportunities and privileges therefore need to be interpreted not only within the context of German women's wartime career prospects, but also in relation to the structures and mentalities of the 'occupation society' in the 'new East'.

Research on the German occupation of eastern Europe during the Second World War has highlighted the way in which invasion and occupation gave the conquerors opportunities for sightseeing and self-enrichment.[10] However, the gratification afforded by such opportunities and by a sense of colonizing mission was often tempered by distaste for the occupied lands and their inhabitants. In encounters with Poles and Polish Jews, the German occupiers were influenced by longstanding prejudices;[11] these negative stereotypes were reinforced by Nazi propaganda.[12] Such influences are manifest in the indifference and malice to be found in accounts by German soldiers and civilians of encounters with Polish poverty and deprivation and the degradation of the Polish Jews.[13]

Most of the evidence on the mentality of the German occupiers focuses on the men who formed the bulk of the civilian administration as well as the security forces. The female employees of the occupation administration, including the SS, and the women who accompanied their husbands to the 'East', have attracted relatively little attention.[14] Gudrun Schwarz sheds light on one category of women within the social world of the Nazi occupiers in her study of SS wives, some of whom went with their husbands to the occupied eastern territories: these women, screened for their ideological commitment to Nazism, lived in close proximity to the perpetrators of violence and sometimes became involved in such crimes themselves.[15] SS wives provide an extreme case of women acting as willing accomplices of Nazi crimes. Probing interview material may help illuminate the outlook of a broader spectrum of 'Reich German' women working in Poland, and the role played in their motivation by reluctant conformity, career-minded opportunism, a patriotic sense of duty, or an ideological commitment to the regime's colonizing 'drive to the East'. The material may also shed light on whether women embraced the chance of new experiences 'on the frontier', or experienced unease at becoming involved in a system that so blatantly oppressed the non-German population; and whether notions of women's work made it easier for women than for men to avoid knowledge of those aspects of occupation policy from which they wished to shield themselves.

Women's Tasks in Occupied Poland

The women who were recruited from the 'old Reich' to educate, assist and lead the ethnic Germans and to support them in their allotted role as colonizers and masters in the newly conquered territories were mobilized by a variety of Party and state agencies,[16] often in liaison with the SS apparatus built up by Himmler in his role as *Reichskommissar für die Festigung deutschen Volkstums* (RKFDV). The women were brought in to set up kindergartens and schools for German children, visit and advise ethnic German women on housekeeping and childcare, and organize village festivals and meetings to generate community spirit and keep up morale.

These activities took place within the context of policies to crush Polish resistance and increase the German population in Poland at the expense of the Poles and Jews. Transfers of population were part of a vast and murderous program to restructure eastern Europe's population.[17] The ethnic Germans in the 'annexed territories' (*eingegliederte Gebiete*) of western Poland became a growing but diverse minority, comprising the native inhabitants registered by the Nazi occupation authorities as ethnic Germans (*Volksdeutsche*), together with Baltic, Volhynian, Galician, Bessarabian and Bukovina German resettlers (*Umsiedler*).[18] This essay focuses on women who were sent to the so-called 'Reichsgau Wartheland', which formed part of the annexed territories. Under its ambitious Gauleiter Arthur Greiser, the 'Reichsgau Wartheland' or 'Warthegau' for short, was a major focus of resettlement efforts that involved the subjugation, displacement and deportation of native Poles and Jews and the confiscation of their property.[19]

The ethnic Germans were regarded by the Nazi authorities as 'material' to be shaped, educated, supported and led. Women from the 'old Reich' were recruited for this pedagogical function partly because men were in short supply (women schoolteachers, for instance, increasingly replaced male schoolteachers), but also because women were seen as having a special mission to take the Nazi message into ethnic German homes and particularly to ethnic German women and children. Women were to combine 'womanly' tasks relating to welfare, education and proper housewifery with the political function of acting as 'model Germans', stiffening settlers' morale. The policy of 'consolidating Germandom' was presented in Nazi propaganda as an unceasing 'struggle' in which constant vigilance regarding the 'alien population' (*fremdes Volkstum*') had to be instilled into the ethnic Germans.[20] One dimension of this 'struggle' was to ensure that the Nazi hierarchy of nationality and race was upheld in daily life, and that social distance was maintained in all interactions between Germans and Poles. The prescribed stance for German women from the Reich was one that combined selfless care for her German protégés with an 'unsentimental' shunning of all those defined as non-German.

Oral History without Heroines: Approaching Memories of Conformity and Complicity

Oral history has often sought to record the lives of those who would otherwise have remained inarticulate: on the basis of this commitment to restoring subjectivity and agency to marginalized and oppressed groups, it has collected narratives that can inspire a progressive politics. Fewer oral historians have concerned themselves with those whose narratives are those of collaboration and compromise with racist movements and repressive regimes; however, such narratives can be enlightening, and not always predictable.[21] Interviewers have found individuals who were actively involved in such movements and regimes sometimes playing down, but sometimes presenting with pride, their past attitudes and actions.[22] Other oral historians, exploring popular memories of life under dictatorship, have traced complex patterns of compromise and consent through narratives in which respondents presented largely 'unpolitical' stories of 'getting on' and 'getting by'.[23]

The sixteen respondents I interviewed between 1994 and 2000[24] were young at the time of their wartime deployment – in their twenties or early thirties – and they were generally middle-class in terms of their family background and education: most had been educated beyond the basic elementary schooling that ended at the age of fourteen. Many would have experienced considerable exposure, through their socialization and training, to Nazi ideology; some though not all were members of the NSDAP or of its affiliated organizations. If they had not been persuaded by what they had heard, they would have learned how to conform. In a sense, therefore, I was interviewing conformists as much as enthusiasts.

The interviews took place mainly in the western part of unified Germany within a political culture predominantly critical of the Nazi past. It seemed likely that these factors would shape the reconstruction of these women's memories for a present-day interviewer; that they might reinterpret any past actions that could be construed as political acts in pursuit of the Nazi agenda in Poland; and that they might play down the degree to which they had personally witnessed acts of persecution or violence carried out against the Polish population.

The interviews yielded insights of various kinds. On the one hand, they provided information about daily routines, colleagues and social networks, and working conditions: describing huge school classes, for instance, or remote and impoverished villages where they were the only 'Reich Germans' for miles around. While some respondents may have played up the strangeness and hardship of their situation to make a better story, such information was partly verifiable through comparison with written sources. The interviews also offered other insights, impossible to verify, about the respondents' motives and feelings. Many, though not all, recounted positive memories that seemed to echo contemporary propaganda accounts of working with happy children and grateful adults. Another recurrent feature was the awkwardness that arose when the interview turned to discussing the situation and fate of the Poles and the Jews; some respondents, however, were prepared to confront the subject directly. Interpreting these memories entailed asking how the interview subjects placed their past experiences both in the overall context of their biography and in the context of recent German history. It involved inferring where positive memories of youthful exploits and achievements might have been magnified by nostalgia and smoothed by frequent telling. It also meant taking into account how German memories of the Second World War and the Holocaust are liable to be distorted or suppressed by collective taboos or an individual sense of shame and unease.

Remembering Wartime Work in Occupied Poland: Three Perspectives

The following analysis focuses on three interviews that were selected from the total of sixteen to illuminate the varied circumstances that surrounded a posting to Poland as well as differences in the respondents' interpretation of their past experiences. The analysis is especially concerned with exploring the respondents' motives for accepting a posting in Poland, their understanding of their role there, and their memories of the treatment of the Poles.

The three respondents, to whom I have given fictitious names, all grew up in the west and the north of prewar Germany, and all worked at some stage during the occupation of Poland in the 'Reichsgau Wartheland'. Anna Ullmann, born in 1922, attended grammar school and obtained the Abitur before training as an elementary school teacher. She was posted as a newly qualified teacher to a district in the south-west of the Warthegau in 1943, and stayed there until January 1945. After the war, she married and continued to work as a teacher. The second respondent, Irmtraud Fischer, born in 1921, also attended grammar school and obtained the Abitur before embarking on teacher training as an elementary school teacher. She was sent to a village in the western Warthegau in summer 1940 as a teacher training student on a compulsory vacation assignment. Having undertaken further study during the war, she worked after the war as a grammar school teacher. The third respondent, Adelheid Bauer, born in 1914, left school at fourteen and worked as a shop assistant before applying to go to the 'Reichsgau Wartheland' in 1941 as a settlement adviser employed by the Nazi women's organization, the *NS-Frauenschaft*; she worked in the north-west of the Warthegau until the end of 1942. After the war, she worked in various occupations.

Of the three respondents, Frau Ullmann and Frau Fischer both belonged to a significant category of women posted to Poland to work with ethnic Germans: these were the middle-class young women with grammar school and Abitur behind them, who were either at university or teacher training college, or newly qualified teachers. Frau Bauer represented a different type: these were women with less formal education, whose career opportunities in the 'new East' arose out of their commitment to the *NS-Frauenschaft* or to the BDM.

An initial point of comparison between the three narratives is to look at where they commented about accepting an assignment in Poland and where they described their work generally. To take Frau Ullmann first: immediately after taking her first qualifying examination as an elementary

school teacher, Frau Ullmann was told that all those who had just qualified except those with aged or sick parents to care for would be sent to
the 'new territories' in the East. She was asked how she felt about being
sent to the 'East':

> *EH*: How did you feel about that, having to go to the East, to the new
> territories?
>
> *U*: Yes, well, with all the stress of the bombing around Hamburg, not a bad
> thing at all. It wasn't bad. Secondly from a purely private angle: my two
> brothers, the one after me had a very difficult development even as a
> small child [. . .] I went to school in C., and my brother failed his second
> year of school and these 'wonderful' neighbors said: what's the girl
> doing at secondary school, shouldn't she be looking after the brother,
> in those days boys counted more than girls, boys have to become
> something, don't they. So this conflict, I could escape it, and another
> thing: the others were all going, why shouldn't I? And my favorite
> subject at school was actually geography, I actually wanted to see
> something of the world as well, and the boys got to go as soldiers –
> wherever, to France or to Finland or to Norway, and that wasn't on offer
> for us, but this way – I was happy to get to know somewhere new.[25]

As Frau Ullmann recounted it, her reaction to the posting to Poland was
what it would offer her as an escape from Allied bombing raids and from
family conflicts, but also as a chance to 'see something of the world' – just
as the men did in the war. She told the story in terms of being disadvantaged as a girl at home: the chance to go to Poland appeared in her account
as a way of getting even as well as getting away. She recalled going to
Poland quite willingly, while conveying a sense that she went without any
thought of the political implications of such a posting and entirely indif-
ferent to any notion of a Germanizing 'mission in the East' that would
involve taking the Nazi message to the ethnic Germans. In her words: 'I
didn't have any such missionary task, I never felt myself to be a missionary, absolutely not'. Asked about what she thought of Nazi propaganda
about 'building the new East', she evaded the question and in subsequent
responses presented a picture of village life and teaching in Poland as a
politics-free zone from which Nazi Party life was virtually absent. She had
positive memories of training sessions and of the school officials in Posen
(Polish: Poznań); of being congratulated on her competence as a teacher;
and of social life in the village. She recalled her function as BDM leader
in the village as a harmless exercise involving only sport and playing the
recorder; when sent propaganda brochures for political training sessions
with the girls, she recalled putting them away in a cupboard and leaving

them there. Generally, she spoke warmly of the village and the school. The landscape was pleasant with attractive woodlands, the neighbors were friendly, the schoolchildren she taught were 'nice, good children' who gave her presents on her birthday, and mastering the art of teaching different age groups in one class gave her satisfaction. Comparing her war experiences to those of her family suffering Allied bombardments, she remembered her good fortune: 'I was fine, I wasn't living in danger, I had friendly people around me, willing children [. . .] things were fine for me there.'

For Frau Fischer, her time in Poland on a short vacation assignment as a teacher training student in the summer of 1940 conjured up fewer positive memories. While for Frau Ullmann the posting to Poland was her major wartime experience, for Frau Fischer the six-week assignment in the Warthegau in 1940 was a minor episode within a sequence of wartime events that took her away from her college training as an elementary school teacher and set her on the road to achieving her longstanding ambition to study and become a grammar school teacher. She accepted the Warthegau assignment because all students in wartime had to perform some form of compulsory vacation 'service', but she recounts that she did not feel particularly drawn to the East or to the task of setting up a village kindergarten on her own responsibility.

> *EH*: Was it more an episode for you, or was it – for some this experience of the Warthegau was a turning point, or a moment when they felt they were somebody for the first time. It meant something positive to some people, and of course I am interested in why that was, but for others I think it meant less.
>
> *F*: It remained an episode for me because my life took this other turn through the chance of further study, and, apart from that, in 1940 I had already had the chance – in the Easter vacation – of doing teaching practice in a school [. . .] and as a teacher, even as a young teacher, you're accepted by the children and you were already somebody. So I didn't have this need to be somebody, I already was. [. . .]
>
> *EH*: And the East: did it so to speak fascinate you, or not so much?
>
> *F*: It was alien to me actually. It was alien to me. And it was the only time I went there. The furthest East I went after that was Berlin.[26]

Recalling the training course in Litzmannstadt (Polish: Łódź) in preparation for her assignment, she remembered being disappointed at the chaotic arrangements for accommodation and shocked at the 'vulgar' behavior of a Nazi official she saw harassing a Polish waitress, particularly since she had taken seriously the message imparted at the training course that 'Reich Germans' were to give a moral and political lead to the ethnic Germans in occupied Poland. In her words: 'One felt the obligation to give assistance and to set an example. So that these people who placed hopes in you were not disappointed, that was the sense of duty that one felt.' Her memories of running the kindergarten were of performing a job competently. She recalled individual children's names and the games they had played, but she presented her memories with some critical distance regarding the way things were done then: she described one of the songs she sang with the children as 'that militaristic song from Kaiser Wilhelm's times'. Recalling the Volhynian German settlers resettled in the 'Reichsgau Wartheland' from eastern, Soviet-occupied Poland, she emphasized their situation as pawns of Nazi policy: she commented on their subsequent fate 'ground between the millstones of history'.

Some obvious contrasts emerge from comparing Frau Ullmann's recollections with those of Frau Fischer. Frau Ullmann recalled being contented doing a job that gave her a sense of pride, and enjoying the status associated with being the village schoolteacher; Frau Fischer portrayed her assignment as an tolerable obligation rather than as something she found fulfilling. Frau Ullmann did not recall seeing her work in the East as a political mission; Frau Fischer remembered being alerted through the training camp to the students' Germanizing mission, and being aware of having a duty as a 'Reich German' to set an example. Frau Fischer thus recognized more readily than Frau Ullmann the political role required of her, but denied having fulfilled the part of activist.

In contrast to both of them, Frau Bauer remembered embracing with great enthusiasm her mission as a settlement adviser:

EH: No hesitation?
B: No, it was a call and there was no going back. I was single and free [. . .] It was completely new territory. We only knew that these are German people who have come to Germany and we had to help them find a homeland. We had the homeland within us and we had to give it to them, and that is what each of us tried, with the heart, not just with the head. With the heart, that was important.[27]

Frau Bauer remembered the 'call' to go East as a sort of annunciation: 'It was a call, somehow from above, from the stars, I must do this and this is what I have to do with my life.' She presented her work in the East as the most fulfilling, and best-paid, work she had ever done; she was working with colleagues she respected, she felt she was helping ethnic Germans who needed her and who were grateful, she was passionately committed to the German cause and felt she was contributing to a historic enterprise. However, even she balked at calling her work 'political': she presented it as being all about looking after ethnic German women and children, reassuring them, giving them a feeling of 'homeland' and 'explaining concepts to them'.

It will already be evident that these three interviews had very different dynamics. Frau Ullmann was reluctant to engage with some of my questions: when asked about the Party organization or Party leaders in occupied Poland, or the degree to which anti-Semitism was preached at her teacher training college, she diverted the conversation on to a different tack. Her self-portrayal as a schoolgirl and young woman growing up in Nazi Germany is as someone who conformed because she had to: she told a story of how her father was arrested by the Gestapo for a couple of days in 1935 as an incident that made a devastating impression upon her as a schoolgirl. When asked whether she liked being a BDM leader, she answered that everyone became a leader if they were more or less intelligent and competent: it wasn't a matter of political commitment. The general tenor of her account of her war years in Poland was bland: she presented her village as a haven, away from bombs and burdensome political meetings. It was difficult to tell whether she was aware of the point of my questions and deliberately evading them, or whether my questions made no sense to her because she had created an 'unproblematic' version of herself as a young woman and of her wartime work. The latter suggestion might be plausible, given that the story she told of her postwar years involved difficulties and obstacles: her membership of the NSDAP, which she remembered joining involuntarily as an ex-BDM member aged 21, threatened briefly to block her teaching career in the early months of Allied occupation; moreover, her personal life was overshadowed by her husband's disability resulting from wartime injuries. One could speculate that these postwar problems led her to construct a pleasant memory of the war years when she had been free, independent and happy in her work.

The interview with Frau Fischer was very different. Frau Fischer had requested to see in advance archival documentation I had found on women students' assignments in the Warthegau as well as an article I had published on the role of German women in wartime Poland.[28] She understood the purpose of my research and was careful to find out what use I was intending to make of her story. The interview turned into a genuine dialogue in which both the archival documentation and my article were discussed. Frau Fischer was more attuned than many of my respondents to the political character of women's assignments in the East, and to the possibility that such assignments could be viewed critically from today's perspective. She was not only prepared to confront her own past self and to take responsibility for what she had done and what she had written; she also had a critical interest in the whole topic of German–Polish relations and the Nazi resettlement program. She was prepared to admit that she had been ready to identify with the notion that she and her fellow-students should act as 'model Germans' in occupied Poland; she felt that she was lucky to have escaped the pressures that might have 'dragged her in deeper' if she had gone on to qualify as an elementary school teacher and had been posted to Poland. She tells her story as that of someone who achieved her life ambitions despite the hindrances of Nazism and the war, and who in the intervening period has left her more uncritical youthful self behind.

Frau Bauer, by contrast, had a very different understanding of my questions. It was as if she had been waiting for someone to come and hear her story, and she was eager to tell of her 'call' to 'bring the homeland' to the newly settled ethnic Germans in the Warthegau. She showed no sign of thinking that I might not share her view of her task. Unlike some other 'unrepentant' former Nazi women activists who have written about their time working in the Warthegau, she had no glib or patronizing comments with which to gloss over the situation of the Poles there;[29] she seemed unprepared for critical questions. The story she wanted to tell was how the 'call' to Poland at the age of 27 took her to a new life of comradeship with like-minded women, inspired by the goal of Germanizing defeated Poland. In her words, 'whoever wasn't committed to it in their hearts was no good'. It seems that the status of the settlement adviser, responsible for several villages and required to undertake home visits over a wide area by bicycle, and the sense of being needed and welcomed by the settlers, was something that appealed strongly to Frau Bauer; even after having given up the job and returned to her home village to have a child, she dreamed of returning to the Warthegau and was on the way there at the beginning of 1945 when she was forced to turn back and join the tide of refugees; she narrowly survived, with her child, the bombing of Dresden. After the war she worked in various occupations, including a number of years as a shop assistant, living with the friend whom she had met in the Warthegau and keeping in touch with other former settlement advisers. It is perhaps understandable that in Frau Bauer's narrative the years of working in Poland appear as a high point. They were, in her words, the 'best years of her life' and something she clung to in the postwar years to blot out her worst experience: Germany's defeat.

Elizabeth Harvey

Memories of the Treatment of the Poles

In each of the three interviews, passages occur where the interviewees recalled of their own accord, or were prompted to recall, the situation and treatment of the Polish population. In pursuing this line of questioning I was seeking to shed light on the issue of Germans' wartime knowledge and awareness of the regime's oppression of the conquered populations in occupied eastern Europe. Germans stationed in the East were clearly in a position to know much more than their compatriots back home about the crimes committed against the Jews and other 'alien' ethnic and national groups. In the case of women employed to work with ethnic Germans as teachers and welfare workers, questions can be posed about the degree to which they were implicated in measures that caused hardship to the subjugated population; for instance whether they knew about or assisted in such acts as the forcible expulsion of Poles from their property; what part they played in the policies to segregate the Germans from the non-Germans; and whether they knowingly appropriated and used the property of those deported and dispossessed.

These are Frau Ullmann's recollections of the Poles in her village in the south-western Warthegau:

> *EH*: You said before that there weren't many Poles in the village.
> *U*: Very few.
> *EH*: So a few were gone.
> *U*: Three farms had been exchanged (*waren ausgetauscht worden*).
> *EH*: Did you hear [. . .]
> *U*: That was before my time.
> *EH*: [. . .] whether those were the better farms, the better farmers?
> *U*: They were all about the same because the estate had been divided up equally under Bismarck. No real difference. And this Polish village street, there were a few laborers who were still working for these farmers, with their families in these little huts. And I know how I learned how to milk with my relatives in the country and no-one believed me so I had to go and sit by the cow (shows picture) – there I am milking the cow. And I can still see this Polish Pablo there gaping in disbelief, he couldn't believe his eyes. There was a rule that Poles and Germans couldn't sit at the same table, we didn't do that in our village. They worked together, they ate together. Where we were they weren't fanatics, not at all.[30]

In this passage, the forcible eviction of three of the village's Polish families is rendered as farms being 'exchanged' (usually, the targets of such evictions were either the more prosperous farmers whose property was the first to be earmarked for incoming Germans, or supposed anti-German activists; often, those evicted were deported to the General Government[31]). Frau Ullmann highlights the good relations existing between Poles and Germans; she adds a touch of comedy in her anecdote about surprising a Polish laborer with her competence at milking. There is no way of verifying her portrayal of this particular village, but one may suspect, given the patterns already identified in her narrative, that she may have presented this benign version of Polish–German neighborly relations as part of her portrayal of the village as a haven where she felt protected from the evils of Nazism and the war.

Frau Fischer, by contrast, was prepared to tackle directly the subject of the Poles and the role of German women in enforcing the social segregation between Poles and Germans. An internal report she had written at the time for the organizers of the student 'eastern assignments' ('*Osteinsatz*') had struck me because of an anecdote at the end: she had written of how a 'little blond Polish girl' 'not at all the usual shifty Polish type' had tried to join in the games of her German kindergarten group. To quote from her 1940 report:

> Something resembling sympathy began to creep over me. I talked to the district nurse about it. She came from Bromberg. Her father was murdered. She described to me the misery and suffering she had undergone. No newspaper report and no radio report can convey this as movingly as a person who speaks from experience. And with that all the stirrings of sympathy within me were gone.[32]

Frau Fischer re-read this report before the interview, and in the interview she discussed what she had felt when she wrote it and how she viewed it now. She wanted me to understand the complexities of the circumstances under which she recorded this incident. In her explanation, she referred to a copy of a 1940 brochure about student assignments in the Warthegau.[33] In the instructions issued by the assignment organizers, reprinted in the brochure, those visiting ethnic German settlers were urged to banish any sympathy that might be shown for Poles, who had after all, according to Nazi atrocity propaganda, shown no mercy towards tens of thousands of Germans in Bromberg (Polish: Bydgosacz) and elsewhere at the beginning of the war: 'Do not allow any sympathy to develop! Explain what the Poles did in West Prussia and what bad farmers they are.'[34] In the light of these 1940 instructions, Frau Fischer discussed the policy of segregating German and Polish children, which initially she could not remember when she re-read her own report:

I asked myself why couldn't you take the Polish child into the group. Someone must have forbidden you to take Polish children, and I found in this printed report an explanation, where it talks about the need for a clear separation, and I thought, at some time perhaps you received such an order, which I can't remember, all that remains is this memory, you mustn't accept this Polish child into the group, although my human feelings and my heart were making me want to take her, because she was standing there so longingly. But I can remember that I had to force myself, or that I had worries at first: can you write this in your report at all, that you have had such feelings? But I had undertaken to write the truth from A to Z, as I say here at the beginning, and I thought, this belongs in the report, but of course I played it down and took some of it back to demonstrate, so to speak, that I was toeing the line.[35]

Thus Frau Fischer remembered the pressure from the student organizers to toe the line, and remembered worrying that even admitting any feelings of sympathy for the Poles might be construed as subversive. This reading of the report restored, so to speak, the reality of her sympathy: the sympathy didn't really vanish, but she had felt compelled to pretend in her report that it had. However, Frau Fischer did not only want to redeem her past self; on the contrary, she also wanted to confront it and to condemn the racist attitudes implicit in the comment 'not at all the usual shifty Polish type'. Unprompted, she commented:

I write here and you've got it too: 'It didn't embody at all the shifty Polish national type, repellent just in its appearance'. And I ask myself of course today, how do I come to say that. Perhaps one ought to say 'the negative type portrayed in propaganda'. At any rate – I ought to have, if I had thought about it, known better [. . .] It is completely untenable, something like that. But – perhaps it contains an element of apology, yes the little Polish girl, first of all it was blond, and I had sympathy with it, but it wasn't, it didn't embody this type, something like that.[36]

Frau Fischer wanted to reassure herself that there were reasons at the time for writing something that she now found unacceptable; she also wanted to reassure me that she now found the anti-Polish policies and the attitudes of the Nazi era repugnant. She regretted having written things that echoed such attitudes; she felt unease (and recalled that she felt unease at the time) at using furniture for her kindergarten that she selected from a stock of goods taken from families deported from the area. This is perhaps an example of how memory sustains, but can disrupt, someone's sense of identity: Frau Fischer's identity today as she presented herself to me was that of an educated, critical, self-reflective person. This entailed distancing herself from thoughtless acts in her youth. At the same time she looked for signs in her earlier self of someone who was more thoughtful than her surroundings allowed her to be, and in whom the roots of the authentic mature self could be found.

How did Frau Bauer, the passionate enthusiast for the German cause in occupied Poland, recall the treatment of the Poles? The issue emerged as Frau Bauer told me how the incoming settlers from the Baltic States, eastern Poland and Bessarabia came to obtain their new farms in the Warthegau. She admitted, after I pressed her, that the forced evictions of Polish farmers left them (with the exception of those involved in a swap of farms with Germans from the General Government) without farms and homes to go to. I then asked her whether she had experienced the operations to evict the Poles and resettle the Germans in the vacated farms:

> *EH*: Can you describe that, how it was when the Germans arrived at the farms?
>
> *B*: Mostly – at night, in the evening, or as night was falling. I don't remember.
>
> *EH*: They came from the camps? (= resettlement camps, EH)
>
> *B*: They came from the camps and were distributed on this farm and that farm. Yes.
>
> *EH*: And you were there, as . . .?
>
> *B*: No, I think when they were being placed on the farms, no, we weren't there ourselves. That was other people, another group, the settlement assistants (= men, EH), they were deployed there for that. But – I can't remember. That is something I have never thought about. I'm sorry about that today. But one didn't think that far in those days – one believed what one was told (*man war gläubig*). One accepted everything at face value. I don't know. After the war, then one was a lot wiser. During the war one took everything to be the truth, just as one knew nothing about concentration camps. One only knew about that after the war.[37]

In this exchange, Frau Bauer told me at what time of day the Germans were brought to the farms, but does not recall witnessing this process herself. As evidence of what women settlement advisers did or did not actually witness, the exchange was inconclusive: written evidence exists that some women settlement advisers were indeed present when the Germans arrived and even when the Poles were being evicted, but Frau Bauer may never have been there herself.[38] However, the exchange did yield critical reflections by Frau Bauer on her former self as someone who 'believed what she was told' and who 'did not think' hard about the inhumane consequences of the resettlement program. However, it could be argued that she was re-containing her unease as soon as she was voicing it. By shifting the emphasis from her field of responsibility to the question of what 'one' knew about the 'concentration camps' (by this she may have meant the concentration camps generally, or specifically the genocide of the Jews) she connected her youthful lack of critical thinking about her work in the Warthegau with the larger issue of many Germans' failure at the time to grasp what crimes the regime was committing. This may have been a self-critical gesture, but it also enabled her to submerge herself within a larger German public, whose exact level of knowledge about the Holocaust still remains disputed. Consciously or unconsciously, she appeared to be leading the conversation away from the question of her individual responsibility and knowledge, from what she surely must have known (the treatment of Polish farming families in the Warthegau) to what she believed she really did not and could not know (the 'concentration camps').

Conclusion

The recollections of the women discussed in this contribution were shaped by their individual biographies, by their interpretation of my questions, and by the particular way in which they engaged with the public memory of Nazism. Of the three respondents, Frau Fischer was the most prepared to engage with the critical public discussion of the Nazi past and with my questions. Her individual biography gave her little reason to cling onto positive memories of her brief stay in Poland, and this together with her general political awareness informed her critical assessment of the students' assignments in the Warthegau and her own role within it. In the case of Frau Ullmann and Frau Bauer, by contrast, elements in their biographies after 1945 suggest that they had more reason to preserve positive memories of their time in the Warthegau. Moreover, both were in Poland for a longer period than Frau Fischer and invested more of their youthful energies in their work there. They recalled being rewarded with a new sense of 'being someone', of feeling respected and needed by the ethnic Germans. Both women highlighted the practical nature and 'harmlessness' of women's wartime tasks in the Warthegau and its 'constructive' and 'worthwhile' quality.

To retain such positive memories of working in occupied Poland, however, is to be at odds with a public memory which constantly recalls the persecution of the Jews and the Poles which took place there. The interviews with Frau Ullmann and Frau Bauer hinted at different ways of responding to that dilemma. Frau Ullmann emphasized that she had no choice in whether she went to Poland: it was a posting, and she had made the best of it. Presenting herself as someone who conformed without enthusiasm to the demands made of her by the regime, she portrayed her corner of rural Poland as something of a refuge from the political pressures of the *Altreich*. Frau Bauer, as a self-confessed enthusiast who volunteered for her posting to the 'Reichsgau Wartheland', did not deny her identification with the Nazi mission to Germanize Poland, but nevertheless presented her work and that of her women colleagues as apolitical, while the evils of Nazi occupation and the violence perpetrated upon the non-German population were portrayed as happening elsewhere and carried out by others. Frau Ullmann did not feel herself to be part of a Germanizing mission at all; Frau Bauer identified with the goal of 'building a German homeland' in the 'Reichsgau Wartheland', but had no recollection that this policy left the non-Germans homeless and impoverished.

It is impossible to tell whether gaps and silences in the stories that respondents tell today are the result of selective perception at the time, or selective recall since. Respondents' positive memories of their work may, as suggested above, have been magnified in the light of what happened subsequently in their lives: memories that were more worrying or uncomfortable may have been filtered out in that process. On the other hand, it is possible that a certain amount of filtering of perceptions was already taking place at the time. The respondents' narratives suggest that working in Poland was experienced by some young German women at the time as a welcome opportunity to demonstrate their independence and their competence as women, to acquire professional experience and to 'see something of the world'; to escape from familial pressures and the stress of living under Allied bombardment, or a humdrum job. Absorbed in their daily tasks with the ethnic Germans, such women probably found it possible to ignore the wider picture of Nazi rule and its consequences. If they constructed their tasks as 'unpolitical' and detached from the affairs of Party and state, such a stance was all the easier.[39] Only the more critical recruits to such tasks recognized that the sphere of 'constructive' womanly work was inseparable from the racist system of domination imposed on wartime Poland, and that the National Socialist 'ethnic struggle' also depended on the efforts of those who helped sustain, in 'harmless' daily routines, the systematic privileging of the German over the non-German population.

Elizabeth Harvey

Notes

I would like to thank the Humboldt-Stiftung, the Nuffield Foundation and the German Academic Exchange Service, who supported the research for this essay. I would also like to thank Karl Christian Führer and Tim Kirk for their comments on an earlier draft.

1. On Nazi ethnic and racial policies in occupied Poland, see Robert H. Koehl, *RKFDV: German Resettlement and Population Policy, 1939–45* (Cambridge, Mass., 1957); Martin Broszat, *Nationalsozialistische Polenpolitik 1939–1945* (Stuttgart, 1961); Czesław Madajczyk, *Die Okkupationspolitik Nazideutschlands in Polen 1939–45* (Cologne, 1988); Götz Aly, *'Endlösung': Völkerverschiebung und der Mord an den europäischen Juden* (Frankfurt a.M., 1995).
2. 'Old Reich' (*Altreich*) referred to Germany in its 1937 borders.
3. On women's work with ethnic Germans in occupied Poland, see Elizabeth Harvey, '"Die deutsche Frau im Osten": "Rasse", Geschlecht und öffentlicher Raum im besetzten Polen,' *Archiv für Sozialgeschichte* 38 (1998): 191–214; see also Jill Stephenson, *The Nazi Organisation of Women* (London, 1981), 190–193; Dagmar Reese, 'Bund deutscher Mädel. Zur Geschichte der weiblichen deutschen Jugend im Dritten Reich,' in *Mutterkreuz und Arbeitsbuch. Zur Geschichte der Frauen in der Weimarer Republik und im Nationalsozialismus*, ed. Frauengruppe Faschismusforschung (Frankfurt a.M., 1981) 163–87, esp. 180–2; and Hans-Christian Harten, *De-Kulturation und Germanisierung. Die nationalsozialistische Rassen- und Erziehungspolitik in Poland 1939–45* (Frankfurt a.M, 1996); for an individual case study, see Johanna Gehmacher, 'Zukunft, die nicht vergehen will. Jugenderfahrungen in NS-Organisationen und Lebensentwürfe österreichischer Frauen,' in *'Sag' mir, wo die Mädchen sind . . .': Beiträge zur Geschlechtergeschichte der Jugend*, ed. Christina Benninghaus and Kerstin Kohtz (Cologne, Weimar and Vienna, 1999), 261–274.
4. For an overview, see Dörte Winkler, *Frauenarbeit im 'Dritten Reich'* (Hamburg, 1977), 102–175.
5. On the ambiguities of wartime gender roles and models of male and female comradeship, see Thomas Kühne, 'Hitlers Soldaten und der Mythos der Kameradschaft,' *Archiv für Sozialgeschichte* 3 (1998): 165–214, esp. 168–169.
6. On women in the German armed forces, see Jeremy Noakes, *Nazism 1919–1945, vol. 4: The German Home Front in World War II* (Exeter, 1998), 338–342; on women as SS auxiliaries, see Gudrun Schwarz,

'Verdrängte Täterinnen: Frauen im Apparat der SS (1939–45),' in *Nach Osten. Verdeckte Spuren nationalsozialistischer Verbrechen,* ed. Theresa Wobbe (Frankfurt a.m., 1992), 197–223, and Gudrun Schwarz, 'Frauen in der SS: Sippenverband und Frauenkorps,' in *Zwischen Karriere und Verfolgung. Handlungsräume von Frauen im nationalsozialistischen Deutschland,* ed. Kirsten Heinsohn, Barbara Vogel and Ulrike Weckel (Frankfurt a.M./New York, 1997), 223–244.

7. On the wartime activities of Nazi women's and girls' organizations, see Reese, 'Bund Deutscher Mädel', 174–184 and Stephenson, *The Nazi Organisation of Women,* 178–213. On the regime's instrumentalization of young women's activism, see Gehmacher, 'Zukunft, die nicht vergehen will.'

8. For debates on women's complicity in Nazi policies, see *Zwischen Karriere und Verfolgung,* ed. Heinsohn, Vogel and Weckel.

9. On the hierarchy of ethnic categories that operated in occupied Poland, including gradations between different categories of Germans, see Broszat, *Nationalsozialistische Polenpolitik,* 125–135; Helmut Krausnick, ed., 'Denkschrift Himmlers über die Behandlung der Fremdvölkischen im Osten (Mai 1940),' *Vierteljahreshefte für Zeitgeschichte* 5 (1957): 194–198; Hans-Erich Volkmann, 'Zur Ansiedlung der Deutschbalten im "Warthegau,"' *Zeitschrift für Ostforschung* 30, no. 4 (1981): 427–558; Hugo Häfner, 'Die Ansiedlung der Umsiedler aus Bessarabien,' *Heimatkalender der Bessarabiendeutschen 1977,* 100–106.

10. On German soldiers in the Second World War as 'tourists' and photographers, see Klaus Latzel, *Deutsche Soldaten – nationalsozialistischer Krieg? Kriegserlebnis – Kriegserfahrung 1939–1945* (Paderborn, 1998), 133–56, and Miriam Yegane Arani, 'Aus den Augen, aus dem Sinn? Publizierte Fotografien aus dem besetzten Warschau 1939 bis 1945 (Teil 1),' *Fotogeschichte* 17 (1997) (Heft 65): 33–58, esp. 41–42.

11. On German anti-Polish stereotypes, see Hubert Orlowski, *'Polnische Wirtschaft': Zum deutschen Polendiskurs der Neuzeit* (Wiesbaden, 1996), 347–369; Peter Fischer, *Die deutsche Publizistik als Faktor der deutsch–polnischen Beziehungen 1919–1939* (Wiesbaden, 1991). On German perceptions of eastern European Jews, see Stephen Aschheim, *Brothers and Strangers: The East European Jew in German and German Jewish Consciousness 1800–1923* (London, 1982).

12. Latzel, *Deutsche Soldaten,* 179–82; Orlowski, *Polnische Wirtschaft,* 347–369.

13. Harvey, 'Die deutsche Frau im Osten,' 199–203; Walter Manoscheck, ed., *'Es gibt nur eines für das Judentum: Vernichtung': Das Judenbild in deutschen Soldatenbriefen 1939–1944* (Hamburg, 1995); Latzel, *Deutsche Soldaten*, 187–190.

14. On female employees of the SS, including secretaries working in the occupied eastern territories for SS Einsatzgruppen, see Gudrun Schwarz, 'Verdrängte Täterinnen,' 203–207. On women working for the German administration in Belorussia in summer 1944, see Bernhard Chiari, *Alltag hinter der Front: Besatzung, Kollaboration und Widerstand in Weißrußland 1941–44* (Düsseldorf, 1998) 61, 72, 86; Christian Gerlach, *Kalkulierte Morde: Die deutsche Wirtschafts- und Vernichtungspolitik in Weißrußland 1941 bis 1944* (Hamburg, 1999), 125, 226, 228. See also Daniel Goldhagen, *Hitler's Willing Executioners: Ordinary Germans and the Holocaust* (London, 1996), 240–245.

15. Gudrun Schwarz, *Eine Frau an seiner Seite: Ehefrauen in der 'SS-Sippengemeinschaft'* (Hamburg, 1997).

16. These included Party organizations such as the Nazi Women's organization (*NS-Frauenschaft*), the Nazi Women Students' organization (*Arbeitsgemeinschaft nationalsozialistischer Studentinnen*), the League of German Girls (*Bund deutscher Mädel*), the Women's Labor Service (*Reichsarbeitsdienst für die weibliche Jugend*) and the Nazi Welfare Organization (*Nationalsozialistische Volkswohlfahrt*). The Reich Education Ministry, too, posted hundreds of young women teachers to occupied Poland.

17. On Nazi plans for the 'East', see, in addition to works cited in note 1 above: Czesław Madajczyk, ed., *Vom Generalplan Ost zum Generalsiedlungsplan* (Munich, 1994); Mechtild Rössler and Sabine Schleiermacher, eds., *Der 'Generalplan Ost': Hauptlinien der nationalsozialistischen Planungs- und Vernichtungspolitik* (Berlin, 1993).

18. On the resettlement program, see Joseph B. Schechtman, *European Population Transfers 1939–1945* (New York, 1946); see also Koehl, *RKFDV*; Aly, *'Endlösung'*; Madajczyk, *Okkupationspolitik*, 441–453.

19. On Nazi policies in the 'Reichsgau Wartheland', see Jerzy Marczewski, *Hitlerowska koncepcja polityki kolonizacyjno-wysiedleńczej i jej realizacja w 'Okręgu Warty'* (Poznań, 1979); Czesław Łuczak, ed., *Położenie ludności polskiej w tzw. Kraju Warty w okresie hitlerowskiej okupacji* (= *Documenta Occupationis* XIII) (Poznań, 1990).

20. Arthur Greiser, 'Der deutsche Osten ein Land des Kampfes. Grundlegende Ausführungen des Gauleiters zum studentischen Einsatz in Posen,' *Litzmannstädter Zeitung*, 2.8.1942.

21. Kathleen Blee, 'Evidence, Empathy and Ethics. Lessons from Oral Histories of the Klan,' in *The Oral History Reader*, ed. Robert Perks and Alistair Thomson (London and New York, 1998), 333–343; for an example of interviews providing insights that challenge assumptions about women's involvement in the racist Right: Annette Skrzydlo, Barbara Thiele and Nikola Wohllaib, 'Frauen in der Partei "Die Republikaner": Zum Verhältnis von Frauen und Rechtsextremismus,' *Beiträge zu feministischer Theorie und Praxis* 33 (1992): 136–146.

22. Kathleen Blee, *Women of the Klan: Racism and Gender in the 1920s* (Berkeley, Los Angeles and Oxford, 1991), 4–7; Claudia Koonz, *Mothers in the Fatherland. Women, the Family and Nazi Politics* (London, 1987), xx–xxxv.

23. Luisa Passerini, *Fascism in Popular Memory: The Cultural Experience of the Turin Working Class* (Cambridge, 1987); Ulrich Herbert, '"Die guten und die schlechten Zeiten": Überlegungen zur diachronen Analyse lebensgeschichtlichen Interviews,' in *'Die Jahre weiß man nicht, wo man die heute hinsetzen soll': Faschismuserfahrungen im Ruhrgebiet*, ed. Lutz Niethammer (Berlin and Bonn, 1983), 67–96.

24. The interviews took place as part of a larger project on women's involvement in Germanization policies in occupied Poland.

25. Interview with Frau Ullmann, January 1999.

26. Interview with Frau Fischer, October 1999.

27. Interview with Frau Bauer, October 1999.

28. The article was the one published in *Archiv für Sozialgeschichte* 38 (1998): see note 3 above.

29. Contrast Helga Schmidt-Thrö (former Gaufrauenschaftsleiterin, Reichsgau Wartheland), letter to Frau N., 24.6.1984, betr. Ihre Fragen betr. Warthegau vom 13.3.1984. BA Berlin-Lichterfelde, NS44, 63; Hildegard Friese, *Unsere Siedler im Kreis Welun* (Wörth über Ellwangen, 1965). Friese had formerly been 'Beauftragte für den BDM-Osteinsatz', Kreis Welun, Reichsgau Wartheland.

30. Interview with Frau Ullmann, January 1999.

31. 'Die Ansiedlungstätigkeit im Kreis Leslau/Weichsel im Jahre 1941': Arbeitsbericht des Beauftragten des RKFDV Arbeitsstab für den Kreis Leslau. Institut für Zeitgeschichte, Archiv, Fb 115.

32. Copy of report in author's possession.

33. 'Facheinsatz Ost der deutschen Studenten: Arbeitsanweisung für die Hausbesuche,' *Die Fachgruppe. Organ des Amtes Wissenschaft und Facherziehung und Mitteilungsblatt der Reichsfachgruppen der Reichsstudentenführung*, no. 4 (April 1941): 94.

34. The actual number of native ethnic Germans who were murdered or who perished as a result of internment during the German military campaign in Poland ran to several thousands in total, but Nazi propaganda talked of 60,000 victims. See Christian Jansen and Arno Weckbecker, *Der 'Volksdeutsche Selbstschutz' in Polen 1939–40* (Munich, 1992), 28.
35. Interview with Frau Fischer, October 1999.
36. Ibid.
37. Interview with Frau Bauer, October 1999.
38. Harvey, 'Die deutsche Frau im Osten', 206–207.
39. On the strategy of defining wartime activism in the service of the Nazi regime in Poland as 'unpolitical', see Gehmacher, 'Zukunft, die nicht vergehen will,' 270–271.

–12–

Erotic Fraternization

The Legend of German Women's Quick Surrender

Susanne zur Nieden

This essay will treat specific aspects of a widespread reaction to the so-called erotic fraternization in postwar Germany. It is not a historic treatise of sexual relations between German women and US American military men.[1] I will neither analyze the reasons for these relationships, nor provide numbers. My real fascination centers on a range of statements about German women and American soldiers which, while stretched out over decades, repeat the same stereotypes. I discovered that there is hardly any difference in basic plot and to a large degree the wording between a factual report from 1947 or a nasty pamphlet dated around the same time, a short story from the 1960s or testimonies from the 1980s and 1990s, in short highly disparate texts in vastly different formal and historical contexts. I will, however, not delve into the actual context of these misogynist and racist accounts, the authors of which are by and large unknown. What I am presenting here is circumstantial evidence pointing to the building of a legend, that of the unconditional surrender of German women to the soldiers of the American occupying forces. I hope I can demonstrate that this legend was based on aggressive clichés which became part and parcel of the German postwar collective memory.

1945: The end of the war in Wahlrod – the arrival of the Americans is the title of a story by Willi H. Grün. In 1997, the story was placed on the Internet as part of a project entitled Living History. Many eyewitnesses, among them Grün, were asked to join the project with the aim of finding out more about the lives of ordinary people during the war and the early postwar years. Although more than fifty years have passed since Germany's defeat, Grün depicts the following episode with remarkable clarity:

No fraternization – that's the slogan. But what's to keep Jimmy from Dakota and Black Johnny from Alabama in their never-ending cavalcade of cars and jeeps from checking out village beauties in the double sense of the word. No small amount of chewing gum is freely thrown from the trucks. For chocolate or coffee, one has to try a bit harder. Which is exactly what happens at the baking house, where the B 8 makes a sharp bend, crosses a little stream, the Gäulsbach, and where two American guards are posted in front of Molly's house. A blond 'lady' from the Prussian regions with her bicycle is a frequent guest here. [. . .] The upper half of the door is left ajar. A Yank jumps up and fidgets with his uniform. I consider it best to withdraw as quickly as I can, to go and warn some friends. Later, we see the 'lady' smoking a cigarette at the partly blinded window. We don't like that either; German women don't smoke. Anyway, that's what we learned in the Third Reich. The pretty blonde gets on her bike and rides towards Altenkirchen. We cut her off at the bunker near the church path. We throw gravel, taken from the roadside, at her. The stones hitting her bike make a clicking sound. 'Yank lover,' we call out. We, too, have our problems with fraternization nowadays.[2]

This story about the end of the war is telling in more ways than one. First, it shows that the issue of fraternization is still considered to be of interest at the end of the twentieth century. The storyteller obviously attaches great value to the episode; it is presented as the first and therefore most important event. Interestingly, the female protagonist's smoking seems enough for the youths of Wahlrod to deem the blonde woman guilty of sexual contact with the victor and to submit her to a form of stoning. In May 1945 this fall from grace was, as our eyewitness involuntarily informs us, already an established story needing but a few keywords. After all, the narrator could not have seen much through a partly blinded window. The passage displays the essential elements of the postwar attitude to so-called Yank lovers (*Amiliebchen*). From spring 1945 onwards, one discovers a consistent desire to tell this story over and over again.

In postwar daily life – in pubs, in the long queues in front of shops, on country journeys in overfilled trains to barter for food – in all kinds of conversations overheard and published by Hans Werner Richter in 1946 (*Unterhaltungen am Schienenstrang*), theme number one was the 'failure of German women' and 'disenchantment with German girls'.[3] It gave everyone something to discuss and released a whole set of emotions.[4] Relationships between German women and American soldiers were ironically called erotic fraternization.[5] Of course, this was also a vicious commentary on the official but ineffective fraternization decree issued at the start of the occupation period. Moreover, women were insulted as

Yank lovers or Yank whores. With the end of the war they seem to have moved to the epicenter of the rage and shame felt by many Germans.

As a rule, judgments on German women involved with American soldiers are, even in retrospect, extremely harsh and most of the time highly exaggerated. Again and again, it was claimed that German women 'threw themselves' at the Americans.[6] The sarcastic epitaph of 'Fräulein Miracle' was another popular term. The 'evidence' for the 'miracle' is usually provided by quoting 'the American soldier' who supposedly stated that women in Germany were the most accessible 'this side of Tahiti'.[7] In any event, the exaggerations indicate the strong emotions surrounding this theme. They show that these women were treated with utter contempt, if not hatred, by German society at large.

I will now trace some of the reasons why the *Fräulein* remained such a hot topic. Both the theme and my questions lead me primarily to popular if not trivial texts. The relationships between members of the American occupation forces and German women have rarely been a topic for in-depth analysis. It wasn't the academic world who held forth on the topic but, rather, 'the people' who endlessly wagged their tongues. A double taboo is at work here, as erotic relations could not be spoken about freely and an all too frank criticism of the Allied victors remained a punishable offense for quite some time. Thus, the theme of sexuality and the occupying armies was mainly treated in texts which relied on irony and sarcasm, as well as a frequent use of vulgar allusions: caricatures and columns, bad jokes, anonymous pamphlets and mediocre short stories or reports written by authors who, on the whole rightly so, have long since been forgotten. What was not forgotten were the memories of many Germans about the 'Yank lover' herself. Her image was repeatedly reproduced in highly stereotypical terms.

I will first present and interpret the basic, recurring plot in a variety of texts: a newspaper report and some pamphlets from the late 1940s, a short story from the 1960s, oral history testimonies from the 1980s and 1990s. It is uncanny to see how the strength of this aggressive resentment was preserved over decades. Obviously, the legend of the quick surrender of 'the German woman', however banal and passé, was passed on from generation to generation. Something which survives for so long must have a specific function and leads me to raise the following question: what purpose was served by this endless stream of reports on so-called Yank lovers? The question leads us to the core of the issue, relations between the sexes in occupied Germany.

Stories about the *Fräulein*

In an article entitled *US-Zone 1947* and published in 1948, Kurt J. Fischer states that he wants to provide an 'unsentimental portrait of the American zone; factual and without any gloss of pathos'. True, the overall tone is factual. However, things change as soon as the writer encounters the theme of fraternization. Ironically, he comments that German girls are seen as 'the prettiest things' by 'GI Joe – as they are all called'. 'The girls, red lips, red fingernails, red toenails, American shoes, high heels, [. . .] presents from half a dozen hands [. . .], from Joe and Jimmy, Charles and another Joe, and from George, blessed with cigarettes and chewing gum, Chanel No. 5, and CARE packages.'[8] The reporter mocks the ease of the transactions. Those girls can't even speak English properly. 'Hallo Fräulein' is the catch-cry, night after night. 'Hallo Fräulein' and along they come, speaking their pidgin English: 'ah, jez'.[9] Further on, Fischer depicts the 'variously shaded erotic relations' and submits the 'Negroes' to a particularly close inspection. For a vivid description of what fraternization really means, the reporter chooses a 'Negro club'.[10]

> The Negro clubs may be found in any suburb of any large, destroyed city along the Rhine. In front, a line-up of girls. Young teenagers, done up to the nines; middle-aged women, dressed fashionably. Letting the Negroes have a good look at them. It's like a belated revenge for the slave markets of last century. The Negroes take their pick, and in they go, into the club. White teeth, grinning broadly. Drinking. Gin. Whisky. [. . .] Wild hurrahs. [. . .] Wild enthusiasm. [. . .] A sweet cloud of cigarette smoke hovering over the wild dancers. Gin. Whisky. The wild rhythms of the Negro band. [. . .] an oversized packet of Pall Mall, a huge glow of red flying towards a girl of barely eighteen, dancing as if possessed to frenetic shouts.[11]

The reporter projects erotic power and potency onto the dancing Blacks, savages devoid of any inhibitions. The rudimentary sentences conjure up their primitiveness: 'White teeth broadly grinning. Drinking. Gin. Whisky.' The streams of alcohol indicate how all inhibition has been thrown overboard. The huge packet of Pall Mall symbolizes prostitution as well as the penetrating phallus. Fischer's scenario of fraternization is that of a world turned upside down. Civilization and social order are dismissed; the slaves of yesteryear are the new masters – 'the Negroes take their pick'– and the women are completely under their spell. Cultural and social differences have become redundant. In the ongoing fraternization the reporter sees a racist nightmare come true: the slaves' revenge on the master race. The tortured creature has risen against civilization. In this context the American victory is interpreted as a domination by social and cultural inferiors. Fraternization is presented as the prime example to prove the point.

An ironic short story by Herbert Eisenreich, *Die neuere (glücklichere) Jungfrau von Orleans* ('The New (Happier) Maid of Orléans') written in the mid-1960s, is a literary confrontation with the topic of fraternization. It deals with the life of a well-to-do woman who, in the 1920s, danced the tango and Charleston, had a bob and several men; in short, the spitting image of the new woman. 'They say she was the first woman who appeared in public with her fingernails polished red; and, naturally, she smoked, a lot in fact.'[12] Her youth disappears and so does her fortune; no man will marry her and physical decay is the revenge for her previous lifestyle. Around this time, the narrator reports, she has changed her identity 'like an actor does'. She has converted to National Socialism, become a keen member of the new community and retained nothing of her former self, 'except smoking'.[13] The alleged reason for this transformation was Adolf Hitler, who happened to shake her hand in a crowd: 'She still had no idea what politics was about, but she believed in the man who shook her hand and stopped thinking about men who would not sleep with her.'[14]

The characterization of this woman is recalled later on in the story, when the arrival of the Americans is depicted. In the face of the immanent surrender, Eisenreich's protagonist becomes a patriotic Joan of Arc, prepared to take up arms and defend her country. Occupying the passenger seat of the motor bike driven by a member of the Hitler Youth, 'four grenades pressed to her bosom, like a mother holding her child, on the way to meet the 3rd US regiment'.[15] The plan is foiled. On seeing a US tank, the driver loses control of his bike. The heroine meets her first GI in a half-faint caused by the fall, while lying unarmed in a field. She sees 'a very tall, solid man [. . .] who holds his short gun, pointed down, as lightly as a whip'.[16] Her will to resist breaks down instantly. With the words, 'at least give me a cigarette, please,' she surrenders.[17] The American summons her to follow him to the next bush. What follows is a prostitution scene with soldiers lined up in front of the haystack to which the heroine has moved. In conclusion, the scene is sarcastically interpreted as a successful strategy for survival. Eisenreich contrasts the national 'misfortune' of Germany's defeat with the 'fortune' of the protagonist.

[. . .] and thus in but a few days, while the military commanders of Germany were signing the documents of surrender, first in Rheims, then in Berlin, and while millions of German soldiers laid down their arms and marched east and west to their imprisonment [. . .] she came to possess well over a hundred packets which helped her through the worst time.[18]

The new (happier) maid of Orléans offers an ironic comparison between its protagonist and the French heroine who was prepared to die for her country. The tragic sacrifice of the saintly Joan of Arc is transformed into a grotesque victory by a 'fallen woman' at the moment of the nation's surrender. By juxtaposing the heroic and the vulgar, Eisenreich suggests that fraternization equals the complete breakdown of patriotic values and moral order.

These stories share a common approach. Both authors use the image of the stranger's greater potency and stronger physical urges. Both make use of obtrusive phallic imagery. And in both polemical descriptions of fraternization, the authors mourn the German defeat as having led to a world turned upside down. When Germany lost the war, it is alleged, slaves turned into masters and the immorality of wayward girls won out. In both stories the women have striking clothes, red nails and lips, and are never without cigarettes.

For One Cigarette – Ready for Anything

In all stories about 'Yank lovers', not only those by Fischer and Eisenreich, the cigarette is a must. In fact, it plays a key role. Cigarettes are no longer just something to enjoy. In the early postwar period they were, of course, the main currency on the black market. In the *Fräulein* stories they always signify the female body as a purchasable commodity. And yet another message, sometimes only hinted at, enters at this point. Eisenreich has made it part of the fable. His heroine forsakes all resistance for one cigarette, giving herself up to the foreign soldiers. The author has thus incorporated a popular phrase according to which German women were ready for anything, for one cigarette.

Catchy phrases like that circulated in pubs and appeared in (dirty) jokes and pamphlets. A satirical poem about Yank lovers, entitled 'Ruins' and published 1947 in the satirical magazine *Kobold*, includes the following lines: 'With what's left of me, I crawl into bed/to put it frankly, to you all: for just a single cigarette/my last bit of clothing, I'll let it fall.'[19] The perpetual strength of the topos of 'one cigarette' can only be related to the fact that it fits in so snugly with the legendary quick surrender of German women. This legend hardly rises above the level of a dirty joke, which may well be the reason for its widespread popularity. An anonymous pamphlet from 1946 reads as follows:

The German woman is shamelessly carrying on with foreigners!
Have you no shame, you German women?
Surely you know you're dragging us all down with you and at the same time
you're staining the honor of the German woman.
We have neither cigarettes nor butter; the foreigner has coffee and sugar. [. . .]
It took six years to besiege the German soldiers, but it took only five minutes
to get the German woman around.[20]

An anonymous letter was sent to a young woman from Hamburg in the
late 1940s, following the announcement of her engagement to an American
soldier in a newspaper. Using some of the same words, it aimed more
directly at US soldiers of color. Interestingly, the anonymous author wrote
his nasty verse on old *Wehrmacht* stationery:

> Dead tired, after weeks so long
> the soldiers are crawling home [. . .]
> She's living it up, the German woman,
> in the worst possible way, we know for a fact.
> In pairs or on their own we see them walk along
> or stand longingly in doorways, in front of houses,
> a seductive smile on a cheery face,
> oh, German women, have you no shame?
> The German soldiers, armless and legless,
> you obviously don't care for them.
> They have neither coffee nor butter,
> the foreigners have the lot, yes, even sugar.
> And if one brings along some chocolate,
> the color of his skin doesn't matter at all;
> five years they needed to besiege us,
> but you, they got around in five minutes. [. . .]
> You're dragging, and you know it, too,
> the honor of German woman through the dirt.[21]

It cannot be stressed enough that the legend of the quick surrender is by
no means merely a thing of the past. In the 1980s, the German historian
Lutz Niethammer evaluated biographical interviews dealing with the early
occupation period. He, too, detected a fixation on the theme of sexuality.
The testimonies of those interviewed display two specific projections:
first, the general expectation that the foreigners, especially the 'uncivilized' ones, would rape all German ('Nordic, blonde') women. Second,
the phantom of national faithlessness, that is the retrospective judgment
of German women who allegedly threw themselves at the victorious

foreigners.[22] Among others, Niethammer interviewed a Social Democratic worker. The latter issued the following as a major point: 'German soldiers fought six years. The German woman, five minutes.' Significantly, he added that a 'Negro' had told him exactly that and emphasized once more: 'It's all true, too. I felt ashamed.'[23]

News reports, short stories, pamphlets and testimonies alike vehemently cite fraternization as the absence of social order and morality, as the women's betrayal of German soldiers, as the dishonor and defilement of a whole nation. What these accusations have in common is that the Nazi past is blotted out entirely. During the postwar period the complex issue of moral decay, guilt and failure of Germans as such was pre-empted by the stories of 'Yank lovers'. It was not the National Socialist regime but, rather, the defeat and occupation of Germany, the lack of national self-determination which was seen as the true cause of the country's moral disaster.

In an essay written in 1947, a twenty-two year old Berlin woman accusingly addresses the occupation forces: '[. . .] do not force the past on us. You will only make enemies! Our fathers and brothers are kept as prisoners. Why don't you return them to us if you want us to lead a normal life?' This is the real reason, she continues, why such 'extreme things' are happening between the German girls and the occupation soldiers. 'Is there no such thing as honor anymore among the German people? The moral breakdown of our young men is inevitable if they come home to a long-desired freedom and see Germany as it is. Someone may lose a war; someone may be humiliated; but there's no need to defile one's honor.'[24]

The American historian Elizabeth Heinemann has rightly pointed out that stories about 'Yank lovers' are essentially about the rejection of guilt.[25] Through the Nuremberg trials, the occupation forces questioned the morality of all Germans. Complaints that the moral decay coincided with the moment of defeat were brought forward as a counter-argument to deflect the real issue of long-lost morals and honor. Undoubtedly, the besieged resented the victors' judgment of collective guilt while attempting to assert the right to 'be left in peace and let the past be'.

By contrasting the quick surrender of the German woman to the long battle of the German soldier, it became possible to shift the time of this particular 'original sin' and, even more importantly, its cause. There can be no doubt about the aim of this thematic shift – from the state of the nation to the war of the sexes; German men, especially those who served in the *Wehrmacht*, were to be exculpated.[26] Another element used in this strategy predates National Socialism. In his study *Nationalism and Sexuality*, George L. Mosse asserts that nationalism in all its varieties tends to enter a liaison with bourgeois morality. He points out that the mightiest and most effective ideology of modern times used the image of the 'virtuous woman' as the 'incorporation of morality' to demonstrate the virtues of its own aims.[27]

Wary Warriors

In the context of the demise of the Third Reich, the image of virtue under threat is highly significant. I am convinced that the process which resulted in the fantasy of the collective faithlessness of German women started during the last few years of the war. Then, the German soldiers who had gone off to conquer Europe increasingly turned into partners and husbands who worried about their families, girlfriends and wives. The ancient image of having to protect the lives (and bodies) of women and children from enemy troops seems to have gained momentum when the Nazi war aims lost credibility. From 1942 onward a process began which I would like to describe as the collective privatization of ideological warfare. Many autobiographical texts, especially letters from the front, support this hypothesis.[28] The final war years should be kept in mind here. The majority of soldiers fighting at the front wanted to forget that they had been in favor of the German war aims and had entered the war convinced of their superiority as a race and as a civilized people, believing they were joining the crusade against Bolshevism.

By 1944, this process seems to have been completed for most. In winter 1942–43 one young *Wehrmacht* soldier at the eastern front wrote: 'Oh yes, every German soldier is longing for his home and his loved ones, for peace and quiet.'[29] The mood described here typifies the mental state of many German soldiers during the final phase of the war. Letters written from the front during the last two years of the war hardly ever display any of the patriotic slogans used in the early, euphoric days of the *Blitzkrieg*. From winter 1942–43 on, with tough battles in the Soviet Union, withdrawal, and growing doubts about a military victory, most men wrote about their desire to return home. Yet 'home' became more and more illusionary. 'At times like these, one starts to realize how good it was at home,' a young German soldier writes from Stalingrad.[30] Worries about families, girlfriends and wives dominate the letters written at this time. Men hoped that whatever was lacking in their current situation would be realized in private life. In a letter from December 1942 we can read: 'If I ever get out of here alive [. . .] then, cost what it may, we will make up for everything. Your husband, your Willi.'[31]

In summer 1944 an officer wrote to his wife: 'Darling, you must know that all the hardships and troubles which I have to endure are for you.'[32] She replies that his view is neither uplifting nor true: 'The hardships which you endure are endured for yourself, for me, for us and, last but not least, for our fatherland.'[33] He counters: 'But knowing that it is also for you makes it easier.'[34]

In another text someone writes, 'for you my dear, and Germany';[35] if mentioned at all, non-private aims rate second. I find it remarkable that as soon as the Nazi regime lost its legitimating power, patterns of behavior were displayed that seem to have been filling an ideological vacuum. Faith in *Führer* and fatherland might be breaking down, yet men were still prepared to fight for love and a better future. While men may have lost sight of the initial war aims, a belief in their male duty to protect homeland, wife and family persisted. The letters written by Gert K., a junior officer, exemplify this development. In 1944 he wrote to a comrade that he had 'somehow changed' during the past year:

> If under fire, you're crawling into the dirt, having to battle to beat off that Russian – all these impressions – something sticks and takes on a new shape. [. . .] Something different has come into my life. It's quite basic. [. . .] I got engaged. With little sister Jutta. [. . .] Believe me, it's good to know where you belong; to have a purpose in life, something to work and even to fight for.[36]

The transformation of the National Socialist warrior into the civilian husband and family man who eventually came to characterize the German Federal Republic obviously started in the trenches during the final war years.[37] But of course without girls and wives remaining faithful to the men who fought at the front and later became prisoners of war, this transformation could not have occurred. And as soon as this faithfulness became doubtful, postwar masculinity was under heavy fire. Forty years after the war, Gertrude B. from Austria (a young woman when the war came to an end), stated in an interview: 'Those soldiers were full of rage, the ones who returned. They had wanted to defend us throughout the war; but no time was lost to get together with the Yanks. And for the soldiers this was the real shock; that they had actually risked their lives for something like that.'[38] A passage from a novel printed in installments by a magazine in 1948 says much the same thing. A young soldier returned from the war who is also the narrator observes a love scene between an occupation soldier and an Austrian woman. Bitterly, he comments: 'In the final analysis, we were also biting the dust somewhere out there between Rostov and the Crimea for you. Yes, for you, too! No doubt about it.'[39]

The vehemence with which the image of 'Yank lovers' was depicted following the end of the war may be seen as a gauge of the fragility of the new male, civilian identity. The legend of the quick surrender of the German woman contributed to the exoneration of German men. The roles of the German soldier and the German girl were clearly defined. He fought for his country, for women and children. She was the fickle female who instead of being grateful offered herself without further ado to the victor. The male ego, insecure after the military defeat, created the ogre of 'national faithlessness' and a new role for himself – that of cuckold.

Conclusion

It wasn't a negotiated peace that ended the war, but instead an unconditional surrender. No legend could be spun out of it as in the case of the First World War, when ostensibly unvanquished troops on the battlefield were said to have been betrayed by their own politicians. The legend of the quick surrender of the German woman is but a variation on the theme. The stab in the back was reformulated as the battle of the sexes, a punch below the belt. It allowed for the implicit understanding that, regardless of military defeat and unconditional surrender, there had been a heroic battle – lost only because the enemy was stronger. The image of female fickleness in facing the enemy (five minutes or the length of a cigarette) served to reinforce an image of male steadfastness (six years).

Finally, the stories about 'Yank lovers' were an attempt to salvage at least part of the German dream of racial superiority. If we follow the work of Margarete and Alexander Mitscherlich, very few Germans had resisted the appeal of belonging to a 'privileged race'.[40] Of course, this self-image was hardly compatible with the acceptance of total defeat. The humiliated losers preferred to mirror themselves in the image of the *Fräulein* succumbing to the erotic power of the stranger, enabling them to feel more civilized and superior after all. In the accounts of fraternization as a world turned upside down – where moral decay paid off and former slaves were masters – Germany's defeat is presented as the victory of formerly subordinate bodies ruling over a society of 'poets and thinkers'. This backdrop, the threat of sheer self-negation when the dream of the superior race came to an unhappy end, explains how the 'failure of German women' could become theme number one in the postwar era.

Notes

Translated by Mai Lef

1. See Heide Fehrenbach's investigation of '"Ami-Liebchen" und "Mischlingskinder". Rasse, Geschlecht und Kultur in der deutschamerikanischen Begegnung', in Klaus Naumann (ed.), *Nachkrieg in Deutschland* (Hamburg, 2001), 178–212. She sheds new light on continuities and ruptures in the concepts of race and gender in postwar Germany by analyzing the reactions of the general population and the authorities towards so-called 'Mischlingskinder'.

2. Internet page: Projekt Jugendkunstwerkstatt Koblenz e.V. und Landesbücherei Rheinland-Pfalz (1997), Webm@ster Christiane Schultzki-Haddouti.

3. Hans Werner Richter, 'Unterhaltungen am Schienenstrang,' *Der Ruf* 1 (1946/47): 6.

4. Ingrid Bauer's study of postwar Austria emphasizes the phenomenon of so-called 'Yank lovers'. A female interview partner is quoted as saying: 'I attended the first returned soldiers' ball [. . .] the conversation was mainly about the Yank whores. That's what they were called.' Ingrid Bauer, 'Die "Ami-Braut" – Platzhalterin für das Abgespaltene? Zur (De-)Konstruktion eines Stereotyps der österreichischen Nachkriegsgeschichte 1945–1955,' *L'Homme. Zeitschrift für feministische Geschichtswissenschaft*, vol. 7, no.1 (1996):107–121, 111. Articles and caricatures published in the *Stars and Stripes* show that, especially during the early occupation years, the Americans themselves were concerned about relations between US soldiers and German women. Caricatures drawn by 'Shep' included a new character, Veronika Dankeschön whose initials VD signaled the danger of venereal disease. The figure played an important role in campaigns launched by military authorities. John Willoughby, 'The Sexual Behavior of American GIs during the Early Years of the Occupation of Germany,' *The Journal of Military History* (Formerly *Military Affairs*), 62, no. 1 (1998): 155–174.

5. Percy Knauth, 'Fraternisation: The Word Takes on a Brand-New Meaning in Germany,' *Life*, 2.7.1945: 26.

6. Cf. Lutz Niethammer, 'Heimat und Front,' in *'Die Jahre weiß man nicht, wo man die heute hinsetzen soll.' Faschismuserfahrungen im Ruhrgebiet. Lebensgeschichte und Sozialkultur im Ruhrgebiet 1930 bis 1960*, vol. 1, ed. Lutz Niethammer and Alexander von Plato (Berlin, 1983), 163–232, 229. Tamara Domentat, *'Hallo Fräulein.' Deutsche Frauen und amerikanische Soldaten* (Berlin,1998): 182–200.

7. Christoph Boyer and Hans Woller, 'Hat die deutsche Frau versagt? Die neue Freiheit der deutschen Frau in der Trümmerzeit 1945,' *Journal für Geschichte*, no. 2 (1983): 32–36.

8. Kurt J. Fischer, 'US-Zone 1947,' in *So lebten wir. Ein Querschnitt durch das Jahr 1947*, ed. Hans Rümelin (Heilbronn, 1948), 3–27, 4.

9. Ibid.

10. See Fehrenbach's observations of the treatment of Black soldiers, 'Amiliebchen'.

11. Fischer, *US-Zone*, 7–8.

12. Herbert Eisenreich, 'Die neuere (glücklichere) Jungfrau von Orléans,' in *Sozusagen* (Gütersloh, 1967), 147–148, 147.

13. Ibid. 149.

14. Ibid. 151.

15. Ibid. 154.

16. Ibid. 156.

17. Ibid. 157.

18. Ibid. 158.

19. H. Hartwig, 'Die Ruine,' *Kobold*, 1, no. 3 (1947): 16.

20. Boyer, Woller, 'Hat die deutsche Frau versagt?', 36. A contemporary pamphlet anonymously distributed in Austria bears a similar text: 'Many an Austrian woman carries on, shamelessly, with foreigners. [. . .] You are dragging each one of us [. . .] through the dirt, even the most decent Austrian woman.' Bauer, 'Die "Ami-Braut"': 113.

21. Domenat, *'Hallo Fräulein'*: 187–188.

22. Lutz Niethammer, 'Privat-Wirtschaft. Erinnerungsfragmente einer anderen Umerziehung,' in *'Hinterher merkt man, daß es richtig war, daß es schief gegangen ist.' Nachkriegserfahrungen im Ruhrgebiet, Lebensgeschichte und Sozialkultur im Ruhrgebiet 1930–1960* , vol. 2, ed. Lutz Niethammer (Berlin/Bonn, 1983), 17–105, 31.

23. Ibid. 29.

24. Quoted in Thurnwald, *Gegenwartsprobleme Berliner Familien* (Berlin, 1948), 156.

25. Elizabeth Heineman, 'The Hour of the Woman: Memories of Germany's "Crisis Years" and West German National Identity,' *American Historical Review* 101, no. 2 (1996): 354–395, 383–384.

26. Analyzing Austrian stories about 'Yank lovers', Ingrid Bauer also points to guilt being shifted from the (male) front to the (female) home front. Bauer, 'Die "Ami-Braut"': 114.

27. George L. Mosse, *Nationalismus und Sexualität. Bürgerliche Moral und sexuelle Normen* (Reinbek, 1987), 111.

28. See Jürgen Reulecke and Thomas Kohut, '"Sterben wie eine Ratte, die der Bauer ertappt". Letzte Briefe aus Stalingrad,' in: Jürgen Reulecke, *'Ich möchte einer werden so wie die . . .'. Männerbünde im 20. Jahrhundert* (Frankfurt am Main/New York, 2001), 177–194.

29. Jens Ebert, *Zwischen Mythos und Wirklichkeit. Die Schlacht um Stalingrad in deutschsprachigen authentischen und literarischen Texten.* Dissertation (Berlin, 1989).

30. Ibid.

31. Ibid.

32. Quoted in Ingrid Hammer, Susanne zur Nieden, eds., *'Sehr selten habe ich geweint.' Briefe und Tagebücher aus dem Zweiten Weltkrieg von Menschen aus Berlin* (Zürich, 1992), 159.

33. Ibid. 161.

34. Ibid. 163.

35. See Ebert, *Zwischen Mythos und Wirklichkeit.*

36. Hammer and zur Nieden, *Sehr selten habe ich geweint,* 181–182.

37. See Robert G. Moeller, '"The Last Soldier of the Great War" and Tales of Family Reunions in the Federal Republic of Germany,' *SIGNS* 24 (1998): 129–145.

38. Bauer, 'Die "Ami-Braut"' 115.

39. Ibid. 116.

40. Alexander and Margarete Mitscherlich, *Die Unfähigkeit zu trauern* (Munich, 1983).

-13-

Cold War Communities

Women's Peace Politics in Postwar
West Germany, 1945–1952

Irene Stoehr

The women who organized women's committees and other political groups in the immediate postwar period had one point in common that united them beyond their political differences: they felt responsible for maintaining peace. The phenomenon of 'women's pacifism'[1] resulted from the combination of a superiority complex and a guilt complex. The women's conviction that men were responsible for both world wars was countered by their admission that they had done nothing to stop them. One or the other of these complexes led many women to postulate that women must now do everything to prevent another war. This 'peace consensus', whether real or imagined, broke down again by 1947 when the East–West conflict began and eventually led to a split in the women's movement.

This essay first examines the peace politics of women's groups that were increasingly oriented toward the politics of the West. My working thesis is that these women's abhorrence of the war was not really related to the Second World War and was therefore not related to National Socialism. Next I examine how gender is constructed in the various arguments for a politics of peace. And finally I analyze examples of the way in which community was imagined by the protagonists of the postwar women's movement as they explicitly addressed the repercussions of the war.

This study focuses on representatives of women's organizations that I will refer to as 'Western-oriented'. This means not only that they were politically active in the Western zones of Germany and in West Berlin, but also that their political position in the East–West conflict was clearly oriented toward the West. These 'West women' who were interested in rebuilding the pre-1933 'bourgeois'[2] women's movement are contrasted with two other women's organizations: the *Demokratischer Frauenbund Deutschlands* (German Democratic Women's League, DFD), which was active in the Soviet Zone of Occupation (*Sowjetische Besatzungszone,*

SBZ) starting in 1947 and increasingly defined itself as communist; and the Central German Office of the World Organization of Mothers of All Nations (WOMAN), which was founded in Hamburg in 1948 and whose goal was to remain politically neutral in the Western zones.[3]

Demands for Peace and Reorganization

Agnes von Zahn-Harnack, the last chairwoman of the *Bund Deutscher Frauenvereine* (Federation of German Women's Associations, BDF) that had been disbanded in 1933, gathered together thirty-three women in the rubble of Berlin on 21 July 1945 in order to found a *Deutscher Frauenbund 1945* (German Women's League of 1945). In her opening address, Zahn-Harnack explicitly stated that she was not interested in 'looking back', explaining succinctly that everyone present 'knows what we have suffered and what we are responsible for'.[4] This example shows that the widespread 'collective silencing' (Hermann Lübbe) of the past was not only fostered by those who had a personal stake in avoiding a look back at the past twelve years. It was precisely those who were considered 'innocent' due to their political behavior during National Socialism[5] who contributed to this collective silencing and the resulting priority of 'beginning anew', which they buttressed with a demonstrative emphasis on reconciliation. The women who organized themselves in independent women's groups rather than political parties had a conviction that further united them, namely that women could or should make a unique contribution to rebuilding Germany.

The idea of women having a special role to play in Germany's reconstruction was widespread among men and women at the end of the war, but the reasoning behind it could be traced to a wide variety of sources. These sources ranged from a tradition that originated with the turn of the century women's movement and their goal to insure the influence of both genders in a world that had thus far been shaped by men,[6] to a popular sentiment widespread in the media according to which the male gender had disqualified itself by inaugurating the two world wars, to a widespread view that women were primarily responsible for allowing the National Socialist regime its rise to power. The different and often contradictory reasoning behind calls for a unique contribution of women in Germany's new political beginning were subject to a fundamental belief in an inherent gender difference that implied 'predestined common tasks' for women 'from which no woman can exempt herself', as it was formulated in the founding statement of the *Hamburger Frauenring* (Hamburg Women's Ring) early in 1946.[7]

Therefore, new organizations found it difficult to deny membership to women who had clearly been complicit in the Nazi regime, despite the fact that the occupying powers demanded a ban on former Nazis. Zahn-Harnack included a clause in the *Deutscher Frauenbund* (German Women's League) statutes that limited membership to 'women who had not been members of the NSDAP or the National Socialist *Frauenschaft*', but this clause was hotly contended during the founding meeting. The women raised the objection that the clause 'robs us of many valuable sources of power'.[8] The same objection had led other new organizations – even the anti-fascist women's committees in the Soviet Zone – to do away with the ban on women known to have been National Socialists. The *Berliner Frauenbund* (Berlin Women's League) that developed out of the planned *Deutscher Frauenbund*, for example, had no such clause in their statutes.[9]

Almost all political organizations founded by women at a local level in Germany between 1945 and 1947 had two points in common. They desired an independent status not tied to a political party, and they placed a high priority on securing peace.[10] A central figure women identified with in the postwar women's movement in the Western zones as well as beyond was the physicist and patent lawyer Freda Wuesthoff. The *Stuttgarter Friedenskreis* (Stuttgart Peace Circle) was founded on Wuesthoff's init- iative in 1946 and continued to meet until 1949. Most of the prominent contemporary representatives of the early bourgeois women's movement in the Western zones and West Berlin were members of this group, includ- ing Gertrud Bäumer, Dorothee von Velsen, Elly Heuss-Knapp, Agnes von Zahn-Harnack, Marie-Elisabeth Lüders and Clara von Simson.[11] The rest included a younger generation of women who were born around 1900 to which, for example, Freda Wuesthoff and Theanolte Bähnisch belonged. Theanolte Bähnisch would later become the first chairwoman of the *Deutscher Frauenring* (German Women's Ring, DFR) that was founded in 1949 as an umbrella organization for the women's movement in the Western zones.[12] The women understood themselves to be conveyers of the ideas that were discussed at the meetings of the *Stuttgarter Friedenskreis*, which they brought back to be discussed in the women's groups. Freda Wuesthoff introduced a 'Plan for Sustainable Peace' at the *Stuttgarter Friedenskreis*, according to which the promotion of peace was posited as a primary task and was to be integrated into politics, research, higher education, schools and child rearing. At the first women's conference in Bad Boll in the Western zone in May 1947, peace was the central issue. Freda Wuesthoff and Agnes von Zahn-Harnack gave official speeches on the subject of peace and mutual understanding among the people and the final resolution of the conference placed peace at the center of its politics.

The role of Freda Wuesthoff should not be underestimated in the formulation of a peace politics among Western-oriented women as well as for the crystallization of these peace politics out of a general, imagined peace consensus. In the years 1947 and 1948, Wuesthoff gave over 100 lectures on the topic of 'atomic energy and peace' to packed audiences.[13] One reason for the strong impact of Wuesthoff, who before 1945 had never been heard of in politics, was hinted at in the impressions of one of her contemporaries when she met Wuesthoff in 1946. Leonore Mayer-Katz was impressed to watch Wuesthoff stewing some plums that she had just 'conquered' and at the same time explicating her thoughts on the nuclear threat to the world.[14] With this type of synthesis of 'a daily practice of conquering groceries and an unusual political appeal',[15] Wuesthoff constituted an ideal postwar image of woman that united a ('feminine') unsentimental competence in daily life with an understanding of a ('masculine') subject pertaining to larger questions of humanity.

It is possible that Wuesthoff's influence on the emerging non-party-affiliated women's movement in the Western zones can be traced to the fact that her pacifist politics were not an explicit reaction to the militarism of National Socialist politics. Wuesthoff refers to the United States' atomic attack on Hiroshima on 6 August 1945 as a key factor that had led to her engagement in civil women's work in the postwar years,[16] which is perhaps no surprise given that Wuesthoff herself was a physicist. Because she was one of the few women who belonged to the scientific community of physicists and had contacts to the earlier women's movement,[17] Wuesthoff was in a position to bring new impulses to the re-emerging 'old' women's movement that was mobilizing around the question of peace. The central role that nuclear warfare played in Wuesthoff's peace politics unintentionally reinforced a tendency in the women's movement to separate peace demands from the National Socialist past. By focussing on the nuclear threat, which was a threat not originating in defeated Germany but rather among the Superpowers (the USA and beginning in 1949 the Soviet Union[18]), Wuesthoff's peace politics opened up a space within the 'peace consensus' to those women who, for whatever reason, did not want to think about the war that had just ended and Germany's responsibility for it.

The phenomenon of 'women's pacifism' in the postwar period must be differentiated in relation to women's experiences of the Second World War, which yields three different positions. The first pacifist position stresses women's and mothers' experiences of suffering during the war and relegates the responsibility for the war to men. The second points to Germany's responsibility for the war, thereby implicating women either implicitly or explicitly. The third variation was a very general and ahistorical position in which peace politics are founded on an objection to 'modern war'.

These three positions cannot be identified exclusively with one or another political organization. Some women strategically took up one position or another depending upon the context, or they combined positions in various ways. The representatives of the Mother's Movement that emerged in the Western zones in 1948 can be most immediately identified with the idea of mothers as the suffering heroines of the war. In a 1951 lecture given by the President of WOMAN, Vilma Mönckeberg, the role of this wartime heroine was extended into the present:

> We saw mothers who gave all their remaining physical strength to save their own or someone else's children from fires, mothers who had outdone themselves for years, who had carried their children into the cellars at night – once, twice, three times – and who stood in endlessly long lines at the stores and lived almost from nothing themselves so that their children would not starve. We experienced the thousand-fold suffering of mothers who lost one or more of their sons but who have become mothers of all children everywhere because the strength of mothers is what is needed today more than ever [. . .][19]

The Western side of the East–West conflict manifested a polarization of the first position described above, which I will refer to as 'maternalistic',[20] versus a second position, which was abstracted from individual experiences of the war. The official (Eastern) discourse on peace as articulated by the DFD also disregarded the Second World War as a point of reference at the same time that they embraced the maternalistic position. 'Women and mothers' was a key phrase in the DFD's peace rhetoric. In the immediate postwar years, the idea of peace was rarely linked to admissions of guilt about the war, with the exception of international contexts in which Germans were arguing for national interests.

Peace and Gender

The way in which peace politics were distanced from the history of the war took many forms as this phenomenon developed parallel to the East–West polarization of women's groups. Among Western organizations not affiliated with political parties, this distancing was related to a perceived need to separate women's demands for peace from their emotions. This trend increasingly had an impact on the way in which gender relations were perceived. One example of this stems from Agnes von Zahn-Harnack, the founder of the *Berliner Frauenbund*. In 1946 she spoke of the 'salvaging effect of women's strengths' and in 1947 continued to argue that women should take on a special role in securing peace because 'according to their nature they strive for reconstruction and preservation' and not for power, as men do.[21] But the conditions for peace were no longer linked to the particular strengths or responsibility of women in a speech by von Zahn-Harnack's on 1 September 1949. In this speech she addressed the women's organizations gathered at a ceremony marking the beginning of the war by reminding them of the intellectual and psychological conditions necessary to establish peace. She gave only brief parenthetical mention of 'men's inherent obsession with adventure' without which 'wars would not likely arise'.[22] In the course of negotiations for a planned Mother's Conference for Peace in Berlin in 1950, she declared mother's organizations 'superfluous' and argued that motherhood and motherliness are 'physiological/psychological facts, but not a political platform for an organization'. Her politics, in other words, were now somewhat different from those articulated in her 1928 standard work on the history of the women's movement, which she described as a movement of 'organized motherliness'.[23]

One of the most influential figures of the postwar Western women's movement had already earlier led the way for the postwar dissociation of peace politics and motherhood. Gabriele Strecker was a 'newcomer'[24] who became director of the Hesse Women's Radio Program in 1946 and was soon a popular speaker at women's meetings. At a women's conference in 1948 she was probably the first to publicly question the notion of a disposition unique to women that predestined them to plead for peace:

> Among our own women's ranks many cheap slogans can be found such as: women as the keepers of life, the preservers of the home, women's strong connection to the earth; it is construed as if women's strengths are tied solely to their gender and their function as bearers of life and as such they serve to a certain extent as a natural bulwark that protects against war. Women are as divided as men by contradictions, interests and the most various differences.[25]

Toward the end of the 1940s, a more gender-neutral idea of peace characterized the politics of the Western women's organizations. In this evolved notion of peace, the experience of the war was only articulated when it could be integrated into 'rational' arguments. For example, Freda Wuesthoff wrote in November 1947 that the recent war had shown that 'women and children not only participated in the suffering of the war to an extent that was previously unimaginable' but that 'women also must bear responsibility for the suffering that they brought to other peoples during the war'.[26] This 'objective' argumentation served to relativize the role of a victim that was both projected onto the women as well as taken up by them.

The 'rational' peace discourse was not influenced most immediately by wartime experiences but instead by two other factors, namely, the intellectual tradition of the women's movement during the First World War and the positioning of women's organizations at the start of the Cold War. The 'Women's National Service' during the First World War, the so-called 'Homefront Army', allowed the majority of the middle-class women's movement to take up the war cause even though they understood themselves as a movement of 'extended' or 'socially engaged motherliness'. This central motif of motherliness was commensurable with an affirmation of war in so far as it was associated with a strong and self-sacrificing image of women whose concerns extended beyond their own immediate families.[27] In 1916 Gertrud Bäumer had taken the notion of women's strength through selflessness to an extreme by demanding that women willingly sacrifice themselves for the fatherland. Her arguments concerning war ethics, which she formulated as a question of Christian brotherly love versus patriotic love for the fatherland, concluded that sacrificing one's life for a purpose higher than an individual's life is 'the most supreme expression of *freedom*'.[28]

This kind of instrumental disregard for human life was obsolete after the Second World War. But the unsentimental tradition of the old women's movement and especially its concept of motherliness still contributed to women's attempts to work through their experience of the war – attempts that ran separately from an imagined pacifist consensus among women. They distanced themselves from women who were (communist) peace proponents and dreamers (and thereby felt justified to declare their cause as that of 'human freedom'). They thereby represented themselves as competent mothers who did not lose their common sense due to an excessive love of mankind. An additional result of their need to distance themselves from communist (or suspected communist) women's organizations was that they increasingly separated the ideas of 'motherhood' and 'peace', which their colleagues in suspected communist organizations continued to invariably link. Beginning in 1947, it was the DFD that drew their suspicion, in 1948 the World Organization of Mothers of All Nations (WOMAN), and in 1951 the West German Women's Peace Movement, all of which were held to be 'communist camouflage organizations'.[29]

The Western-oriented women adapted their concept of peace in response to public opinion in the Western zones. They rejected such general notions of 'peace at all cost' and 'peace at the cost of freedom'. They even increasingly doubted various public demands for peace, questioning both the underlying 'true' motives of such demands, as well as their efficacy. In particular, they were eager to point to the communists' arguments for peace as insincere 'tattle'. The evolving changes in public opinion did not develop constantly nor without contradiction, and it can be assumed that these changes evolved more slowly among women's organizations than among male-dominated organizations because the women held onto the idea of a 'peace consensus' among all women.

The search for a distinguishing justification for women's civic organizations was articulated by these women in the form of a 'feminine touch' inserted into the dominant civic understanding of peace as a relative term or by the addition of terms that related to everyday family life. An example of this came in response to the comment of the Soviet Commanding Officer of Berlin that peace 'must be created by the hearts of women'. Else Ulich-Beil, chairwoman of the *Staatsbürgerinnenverband* (Women's Citizen Association), replied that peace is 'like a good marriage', i.e. one can't do it alone, both partners must want it.[30]

The above reply manifests a certain pedagogical rigor that was also intrinsic to the old concept of 'organized motherliness'. This was sometimes expressed through a scolding of mothers who did not understand their role as housewives to be a socially responsible 'profession'. This critique recalled the way in which veterans of the old women's movement warned fellow women during the Cold War not to 'fall for' the 'dangerous' offers of reconciliation and the calls to peace made by communist women. 'State civic education' increasingly took the highest priority in the agendas of Western-oriented women's associations. This was in part the result of the above-mentioned pedagogical and political disposition transported from the old 'organized motherliness' into a contemporary context in which an explicitly maternal position was no longer taken seriously in the West. Because women were purportedly more oriented towards reconciliation, they were thought to be more susceptible to communist 'infiltration'. Civic women's work was thus closely tied to anti-communist education in the Federal Republic in the 1950s. This work was oriented around the image of the responsible female citizen who approached political offers not with a 'hot heart' but with cool reason, thereby learning to differentiate and appropriately judge political systems rather than ignoring their differences due to a flood of motherly feelings. The Western-oriented women's movement had thus established their civic duty as an educational endeavor that was no longer compatible with an unconditional 'women's peace politics'.[31]

In contrast, by 1950 the rhetoric linking women, mothers and peace was ritualized by the DFD in the SBZ and in the GDR as the women's organization gradually lost its autonomy from the *Sozialistische Einheitspartei Deutschlands* (Socialist Unity Party, SED).[32] Eastern-oriented peace discourse was structured around an ethical contrast of societies oriented toward either war or peace in which reference to the Second World War was omitted. The East's ideology of internationalism fostered a concept of peace in which an intention of war or a desire for peace was projected onto political elites while 'the people' of all nations were assumed to be peace-loving and friendly towards each other. This was assumed also of the 'women and mothers' of all nations. The members of the mass political peace organization of the GDR, the DFD, were defined from the beginning as 'fighters for peace'. The anti-fascist self-image of the politically active citizens in the SBZ, which had been increasingly divorced from the historical context since the beginning of the 1950s,[33] contributed to the dehistoricization of peace discourses.

After the Korean War broke out in the spring of 1950, the DFD developed a powerful peace rhetoric based on the principles of allegiance and self-sacrifice and with clearly defined enemies and victims. As such, it was characteristic of postwar socialist systems:

> The attack of Anglo-American imperialists on the peace-loving North Korean population is a signal for all peace-loving people in the world to strengthen and spread with even greater conviction and vigor the mighty peace camp led by the Soviet Union. Thus the DFD [. . .] will commit itself even more passionately than previously to using all its power to insure that every woman and mother in all of Germany will become a conscious champion of peace.[34]

The meaning and impact of the gender-specific aspect of such entreaties is difficult to assess. On the one hand, the recurring appeal to 'women and mothers' appears oddly conspicuous. On the other hand, this separate appeal to women's responsibility in the peace endeavor is never problematized nor further explicated, thus indicating an unbroken social consensus on gender difference that contrasts with the questioning of gender that proponents of the women's movement in the Western zones were engaged with in the late 1940s. The stereotyped doubling of 'women and mothers' in DFD discourse could be interpreted in a favorable light as an indication that while the image of woman was inseparable from women's roles as mothers, it was nonetheless unacceptable to equate the two.

The extent to which an unproblematic, naturalized gender difference lost its hold within the women's movement and the political public sphere of the Western zones can ultimately be measured by considering the emergence and development of an independent *Weltmütterbewegung* (Mother's of the World Movement) in the Western zones. This movement explicitly and elaborately constructed the centrality of motherliness for establishing peace. In 1948 the *Deutschlandzentrale* (Central German Branch) of the American-based organization WOMAN was founded in Hamburg. In the same year the pedagogy professor Klara Marie Faß-binder founded a German branch of the French *Mouvement Mondial des Meres* (MMM), which was subsumed by the *Westdeutsche Frauenfried-ensbewegung* (West German Women's Peace Movement, WFFB) in 1951.[35] The Mother's Charter that was drawn in 1947 by the *Weltbewegung der Mütter* (MMM) had as its goal 'establishing the assurance of true peace. Securing peace on earth is dependent upon a harmony of forces that can only develop if motherly forces govern the world.'[36]

While the MMM was grounded in a Catholic Christian tradition and thus emphasized a 'divine' source of 'peace on earth', WOMAN imagined a sacral community of mothers, as the following excerpt from the WOMAN Manifesto reveals:

> The mothers of the world have until now constituted a silent community. For them there are no borders between peoples, races or classes. Every mother knows of all other mothers that their children's lives are more important than their own. Their common task is rooted in a common feeling: protecting and preserving the life of the human race. Even the war cannot destroy this community. The battles rage between the men [. . .] Every woman and mother knows that since the beginning of history war has been her arch enemy; it destroys the home, which is the center of the family, and it eradicates the meaning of all human activity.[37]

The international orientation that distinguished WOMAN from most other women's organizations of the time is nonetheless conspicuously limited. This is less apparent in the essentialist materialism of the above statement than in its invocation of a collective identity.

Community Building and the Politics of the Past

The more women's organizations specifically invoked the war and/or its immediate consequences, the more they positioned themselves in communities that were gendered as feminine. Evidence of this can be found in the spontaneous emergence of numerous women's committees that supported local authorities in servicing communities beginning in 1945, as well as the constructed image of the '*Trümmerfrauen*' who participated in the communal labor of cleaning up the ruins after the war. A 1946 feature in a women's journal about the 'women of Berlin's construction sites' reported that the workers interviewed specifically requested that it be made clear that they are not 'Nazi wives', as they were often called by people passing by. When they were asked to elaborate on this, the report said that it was 'one of the youngest' workers who added that even former 'Nazi women' should not be treated this way 'because everyone who lends an honest hand in our reconstruction shows that they want to make good their mistakes. And they should not be scolded but rather helped.'[38] This report serves as an example of the dominant postwar moral tenor in all of Germany according to which past mistakes could be atoned through energetic participation in reconstruction. This moral code was the same one found in the previously mentioned politics of the first postwar women's organizations who were reluctant to ban women who had been active National Socialists. The '*Trümmerfrauen*', like the women's committees and their 'bread and potatoes' politics, understood themselves as 'reconstruction communities'. In contrast to the 'community of mothers' propagated by the WOMAN Manifesto, their politics were not grounded in a common 'biological' experience from which a moral code of conduct was purportedly derived. Instead, they judged fellow citizens on the basis of their participation in reconstruction, which they posited as a necessary precondition for rebuilding a national political identity for 'the people'. This moral code was gender neutral, yet at the same time it is apparent that the community-building spirit of the women's organizations was more pronounced due not only to their independence from political parties but also to their self-image as proponents of reconciliation. The next two examples will further explore this nexus of community, nation and gender.

Dorothee von Velsen, one of the prominent members of the 'old' women's movement who most clearly opposed the National Socialist regime,[39] recalled in the mid-1950s that peace was more difficult for her than war because '[w]e got the feeling that we were a nation of criminals who all together were responsible for having caused the present misfortune.'[40] Von Velsen had retreated from Berlin just after the National Socialists came to power, settling in a Bavarian village where she was active in rebuilding the women's movement in Southern Germany starting in 1945. Looking back at the years 1945 and 1946, she felt herself implicated in the critique of 'the Germans' that was coming from other nations, and she identified herself correspondingly with the German people and not with a 'community of women': 'Of all the charges launched by the American press against us, [. . .] none of them were more directed against our self-confidence than the constant denunciation of our "self-pity".'[41]

Von Velsen's redefinition of this 'self-pity' as an inability to understand the consequences of the war ('it must be admitted that a great part of the population simply didn't understand the consequences of the war') posited an imaginary majority of Germans who were not guilty of National Socialism. She considered herself a part of this majority of Germans who 'had inwardly resisted National Socialism and had suffered under it' and who 'foolishly' believed, as she added with (self-)irony, 'that they deserved reparations for these years'. It did not occur to them (nor to her) that:

> they had been expected to risk our lives to fight against the dictatorship. Now, instead of becoming introspective with extreme regret and offering up an admission of guilt, they raised complaints against the constant privations and the exploitations of the occupying powers. Psychologically this seemed convincing, and nothing could hurt us more than the standard reply that the Germans are self-confident and arrogant in good times and pitiful beggars in times of misfortune.[42]

In order to explain what she imputes as the logical consequences of the war, according to which the Germans should have been compensated for the suffering they endured, she temporarily leaves the first person plural form 'we'. But she does not completely give up the identification as if she would then use irony from the perspective of a detached critic. She instead creates the impression that she belongs to a political elite that can raise itself above the community, not in order to distance oneself from it but in order to speak for it. Von Velsen's critique of the International Military Tribunal's Nuremberg trials of the principal war criminals was also characterized by a peculiarly strong identification:

> The German people failed to take justice into their own hands. They were then forced to listen as guilt for the preparation and the execution of the war was hoisted upon the accused. There were those among them whom we looked upon with heavy aversion, but also many who were clearly tied up in situations that were no different from those of people in other countries.[43]

The trials that condemned twenty-four leading representatives of the NSDAP, the German state and army, and six National Socialist organizations were observed by many Germans who similarly held the suspicion that 'the justice sought by the victors will prove to be a vengeful one'. Yet most Germans were so shocked by the crimes exposed during the trials that they largely agreed with the judgements against the 'principal war criminals'.[44] Even when it is taken into account that von Velsen wrote her memoirs during the mid-1950s when public acceptance of the Nuremberg judgements was relativized by the process of 'denazification' and by the follow-up trials in Nuremberg,[45] her aggressive identification with the accused still comes across as astoundingly extensive. The official coverage of the trials issued under control of the occupying authorities was characterized by von Velsen as 'dominated by the victors'. She found it 'scandalous' and 'barbaric' that 'the plaintiffs were also the judges'. And she claimed that on the night of the executions 'many of us who had nothing in common with Hitler's government still couldn't get to sleep'.[46]

Not only did von Velsen confidently publish such reflections in her 1956 memoirs, she also relied on them in her political work in the women's movement. One example of this stems from a letter von Velsen wrote in May 1951 reporting as chairwoman of the *Frauenring Südbayern* (Southern Bavarian Women's Ring) to the chairwoman of the *Berliner Staatsbürger-innen Verband* (Berlin Women's Citizen Association), Else Ulich-Beil, in which she describes her meeting with a group of high-level representatives of American women's organizations who were invited to a six-week 'Panel Visit' in West Germany and West Berlin. Von Velsen reports that at one of the first meetings in Frankfurt the American women had been surprised that they were received with reservations in Germany despite their coming 'with the Marshall Plan'. Von Velsen writes that her response to the American women was that 'they didn't come with the M Plan etc.' but instead they came 'with the denazification, the dismantling, the Nuremberg trials and the terrible, moralizing defamation'. She further explicated to her American colleagues 'how willing the German people were in 1945 to recognize the injustice they had done and to admit it, and how in all their political ignorance they had expected to be welcomed by the other side with open arms'. She reports that her words had been 'very supported' by one of the women, while some of the others had told her later that 'they knew nothing about all this and just now had begun to understand the situation'.[47]

Dorothee von Velsen was one of the most influential and recognized personalities of the West German women's movement even as she reached age 70. She was in a good position to expect the approval of the addressee of her letter, Ulich-Beil, who was her contemporary and had long accompanied her in her political activism for women. But her position may not be described as representative for the 'politics of the past' among the West German women's movement, despite the fact that she gave public voice to the unspoken convictions of some other women. Agnes von Zahn-Harnack, for example, was of a completely different opinion in her somewhat pathetic 1949 speech marking the start of the war ten years earlier: 'We betrayed the Western world [*das Abendland*], we forced the victors to sacrifice blood and goods. [. . .] During these years a jungle of dangerous, poisonous weeds sprang up. The postwar years of hunger brought us a vulgar, unscrupulous materialism, and our disappointment with the occupying powers brought an unjustified bitterness [. . .]'[48] In her recollections of a women's meeting in the fall of 1945, Gabriele Strecker even reported her 'view of the German woman's soul [. . .] with a strange mixture of self -pity, bad conscience, stubborn prancing, and so many, so many good intentions to help in the reconstruction'. Although her memoir was published in 1981, it can still be contrasted to von Velsen's position above that spoke for a reproachful German community, because Strecker attempts to see from the perspective of the Americans.[49]

A third position in community politics and the politics of the past was represented by the mother's organization WOMAN. Because their 'German Central Office' was only founded in 1948, they did not articulate a position on the Nuremberg trials. But the American journalist Dorothy Thompson, who had founded WOMAN in the USA in 1946, was one of the few prominent Americans who was critical of the Nuremberg trials. Already in 1945, she registered her reservations about a trial 'in which the judges are also the plaintiffs and the "executioners".'[50]

It is possible that the *Frauendank* (Women Give Thanks) ceremony that the German WOMAN founders planned as one of their first political actions was inspired by a compensatory 'sense of justice' articulated by Thompson. On 16 December 1948 the mothers' organization initiated a rally in the Hamburg Music Hall that was attended by over 2,000 women who came to give thanks to the foreign organizations and individuals for the various forms of help they had given Germany since the end of the war.[51] This demonstration was clearly in opposition to the type of reproachful position represented by Dorothee von Velsen that was in fact widespread among the German public during denazification (i.e. late in 1948). The *Frauendank* demonstration emphasized instead the positive side of Germany's foreign relations. Thanks were given in particular for the care packages from the USA, the food supplied to schools by the Quakers and other aid organizations, the children's homes provided by English women in the British zone, packages from Argentina and Canada as well as donations and funds for German families in Switzerland, England, Scandinavia, and the USA, and invitations for children to spend the holidays in Switzerland or for students to study in Sweden, Denmark, and England.

The initiators of the rally distanced themselves from the idea of a German community based on their suffering or victim-status. Instead they propagated a 'community of thanks', according to the retired school supervisor Emmy Beckmann in her speech at the Hamburg rally in the name of 'those who do intellectual work'.[52] This idea of community not only upheld an identification with Germany (rather than an identification with 'world motherhood'), the Hamburg women understood themselves to represent all of Germany not as a nation that protests, challenges, complains and judges the foreign community, but one that greets it with thankfulness. This identification with a positive image of Germany was apparent in the opening speech by Vilma Mönckeberg, the chairwomen of WOMAN. She replied to what she imagined to be the 'voices from abroad' that accused the Germans of a preference for taking rather than thanking: 'We can answer you in good conscience and with our heads held high: yes, we like to give thanks. We prefer giving thanks to just taking. And rather than taking we would prefer to give. But a hope lives in our hearts that we Germans will some day be givers again, both materially and spiritually.'[53] This community representing the Germans as givers of thanks apparently harbored a latent feeling of national shame at being dependent upon foreign aid. On the other hand, the representatives of a '*world* mother's movement' could more easily overcome the shame of being helped by 'foreigners'. Thus 'national interests' could to be linked to the international interests of all mothers everywhere and thereby be considered legitimate.

As the representative of a *mother's* movement, WOMAN was able to position itself at the center of a popular moral movement aimed at 'drawing the line' by leading a campaign supporting eight war criminals imprisoned and sentenced to death in France. The eight soldiers were considered 'innocent' by the German public because their individual participation in a massacre in a French border town could purportedly not be proved. French opinion held that this proof was irrelevant because the army formation that they belonged to and that carried out the massacre had been designated a 'criminal organization' at the Nuremberg trials. For WOMAN, the accused were innocent by the mere fact that by the end of the war they had 'not yet outgrown adolescence and so in the eyes of mothers were not responsible for deeds carried out at the command of their superiors'.[54] A WOMAN brochure that published letters from the accused was introduced with an anonymous 'voice from the press' that granted an emphatic legitimacy to the action of the mothers on behalf of the soldiers condemned in a foreign country because, '[t]hey speak not a political language but a *mother*-tongue that is that same everywhere and is understood by every nation despite differences in national languages.'[55] The idea of a world-wide – and, it must be added, a correspondingly simple – 'mother-tongue' was used to rescue lost German sons by representing a national interest as an international affair.

Their support for the war criminals accused in French courts led WOMAN to sypathize with the activities of Princess von Isenburg, who was called the 'Mother of the Landberger Prisoners' by her followers.[56] She was an advocate for the amnesty of the last remaining war criminals imprisoned in the Landsberg prison, who had been sentenced to death in 1946 by an American military court. As members of the 1st SS Armor Division '*Leibstandarte Adolf Hitler*', these men participated in the murder of seventy-two unarmed Americans in the Belgian town of Malmedy in December 1944.[57] Helene Wessel, the contentious *Bundestag* Centrist Party representative[58] who was closely tied to the Mothers' Movement, also supported Isenburg's *Arbeitsring für Wahrheit und Gerechtigkeit* (Working Group for Truth and Justice), also known as the *Arbeitsgemeinschaft zur Rettung der Landsberger Häftlinge* (Working Group to Save the Landsberger Prisoners).[59] Some influential members of the Western-oriented women's movement voiced their skepticism of these solidarity groups. In the official organ of the Western-oriented women's citizen associations called *Informationen für die Frau*, for example, a radio commentary by Gabriele Strecker (once again) pointed out that the seven men in Landsberg sentenced to death were mass murderers. Strecker's criticism of the communist peace enthusiasts was similar to her critique of the erroneous sympathy that had been aroused among the women in the Landsberg solidarity groups.[60]

In the eyes of many West German women, the women from the SBZ/GDR had discredited community thinking on the basis of their position on yet another issue. In 1947 they had campaigned for a unified German women's movement with the DFD as its umbrella organization. This was interpreted by the leading Western women as a totalitarian usurpation. Beyond this, the women in the Eastern zone attempted to link the 'unity of the women's movement' with the 'reunification' of Germany, which was a high priority on the public agendas of both Germanies. They also tried to capitalize on a critique of the (Western women's) willingness to reconcile with women who had been National Socialists.[61]

Conclusion

Women's political engagement for securing peace and simultaneously reconstructing Germany as well as their goal of working together independent of political parties constituted the factors that contributed to the willingness of most women's organizations founded or re-founded just after 1945 to work together with women who had formerly been active National Socialists. This led to a need to repress the past, despite the fact that doing so also went against their common desire to create the conditions that could lead to sustainable peace. A bridge between these two apparently divergent interests was created in the Western zones by a peace politics predicated not on the problematic of the Second World War, but instead on the threat of nuclear war – a threat that had first become acute at the end of the war in 1945 and which had not been initiated by Germany. These politics were easily united with the Western organizations' increasing desire to distance themselves from the communist-dominated DFD, whose peace speeches were denounced throughout the East–West conflict as a 'politics of feelings' that aimed only at women's hearts while neglecting to cultivate their reason. The peace rhetoric of the women in the East and the West became polarized around the question of the 'conditionality' of peace and around the meaning of gender. On neither side, however, did their rhetoric condense around the National Socialist past and the Second World War, which were marginalized in the discourses of both.

In the immediate postwar period, politically active women positioned themselves in communities with very different characteristics. As members of a defeated nation, many women identified with a community of fellow sufferers and victims who expected to be compensated because they had been treated with 'injustice'. As part of a community of 'mothers of the world' with common feelings, as well as part of a service community of a special nature, or as a 'community of thanks', they identified with women who contributed materially or intellectually to Germany's reconstruction. The notions of community suggested here continued to develop with various accents and new links in the rhetoric of reunification that ensued and as both sides continued to distance themselves from the other. An analysis of the gendering of these developments still remains to be done.

Notes

Translated by Christina M. White

1. Anette Kuhn, 'Frauen suchen neue Wege der Politik,' in *Frauen in der deutschen Nachkriegszeit*, vol. 2, ed. Anette Kuhn (Düsseldorf, 1986). Kuhn, however, uses the term 'feminist pacifism'.

2. The common reference to the pre-1933 women's movement as 'bourgeois' is problematic not least because the majority of middle-class women who constituted it did not necessarily have access to their family's money.

3. The *Westdeutsche Frauen-Friedensbewegung* (West German Women's Peace Movement, WFFB) was not included because it was only founded in 1952 and positioned itself above all against the Federal Republic of Germany's rearmament. Cf. Irene Stoehr 'Phalanx der Frauen? Wiederaufrüstung und Weiblichkeit in Westdeutschland 1950–1957,' in *Soziale Rekonstruktionen – Militär und Geschlechterverhältnis*, ed. Christine Eifler and Ruth Seifert, (Münster, 1999), 187–204.

4. 'Protokoll der Gründungsversammelung des Deutschen Frauenbundes 1945,' Landesarchiv Berlin, HLA/BFB, Nr. 10.

5. On Zahn-Harnack's political integrity see Ilse Meseberg-Haubold, Agnes von Zahn-Harnack (Manuscript, 1992); Irene Stoehr, 'Agnes von Zahn-Harnack,' in *Frauenpolitik und politisches Wirken im Berlin der Nachkriegszeit 1945–1949*, ed. Renate Genth et al. (1996), 348–358.

6. Helene Lange, "Das Endziel der Frauenbewegung" (1904), in Helene Lange, *Kampfzeiten*, vol. 1 (Berlin, 1928), 72–85.

7. 'Fünf Jahre Hamburger Frauenring,' in *Informationsdienst für die Frau*, 8–10 (December 1951): 23.

8. 'Protokoll der Gründungsversammlung,' 3.

9. An exception was the '*Süddeutsche Frauen-Arbeits-Kreis*', founded in 1945, which according to its statutes only accepted women 'who were did not belong to National Socialist organizations nor share their sentiments' (Archiv der Sozialen Demokratie der Friedrich-Ebert-Stiftung, Bonn, Else Reventlow Papers). This group, which led to the founding of the *Arbeitsgemeinschaft der Wählerinnen* (Working Group of Women Voters, AdW), had a unique position in the postwar women's movement. The AdW members, for example, refused to hold joint membership in umbrella organizations such as the DFR or the *Deutschen Staatsbürgerinnenverband* (the Citizen's League of German Women).

10. 'The first thing that we demand as women and mothers is to secure peace', according to the first calls for a central women's committee in Berlin that was signed by representatives of all the political parties (SPD, KPD, CDU and LDP). *Deutsche Volkszeitung* (DVZ), 9 November 1945.

11. Gertrud Bäumer (born 1873) was the chair of the *Bund Deutscher Frauenvereine* from 1910 to 1919 and remained a proponent of the women's movement until 1933; Dorothee von Velsen (born in 1883), the former chair of the *Deutscher Staatsbürgerinnnenverband* from 1921 to 1933, was a leading figure in the development of the women's movement in Bavaria. Elly Heuss-Knapp, the wife of a later president of the FRG, belonged to the informal political circle of Gertrud Bäumer and later founded the *Deutsche Müttergenesungswerk* in 1950; concerning Agnes von Zahn-Harnack (born 1884) see note 5; Marie-Elisabeth Lüders (born 1878) was first Prussian housing inspector and director of the Central Office for Women's Work during the First World War, City Social Advisor in West-Berlin from 1949 to 1951, and starting in 1953 served as the Parliament Eldest in the West German government (FDP); the physicst Clara von Simson was the director of the peace commission of the *Berliner Frauenbund* (the Berlin Women's League).

12. The lawyer Theanolte Bähnisch was governing president of the state of Lower Saxony in Hanover. On the founding of the DFR see Barbara Henicz and Margrit Hirschfeld, '"Wenn die Frauen wüßten, was sie könnten, wenn sie wollten" – Zur Gründungsgeschichte des Deutschen Frauenrings,' in *Frauen in der deutschen Nachkriegszeit*, 135–156.

13. Ingrid Schmidt-Harzbach, "Freda Wuesthoff – Vorkämpferin gegen atomare Aufrüstung. Versuch eines Porträts," in *Frauen in der Geschichte* V, ed. Anna-Elisabeth Freier and Anette Kuhn (Düsseldorf, 1984), 410–444 and 422.

14. Leonore Mayer-Katz, *Sie haben zwei Minuten Zeit! Nachkriegsimpulse aus Baden* (Freiburg, 1981), 134.

15. Nori Möding, "Die Stunde der Frauen? Frauen und Frauenorganisationen des bürgerlichen Lagers," in *Von Stalingrad zur Währungsreform. Zur Sozialgeschichte des Umbruchs in Deutschland*, ed. Martin Broszat (Munich, 1988), 619–647 and 636.

16. Mayer-Katz, *Sie haben zwei Minuten*, 132–156; Günther Berthold, *Freda Wuesthoff. Eine Faszination* (Freiburg, 1982).

17. Wuesthoff met Marie-Elisabeth Lüders, Agnes von Zahn-Harnack and other representatives of the 'old women's movement' during the First World War in the '*Nationaler Frauendienst*' (National Women's Service) when she was 19 years old, and as director of the war office's *Hilfsdienst für Frauen in der Etappe* (Aid for Women in the Rear Army) when she was 21 years old. During the years that followed, she studied and then began her career and was not active in the women's movement.

18. The Soviet Union first detonated an atom bomb on 25 September 1949.

19. Vilma Mönckeberg's lecture in November 1951 in Winterthur und Olten, WOMAN-Archive Wilhelmshaven.

20. For the history of maternalist politics see Seth Koven and Sonya Michel, 'Womanly Duties: Maternalist Politics and the Origins of Welfare States in France, Germany, Great Britain and the United States, 1880–1920,' *American Historical Review* 95 (1990) and Seth Koven and Sonya Michel, eds, *Mothers of a New World: Maternalist Politics and the Origins of Welfare States* (London, 1993).

21. Quoted in Henicz and Hirschfeld, 'Wenn die Frauen wüßten,' 136.

22. Agnes von Zahn-Harnack, 'Zum 1. September 1949!' Manuscript, Landesarchiv Berlin, BFB-Rep 235, p. 3, printed in Genth et al., *Frauenpolitik*, Appendix 17, 484–488.

23. Agnes von Zahn-Harnack, *Die Frauenbewegung. Geschichte – Probleme – Ziele* (Berlin, 1928). On the planned 'Mother's Conference' cf. Irene Stoehr, 'Der Mütterkongreß fand nicht statt. Frauenbewegung, Staatsmänner und Kalter Krieg 1950,' *WerkstattGeschichte* 17 (1997): 66–82.

24. Gabriele Strecker (born 1905) was a doctor until 1945 and only took up contact with representatives of political women's organizations after the Second World War via an American woman who was a US officer. In 1946 the American army forces appointed her as director of the women's radio program 'Radio Frankfurt'. Gabriele Strecker, *Überleben ist nicht genug. Frauen 1945–1950* (Freiburg, 1981), 14ff.

25. Gabriele Strecker, 'Was steht im Wege?' *Die Welt der Frau* 3, 1 (1948): 1–3.

26. Freda Wuesthoff to the *Frauenring Baden-Baden*, 26 November 1947, NL Schmidt-Harzbach, private document.

27. Cf. Irene Stoehr, '"Organisierte Mütterlichkeit." Zur Politik der deutschen Frauenbewegung um 1900,' in *Frauen suchen ihre Geschichte*, ed. Karin Hausen (Munich, 1987), 225–253.

28. 'Nachwort,' in Gertrud Bäumer and Gesine Nordbeck, Zwischen zwei Gesetzen! *Die Frau* (January 1916): 221–225 and 224. (My emphasis here. – I.St.)

29. Cf. Stoehr, *Phalanx der Frauen*, 194ff.

30. Else Ulich-Beil, *Ich ging meinen Weg. Lebenserinnerungen* (Berlin, 1961), 165ff.

31. Irene Stoehr, '"Feministischer Antikommunismus" und weibliche Staatsbürgerschaft in der Gründungsdekade der Bundesrepublik,' *Feministische Studien* 1 (1998): 86–94.

32. Rita Pawlowski, 'Der Demokratische Frauenbund Deutschlands (DFD),' in *Frauenpolitik*, 75–98 and 93ff.
33. Anette Leo has analyzed this process in relation to 'antisemitic tendencies' in dealing with the opposition in the GDR. Cf. Anette Leo, 'Antifaschismus und Kalter Krieg. Eine Geschichte von Einengung, Verdrängung und Erstarrung,' *Brandenburgische Gedenkstätten für die Verfolgten des NS-Regimes* (Berlin, 1992), 74–80.
34. Public notice of the *Demokratischer Frauenbund Deutschlands* for the Second World Peace Conference 1950, *Bundesarchiv Berlin, DY 31/105.*
35. On political materialism in the two 'mother countries' of the West German postwar mother's movement cf. Joanne Meyorowitz, 'Beyond the Feminine Mystique. A Reassessment of Postwar Mass Culture,' *The Journal of American History* (1993): 1455–1482 and 1468; Silvie Chaperon, 'Geschlechtergeschichte der Nachkriegszeit in Frankreich. Ein historiographischer Abriß aus der Sicht der Geschichte der Frauenverbände' (unpublished lecture at the Free University in Berlin, 1995).
36. 'Die Charta der Mütter,' in *Frauen in der deutschen Nachkriegszeit*, 176f.
37. 'Manifest der WOMAN,' in *Der Ruf der Mütter*, ed. Barbara Nordhaus Lüdecke (München, 1949), 213–218; 213f. This was apparently a free translation of the following passage from 'A Woman's Manifesto' by Dorothy Thompson:

> Thus there is on this earth a solidarity which has hitherto been largely silent. It needs no governments, nor unions nor organized associations to bring it into being. It needs no flag to raise. No boundaries delineate it, weather these be boundaries of nation race or class. It is the solidarity between women as mothers. It is the solidarity of a function transcending all ephemeral patterns of organized society – the function of protecting through nurture, the human race. Even war does not destroy it nor the hates of war obliterate it.The woman knows that war is the cancer of society, the running amok of its cells, the destroyer of its focussing point, the home, and as such the violator of the purposes of all human activity. (New York (no date given), *Swarthmore College Peace Collection*)

38. 'Kiek ma die Naziweiba! Unter uns: Es sind gar keine,' *Die Welt der Frau* 2, March 1946.
39. After 1940 she mentioned to Gertrud Bäumer, the editor of the magazine *Die Frau* (an organ of the earlier women's movement that was able to be published until 1944) 'in recurring harsh debates' to

be wary of 'the dangerous affinities to National Socialist ideas'. Cf. Angelika Schaser, *Helene Lange und Gertrud Bäumer. Eine politische Lebensgemeinschaft* (Cologne/Weimar/Vienna, 2000), 302f.

40. Dorothee von Velsen, *Im Alter die Fülle. Erinnerungen* (Tübingen, 1956), 366.
41. Ibid. 367.
42. Ibid.
43. Ibid. 369.
44. Norbert Frei, *Vergangenheitspolitik. Die Anfänge der Bundesrepublik und die NS-Vergangenheit* (Munich, 1997), 133.
45. Ibid., 136.
46. Velsen, *Im Alter die Fülle*, 369.
47. Velsen an Else Ulich-Beil, Munich, 19.5.1951, *Archiv des Deutschen Staatsbürgerinnenverbandes Berlin.*
48. Zahn-Harnack, 'Zum 1. September,' 2.
49. Strecker, *Überleben*, 15.
50. Frei, *Vergangenheitspolitik*, 136
51. '"Frauendank" für das geleistete Liebeswerk des Auslandes. Kundgebung der Hamburger Frauen am 16. Dezember 1948,' a report by Vilma Mönckeberg, WOMAN-Archiv Wilhelmshaven.
52. Ibid. 11. The school supervisor Emmy Beckmann belonged to the veterans of the 'old' women's movement. From 1921 to 1933 she took over her predecessor Helene Lange's position as chair of the *Allgemeiner Lehrerinnenverein* (General Teachers' Association) and became chair of the re-established *Deutscher Akademikerinnenbund* (Association of German Female Academics).
53. Ibid. 5.
54. 'Zum Tode verurteilt von Müttern betreut' (undated, unpublished brochure, no place of publication, n.p.), *WOMAN-Archiv Wilhelmshaven.* The eight accused were between 19 and 27 years old at the end of the war.
55. Ibid.
56. Ella Schirmacher to Vilma Mönckeberg, 3 June 1954, *WOMAN-Archiv Wilhelmshaven.*
57. Most of the 73 accused have since been pardoned. Frei, *Vergangenheitspolitik*, 142.
58. Wessel was one of the four women who were members of the Parliamentary Council that formulated the Constitution for the FGR in 1948/49. After the Centrist Party was dissolved, starting in 1953 Wessel was an elected representative of the *Gesamtdeutsche Volkspartei* (The All-German People's Party, GVP) that she founded

together with Gustav Heinemann. After the dissolution of the GVP, Wessel was an elected representative of the SPD starting in 1957.

59. Frei, *Vergangenheitspolitik*, 284.
60. Gabriele Strecker, 'Rundfunkkommentar zu Landsberg,' *Informationen für die Frau* (March/April 1951), 17f.
61. During the West German women's conference in Bad Boll in 1947 during which Wuesthoff und Zahn-Harnack held their speeches on peace, the DFD delegates complained that 'the women in the West don't want to hear anything about the German women in the East' and that nothing was said about 'uniting Germany' but instead they had 'discussions hours long about the fascists who had been released from the internment camp in Ludwigsburg'. Report by Maria Rentmeister to the SED Women's Secretariat (private archive of Rita Pawlowski, 1947).

-14-

Men of Reconstruction – The Reconstruction of Men

Returning POWs in East and West Germany, 1945–1955[1]

Frank Biess

This essay discusses the relationship between East and West German confrontations with consequences of the Second World War and the 'remasculinization' of postwar society.[2] In particular, the essay addresses the reception and experiences of the approximately two million soldiers who returned from Soviet POW camps between 1945 and 1955 to one of the two German postwar societies. In so doing, the essay focuses on two larger conceptual problems of writing a comparative history of postwar Germany. The first concerns the aftermath of the war of annihilation and its immediate impact on both German postwar societies. This is an issue that until now has not received adequate attention in the literature on postwar history. Ever since the Swiss publicist Fritz Rene Allemann coined the slogan 'Bonn is not Weimar' in his 1957 publication, West German commentators (as well as later historians) have celebrated the mastering of the consequences of the war as one of the hallmarks of a West German success story that clearly distinguished the second from the first German democracy. A similar narrative of overcoming the consequences of the war was very much part of the self-representation of the East German dictatorship, which was by definition predicated on shaping the future rather than on seriously confronting the past.[3] More recently, the dominant paradigms of postwar historiography such as 'modernization', 'Americanization' or 'Westernization' for the West, and 'Stalinization' or 'Sovietization' for the East have emphasized, for perfectly legitimate reasons, the dynamic transformations of both German societies since the late 1940s.[4] Seen in this way, the first postwar decade appears primarily as the fulcrum of an Americanized consumer society in the West, and a Stalinist dictatorship in the East. While these paradigms have yielded a host of important insights, they are, however, less well suited to capture the after-effects and consequences of unprecedented collective experiences of violence and destruction. This essay thus builds on an emerging literature that has begun to bring into focus post-1945 history specifically as *postwar* history.[5]

Returning POWs from the Soviet Union offer a particularly worthwhile object of study when trying to understand both German societies as postwar societies. Next to expellees from Eastern Europe, returning POWs from the Soviet Union represented that segment of the former German 'national community' (*Volksgemeinschaft*) most deeply affected by the experiences of war and defeat. The collective experience of these returning POWs combined an active experience of violence as soldiers on the eastern front engaged in ideological warfare with a more passive experience of violence in Soviet prisoner-of-war camps.[6] The protracted return of the POWs, which lasted the entire first postwar decade, thus compelled both postwar societies to confront these successive experiences of violence during their formative periods of postwar reconstruction. The confrontation was a dynamic one. Both East and West German attempts to come to terms with war and defeat were closely intertwined with the process of reconstruction, and in both postwar societies, the link between reconstruction and overcoming the past manifested itself particularly clearly in the formulation of new ideals of masculinity. As men in the 'best years of their lives' who were to assume a crucial function in the respective reconstruction efforts, returning POWs provided an important surface onto which these postwar ideals of masculinity could be projected.

The second major focus of this essay is the comparison between East and West Germany. In both postwar societies, the confrontation with the consequences of war and defeat was decisively shaped by the German–German context. Returning POWs represented one of the problems facing both German societies due to their shared past. After 1945, both German societies needed to transform former *Wehrmacht* soldiers and returning POWs into male citizens on opposite sides of the Cold War. Consequently, East and West German attitudes toward the returning POWs help elucidate the dialectical interaction between these societies that Christoph Klessmann has characterized as 'demarcation and interweaving' (*Abgrenzung und Verflechtung*).[7] Through their respective attitudes toward the returning men, both societies attempted to distance themselves from one another and from their shared past. But at the same time, East and West German responses to the returning POWs reveal similarities, which resulted from their common nature as successor-societies to the Third Reich. The emphasis on the shared character of both German societies as 'postfascist' and 'postwar' thus also directs attention to their structural and functional similarities that were located, as it were, below the surface of ideological antagonisms of the Cold War.

This essay analyzes perceptions of returning POWs in East and West Germany, and examines how these men in turn responded to their 'reception' in both postwar societies. Here it should be noted that West German reactions and perceptions were clearly more pluralistic than East German ones. My analysis of the West German situation therefore draws on a variety of different sources including interest groups, churches, charitable organizations, and medical and psychiatric experts. In contrast, the East German reception of the returning POWs was determined increasingly by the Socialist Unity Party (SED). Even in the West, however, official responses to the returnees, despite the heterogeneity of the forces involved, exhibited a remarkable homogeneity in terms of content. The first section of the essay examines two distinctly different concepts of liminality in both postwar societies. It focuses in particular on the importance of a comprehensive medical-psychiatric discourse in West Germany in defining the returning men as 'victims' of war and captivity. The second section explores East and West German strategies for assigning the returning POWs some positive ways of interpreting their experiences that were compatible with the symbolic and ideological requirements of East and West German reconstruction. In the final section of the essay, I consider how these 'official' interpretative schemes contributed to the reconstruction of male subjectivity in postwar Germany.

Pathologizing Returning POWs and the 'Crisis of Masculinity' in West and East Germany

During the early postwar period, East and West German perceptions of returning POWs initially emphasized their liminality. This liminality manifested itself in the enduring effects of war and imprisonment on returnees' body, psyche and consciousness. The term 'liminality' derives from the anthropological model of a 'rite of passage' by Arnold von Gennep and Victor Turner, and refers to a transitional period between two stages of life. In East and West German perceptions, returning POWs appeared caught in the transition from military soldiers into East and West German citizens.[8] This shared emphasis on the liminality of the returning POWs highlighted the protracted consequences of the war in both societies. At the same time, the respective definitions of returning POWs' liminality in East and West revealed two distinctly different perceptions of the war's aftereffects. In the West, liminality was defined primarily in terms of physical and mental characteristics, whereas in the East, it referred to ostensible political or ideological deficiencies. In both societies, deficient masculinity was a key component of liminality.

The clearest indication of returnees' liminality in the West was an extensive discussion of the trauma they had experienced in Soviet captivity. Originating in medical and psychiatric professional literature, the issue of returnees' trauma was then taken up by charitable organizations, state offices and the print media. This medical-psychiatric discourse set in immediately after the start of the mass repatriation of German POWs from the Soviet Union in the summer of 1946, and concentrated primarily on the poor physical and mental condition of the first returning veterans. These men were diagnosed as suffering from a specific 'returnee disease' (*Heimkehrerkrankheit*) whose primary symptoms were the physical and mental effects of malnutrition in Soviet POW camps. In the professional literature of the time, the illness received the name of 'dystrophy'. This diagnosis also included such mental or emotional symptoms as apathy, depression, underachievement, and a tendency to become easily agitated, any and all of which persisted even after their initial somatic cause – malnutrition – had ceased to exist.[9] While the health of the returning POWs improved considerably after 1947/48, the discussion of physical and mental aftereffects of the prisoner-of-war camp experience continued well into the late 1950s. The 'medical-scientific advisory board' of the Association of Returnees (*Verband der Heimkehrer*), for example, published a multi-volume series in the 1950s on 'extreme living conditions and their consequences', and in 1958 the Federal Labor Ministry (*Bundesministerium für Arbeit und Soziales*) put out a volume of essays on the 'long-term consequences' and 'permanent damage' resulting from dystrophy in Soviet captivity.[10]

The very existence of these writings on dystrophy into the late 1950s runs counter to the assumption of a rapid, unproblematic overcoming of the war in the postwar period, and it testifies to the existence of genuine pain and suffering among former soldiers and POWs. At the same time, the dystrophy diagnosis served a functional purpose by assisting returning POWs in gaining access to benefits provided under the Federal War Victims' Law (*Bundesversorgungsgesetz*, BGV). The dystrophy diagnosis became especially important in the case of returnees' frequent mental or emotional suffering, which by itself did not entitle a patient to any material compensation during the 1950s. If diagnosed as dystrophy, however, this mental suffering could be traced back to somatic causes; and as such, it actually fell under the provisions of the BGV.[11]

Publications on dystrophy, however, represented more than an objective reflection of the mental and physical health of returning German POWs
after the Second World War. While psychotherapeutic professional literature on trauma proceeds from the premise of a strong psycho-biological
continuum, historians have consistently emphasized that perceptions of
trauma are both culturally and historically determined.[12] Historicizing the
diagnosis of dystrophy seems also necessary in light of the extent to
which some leading medical and psychiatric authorities on the so-called
'returnee-disease' were politically tainted. The author of the first mono-
graph on dystrophy, Kurt Gauger, was, for instance, according to Geoffrey
Cocks an 'enthusiastic Nazi' who in 1934 had already expressed his views
on the connection between 'psychotherapy and political world view'.[13]
Another dystrophy expert, the physician Ernst Guenter Schenk, had been
an SS nutrition inspector during the war, and in this capacity he had
overseen nutritional conditions in Nazi concentration camps.[14] This is not
say that the dystrophy diagnosis as a whole was 'infected' with National
Socialist ideas, or that it did not refer to actual mental and physical symptoms. But the ideological bias of some of the leading authors on dystrophy
does suggest that after 1945, as after the First World War, the diagnosis,
interpretation and treatment of war-related trauma were intimately connected with the West German culture of remembrance, and with specific
conceptions of masculinity.

Among psychiatric and medical professionals, but also in charitable
organizations, the diagnosis of physical and mental damage among
returning POWs strongly resembled earlier eugenic theories.[15] Following
a firmly established view in the German neuropsychiatric tradition, these
writings on dystrophy often coupled individual pathologies with the
notion of the 'collective health of a people' (*Volksgesundheit*).[16] In the
year the Federal Republic of Germany was founded, for instance, one
medical observer called it 'of the utmost importance for the health of our
entire population that these hundreds of thousands of veterans, supposedly in the prime of life, regain their physical and mental potential as soon
as possible'.[17] Writers on dystrophy also saw in the weakened constitution
of the returning POWs the danger of an increased susceptibility to criminal behavior; they warned further that dystrophy might reduce the postwar
society's capacity for resistance in the Cold War.[18]

The diagnosis of physical and mental deficiencies among returning
POWs reflected historically specific notions of normalcy and deviance.
Perceptions of these traumatized men repeatedly associated their mental
and emotional problems with their presumed 'Russification' in Soviet
prisoner-of-war camps. An analysis of the men's 'physical and mental

state' carried out by a church-run veterans' facility viewed the former soldiers as so dramatically altered by their 'terrible existence in captivity' that their 'character and facial expression have become Russian', and that they had 'lost much of their actual humanity'.[19] This destruction of the men's collective identity in Soviet prisoner-of-war camps also meant the destruction of their masculinity. A central component of the dystrophy diagnosis was the presumed 'desexualization' of returning men who while imprisoned had needed to concentrate all their energy on satisfying their hunger, and therefore displayed a 'eunuch-like absence of sexual desire' upon their return home.[20] Kurt Gauger claimed that among returning POWs he had even seen the beginning of female breasts and 'pubic hair of the female type'.[21]

By the late 1940s the nutritional situation in the Soviet POW camps had improved; as a result, so had the physical health of returning German POWs. Now, the diagnosis of absent sexuality became infused with speculation about the men's potential homosexuality. According to estimates of the psychiatrist Hans Kilian, roughly 15 per cent of POWs committed homosexual acts in the East, while other authors noted the danger of homosexuality among veterans following their failed 'resexualization' upon returning home.[22] Thus, 'deficient' or 'misdirected' male sexuality was a key element in the diagnosis of returnees' trauma.[23]

Pathologizing the returning POWs in this medical and psychiatric discourse served an important function in the West German culture of remembrance. The diagnosis of former POWs' emotional problems always located the etiology of the trauma in the Soviet prisoner-of-war camp or in their confrontation with a radically changed homeland, but never in the war itself. As after the First World War, the majority of German psychiatrists refused to assign a traumatizing function to the war itself.[24] Instead, the portrait of returning POWs as 'denationalized' and 'desexualized' men in writings on dystrophy separated them from the image of the hypermasculine, militarized National Socialist frontline soldier as an ideal representative of the Nazi *Volksgemeinschaft*. As returning POWs, former soldiers acquired in the literature on dystrophy the physical and mental characteristics of Nazi victims. Indeed, one of the recurring *topoi* of this literature was a comparison between the effects of POW camps and concentration camps. The dystrophy diagnosis thus lent a certain scientific authority to the widespread equation between 'victims of the Germans' and 'German victims'. As such, it made a decisive contribution to what Robert Moeller calls the West German 'rhetoric of victimization'.[25]

East German perceptions of returning POWs ignored their physical, mental and sexual condition almost entirely. Instead, they defined the men's liminality almost exclusively in political and ideological terms. To the Communist Party of Germany (KPD/SED), the former soldiers of the 'fascist army' at first seemed to pose a serious threat to the antifascist democratic reconstruction in the Soviet Zone of Occupation (*Sowjetische Besatzungszone*, SBZ). Faced with the impending mass repatriation of German POWs from the Soviet Union, the party was seized by genuine panic. At the end of 1945, party functionary Karl Lewke warned the SED leadership in Berlin about the assault of 'a million anti-Bolshevists' who represented the 'gravest danger for the democratic reconstruction of Germany'.[26] While East German views of returning POWs differed diametrically from those in West Germany in terms of content, they nonetheless attributed to the men an equally marked weakness of (political) will and character, which allowed them to be easily 'influenced by former Nazis and other enemy elements'.[27]

In addition, these perceptions of returning POWs as politically backward were linked with notions of deficient masculinity. Unlike in the West, however, where 'deficiency' referred to the men's reproductive functions, here it referred to political apathy and indifference. In sharp contrast stood the public presence and political activity of women in the SBZ during the early postwar years, as evidenced by the work of over 6,000 antifascist-democratic women's committees.[28] East German reactions to returning POWs in the postwar period thereby showed a fundamental reversal of earlier Communist gender stereotypes: since the 1920s the KPD had contrasted the militancy and activism of male party members with the passivity of women, but in the early years of the SBZ, the images were reversed.[29] Visiting a POW transition camp in Gronefeld in August 1946, the director of an SED delegation of women was outraged at the self-pitying attitude of the returning POWs there. In her view, these men were 'consumed by the idea that they would remain ruined forever. We told them what we women here in Berlin had been through, and that in the returning men we expected to find good comrades who would help us with the work of reconstruction.'[30]

In the East as in the West, emphasizing the liminality of the returning POWs served an important, albeit different, purpose in the politics of memory. The alleged political and ideological immaturity of the returnees helped support the self-image of the KPD/SED as the revolutionary avantgarde who could not afford to allow the East German populace any real democratic participation; instead, they set about re-making former Nazi comrades into antifascist citizens by subjecting them to a Leninist educational dictatorship.[31]

Frank Biess

East and West German Strategies of 'Remasculinization'

While the emphasis on the returning POWs' liminality played an important role in the politics of memory in both societies, pathologizing the men
in this way was also deeply problematic. Whether styled as dehumanized
and desexualized victims in the West or as unreconstructed fascists in the
East, returning POWs were ill-suited for participation in the rebuilding of
the two destroyed societies. Therefore, the reconstruction of both societies
at the forefront of the Cold War demanded the transformation of returned
POWs from liminal figures into East and West German citizens. In both
societies this metamorphosis involved the creation of collective memories
of war and captivity that were compatible with the respective social and
political orders in the East and West. These official interpretations of
returning POWs' experiences were in turn closely related to the development of new prescriptive ideals of masculinity. The new ideals differed
both from each other and from the two dominant images of masculinity
that had preceded them, namely, the hypermasculine, militarized ideal of
the National Socialist front-line soldier and the threatened, even shattered
masculinity of the early postwar period. As in the earlier pathologizing of
returning POWs, their subsequent 'remasculinization' linked collective
memories of war and captivity with specific ideas about masculinity. The
different diagnoses of a 'crisis of masculinity' during the early postwar
period now helped determine specific strategies of remasculinization in
East and West Germany respectively.

Drawing on Elizabeth Heineman's notion of a feminization of war
memories in the early postwar period,[32] it is possible to see East and West
German interpretations of the returning POWs' experiences as parallel
processes of universalizing what had been a specifically male experience.
In the course of their social and symbolic reconstruction, both societies
claimed that the almost exclusively male experience of war and captivity
in POW camps held significance for all Germans. The 'remasculinization'
of memories of war and defeat, however, necessitated that returning
POWs were 'decontaminated' (Bernd Weisbrod) of their active experience of violence in the war of annihilation.[33] Both societies therefore
developed models that interpreted the men's passive experience of violence in POW camps as a prerequisite for their religious, moral or political
renewal. These perceptions of the POW camp experience can be seen as
an indirect form of communication about the war itself. While public
discussion of actual war experiences (and thereby any actual participation
in the war of annihilation) became taboo, in both postwar societies the
topic 'prisoner-of-war camp' enjoyed a decidedly prominent place in

public discourse. In other words, public communication about the Second World War centered not on the war itself, but rather on its impact on both individuals and society as a whole.

In the West, redemptive memories of the POW experience overlapped somewhat with the discourse of victimization that both preceded it and continued on through the entire first postwar decade. And yet, the ubiquitous view of returning POWs as 'victims' gave way increasingly to the image of the 'survivor', which foregrounded the regenerative function of the former soldiers' experience as prisoners-of-war. As part of a broad-based strategy of re-Christianization, both churches began in the late 1940s to aggressively promote an interpretation of the captivity experience that followed the Christian model of atonement and conversion. Returning POWs were cast as modern Christ figures whose suffering in prisoner-of-war camps was the necessary prerequisite for their redemption. They became the ideal representatives of a 'Christian Occident'.[34] A secularized version of this Christian view was also disseminated by West German returnee organizations beginning in the early 1950s. According to this version, it was precisely their adherence to supposedly timeless German values such as German culture and German quality work that had enabled the POWs to survive the Soviet camps. As survivors of both National Socialist and Stalinist forms of totalitarianism, they emerged as ideal citizens of a post-totalitarian, liberal-democratic republic.[35] The enthusiastic welcome given the last returning POWs in 1955–56, who were celebrated virtually as 'heroes', concluded this metamorphosis of the POWs from 'victims' into 'survivors' in West German public discourse.[36]

A similar reevaluation of the POW experience also occurred in the official discourse of the SED; it was different in content, but structurally similar in its positive tone. In the course of transforming itself into a Leninist 'party of the new type' and solidifying the division of Germany after 1947/48, the SED placed increasing emphasis on the returning POWs' role as citizens of the new 'antifascist-democratic' order. This view included primarily those returning POWs who had attended antifascist schools in the Soviet Union. They formed an important cadre of reserves who during the extensive party purges of the late 1940s and early 1950s were promoted over 'Old Communists' now out of political favor.[37] In addition, antifascist returnees assumed an important symbolic function in that they demonstrated to all East Germans how former members of a National Socialist 'national community' could become good antifascist citizens. This symbolic role was demonstrated nowhere more clearly than in a series of so-called 'returnee conferences', held in the summer and fall of 1949, where antifascist returnees reported on their political conversion in Soviet prisoner-of-war camps. Not coincidentally, the conferences took place at the same time the GDR was officially established; they represented a constitutive act in the founding of the SED-state.[38]

East and West German attitudes alike distanced the returning POWs from the specific past of the war of annihilation. In the West, interpreting the POWs' internment as a (universal) form of moral and religious regeneration eliminated any reference to actual victims and actual perpetrators on the eastern front. The appeal to religious, moral and psychological categories likewise served to de-ideologize the consequences of a highly ideological war in West Germany. It thus became possible to integrate memories of the war of annihilation and its consequences into a Western community of values that at the end of the 1950s proclaimed the 'end of ideologies'.[39]

The depoliticizing and psychologizing tendencies in the West stood diametrically opposed to the extreme politicization of the POW experience in the East. Unlike in the West, the official East German interpretation saw the POW camp experience as firmly rooted within the larger context of the war against the Soviet Union. Even so, East Germans always defined guilt and responsibility for genocidal warfare historically and collectively rather than in terms of individuals, which meant that, ultimately, neither moral nor legal responsibility was entailed. At the returnee conferences, for instance, antifascist returning POWs admitted to their historical guilt as former members of the 'fascist military', yet they consistently portrayed their individual role in the war as passive and – in the words of one veteran – 'virtually unconscious'.[40] It was only in Soviet captivity that they had discovered their 'true' antifascist selves and thereby had been able to make the leap to the victor's side of history.

These interpretations of the returnees' experiences not only gave a specifically male experience a paradigmatic status in the reconstruction of collective identities in East and West Germany, they were also closely linked to specifically East and West German ideals of masculinity. It was admittedly no simple matter to restore the link between masculinity and the nation that had been firmly established in the early nineteenth century.[41] The refashioning of returning POWs into ideal East and West German citizens thus took place not in the vocabulary of the nation, but by invoking the more universal languages of Christianity and antifascism.[42] Accordingly, conceptions of masculinity after 1945 used pre- or supranational orders as their point of reference rather than the nation.

In the West this almost always meant the family. Returning POWs were viewed primarily as actual or potential fathers and husbands who were to transform 'incomplete' families into 'complete' ones. The reconstruction of the family through the return of the POWs therefore became the focal point for the ideological, social, moral and social stabilization of West Germany.[43] Christian charitable organizations, for example, felt that their main goal when counseling returnees was to help make these men suited for family life once again. This also meant that they should turn away from all-too authoritarian and patriarchal notions. One Catholic memorandum encouraged returning men to forgive any indiscretions their wives may have committed, and not adopt too military a tone with their children, in view of their own behavior during the war.[44] Hence these religious organizations promoted tamed, civil, even 'gentle' masculinities.

Nevertheless, the ultimate goal in reconstructing returning POWs as fathers and husbands was to restore patriarchal authority, an authority which until the end of the 1950s was firmly anchored in the West German basic law. If necessary, women were to voluntarily relinquish their positions of power within the family in order to reestablish male authority in the family. This kind of self-imposed limitation of the part of women also appeared to be the most promising form of treatment for persistent sexual problems among returnees. At the 1957 conference of the German Society for Research on Sexuality, for instance, the Berlin doctor Eberhard Schaetzing explained that 'by and large, we doctors possess in the wives the sole effective medicine for the wounded soul of the returnee'.[45] Similar prescriptions were given by West German marriage counseling agencies in the 1950s.[46] But many women, too, saw in the POWs' return the possibility of creating or returning to a bourgeois family life that had been lost during the crisis of the war and the postwar period. This desire became apparent not least during the return of the last POWs in the fall of 1955, when hundreds of single women addressed requests for partners to the POW discharge camp in Friedland.[47] The West German focus on the role of returnees as fathers and husbands defined masculinity chiefly in civilian terms, and thereby broke with the traditional coupling of masculinity and militarism. At the same time, the image of these veterans as civilian family men repressed the altogether 'uncivil' past of some returning POWs, thus easing the return of NS-perpetrators to their lives as upstanding bourgeois citizens in the 1950s.[48]

In contrast to West Germany, the family in East Germany appeared as one of the greatest obstacles to remasculinizing returning POWs, not as its focal point. Unlike in the West, masculinity in the East was defined not in terms of a depoliticized private realm, but within the framework of an extremely politicized public sphere. The ideal male citizen was a producer and party activist, not a father and husband. A photo series produced by the SED-dominated East Berlin committee for returning POWs documented the ideal path of veteran L. from a discharge camp for POWs in Gronenfelde to 'integration into the production process' in the Bergmann-Borsig locomotive works.[49] SED functionaries at the same time repeatedly criticized the influence of families, and especially wives, as detrimental to the political conversion that antifascist returnees had presumably undergone in Soviet captivity. This critique suggested a restoration of traditional Communist gender stereotypes in the SBZ/GDR. Whereas in the early postwar period women's public role was set up as a model for returning men, now – more in keeping with older Weimar tradition – it was 'politically blind women' who supposedly threatened to undermine the political engagement of converted returning POWs.[50] Unlike in the West, East German notions of masculinity also remained more closely linked to military virtues, which were now based on antifascist rather than fascist premises. Thus the antifascist returnees could present themselves at the above-mentioned conferences as 'ardent fighters for peace' who would impose this 'peace on imperialists, by force if necessary'.[51] Despite all the emphasis on the notion of radical transformation in the SBZ/GDR, these militarized ideals of masculinity represented important continuities between the Nazi and the East German dictatorship. Militarized masculinities had been part of the former soldiers' socialization in the Third Reich, and they were now carried over into the antifascist-democratic republic. In this regard, East German ideals of masculinity revealed greater continuity with Prussian-German traditions than did West German ones.

Returning POWs and the Reconstruction of Male Subjectivity in Postwar Germany

The discursive constructs of masculinity analyzed thus far say very little about the male subjectivity of the returning POWs. In both societies, the reconstruction of this subjectivity took place by means of very complex processes of mediation between discursive prescriptions and the returning men's own perceptions of themselves.[52] Within the general framework of this analysis, it is impossible to address all the potential differentiations along the lines of social status, family status, age and religion that might have influenced returnees' sense of self. I would instead like to discuss the process of subject formation in an admittedly somewhat more impressionistic fashion by identifying several of the paradigms invoked by returning POWs in their confrontation with both postwar societies.

In contemporary reports and later memoirs alike, returnees described the day of their return from POW camps as a decisive rupture in their lives. Coming home seemed on the one hand like 'a second birthday' or 'the most momentous day of my life'.[53] On the other hand, reports on returning POWs also note the shock they felt upon confronting the image of a destroyed, fundamentally altered home. A pilot shot down over Russia in 1943 found 'much greater misery and poverty than we had imagined' on his 1948 return to the Western zones.[54] This discrepancy between expectations about returning home and the disappointment that often followed appears to have triggered in many returnees a sense of existential uncertainty and a strong need to locate their identities in a continuum of past, present and future. The Protestant theologian Hellmuth Gollwitzer expressed this feeling in a 1951 report on captivity and homecoming in the following way: 'What kind of wall of glass is this, that divides the past from the present, which can yet touch each other within me, since I am still both the "then" and "now", the former no less than the latter? What is time? What is the meaning of past and present? What does our existence in time mean?'[55] The interpretive frameworks available in both postwar German societies should therefore also be considered in terms of the extent to which they helped returning POWs preserve the continuity of the self in times of existential uncertainty and radical historical discontinuity. In the West, anti-Communism served as the decisive ideological link between past and present. As the crucial ideology of legitimation in the Federal Republic, anti-Communism made it possible for returnees to keep the image of the anti-Bolshevist enemy as propagated during the Third Reich intact in the Bonn Republic.[56] This continuity became apparent in a letter that returnee Alfons H. sent to Chancellor Konrad Adenauer after his return from Soviet captivity through the GDR in May 1950:

And now we continued, not through Germany, oh no, though it was indeed through a German country with German people – but it was not Germany. Russians everywhere with carbines [. . .] Germany's marked off Eastern Zone – the very image of Russia. The population under the pressure of informers, and the police made up of former concentration camp inmates. [. . .] Early on April 26, 1950, after many years of disgrace and shame, we crossed the zonal border and with tears in our eyes, sang our old national anthem '*Deutschland, Deutschland über alles*', which we had not heard for so long. Only now did we begin to feel any love for our home (*Heimat*), we who had been believed missing or condemned, even given up for dead.[57]

In this homecoming experience, it was precisely the distancing from Soviet occupation and East German antifascism through a familiar and still rather Nazified language ('informers', 'concentration camp inmates') that allowed a renewed identification with the Federal Republic as the 'true' Germany.[58]

Despite the official emphasis on the ideological transformation of returnees, East German interpretive schemata also offered the men some starting points for constructing biographical continuities between past and present. Militant official antifascism in the SBZ/GDR allowed the continuity of militarized mentalities, which had shaped the socialization process of these former soldiers before 1945.[59] To be sure, these mentalities did need to shift their focus away from the 'racial enemy' (*Rassenfeind*) on the Eastern front and toward the 'class enemy' (*Klassenfeind*) in the West. In a poem entitled 'Struggle' (*Kampf*), for example, the antifascist returnee Werner K. described his return to Erfurt in December 1948 in this way: 'Fight! Fight and win! Fight and win! Loyally following the red flag through the din of the last battle, until, a shining beacon, it pierces the peoples' night.'[60] This antifascist returning POW had by no means given up hope of a final victory; he had merely given it a new orientation.

In self-descriptions of returning POWs what we find more often than references to the official ideologies of legitimation in both German states is an appeal to the supposedly apolitical notion of *Heimat* or homeland. *Heimat* referred neither to a fatherland defined in national terms, nor to a socio-politically defined social order.[61] Instead, the 'beloved *Heimat*' meant 'the German language, the old customs and German folksongs we had been forced to do without for so long'.[62] Returning POWs' self-descriptions recalled the 'gentle waves of the Oder mountains' or the 'smell of the woods at home' as sources of uncorrupted Germanness that had remained untainted by fascism, war and defeat.[63] The concept of *Heimat* offered especially returnees in East Germany a more concrete, physically tangible image of the country to which they returned than the abstract, officially approved concept of an 'antifascist-democratic' order.

The notion of *Heimat* also included the promise of predominantly traditional gender roles, and helped compensate for the uncertainty of male subjectivity in the wake of war and defeat. No one documented this more clearly than the returnee Karl T., who upon coming home to the Soviet zone of occupation thanked 'the German woman' for her service to the *Heimat* with the following words:

You German woman, so pure and good, in character so unique
With unbroken courage you will show your loyalty to the *Heimat*. [. . .]
You know no peace, no rest
shrink not from time or effort
You ease the woe, the pains
of men returning from far-off lands who, sick in body yet stout of heart
found their way back to the *Heimat*.[64]

Given the dissolution of the boundaries between front and homefront during the Second World War, this male fantasy of a *Heimat* which in the hands of 'the German woman' had remained intact and awaited the return of the men had nothing to do with the reality of postwar Germany.[65] Nonetheless, this invocation of an idealized, feminized *Heimat* documented emotional and psychological needs of a male subjectivity that were compatible neither with the Nazi frontline soldier *nor* with the martial ideal of the antifascist fighter in the East; rather, these needs were more consistent with the masculine ideal of the bourgeois family man in the West.

In addition to the appeal to an idealized *Heimat*, 'work' became a key concept in reconstructing male subjectivity in both societies. The emphasis on work reflected the parallel requirements in East and West connected with rebuilding a destroyed country, but also the self-perceptions of the returning men. Reports from East and West German employment offices frequently mentioned that many returnees were highly motivated to work.[66] Returning POWs thus displayed the hopes for social advancement that had been present already in the 1930s, and which had received new impetus (among soldiers) from the military successes of the early war years.[67]

The importance of social factors like work meant that for returnees trying to reestablish themselves, the political and ideological opposition between East and West Germany as presented in the official interpretive schemata of the POW experience receded into the background. For instance, the exceptionally high social mobility in the SBZ/GDR during the early postwar period meant that returnees enjoyed many possibilities of advancement which prompted them to remain in the Eastern zone even if they kept their ideological distance from the KPD/SED.[68] The rhetoric of East German reconstruction also offered returnees possible mental continuities: this antifascist republic – similar to National Socialism – justified individual initiative (e.g. in the activist movement that began in 1948) by always relating it to the 'greater whole'. A returning soldier thus characterized his 'first impression' of East Germany with these words:

'Under the Nazis there was always talk of community (*Volksgemeinschaft*) but no action. Now, people talk less, but they demonstrate this community all the more clearly in deeds.'[69] Another returning POW makes clear just how seamless the transition could be from the 'achievements' of former soldiers and POWs under the first dictatorship to political engagement in the second. In an interview, he presented his Iron Cross earned in the war together with a medal from the SED in recognition of his 'lifetime achievement' without suggesting in any way that some tension might exist between these two honors by ideologically anatagonistic regimes.[70]

'Work' held a similar importance for POWs returning to the West, and they doubtless enjoyed similar opportunities for social advancement in the context of the West German 'economic miracle'. And yet, the files of welfare offices document a large number of shattered hopes of advancement, especially among returning soldiers from middle-class backgrounds. In view of the difficult social and economic situation, the well-established image of the provider and bourgeois family man meant that many returnees were faced with virtually impossible tasks. Having returned from a Soviet prisoner-of-war camp in 1949, the pharmacist Friedrich W. lamented in a letter of January 1951 to the minister of social affairs in North Rhine-Westphalia that any return to a middle-class existence still remained impossible. When he married in 1942, he wrote, he had still felt himself to be in a 'secure middle-class situation' with a guaranteed future. Yet even two years after returning home, he finds it impossible to establish an independent household, and after thirteen years he is still incapable of 'leading a normal family life'. 'As a man and a father' he can no longer tolerate that his wife and children are 'morally and psychologically depressed, their health ruined'.[71] Not infrequently, this discrepancy between the social reality and a prescriptive masculine ideal of provider and middle-class father-figure also contributed to the returnees' view of themselves as 'victims' of war and dictatorship.[72] In short, the West German discourse of victimization was based not only on real or perceived suffering in war and captivity, but also on the social degradation that especially men from the middle class experienced only after returning home from POW camps.[73]

This significance of work also points to the central importance of the family for the social integration of returning POWs in both postwar societies. In this connection Vera Neumann has recently noted the 'family work' done primarily by women as a crucial factor in the West German economic miracle.[74] This 'family work' involved caring for returnees with long-term or permanent disabilities, and reintegrating former participants in the war into the work force, which often entailed abandoning any professional hopes of their own. In both German societies the adjustment problems experienced by returning POWs were thus transferred out of society and into the families. The 'privatization of the consequences of the war' meant that unlike after the First World War, returnees' difficulties in adapting to postwar conditions became atomized and thereby less socially and politically disruptive.[75] At the same time, the consequences of war and captivity remained present within the families for an extended period of time and thus shaped both gender relations and the relationship between generations. While the internal dynamics of East German families have yet to be researched in any detail, generational conflicts of the 1950s and above all in the 1960s in the West might be understood as a societal re-thematization of these intrafamilial conflicts.[76] The privatization of the consequences of war thus became one of the preconditions for a massive politicization of the generational conflict in West Germany.

Conclusion

On the whole, redemptive memories of the POW experience contributed only marginally to the reconstruction of male subjectivity in postwar Germany. Returnees' male subjectivity related less to regenerative remembrance of the war, internment and related notions of masculinity than it did to idealized notions of *Heimat* and to the confrontation with societal realities in the workplace and the family. While the commemorative practices in both postwar societies aimed to win the war retroactively and thereby leave it behind, the consequences of war, defeat and internment were not so easily dismissed from the individual lives of returning POWs after 1945. Rather, their biographies document a 'protracted German postwar period' that extends – as ongoing controversies surrounding memories of the Second World War confirm – even into the present.[77]

Notes

I would like to thank Elizabeth Berdeck for translating the bulk of the original German version of this essay into English.

1. This essay is based on material from Frank Biess, 'The Protracted War. Returning POWs and the Making of East and West German Citizens, 1945–1955' (Ph.D. Diss., Brown University, 2000).

2. Susan Jeffords defines remasculinization as the 'regenerations of the concepts, constructions, and definitions of masculinity [...] and of the gender system for which [they are] formulated', see Susan Jeffords, *The Remasculinization of America. Gender and the Vietnam War* (Bloomington, 1989), 51; for the application of this concept to postwar Germany, see Robert Moeller, 'The "Remasculinization" of Germany: An Introduction,' *Signs* 24 (1998): 101–06.

3. Allemann, Fritz René. *Bonn ist nicht Weimar* (Cologne, 1956). On the virtual omission of any extended discussion of the consequences of the war in recent syntheses, see Adolf Birke, *Nation ohne Haus. Deutschland 1945-1961* (Berlin, 1989) or Gerhard A. Ritter, *Über Deutschland. Die Bundesrepublik in der deutschen Geschichte* (Munich, 1998).

4. See Anselm Doering-Manteuffel, 'Deutsche Zeitgeschichte nach 1945. Entwicklung und Problemlagen der historischen Forschung,' *Vierteljahreshefte für Zeitgeschichte* 41 (1993): 1–29.

5. See, for example, Michael Geyer, 'Das Stigma der Gewalt und das Problem der nationalen Identität,' in *Von der Aufgabe der Freiheit. Politische Verantwortung und bürgerliche Gesellschaft*, ed. Christian Jansen, Lutz Niethammer and Bernd Weisbrod (Berlin, 1995), 673–698; Klaus Naumann, ed., *Nachkrieg in Deutschland* (Hamburg: Hamburger Edition, 2001); 1999). For a similar emphasis regarding post-1945 European history in general. see Tony Judt, 'Preface' in *The Politics of Retribution in Europe: World War II and Its Aftermath*, eds. Istvan Deak, Jan Gross and Tony Judt (Princeton, 2000), vii–xii; see also Mark Mazower, 'Changing Trends in the Historiography of Postwar Europe, East and West,' *International Labor and Working Class History* 58 (Fall 2000): 261–274.

6. On the war experience, see Omer Bartov, *Hitler's Army. Soldiers, Nazis, and War in the Third Reich* (New York, 1990) und Klaus Latzel, *Deutsche Soldaten – Nationalsozialistischer Krieg, Kriegserlebnis – Kriegserfahrung 1939–1945* (Paderborn, 2000); on Soviet captivity, see Andreas Hilger, *Deutsche Kriegsgefangene in der Sowjetunion 1941–1956. Kriegsgefangenenpolitik, Lageralltag und Erinnerung* (Essen, 2000).

7. Christoph Kleßmann, 'Abgrenzung und Verflechtung: Aspekte der geteilten und zusammengehörigen deutschen Nachkriegsgeschichte,' *Aus Politik und Zeitgeschichte* 29/30 (1993): 30–41. For instructive comments on conceptualizing the East/West German comparison, see Uta Poiger, *Jazz, Rock, and Rebels. Cold War Politics and American Culture in Divided Germany* (Berkeley, 2000).

8. Arnold van Gennep, *The Rites of Passage*, Sixth Edition (Chicago, 1972); Victor Turner, 'Betwixt and Between: The Liminal Period in Rites de Passage,' in ibid., *Forest of Symbols*. *Aspects of Ndembu Ritual* (Ithaca,1967), 93–111.

9. On these symptoms, see Manfred Balderman, 'Die psychischen Grundlagen der Heimkehrerdystrophien und ihre Behandlung,' *Münchner Medizinische Wochenschrift* 93 (1951): 2187–2190.

10. E.G. Schenk and W. von Nathusis, eds., *Extreme Lebensverhältnisse und ihre Folgen: Handbuch der ärztlichen Erfahrung aus der Gefangenschaft*, 8 vols., Schriftenreihe des ärztlich-wissenschaftlichen Beirats des Verbandes der Heimkehrer Deutschlands (n.p., 1958–1959); Bundesministerium für Arbeit und Sozialordnung, ed., *Die Dystrophie. Spätfolgen und Dauerschäden* (Stuttgart, 1958).

11. See Heinz Harro Rauschelbach, 'Zur versorgungsrechtlichen Beurteilung der Spätheimkehrer unter besonderer Berücksichtigung der Dystrophiefolgenzustände,' *Die Medizinische* 50 (1954): 1678–1682.

12. Paul Lerner and Mark Micale, eds., *Traumatic Pasts: History, Psychiatry, and Trauma in the Modern Age, 1870–1930* (Cambridge, 2001); Allan Young, *The Harmony of Illusions. Inventing Post-Traumatic Stress Disorder* (Princeton, 1995); Cathy Caruth, *Unclaimed Experience. Trauma, Narrativity, and History* (Baltimore, 1995).

13. On Gauger, see Geoffrey Cock, *Psychotherapy in the Third Reich* (New York, 1986), 126; Kurt Gauger, 'Psychotherapy and Political World View,' in *Nazi Culture*, ed. George Mosse (New York, 1966), 215–217; Kurt Gauger, *Die Dystrophie* (Munich, 1951).

14. See Ernst Klee, *Auschwitz, die NS Medizin und ihre Opfer* (Frankfurt, 1997), 179–89.

15. See Svenja Goltermann, 'Verletzte Körper oder "Building National Bodies". Kriegsheimkehrer, "Krankheit" und Psychiatrie in der westdeutschen Nachkriegsgesellschaft, 1945–1955,' *Werkstatt Geschichte* 24 (1999): 83–98.

16. Paul Weindling, *Health, Race, and German Politics between National Unification and Nazism, 1870–1945* (New York, 1989).

17. Gerd Sedlmayer, 'Wandlungen im Krankheitsbild der Ostheimkehrer,' *Medizinische Klinik* 44 (1949): 1223–25.

18. On the alleged susceptibility of returnees to crime, see Hans Kilian, 'Zur Psychopathologie der Heimkehrer,' *Deutsche Medizinische Rundschau* 3 (1949): 12; Gauger even warned of a 'future use of planned Dystrophication of entire peoples during the Cold War', see Gauger, *Die Dystrophie*, 134.

19. 'Die psychische und physische Situation der Ostheimkehrer (Beobachtungen und Erfahrungen im Heimkehrerhotel Willingen),' Evangelisches Zentralarchiv 2/529.
20. Hans Malten, 'Heimkehrer,' *Medizinische Klinik* 41 (1946): 598.
21. Gauger, *Dystrophie*, 64.
22. Hans Kilian, 'Das Wiedereinleben der Heimkehrer in Ehe, Familie und Beruf,' in *Die Sexualität der Heimkehrer*, ed. Hans Bürger-Prinz and Hans Giese (Stuttgart, 1957), 27–38.
23. This confirms an observation by Dagmar Herzog who recently argued: '[. . .] male bodies were called to a kind of public visibility and accountability that most scholars of the history of sexuality generally assume to be reserved for women'; see Dagmar Herzog, '"Pleasure, Sex, and Politics Belong Together": Post-Holocaust Memory and the Sexual Revolution in West Germany,' *Critical Inquiry* 24 (1998): 398.
24. On the First World War, see Paul Lerner, 'Hysterical Men. War, Neurosis, and German Mental Medicine' (Ph.D. Dissertation, Columbia University, 1996).
25. Robert Moeller, *War Stories. The Search for a Usable Past in the Federal Republic of Germany* (Berkeley, 2001), 48.
26. Karl Lewke an KPD Berlin, 2 December 1945, BA-SAPMO, DY30/IV2/11/211.
27. Bericht von Gronenfelde, 15 November 1945, BA-SAPMO, DY30/IV2/11/211, 1.
28. See Norman Naimark, *The Russians in Germany. A History of the Soviet Zone of Occupation* (Cambridge, Mass., 1995), 131–132.
29. See Eric Weitz, *Creating German Communism. From Popular Protest to Socialist State* (Princeton, 1997), 188–233.
30. Edith Hönig, 'Stimmungsbild aus dem Rückkehrerlager der aus russischer Kriegsgefangenschaft heimkehrenden Deutschen in Frankfurt/Oder,' 2 August 1946, BA-SAPMO, DY30/IV2/17/56.
31. Jeffrey Herf, *Divided Memory. The Nazi Past in the Two Germanys* (Cambridge, 1997).
32. Elizabeth Heineman, 'The Hour of the Woman. Memories of Germany's 'Crisis Years' and West German National Identity,' *American Historical Review* 101 (1996): 354–396.
33. Bernd Weisbrod, "The Moratorium of the Mandarins. The Denazification of the German Academic Mind," unpublished paper, Rutgers Center for Historical Analysis.
34. See, for example, Erich Müller-Gangloff, *Christen in der Kriegsgefangenschaft* (Berlin, 1948) as well as the essays in *Heimatvertriebene*

und Heimkehrer Vorträge und Anregungen der VII. überdiözesanen Aussprache-Konferenz für Männerseelsorge in Fulda, 9–12 May 1950 (Augsburg, 1950).

35. See, for example, the exhibition of the Association of Returnees 'Wir Mahnen' ('We Admonish'), which toured through sixty German cities between 1951 and 1958.

36. See, for example, the analysis on West German responses to the return of the last POWs in Moeller, *War Stories*, 105–122.

37. The actual recruitment of antifascist returnees for the party, however, remained behind the high expectations of the SED-leadership, see Jörg Morré, 'Kader für Deutschland? Die Bemühungen der SED um die Repatriierung deutscher Kriegsgefangener,' in *Heimkehr 1948. Geschichte und Schicksal deutscher Kriegsgefangener*, ed. Annette Kaminsky (Munich, 1998), 217–231.

38. On these returnee conferences, see BA-SAPMO, DY32/10057.

39. On 'depoliticization' as the crucial aspect of West German reconstruction, see Poiger, *Jazz, Rock, and Rebels*.

40. 'Heimkehrer Ludwig Sulek beim Heimkehrertreffen im Saal des Landratsamtes Guben,' 26 July 1949, BLHA, Landratsamt Guben, Rep. 250/284.

41. Ute Frevert, 'Soldaten, Staatsbürger: Überlegungen zur historischen Konstruktion von Männlichkeit,' in *Männergeschichte-Geschlechtergeschichte*, ed. Thomas Kühne (Göttingen, 1996), 69–87.

42. Ute Frevert, 'Die Sprache des Volkes und die Rhetorik der Nation. Identitätssplitter in der deutschen Nachkriegszeit,' in *Doppelte Zeitgeschichte. Deutsch–Deutsche Beziehungen*, ed. Arnd Bauernkämper, Martin Sabrow and Bernd Stöver (Berlin, 1998), 18–31.

43. Robert Moeller, *Protecting Motherhood. Women and the Family in the Politics of Postwar West Germany* (Berkeley, 1993); Elizabeth Heineman, 'Complete Families, Half Families, No Families at All. Female Headed Households and the Reconstruction of the Family in the Early Federal Republic,' *Central European History* 29 (1996): 29–60.

44. 'Richtlinien für die Pastoration der Heimkehrer,' Archiv des Caritasverbandes, 372.025, Fasz.3.

45. Eberhard Schaetzing, 'Die Frau des Heimkehrers,' in *Die Sexualität der Heimkehrer*, 42.

46. Franka Schneider, 'Ehen in Beratung,' in *Heimkehr 1948*, 192–216.

47. See Biess, 'The Protracted War,' chapter V and Moeller, *War Stories*, 88–122.

Frank Biess

48. On the highly compromised past of some 1955 returnees, see Ulrich Brochhagen, *Nach Nürnberg. Vergangenheitsbewältigung in der Ära Adenauer* (Hamburg, 1994), 250–55.
49. Photo report 'Frankfurt bis Bergmann Borsig,' Landesarchiv Berlin (Ost), Rep.061, Nr. 3.
50. 'Die Stellung der Frau zum Heimkehrer,' BA-SAPMO, DY30/IV2/11/211.
51. 'Protokoll über das Heimkehrertreffen im Saal des Landratsamtes Guben, Brandenburgisches Landeshauptarchiv,' Rep. 250/284.
52. See Kathleen Canning, 'Historicizing "Discourse" and "Experience." Feminist History after the Linguistic Turn,' *Signs* 19 (1994): 368–404; Joan Scott, 'The Evidence of Experience,' *Critical Inquiry* 17 (1991): 772–797; and Ute Daniel, 'Erfahrung – (k)ein Thema der Geschichtstheorie?' *L'Homme* 11 (2000): 120–123.
53. Interview with Thomas G., 4 November 1996; Gustav M., Heimkehrer aus Polen, an Ausschuß für Kriegsgefangenenfragen, 4 June 1949, BAK, B150/331.
54. G. Francke, Erlebnisbericht, 22 March 1949, ADW, HGst, Allg.S., B 456.
55. Helmut Gollwitzer, . . . *und führen, wohin du nicht willst. Bericht einer Gefangenschaft* (Munich, 1951), 339.
56. Eric Weitz, 'The Ever-Present Other. Communism in the Making of West Germany,' in *The Miracle Years. A Cultural History of West Germany, 1945–1968*, ed. Hanna Schissler (Princeton, 2001), 219–32.
57. Alfons H. to Bundeskanzler Adenauer, 23 May 1950, Politisches Archiv des Auswärtigen Amtes (PAA), B10/2/1977.
58. See also the results of the study by the Frankfurter Institut für Sozialforschung, *Zum politischen Bewußtsein ehemaliger Kriegsgefangener* (Frankfurt, 1957) which detected similar ideological continuities among returnees.
59. See Lutz Niethammer, 'Erfahrungen und Strukturen: Prolegomena zu einer Geschichte der Gesellschaft der DDR,' in *Sozialgeschichte der DDR*, ed. Jürgen Kocka (Stuttgart, 1993), 95–115.
60. Werner K., Kampf, der SED, Kreis Erfurt, gewidmet, 26 December 1948, BA, DO2/77.
61. On the notion of *Heimat*, see Celia Applegate, *A Nation of Provincials. The German Idea of Heimat* (Berkeley, 1990) and Alon Confino, *The Nation as a Local Metaphor. Württemberg, Imperial Germany, and National Memory* (Chapel Hill, 1997).
62. Gustav M., Heimkehrer aus Polen, an Ausschuß für Kriegsgefangenenfragen, 4 June 1949, BAK, B150/331.

63. Dr. Heinz S. aus Weimar, Heimkehr aus der Kriegsgefangenschaft, 1 September 1946, BA-SAPMO, NY4182/1160.

64. Gedicht des Heimkehrers Karl T., Die deutsche Frau, BA-SAPMO, DY34/40/61/4508.

65. On gender relations during the war, see Birthe Kundrus, *Kriegerfrauen. Familienpolitik und Geschlechterverhältnisse im Ersten und Zweiten Weltkrieg* (Hamburg, 1995); on postwar gender projections see the contribution of Susanne zur Nieden to this volume.

66. See the reports of the employment office in Saxony in BA, DQ 2/ 1933 and of North Rhine-Westphalian offices in NRWHStA-Kalkum, LA NW 36/1.

67. Ulrich Herbert, '"Die guten und die schlechten Zeiten." Überlegungen zur diachronen Analyse lebensgeschichtlicher Interviews,' in '*Die Jahre weiß man nicht wo man die heute hinsetzen soll.' Faschismuserfahrungen im Ruhrgebiet*, ed. Lutz Niethammer (Bonn, 1986), 67–96; Klaus Latzel, '"Freie Bahn den Tüchtigen." Kriegserfahrung und Perspektiven für die Nachkriegszeit in Feldpostbriefen aus dem Zweiten Weltkrieg,' in *Lernen aus dem Krieg. Deutsche Nachkriegszeiten 1918–1945*, ed. Gottfried Niedhardt and Dieter Riesenberger (Munich, 1997), 331–343.

68. On social mobility in the early history of the GDR, see Heike Solga, *Auf dem Weg in eine klassenlose Gesellschaft? Klassenlagen und Mobilität zwischen den Generationen* (Berlin, 1995).

69. Heimkehrer Heinz P., Der erste Eindruck in der Heimat, BLHA, Rep.332, Nr.578, 233.

70. Interview with 'Hans M.', 7 December 1996.

71. Friedrich Wilhelm W. to the Minister of Social Affairs in the state of North-Rhine Westphalia, 31 January 1951, Nordrhein-Westfälisches Hauptstaatsarchiv, NW42/1183.

72. A specific middle-class way of coping with the experience of war and captivity constitutes one of the main results of the study by the Frankfurter Institut für Sozialforschung, *Zum politischen Bewußtsein ehemaliger Kriegsgefangener.*

73. It is likely, however, that many of these experiences of degradation presumably reversed themselves in the course of the 1950s through a combination of economic upturn and socio-political measures. In the Frankfurt study, two-thirds of former POWs described their economic situation as 'satisfactory', see Frankfurter Institut für Sozialforschung, *Zum politischen Bewußtsein ehemaliger Kriegsgefangener*, 18–19.

74. Vera Neumann, *Nicht der Rede Wert. Die Privatisierung der Kriegsfolgen in der frühen Bundesrepublik* (Münster, 1998).
75. On veterans after the First World War, see the excellent work by Deborah Cohen, *The War Come Home. Disabled Veterans in Britain and Germany, 1914–1939* (Berkeley, 2001).
76. See the pioneering work by Dorothee Wierling, 'Mission to Happiness. The Cohort of 1949 and the Making of East and West Germans,' in *The Miracle Years*, 110–125.
77. See the instructive comments in Klaus Naumann, 'Die Frage nach dem Ende. Von der unbestimmten Dauer der Nachkriegszeit,' *Mittelweg* 36. 8 (1998): 21–33.

The Military, War and Gender in Nineteenth- and Twentieth-Century Germany

A Selected Bibliography

Karen Hagemann and
Stefanie Schüler-Springorum

The choice of literature for this bibliography has been limited to the most important recent publications on the military, war and gender in nineteenth- and twentieth-century Germany. It is intended to provide general orientation and makes no claims to be exhaustive. In addition, we have included international standard works on related themes from various disciplines as well as innovative studies in the gender history of other countries involved in the First and Second World and more general introductions to the history of the military and war. Essays from collections are listed in the bibliography only if the volume in which they appeared is not included.

The Selected Bibliography is organized as follows:

I: Reviews and Bibliographies
II: Theories and Methods – International Classics and Innovators
III: Overviews – Thematic Monographs and Essay Collections
IV: Nineteenth-Century Germany
V: The First World War
VI: The Weimar Republic
VII: The Third Reich
VIII: The Postwar Germanies

I: Reviews and Bibliographies

BARTOV, OMER (1997), 'German Soldiers and the Holocaust. Historiography, Research and Implications,' *History and Memory* 9, nos. 1–2: 162–188.

Karen Hagemann and Stefanie Schüler-Springorum

BIBLIOGRAPHY: Military/War (1991), *Journal of Women's History* 3: 140–159.

BUDGE, ALICE and PAM DIDUR (1990), 'Women and War. A Selected Bibliography,' *Mosaic* 23: 151–173.

GOLDENBERG, MYRNA (1996), '"From a World Beyond". Women in the Holocaust,' *Feminist Studies* 22, no. 3: 667–687.

HAGEMANN, KAREN (1997), 'Militär, Krieg und Geschlechterverhältnisse. Untersuchungen, Überlegungen und Fragen zur Militärgeschichte der Frühen Neuzeit,' in *Klio in Uniform? Probleme und Perspektiven einer modernen Militärgeschichte der Frühen Neuzeit*, ed. Ralf Pröve, Cologne, 35–88.

—— (1998), 'Venus und Mars. Reflexionen zu einer Geschlechtergeschichte von Militär und Krieg,' in *Landsknechte, Soldatenfrauen und Nationalkrieger. Militär, Krieg und Geschlechterordnung im historischen Wandel*, ed. Karen Hagemann and Ralf Pröve, Frankfurt a.M., New York, 13–48.

—— (2001), 'Von Männern, Frauen und der Militärgeschichte,' *L'Homme* 12: 144–154.

HÄMMERLE, CHRISTA (2000), 'Von den Geschlechtern der Kriege und des Militärs. Forschungseinblicke und Bemerkungen zu einer neuen Debatte,' in *Was ist Militärgeschichte?*, ed. Thomas Kühne and Benjamin Ziemann, Paderborn, 229–262.

KÜHNE, THOMAS (1999), 'Der nationalsozialistische Vernichtungskrieg und die "ganz normalen" Deutschen. Forschungsprobleme und Forschungstendenzen der Gesellschaftsgeschichte des Zweiten Weltkriegs. Erster Teil,' *Archiv für Sozialgeschichte* 39: 580–662.

—— (2000), 'Der nationalsozialistische Vernichtungskrieg im kulturellen Kontinuum des 20. Jahrhunderts. Forschungsprobleme und Forschungstendenzen der Gesellschaftsgeschichte des Zweiten Weltkriegs. Zweiter Teil,' *Archiv für Sozialgeschichte* 40: 440–486.

—— and BENJAMIN ZIEMANN, ed. (2000), *Was ist Militärgeschichte?*, Paderborn.

KUNDRUS, BIRTHE (1996), 'Frauen und Nationalsozialismus. Überlegungen zum Stand der Forschung,' *Archiv für Sozialgeschichte* 36: 481–499.

—— (1999), 'Nur die halbe Geschichte. Frauen im Umfeld der Wehrmacht zwischen 1939 und 1945 – Ein Forschungsbericht,' in *Die Wehrmacht. Mythos und Realität*, ed. Rolf-Dieter Müller and Hans-Erich Volkmann, Munich, 719–735.

—— (2000), 'Widerstreitende Geschichte. Ein Literaturbericht zur Geschlechtergeschichte des Nationalsozialismus,' *Neue Politische Literatur* 45, no. 2: 67–92.

LECK, RALPH M. (2000), 'Conservative Empowerment and the Gender of Nazism. Paradigms of Power and Complicity in German Women's History,' *Journal of Women's History* 12, no. 2: 147–169.

NONN, CHRISTOPH (2000), 'Oh What a Lovely War? German Common People and the First World War,' *German History* 18: 97–111.

NORDSTROM, CAROLYN (1991), 'Women and War. Observations from the Field,' *Minerva* 9: 1–15.

PIERSON, RUTH ROACH (1989), 'Beautiful Soul or Just Warrior. Gender and War,' *Gender & History* 1: 77–86.

SALDERN, ADELHEID v. (1994), 'Victims or Perpetrators? Controversies about the Role of Women in the Nazi State,' in *Nazism and German Society, 1933–1945*, ed. David F. Crew, London, New York, 141–165.

SCHUMANN, DIRK (1997), 'Gewalt als Grenzüberschreitung. Überlegungen zur Sozialgeschichte der Gewalt im 19. und 20. Jahrhundert,' *Archiv für Sozialgeschichte* 37: 366–386.

SEIFERT, RUTH (2001), 'Militär und Geschlecht in den deutschen Sozialwissenschaften. Eine Skizzierung der aktuellen Forschungssituation,' *L'Homme* 12: 134–143.

SUMMERFIELD, PENNY (1998), 'Research on Women in Britain in the Second World War. A Historiographical Essay,' *Cahiers d'Histoire du Temps Présent* 4: 207–226.

TAYLOR ALLEN, ANN (1997), 'The Holocaust and the Modernization of Gender: A Historiographical Essay,' *Central European History* 30: 349–364.

II: Theories and Methods – International Classics and Innovators

ADAMS, MICHAEL C.G. (1990), *The Great Adventure. Male Desire and the Coming of World War I*, Bloomington.

ARDENER, SHIRLEY et al., eds. (1987), *Images of Women in Peace and War. Crosscultural and Historical Perspectives*, London.

AUDOIN-ROUZEAU, STÉPHANE (1992), *Men at War, 1914–1918. National Sentiment and Trench Journalism in France during the First World War*, Oxford, New York.

BERKIN, CAROL R. AND CLARA M. LOVETT, ed. (1980), *Women, War, and Revolution*, New York, London.

BOURKE, JOANNA (1996), *Dismembering the Male. Men's Bodies, Britain and the Great War*, London.

—— (1999), *An Intimate History of Killing. Face-to-Face Killing in Twentieth-Century Warfare*, London.

BRAYBON, GAIL and PENNY SUMMERFIELD, ed. (1987), *Out of the Cage. Women's Experiences in Two World Wars*, London, New York.

BROWNMILLER, SUSAN (1976), *Against our Will. Men, Women and Rape*, New York.

CARDINAL, AGNES et al., eds. (1999), *Women's Writing on the First World War*, Oxford.

COOKE, MIRIAM (1996), *Women and the War Story*, Berkeley.

—— and ANGELA WOOLLACOTT, eds. (1993), *Gendering War Talk*, Princeton.

COOPER, HELEN M. et al., eds. (1989), *Arms and the Woman. War, Gender and Literary Representation*, Chapel Hill, London.

CREVELD, MARTIN VAN (2001), *Men, Women and War*, London.

D'AMICO, FRANCINE and LAURIE WEINSTEIN, eds. (1999), *Gender Camouflage. Women and the US Military*, New York.

DAMOUSI, JOY (1999), 'Private Loss, Public Mourning. Motherhood, Memory and Grief in Australia during the Inter-war Years,' *Women's History Review* 8, no. 2: 365–337.

—— and MARILYN LAKE, eds. (1995), *Gender and War. Australians in the Twentieth Century*, New York.

DARROW, MARGARET H. (2000), *French Women and the First World War. War Stories of the Home Front*, Oxford, New York.

DAWSON, GRAHAM (1994), *Soldier Heroes. British Adventures, Empire and the Imagining of Masculinities*, London, New York.

DELANO, PAGE DOUGHERTY (2000), 'Making up for War. Sexuality and Citizenship in Wartime Culture,' *Feminist Studies* 26, no. 1: 33–68.

DOMBROWSKI, NICOLE ANN, ed. (1999), *Women and War in the Twentieth Century. Enlisted without Consent*, New York, London.

DUCHEN, CLAIRE and IRENE BANDHAUER-SCHOFFMANN, eds. (2000), *When the War was Over. Women, War, and Peace in Europe, 1940–1956*, London, New York.

EHRENREICH, BARBARA (1997), *Blood Rites. Origins and History of the Passions of War*, New York.

ELSHTAIN, JEAN BETHKE (1987), *Women and War*, New York.

—— and SHEILA TOBIAS, eds. (1990), *Women, Militarism, and War. Essays in History, Politics, and Social Theory*, Savage, MD.

ENLOE, CYNTHIA (1980), *Bananas, Beaches & Bases. Making Feminist Sense of International Politics*, London.

—— (1988), *Does Khaki Become You? Militarization of Women's Lives*, London.

—— (2000), *Maneuvers. The International Politics of Militarizing Women's Lives*, Berkeley etc.

A Selected Bibliography

FEINMAN, ILENE ROSE (2000), *Citizenship Rites. Feminist Soldiers and Feminist Antimilitarists*, New York, London.

FENNER, LORRY M.and MARIE E. DE YOUNG (2001), *Women in Combat. Civic Duties or Military Liability*, Washington.

FORTY, GEORGE AND ANNE (1997), *Women War Heroines*, London, New York.

FRASER, T.G. AND KEITH JEFFERY, eds. (1993), *Men, Women and War*, Dublin.

FUSSEL, PAUL (1977), *The Great War and Modern Memory*, London etc.

GEYER, MICHAEL (1995a), 'Das Stigma der Gewalt und das Problem der nationalen Identität,' in *Von der Aufgabe der Freiheit. Politische Verantwortung und bürgerliche Gesellschaft*, ed. Christian Jansen et al., Berlin, 673–698.

—— (1995b), 'Eine Kriegsgeschichte, die vom Tod spricht,' in *Physische Gewalt. Studien zur Geschichte der Neuzeit*, ed. Thomas Lindenberger and Alf Lüdtke, Frankfurt a.M., 136–162.

GOLDMAN, DOROTHY, ed. (1993), *Women and World War I. The Written Response*, London.

GOLDMAN, NANCY LORING, ed. (1982), *Female Soldiers. Combatants or Non-combatants? Historical and Contemporary Perspectives*, Westport, London.

GOLDSTEIN, JOSHUA (2001), *War and Gender. How Gender Shapes the War System and Vice Versa*, Cambridge.

GRAYZEL, SUSAN (1997), 'The Outward and Visible Sign of her Patriotism. Women, Uniforms and National Service during the First World War,' *Twentieth Century British History* 8 (1997): 145–164.

—— (1999), *Women's Identities at War. Gender, Motherhood and Politics in Britain and France During the First World War*, Chapel Hill, London.

GULLACE, NICOLETTE F. (1997), 'Sexual Violence and Family Honor. British Propaganda and International Law during the First World War,' *American Historical Review* 102: 714–747.

HARRIS, RUTH (1993), 'The "Child of the Barbarian". Rape, Race, and Nationalism in France during the First World War,' *Past & Present* 141: 170–206.

HIGONNET, MARGARET R., ed. (1999), *Lines of Fire. Women Writers of World War I*, New York.

HIGONNET, MARGARET RANDOLPH et al., eds. (1987), *Behind the Lines. Gender and the Two World Wars*, New Haven, London.

HORNE, JOHN, ed. (1997), *State, Society and Mobilization in Europe during the First World War*, Cambridge.

ISAKSSON, EVA, ed. (1988), *Women and the Military System*, New York.
JEFFORDS, SUSAN (1989), *The Remasculinization of America. Gender and the Vietnam War*, Berkeley.
JONES, DAVID E. (1997), *Women Warriors. A History*, London, Washington.
KENNEDY, KATHLEEN (1999), *Disloyal Mothers and Scurrilous Citizens. Women and Subversion during World War I*, Bloomington.
KENT, SUSAN KINGSLEY (1993), *Making Peace. The Reconstruction of Gender in Interwar Britain*, Princeton.
KUHLMAN, ERIKA A. (1997), *Petticoats and White Feathers. Gender Conformity, Race, the Progressive Peace Movement, and the Debate over War, 1895–1919*, Westport, Conn.
LATZEL, KLAUS (1997), 'Vom Kriegserlebnis zur Kriegserfahrung. Theoretische und methodische Überlegungen zur erfahrungsgeschichtlichen Untersuchung von Feldpostbriefen,' *Militärgeschichtliche Mitteilungen* 56: 1–30.
LEED, ERIC J. (1979), *No Man's Land. Combat and Identity in World War I*, Cambridge.
LEVINE, PHILIPPA (1998), 'Battle Colors. Race, Sex, and Colonial Soldiery in World War I,' *Journal of Women's History* 9, no. 4: 104–130.
LOMAS, JANIS (2000), '"Delicate Duties". Issues of Class and Respectability in Government Policy towards the Wives and Widows of British Soldiers in the Era of the Great War,' *Women's History Review* 9, no. 1: 123–147.
LORENTZEN, LOIS ANN and JENNIFER TURPIN, eds. (1998), *The Women and War Reader*, New York, London.
MELMAN, BILLIE, ed. (1998), *Borderlines. Genders and Identities in War and Peace, 1870–1930*, New York, London.
NIVA, STEVE (1998), 'Tough and Tender. New World Order Masculinity and the Gulf War,' in *The 'Man' Question in International Relations*, ed. Marysia Zalewski and Jane Parpart, Boulder, 109–128.
POIS, ANNE MARIE (1999), 'Perspectives on Twentieth-Century Women's International Activism: Peace, Feminism, and Foreign Policy,' *Journal of Women's History* 11, no. 3: 213–222.
ROBERTS, KRISZTINA (1997), 'Gender, Class and Patriotism. Women's Paramilitary Units in First World War Britain,' *International History Review* 19: 52–65.
ROBERT, MARY LOUISE (1994), *Civilization without Sexes. Reconstructing Gender in Postwar France, 1917–1927*, Chicago.
ROSE, SONYA O. (1998), 'Sex, Citizenship and the Nation in World War II Britain,' *American Historical Review* 103 (October): 1147–1176.

SCARRY, ELAINE (1985), *The Body in Pain. The Making and Unmaking of the World*, Oxford, New York.

SHERMAN, DANIEL J. (1996), 'Monuments, Mourning and Masculinity in France after World War I,' *Gender & History* 8: 83–107.

SHUKERT, ELFRIEDA and BARBARA SCIBETTA (1988), *War Brides of World War II*, Novato.

SEIFERT, RUTH (1996), *Militär – Kultur – Identität. Individualisierung, Geschlechterverhältnisse und die soziale Konstruktion der Soldaten*, Bremen.

SKOCPOL, THEDA (1993), *Protecting Soldiers and Mothers. The Political Origins of Social Policy in the United States*, Cambridge.

STONE, TESSA (1999), 'Creating a (Gendered?) Military Identity. The Women's Auxiliary Air Force in Great Britain in the Second World War,' *Women's History Review* 8, no. 4: 605–624.

STOVALL, TYLER (1998), 'The Color Lines behind the Lines. Racial Violence in France during the Great War,' *American Historical Review* 103, no. 3: 737–769.

SUMMERFIELD, PENNY (1998), *Reconstructing Women's Wartime Lives*, Manchester, New York.

—— and CORINNA PENISTON-BIRD (2000), 'Women in the Firing Line. The Home Guard and the Defence of Gender Boundaries in Britain in the Second World War,' *Women's History Review*, no. 2: 231–255.

SUMMERS, ANNE (1988), *Angels and Citizens. British Women as Military Nurses 1854–1914*, New York.

THOM, DEBORAH (1998), *Nice Girls and Rude Girls. Women Workers in World War I*, London etc.

ULRICH, BERND (1994), 'Feldpostbriefe des Ersten Weltkrieges. Möglichkeiten und Grenzen einer alltagsgeschichtlichen Quelle,' *Militärgeschichtliche Mitteilungen* 53: 73–83.

—— (1996), '"Militärgeschichte von unten". Anmerkungen zu ihren Ursprüngen, Quellen und Perspektiven im 20. Jahrhundert,' *Geschichte und Gesellschaft* 22: 473–503.

WEBSTER, ALEXANDER F.C. (1991), 'Paradigms of the Contemporary Soldier and Women in the Military,' *Strategic Review* 3: 22–30.

WHEELWRIGHT, JULIE (1989), *Amazons and Military Maids, Women Who Dressed as Men in the Pursuit of Life, Liberty and Happiness*, London.

WITTNER, LAWRENCE (2000), 'Gender Roles and Nuclear Disarmament Activism, 1954–1965,' *Gender & History* 12: 197–222.

YUVAL-DAVIS, NIRA (1997), *Gender and Nation*, London.

ZEIGER, SUSAN (2000), *The Uncle Sam's Service. Women Workers with the American Expeditionary Force, 1917–1919*, Ithaca.

III: Overviews – Thematic Monographs and Essay Collections

AMBERGER, WALTRAUD (1984), *Männer, Krieger, Abenteurer. Der Entwurf des 'soldatischen Mannes' in Kriegsromanen über den Ersten und Zweiten Weltkrieg*, Frankfurt a.M.

BEHRENBECK, SABINE (1996), *Der Kult um die toten Helden. Nationalsozialistische Mythen, Riten und Symbole 1923–1945*, Cologne.

BERDING, HELMUT et al., eds. (2000), *Krieg und Erinnerung. Fallstudien zum 19. und 20. Jahrhundert*, Göttingen.

BRIEDENTHAL, RENATE et al. (1984), *When Biology Became Destiny. Women in Weimar and Nazi Germany*, New York.

BRÖCKLING, ULRICH and MICHAEL SIKORA, eds. (1998), *Armeen und ihre Deserteure. Vernachlässigte Kapitel einer Militärgeschichte der Neuzeit*, Göttingen.

BUSCHMANN, NIKOLAUS and HORST CARL, eds. (2001), *Die Erfahrung des Krieges. Erfahrungsgeschichtliche Perspektiven von der Französischen Revolution bis zum Zweiten Weltkrieg*, Paderborn.

COHEN, DEBORAH (2001), *The War Comes Home. Disabled Veterans in Great Britain and Germany, 1914–1939*, Berkeley etc.

DEIST, WILHELM, ed. (1985), *The German Military in the Age of Total War*, Leamington Spa.

EIFLER, CHRISTINE and RUTH SEIFERT, eds. (1999), *Soziale Konstruktionen. Militär und Geschlechterverhältnis*, Münster.

FERGUSON, NIALL (1999), *The Pity of War*, New York.

FREVERT, UTE (1995), *Men of Honour. A Social and Cultural History of the Duel*, Cambridge.

—— ed. (1997), *Militär und Gesellschaft im 19. und 20. Jahrhundert*, Stuttgart.

—— (2001), *Die kasernierte Nation. Militärdienst und Zivilgesellschaft in Deutschland*, Munich.

FRITZSCHE, PETER (1992), *A Nation of Fliers. German Aviation and the Popular Imagination*, Cambridge.

GERSDORFF, URSULA v. (1969), *Frauen im Kriegsdienst 1914–1945*, Stuttgart.

GESTRICH, ANDREAS, ed. (1996), *Gewalt im Krieg. Ausübung, Erfahrung und Verweigerung von Gewalt in Kriegen des 20. Jahrhunderts*, Münster etc.

A Selected Bibliography

HACKER, HANNA (1998), *Gewalt ist: keine Frau. Der Akteurin oder eine Geschichte der Transgressionen*, Königstein i.T.

HAGEMANN, KAREN, ed. (2001), *Nach – Kriegs – Helden. Kulturelle und politische Demobilmachung in deutschen Nachkriegsgeschichten*, Special Issue: *Militärgeschichtliche Zeitschrift* 60, no. 2.

—— (2002), 'Jede Kraft wird gebraucht'. Militäreinsatz von Frauen im Ersten und Zweiten Weltkrieg, in *Krieg – Kriegserlebnis – Kriegserfahrung in Deutschland 1914–1945*, ed. Bruno Thoss, Paderborn.

—— and Ralf Pröve, eds. (1998), *Landsknechte, Soldatenfrauen und Nationalkrieger. Militär, Krieg und Geschlechterordnung im historischen Wandel*, Frankfurt a.M., New York.

HEINEMAN, ELIZABETH (1999), *What Difference Does a Husband Make? Marital Status in Germany, 1933–1961*, Berkeley.

HOLL, KARL (1988), *Pazifismus in Deutschland*, Frankfurt a.M.

KÄMPER, GABRIELE (2000), 'Der "Kult der Kälte". Figurationen von Faszination und Männlichkeit im Rückblick auf Ernst Jünger. Ein Nachruf auf die Nachrufe,' *Feministische Studien* 18, no. 2: 20–34.

KOLLER, CHRISTIAN (2001), *'Von Wilden aller Rassen niedergemetzelt'. Die Diskussion um die Verwendung von Kolonialtruppen in Europa zwischen Rassismus, Militär- und Kolonialpolitik (1914–1930)*, Stuttgart.

KOSELLECK, REINHART and MICHAEL JEISMANN, eds. (1994), *Der politische Totenkult. Kriegerdenkmäler in der Moderne*, Munich.

KÜHNE, THOMAS, ed. (1996), *Männergeschichte – Geschlechtergeschichte. Männlichkeit im Wandel der Moderne*, Frankfurt a.M., New York.

KUNDRUS, BIRTHE (1995), *Kriegerfrauen. Familienpolitik und Geschlechterverhältnisse im Ersten und Zweiten Weltkrieg*, Hamburg.

LORRAIN, SOPHIE (1999), *Des Pacifistes français et allemands, pionniers de l'entente franco-allemande, 1871–1925*, Paris.

MARßOLEK, INGE (1999), '"Ich möchte Dich zu gern mal in Uniform sehen". Geschlechterkonstruktionen in Feldpostbriefen,' *Werkstatt-Geschichte* 22: 41–59.

MOSSE, GEORGE L. (1985), *Nationalism and Sexuality. Middle-class Morality and Sexual Norms in Modern Europe*, Madison.

—— (1990), *Fallen Soldier. Reshaping the Memory of the World Wars*, Oxford, New York.

—— (1996), *The Image of Man. The Creation of Modern Masculinity*, Oxford, New York.

OVERMANS, RÜDIGER, ed. (1999), *In der Hand des Feindes. Kriegsgefangenschaft von der Antike bis zum Zweiten Weltkrieg*, Cologne.

RIESENBERGER, DIETER (1992), *Für Humanität in Krieg und Frieden. Das Internationale Rote Kreuz 1863–1977*, Göttingen.

SCHILLING, RENÉ (2002), *Heroische Männlichkeit. Die Konstruktion des Kriegshelden in Deutschland zwischen 1813 und 1945 am Beispiel der Rezeptionsgeschichte Körners, Friesens, Richthofens und Weddigens*, Paderborn.

SCHULTE, REGINA (1998), *Die verkehrte Welt des Krieges. Studien zu Geschlecht, Religion und Tod*, Frankfurt a.M., New York.

SEIDLER, FRANZ W. (1978), *Frauen zu den Waffen? Marketenderinnen, Helferinnen, Soldatinnen*, Koblenz, Bonn.

TERNON, YVES (1995), *L'Etat criminel. Les génocides au XXe siècle*, Paris.

THEWELEIT, KLAUS (1987), *Male Fantasies*, 2 vols, Minneapolis.

TUTEN, JEFF M. (1982), 'Germany and the World Wars,' in *Female Soldiers. Combatants or Non-combatants? Historical and Contemporary Perspectives*, ed. Nancy Loring Goldman, Westport, London, 47–60.

ULRICH, BERND (1997), *Die Augenzeugen. Deutsche Feldpostbriefe in Kriegs- und Nachkriegszeit 1914–1933*, Essen.

WALLER, MARGUERITE R. and JENNIFER RYCENGA, eds. (2000), *Frontline Feminisms. Women, War, and Resistance*, New York.

WETTE, WOLFRAM, ed. (1992), *Der Krieg des kleinen Mannes. Eine Militärgeschichte von unten*, Munich.

—— ed. (1999), *Militarismus in Deutschland 1871 bis 1914. Zeitgenössische Analyse und Kritik*, Münster etc.

WHALEN, ROBERT WELDON (1984), *Bitter Wounds. German Victims of the Great War, 1914–1939*, Ithaca, London.

WINTER, JAY (1995), *Sites of Memory, Sites of Mourning. The Great War in European Cultural History*, Cambridge.

—— and EMMANUEL SIVAN, eds. (1999), *War and Remembrance in the Twentieth Century*, Cambridge.

IV: Nineteenth-Century Germany

BOEMEKE, MANFRED F., ROGER CHICKERING and STIG FÖRSTER, eds. (1999), *Anticipating Total War. The German and American Experiences, 1871–1914*, Cambridge.

CHICKERING, ROGER (1988), '"Casting their Gaze More Broadly". Women's Patriotic Activism in Imperial Germany,' *Past & Present* 118: 156–185.

FÖRSTER, STIG and JÖRG NAGLER, eds. (1997), *On the Road to Total War. The American Civil War and the German War of Unification 1861–1871*, Cambridge.

GÖTSCH, SILKE (1998), '"Der Soldat, der Soldat ist der erste Mann im Staat . . .". Männerbilder in volkstümlichen Soldatenliedern 1855– 1875,' in *MannBilder. Ein Lese- und Quellenbuch zur historischen Männerforschung*, ed. Wolfgang Schmale, Berlin, 131–154.

HAGEMANN, KAREN (1996), 'Nation, Krieg und Geschlechterordnung. Zum kulturellen und politischen Diskurs in der Zeit der antinapoleonischen Erhebung Preußens 1806–1815,' *Geschichte und Gesellschaft* 22: 562–591.

—— (1997), 'Of "Manly Valor" and "German Honor". Nation, War and Masculinity in the Age of the Prussian Uprising against Napoleon,' *Central European History* 30: 187–220.

—— (2000a), '"Deutsche Heldinnen". Patriotisch-nationales Frauenhandeln in der Zeit der antinapoleonischen Kriege,' in *Nation, Politik und Geschlecht. Frauenbewegungen und Nationalismus in der Moderne*, ed. Ute Planert, Frankfurt a.M., New York, 86–112.

—— (2000b), 'A Valorous *Volk* Family. The Nation, the Military, and the Gender Order in Prussia in the Time of the Anti-Napoleonic Wars, 1806–15,' in *Gendered Nations. Nationalisms and Gender Order in the Long Nineteenth Century*, ed. Ida Blom et al., Oxford, New York, 179– 205.

—— (2002), *'Mannlicher Muth und Teutsche Ehre'. Nation, Militär und Geschlecht zur Zeit der Antinapoleonischen Kriege Preußens*, Paderborn.

KLENKE, DIETMAR (1994), 'Nationalkriegerisches Gemeinschaftsgefühl als politische Religion. Zum Vereinsnationalismus der Sänger, Schützen und Turner am Vorabend der Einigungskriege,' *Historische Zeitschrift* 260: 395–448.

—— (1994), 'Zwischen nationalkriegerischem Gemeinschaftsideal und bürgerlich-ziviler Modernität. Zum Vereinsnationalismus der Sänger, Schützen und Turner im Deutschen Kaiserreich,' *Geschichte in Wissenschaft und Unterricht* 45: 207–223.

LENGWILER, MARTIN (2000), *Zwischen Klinik und Kaserne. Die Geschichte der Militärpsychiatrie in Deutschland und der Schweiz 1870–1914*, Zurich.

MONCURE, JOHN (1993), *Forging the King's Sword. Military Education Between Tradition and Modernization. The Case of the Royal Prussian Cadet Corps 1871–1918*, New York, Berlin.

PARIS, MICHAEL (1993), 'The Rise of the Airmen. The Origins of Air Force Elitism, c. 1890–1918,' *Journal of Contemporary History* 28: 123–141.

REDER, DIRK (1998), *Frauenbewegung und Nation. Patriotische Frauenvereine in Deutschland im frühen 19. Jahrhundert (1813–1830)*, Cologne.

RIESEBERGER, DIETER (1994), 'Zur Professionalisierung und Militarisierung der Schwestern vom Roten Kreuz vor dem Ersten Weltkrieg,' *Militärgeschichtliche Mitteilungen* 53: 49–72.

ROHKRÄMER, THOMAS (1990), *Der Militarismus der 'kleinen Leute'. Die Kriegervereine im Deutschen Kaiserreich, 1871–1914*, Munich.

—— (1990), 'Mannesstolz und Kriegsverdrossenheit. Autobiographische Erinnerungen an die Einigungskriege,' *Krieg und Literatur* 2: 19–36.

—— (1995), 'Das Militär als Männerbund? Kult der soldatischen Männlichkeit im Deutschen Kaiserreich,' *Westfälische Forschungen* 45: 169–187.

TROX, ECKARD (1992), 'Kriegerfeste, militärische Männerbünde und politische Offiziere. Aspekte preußischer Militärgeschichte in der ersten Hälfte des 19. Jahrhunderts als Geschichte konservativer Modernisierung,' *Militärgeschichtliche Mitteilungen* 51: 23–46.

VOGEL, JAKOB (1997), *Nationen im Gleichschritt. Der Kult der Nation in Waffen in Deutschland und Frankreich, 1871–1914*, Göttingen.

V: The First World War

BERGHAHN, VOLKER (1993), *Germany and the Approach of War in 1914*, Basingstoke, Hampshire.

CHICKERING, ROGER (1998), *Imperial Germany and the Great War, 1914–1918*, Cambridge.

—— and STIG FÖRSTER, eds. (2000), *Great War, Total War. Combat and Mobilization on the Western Front, 1914–1918*, Cambridge.

DANIEL, UTE (1997), *The War from Within. German Working-class Women in the First World War*, Oxford, New York.

DAVIS, BELINDA (1998), 'Geschlecht und Konsum. Rolle und Bild der Konsumentin in den Verbraucherprotesten des Ersten Weltkrieges,' *Archiv für Sozialgeschichte* 38: 119–139.

—— (2000), *Home Fires Burning. Food, Politics, and Everyday Life in World War I Berlin*, Chapel Hill, London.

DOMANSKY, ELISABETH (1996), 'Militarization and Reproduction in World War I Germany,' in *Society, Culture, and the State in Germany, 1870–1930*, ed. Geoff Eley, Ann Arbor, 426–454.

EKSTEINS, MODRIS (1989), *Rites of Spring. The Great War and the Birth of the Modern Age*, Boston.

FELDMAN, GERALD (1992), *Army, Industry and Labour in Germany, 1914–1918*, Oxford, New York.

FRIDENSON, PATRICK (1993), *The French Home Front, 1914–1918*, Oxford, New York.

GREENHUT, JEFFREY (1981), 'Race, Sex and War. The Impact of Race and Sex on Morale and Health Services on the Western Front 1914,' *Military Affairs* 45: 71–74.

GUTTMANN, BARBARA (1989), *Weibliche Heimarmee. Frauen in Deutschland 1914–1918*, Weinheim.

HÄMMERLE, CHRISTA (1992), '"Wir strickten und nähten Wäsche für Soldaten . . .". Von der Militarisierung des Handarbeitens im Ersten Weltkrieg,' *L'Homme* 3: 88–128.

—— (1997), '"Habt Dank, Ihr Wiener Mägdelein . . .". Soldaten und weibliche Liebesgaben im Ersten Weltkrieg,' *L'Homme* 8: 132–154.

—— (1998), '". . . wirf ihnen alles hin und schau, daß du fort kommst." Die Feldpost eines Paares in der Geschlechter(un)ordnung des Ersten Weltkriegs,' *Historische Anthropologie* 6: 431–458.

HIRSCHFELD, GERHARD et al., eds. (1993), *'Keiner fühlt sich hier mehr als Mensch . . .' Erlebnis und Wirkung des Ersten Weltkriegs*, Essen.

—— et al., eds. (1997), *Kriegserfahrungen. Studien zur Sozial- und Mentalitätsgeschichte des Ersten Weltkrieges*, Essen.

JAHR, CHRISTOPH (1998), *Gewöhnliche Soldaten. Desertion und Deserteure im deutschen und britischen Heer 1914–1918*, Göttingen.

KIENITZ, SABINE (1999), 'Die Kastrierten des Krieges. Körperbilder und Männlichkeitskonstruktionen im und nach dem Ersten Weltkrieg,' *Zeitschrift für Volkskunde* 95: 63–82.

KOCKA, JÜRGEN (1984), *Facing Total War. German Society, 1914–1918*, Cambridge.

KOLLER, CHRISTIAN (2000), '"Alsacien, Déserteur!". Die Kriegserfahrung des Elsässer Bauern Dominik Richert im Spiegel seiner Memoiren,' *BIOS* 13: 225–239.

KRUSE, WOLFGANG, ed. (1997), *Eine Welt von Feinden. Der große Krieg 1914–1918*, Frankfurt a.M.

LERNER, PAUL (1998), 'Hysterical Cures. Hypnosis, Gender and Performance in World War I and Weimar Germany,' *History Workshop Journal* 45: 79–101.

LINDER, ANN P. (1996), *Princes of the Trenches. Narrating the German Experience of the First World War*, New York.

LIPP, ANNE (1996), 'Friedenssehnsucht und Durchhaltebereitschaft. Wahrnehmungen und Erfahrungen deutscher Soldaten im Ersten Weltkrieg,' *Archiv für Sozialgeschichte* 36: 279–292.

LIULEVICIUS, VEJAS GABRIEL (2000), *War Land on the Eastern Front. Culture, National Identity, and German Occupation in World War I,* Cambridge.

MAß, SANDRA (2001), 'Der Traum des weißen Mannes. Afrikanische Kolonialsoldaten in propagandistischen Texten, 1914–1923,' *L'Homme* 12: 11–33.

O'BRIEN, CATHERINE (1997), *Women's Fictional Responses to the First World War. A Comparative Study of Selected Texts by French and German Writers,* New York.

SCHUBERT-WELLER, CHRISTOPH (1998), *'Kein schöner Tod . . .' Die Militarisierung der männlichen Jugend und ihr Einsatz im Ersten Weltkrieg 1890–1918,* Weinheim, Munich.

SCHULTE, REGINA (1996), 'Käthe Kollwitzs Sacrifice,' *History Workshop Journal* 41: 193–221.

SPIKER, ROLF and BERND ULRICH, eds. (1998), *Der Tod als Maschinist. Der industrialisierte Krieg 1914–1918,* Bramsche.

STRACHAN, HEW, ed. (1998), *World War I. A History,* Oxford.

—— (2001), *The First World War,* Oxford.

THÉBAUD, FRANÇOISE (1994), The Great War and the Triumph of Sexual Division, in *A History of Women in the West,* vol. 5: *Towards a Cultural Identity in the Twentieth Century,* ed. Françoise Thébaud, Cambridge, London, 20–75.

ULRICH, BERND and BENJAMIN ZIEMANN, eds. (1994), *Frontalltag im Ersten Weltkrieg. Wahn und Wirklichkeit, Quellen und Dokumente,* Frankfurt a.M.

—— (1997), *Die Augenzeugen. Deutsche Feldpostbriefe in Kriegs- und Nachkriegszeit 1914–1933,* Essen.

VAN DER LINDEN, MARCEL and GOTTFRIED MERGNER, eds. (1991), *Kriegsbegeisterung und mentale Kriegsvorbereitung. Interdisziplinäre Studien,* Berlin.

VERHEY, JEFFREY (2000), *The Spirit of 1914. Militarism, Myth and Mobilization in Germany,* Cambridge.

WINTER, JAY and RICHARD WALL, eds. (1988), *The Upheaval of War. Family, Work and Welfare in Europe, 1914–1918,* Cambridge.

WINTER, JAY and JEAN-LOUIS ROBERT, eds. (1997), *Capital Cities at War. Paris, London, Berlin, 1914–1919,* Cambridge.

WINTER, JAY et al., eds. (2000), *The Great War and the Twentieth Century,* New Haven.

ZIEMANN, BENJAMIN (1996), 'Fahnenflucht im deutschen Heer 1914–1918,' *Militärgeschichtliche Mitteilungen* 55: 93–130.
—— (1997), *Front und Heimat. Ländliche Kriegserfahrungen im südlichen Bayern 1914–1923*, Essen.

VI: The Weimar Republic

BERGHAHN, VOLKER R. (1966), *Der Stahlhelm. Bund der Frontsoldaten 1918–1935*, Düsseldorf.
BESSEL, RICHARD (1983), '"Eine nicht allzu große Beunruhigung des Arbeitsmarktes". Frauenarbeit und Demobilmachung in Deutschland nach dem Ersten Weltkrieg,' *Geschichte und Gesellschaft* 9: 211–229.
—— (1993), *Germany after the First World War*, Oxford.
—— (1995), 'The "Front Generation" and the Politics of Weimar Germany,' in *Generations in Conflict. Youth Revolt and Generation Formation in Germany 1770–1968*, ed. Mark Roseman, Cambridge, 121–136.
DIEHL, JAMES M. (1977), *Paramilitary Politics in Weimar Germany*, Bloomington.
DUPPLER, JÖRG and GERHARD P. GROß, eds. (1999), *Kriegsende 1918. Ereignis, Wirkung, Nachwirkung*, Munich.
GEYER, MICHAEL (1980), *Aufrüstung oder Sicherheit. Die Reichswehr in der Krise der Machtpolitik, 1924–1936*, Wiesbaden.
—— (1983), 'Ein Vorbote des Wohlfahrtsstaates. Die Kriegsopferversorgung in Frankreich, Deutschland und Großbritannien nach dem Ersten Weltkrieg,' *Geschichte und Gesellschaft* 9: 230–277.
HAGEMANN, KAREN (1990), *Frauenalltag und Männerpolitik, Alltagsleben und gesellschaftliches Handeln von Arbeiterfrauen in der Weimarer Republik*, Bonn.
—— (1993), 'Men's Demonstrations and Women's Protest. Gender in Collective Action in the Urban Working-Class Milieu during the Weimar Republic,' *Gender & History* 5: 101–119.
HARVEY, ELIZABETH (2000), 'Pilgrimages to the "Bleeding Border". Gender and Rituals of Nationalist Protest in Germany, 1919–39,' *Women's History Review* 9, no. 2: 201–229.
HAUSEN, KARIN (1994), 'Die Sorge der Nation für ihre "Kriegsopfer". Ein Bereich der Geschlechterpolitik während der Weimarer Republik,' in *Von der Arbeiterbewegung zum modernen Sozialstaat*, ed. Jürgen Kocka et al., Munich, 719–739.
HOLL, KARL and WOLFRAM WETTE, eds. (1981), *Pazifismus in der Weimarer Republik. Beiträge zur Historischen Friedensforschung*, Paderborn.

KRUMEICH, GERD, ed. (2001), *Versailles 1919. Ziele – Wirkung – Wahrnehmung*, Essen.

ROHE, KARL (1966), *Das Reichsbanner Schwarz Rot Gold. Ein Beitrag zur Geschichte und Struktur der politischen Kampfverbände zur Zeit der Weimarer Republik*, Düsseldorf.

ROSENHAFT, EVE (1983), *Beating the Fascists? The German Communists and Political Violence, 1929–1933*, Cambridge.

ROUETTE, SUSANNE (1993), *Sozialpolitik als Geschlechterpolitik. Die Regulierung der Frauenarbeit nach dem Ersten Weltkrieg*, Frankfurt a.M., New York.

—— (1997), 'Mothers and Citizens. Gender and Social Policy in Germany after the First World War,' *Central European History* 30: 48–66.

SCHMIDT, JENS (2000), *'Sich hart machen, wenn es gilt'. Männlichkeitskonzeptionen in Illustrierten der Weimarer Republik*, Münster.

SCHUHMANN, DIRK (2001), *Politische Gewalt in der Weimarer Republik 1918–1933. Kampf um die Straße und Furcht vor dem Bürgerkrieg*, Essen.

SEIFFERT, ANJA (1995), 'Männer – Soldaten – Krieger. Zur Männlichkeitskonstruktion im Frühwerk Ernst Jüngers,' *Widersprüche* 15: 129–143.

ULRICH, BERND and BENJAMIN ZIEMANN, eds. (1997), *Krieg im Frieden. Die umkämpfte Erinnerung an den Ersten Weltkrieg*, Frankfurt a.M.

WEISBROD, BERND (1992), 'Gewalt in der Politik. Zur politischen Kultur in Deutschland zwischen den beiden Weltkriegen,' *Geschichte in Wissenschaft und Unterricht* 43: 391–404.

—— (2000), 'Military Violence and Male Fundamentalism. Ernst Jünger's Contribution to the Conservative Revolution,' *History Workshop Journal* 49: 69–94.

WEITZ, ERIC D. (1997), *Creating German Communism, 1890–1990. From Popular Protest to Socialist State*, Princeton.

ZIEMANN, BENJAMIN (1998), 'Republikanische Kriegserinnerungen in einer polarisierten Öffentlichkeit. Das Reichsbanner Schwarz–Rot–Gold als Veteranenverband der sozialistischen Arbeiterschaft,' *Historische Zeitschrift* 267: 357–398.

VII: The Third Reich

BARTOV, OMER (1991), *Hitler's Army. Soldiers, Nazis, and War in the Third Reich*, Oxford, New York.

—— (2000a), *Mirrors of Destruction. War, Genocide, and Modern Identity*, Oxford, New York.

—— (2000b), *Murder in Our Midst. The Holocaust, Industrial Killing, and Representation*, Oxford, New York.

BECK, BIRGIT (1999), 'Sexuelle Gewalt und Krieg. Geschlecht, Rasse und der nationalsozialistische Vernichtungsfeldzug gegen die Sowjetunion, 1941–1945,' in *Geschlecht hat Methode. Ansätze und Perspektiven in der Frauen- und Geschlechtergeschichte*, ed. Veronika Aegerter et al., Zurich, 223–234.

BOCK, GISELA (1986), *Zwangssterilisation im Nationalsozialismus. Studien zur Rassenpolitik und Frauenpolitik*, Opladen.

BOOG, HORST et al. (1987), *Der Angriff auf die Sowjetunion*, Stuttgart (vol. 4 of *Das Deutsche Reich und der Zweite Weltkrieg*).

—— et al. (1990), *Der globale Krieg. Die Ausweitung zum Weltkrieg und der Wechsel der Initiative 1941–1943*, Stuttgart (vol. 6 of *Das Deutsche Reich und der Zweite Weltkrieg*).

—— et al. (2001), *Das Deutsche Reich in der Defensive. Strategischer Luftkrieg in Europa. Krieg im Westen und in Ostasien, 1944/45*, Stuttgart (vol. 7 of *Das Deutsche Reich und der Zweite Weltkrieg*).

BROWNING, CHRISTOPHER R. (1992a), *Ordinary Men. Reserve Police Battalion 101 and the Final Solution in Poland*, New York.

—— (1992b), *The Path to Genocide. Essays on Launching the Final Solution*, Cambridge.

—— (2000), *Nazi Policy, Jewish Workers, German Killers*, Cambridge.

BUNTING, MADELEINE (1996), *The Model Occupation. The Channel Islands under German Rule, 1940–1945*, London.

CAMPBELL, D'ANN (1993), 'Women in Combat. The World War II Experience in the United States, Great Britain, Germany, and the Soviet Union,' *Journal of Military History* 57: 301–323.

CHIARI, BERNHARD (1998), *Alltag hinter der Front. Besatzung, Kollaboration und Widerstand in Weißrußland 1941–44*, Düsseldorf.

DEIST, WILHELM et al. (1979), *Ursachen und Voraussetzungen der deutschen Kriegspolitik*, Stuttgart (Nachdruck 1991) (vol. 1 of *Das Deutsche Reich und der Zweite Weltkrieg*).

DÖRR, MARGARETE (1998), *'Wer die Zeit nicht miterlebt hat . . .' Frauenerfahrungen im Zweiten Weltkrieg und in den Jahren danach*, 3 vols, Frankfurt a.M., New York.

DROLSHAGEN, EBBA D. (1998), *Nicht ungeschoren davongekommen. Das Schicksal der Frauen in den besetzten Ländern, die Wehrmachtssoldaten liebten*, Hamburg.

EBBINGHAUS, ANGELIKA, ed. (1996), *Opfer und Täterinnen. Frauenbiographien des Nationalsozialismus*, Frankfurt a.M.

GEHMACHER, JOHANNA (1998), *'Völkische Frauenbewegung'. Deutschnationale und nationalsozialistische Geschlechterpolitik in Österreich*, Wien.

GERBER, PIA (1996), *Erwerbsbeteiligung von deutschen und ausländischen Frauen 1933–1945 in Deutschland*, Frankfurt a.m.

GERLACH, CHRISTIAN (1999), *Kalkulierte Morde. Die deutsche Wirtschafts- und Vernichtungspolitik in Weißrußland 1941 bis 1944*, Hamburg.

GOLDHAGEN, DANIEL (1996), *Hitler's Willing Executioner. Ordinary Germans and the Holocaust*, New York.

GRAVENHORST, LERKE and CARMEN TATSCHMURAT, eds. (1990), *TöchterFragen. NS-Frauen-Geschichte*, Freiburg.

HACHTMANN, RÜDIGER (1993), 'Industriearbeiterinnen in der deutschen Kriegswirtschaft 1936–1944/45,' *Geschichte und Gesellschaft* 19: 332–366.

HAMBURGER INSTITUT FÜR SOZIALFORSCHUNG, ed. (2002), *Verbrechen der Wehrmacht. Dimensionen des Vernichtungskriegs, 1941–1944. Ausstellungskatalog*, Hamburg.

HAMMER, INGRID and SUSANNE ZUR NIEDEN, eds. (1992), *'Sehr selten habe ich geweint.' Briefe und Tagebücher aus dem Zweiten Weltkrieg von Menschen aus Berlin*, Zurich.

HARVEY, ELIZABETH (1998), '"Die deutsche Frau im Osten". "Rasse", Geschlecht und öffentlicher Raum im besetzten Polen 1940–1944,' *Archiv für Sozialgeschichte* 38: 191–214.

HEER, HANNES (1999), *Tote Zonen. Die deutsche Wehrmacht an der Ostfront*, Hamburg.

HEINEMAN, ELIZABETH D. (2001), 'Whose Mothers? Generational Difference, War, and the Nazi Cult of Motherhood,' *Journal of Women's History* 12, no. 4: 138–163.

HEINSOHN, KIRSTEN et al., eds. (1997), *Zwischen Karriere und Verfolgung. Handlungsräume von Frauen im nationalsozialistischen Deutschland*, Frankfurt a.M., New York.

HERBERT, ULRICH (1990), *A History of Foreign Labor in Germany, 1880–1980. Seasonal Workers, Forced Laborers, Guest Workers*, Ann Arbor.

—— (1997), *Hitler's Foreign Worker. Enforced Foreign Labor in Germany under the Third Reich*, Cambridge.

—— ed. (2000), *National Socialist Extermination Policies. Contemporary German Perspectives and Controversies*, New York.

HUMBURG, MARTIN (1998), *Das Gesicht des Krieges. Feldpostbriefe von Wehrmachtssoldaten aus der Sowjetunion 1941–1944*, Opladen.

A Selected Bibliography

JUREIT, ULRIKE (1999), 'Zwischen Ehe und Männerbund. Emotionale und sexuelle Beziehungsmuster im Zweiten Weltkrieg,' *Werkstatt-Geschichte* 22: 61–73.

KOCK, GERHARD (1997), *'Der Führer sorgt für unsere Kinder . . .' Die Kinderlandverschickung im Zweiten Weltkrieg*, Paderborn.

KOONZ, CLAUDIA (1986), *Mothers in the Fatherland. Women, the Family, and Nazi Politics*, New York.

KROENER, BERNHARD R. et al. (1988), *Organisation und Mobilisierung des deutschen Machtbereichs. Kriegsverwaltung, Wirtschaft und personelle Ressourcen 1939–1941*, Stuttgart (vol. 5.1: Das Deutsche Reich und der Zweite Weltkrieg).

—— (1999), *Organisation und Mobilisierung des deutschen Machtbereichs. Kriegsverwaltung, Wirtschaft und personelle Ressourcen 1942–1944/45*, Stuttgart (vol. 5.2 of *Das Deutsche Reich und der Zweite Weltkrieg*).

KÜHNE, THOMAS (1996), '"Kameradschaft – Das Beste im Leben des Mannes". Die deutschen Soldaten des Zweiten Weltkrieges in erfahrungs- und geschlechtergeschichtlicher Perspektive,' *Geschichte und Gesellschaft* 22: 504–529.

—— (1998), 'Zwischen Männerbund und Volksgemeinschaft. Hitlers Soldaten und der Mythos der Kameradschaft,' *Archiv für Sozialgeschichte* 38: 165–189.

KUNDRUS, BIRTHE (1997), 'Loyal, weil satt. Die innere Front im Zweiten Weltkrieg,' *Mittelweg* 36: no. 5, 80–93.

LATZEL, KLAUS (1998), *Deutsche Soldaten – Nationalsozialistischer Krieg, Kriegserlebnis – Kriegserfahrung 1939–1945*, Paderborn.

MEINEN, INSA (1999), 'Wehrmacht und Prostitution – Zur Reglementierung der Geschlechterbeziehungen durch die deutsche Militärverwaltung im besetzten Frankreich 1940–1944,' *1999. Zeitschrift für Sozialgeschichte des 20. und 21. Jahrhunderts* 14: 35–55.

MESSERSCHMIDT, MANFRED (1996), *Was damals Recht war . . . NS-Militär- und Strafjustiz im Vernichtungskrieg*, Essen.

MÜLLER, ROLF-DIETER and HANS-ERICH VOLKMANN, eds. (1999), *Die Wehrmacht. Mythos und Realität*, Munich.

OFER, DALIA and LEONORE J. WEITZMAN, eds. (1998), *Women in the Holocaust*, New Haven, London.

OVERMANS, RÜDIGER (1999), *Deutsche militärische Verluste im Zweiten Weltkrieg*, Munich.

—— and GÜNTHER BISCHOF, eds. (1999), *Kriegsgefangenschaft im Zweiten Weltkrieg. Eine vergleichende Perspektive*, Ternitz-Potschach.

Karen Hagemann and *Stefanie Schüler-Springorum*

PAUL, CHRISTA (1994), *Zwangsprostitution. Staatlich errichtete Bordelle im Nationalsozialismus*, Berlin.

PINE, LISA (1997), *Nazi Family Policy, 1933–1945*, Oxford, New York.

POHL, KARL HEINRICH, ed. (1999), *Wehrmacht und Vernichtungspolitik. Militär im nationalsozialistischen System*, Göttingen.

REAGIN, NANCY R. (2001), '*Marktordnung* and Autarkic Housekeeping. Housewives and Private Consumption under the Four-Year Plan, 1936–1939,' *German History* 19, no. 2: 162–184.

RINGELHEIM, JOAN et al., eds. (1993), *Different Voices. Women and the Holocaust*, New York.

RUPP, LEILA J. (1980), '"I Don't Call that Volksgemeinschaft". Women, Class and War in Nazi Germany,' in *Women, War, and Revolution*, ed. Carol R. Berkin and Clara M. Lovett, London, New York, 37–53.

—— (1980), *Mobilizing Women for War. Germany and American Propaganda, 1939–1945*, Princeton.

SCHWARZ, GUDRUN (1997), *Eine Frau an seiner Seite. Ehefrauen in der 'SS-Sippengemeinschaft'*, Hamburg.

SEIDLER, FRANZ W. (1977), *Prostitution. Homosexualität. Selbstverstümmelung. Probleme der deutschen Sanitätsführung 1939–1945*, Neckargemünd.

SPANGER, RINCO et al., eds. (1999), *Zur Arbeit gezwungen. Zwangsarbeiter in Deutschland 1940–1945*, Bremen.

STEPHENSON, JILL (1975), *Women in Nazi Society*, London.

—— (1981), *The Nazi Organisation of Women*, London.

STROBL, INGRID (1989), '*Sag nie, Du gehst den letzten Weg.' Frauen im bewaffneten Widerstand gegen Faschismus und deutsche Besatzung*, Frankfurt a.M.

—— (1998), *Die Angst kam erst danach. Jüdische Frauen im Widerstand in Europa 1939–1945*, Frankfurt a.M.

UEBERSCHÄR, GERD R. and WOLFRAM WETTE, eds. (2001), *Kriegsverbrechen im 20. Jahrhundert*, Darmstadt.

WEINBERG, GERHARD L. (1994), *A World at Arm. A Global History of World War II*, Cambridge, New York.

WETTE, WOLFRAM, ed. (1995), *Deserteure der Wehrmacht. Feiglinge – Opfer – Hoffnungsträger. Dokumentation eines Meinungswandels*, Essen.

WILDMANN, DANIEL (1998), *Begehrte Körper. Konstruktion und Inszenierung des 'arischen' Männerkörpers im 'Dritten Reich'*, Würzburg.

WILLMOT LOUISE (1985), 'Women in the Third Reich. The Auxiliary Military Service Law of 1944,' *German History* 2: 10–20.

A Selected Bibliography

WINKLER, DÖRTE (1977), *Frauenarbeit im "Dritten Reich"*, Hamburg.
WOBBE, THERESA, ed. (1992), *Nach Osten. Verdeckte Spuren national-sozialistischer Verbrechen*, Frankfurt a.M.
ZIPFEL, GABY (1995), 'Wie führten Frauen Krieg?' in Hannes Heer, Klaus Naumann, eds., *Vernichtungskrieg. Verbrechen der Wehrmacht 1941 bis 1944*, Hamburg, 460–474.
ZUR NIEDEN, SUSANNE (1993), *Alltag im Ausnahmezustand. Frauentagebücher im zerstörten Deutschland 1943 bis 1945*, Berlin.

VIII: The Postwar Germanies

BALD, DETLEF (1993), '"Bürger in Uniform". Tradition und Neuanfang des Militärs in Westdeutschland,' in *Modernisierung im Wiederaufbau. Die westdeutsche Gesellschaft der 50er Jahre*, ed. Axel Schildt and Arnold Sywottek, Bonn, 392–402.
BANDHAUER-SCHÖFFMANN, IRENE and ELA HORNUNG (1990), 'Trümmerfrauen – ein kurzes Heldinnenleben? Nachkriegsgesellschaft als Frauengesellschaft,' in *Zur Politik des Weiblichen. Frauen, Macht und Ohnmacht*, ed. Andrea Graf, Vienna, 93–120.
BARNOUW, DAGMAR (1996), *Germany 1945. Views of War and Violence*, Bloomington.
BAUER, INGRID (1996), 'Die "Ami-Braut" – Platzhalterin für das Abgespaltene? Zur (De)Konstruktion eines Stereotyps der österreichischen Nachkriegsgeschichte 1945–1955,' *L'Homme* 7: 107–121.
BAUMGARTNER, MARIANNE (1994), '*Jo, des waren halt schlechte Zeiten . . .' Das Kriegsende und die unmittelbare Nachkriegszeit in den lebensgeschichtlichen Erzählungen von Frauen aus dem Mostviertel*, Frankfurt a.M. etc.
BERGER, FRANZ SEVERIN and CHRISTIANE HOLLER (1994), *Trümmerfrauen. Alltag zwischen Hamstern und Hoffen*, Vienna.
BIESS, FRANK (1999), '"Pioneers of a New Germany?" Returning POWs from the Soviet Union and the Making of East German Citizens, 1945–1950,' *Central European History* 32: 143–180.
—— (2001), 'Survivors of Totalitarianism. Returning POWs and the Reconstruction of Masculine Citizenship in West Germany, 1945–1955,' in *The Miracle Years Revisited. A Cultural History of West Germany, 1949–1968*, ed. Hanna Schissler, Princeton, 57–82.
CARTER, ERICA (1997), *How German Is She? Postwar German Reconstruction and the Consuming Women*, Ann Arbor.
COOPER, ALICE HOLMES (1996), *Paradoxes of Peace. German Peace Movements since 1945*, Ann Arbor.

– 379 –

DANYEL, JÜRGEN, ed. (1995), *Die geteilte Vergangenheit. Zum Umgang mit Nationalsozialismus und Widerstand in beiden deutschen Staaten*, Berlin.

DIEHL, JAMES M. (1993), *The Thanks of the Fatherland. German Veterans after the Second World War*, Chapel Hill, London.

DOMANSKY, ELISABETH and JUTTA DE JONG (2000), *Der lange Schatten des Krieges. Deutsche Lebensgeschichten nach 1945*, Münster.

DOMENTAT, TAMARA (1998), *'Hallo Fräulein'. Deutsche Frauen und amerikanische Soldaten*, Berlin.

FEHRENBACH, HEIDE (1995), *Cinema in Democratizing Germany. Reconstructing National Identity after Hitler*, Chapel Hill, London.

—— (1998), 'Rehabilitating Fatherland. Race and German Remasculinazation,' *SIGNS* 24: 102–127.

FREI, NORBERT (1996), *Vergangenheitspolitik. Die Anfänge der Bundesrepublik und die NS-Vergangenheit*, Munich.

GOLTERMANN, SVENJA (1999), 'Verletzte Körper oder "Building National Bodies". Kriegsheimkehrer, "Krankheit" und Psychiatrie in der westdeutschen Nachkriegsgesellschaft, 1945–1955,' *Werkstatt-Geschichte* 24: 83–98.

—— (2000), 'Die Beherrschung der Männlichkeit. Zur Deutung psychischer Leiden bei den Heimkehrern des Zweiten Weltkriegs 1945–1956,' *Feministische Studien* 18, no. 2: 7–19.

GRAVENHORST, LERKE (1997), *Moral und Geschlecht. Die Aneignung der NS-Erbschaft. Ein soziologischer Beitrag zu Selbstverständigungen vor allem in Deutschland*, Freiburg.

GROSSMANN, ATINA (1998), 'Trauma, Memory, and Motherhood. Germans and Jewish Displaced Persons in Post-Nazi Germany, 1945–1949,' *Archiv für Sozialgeschichte* 38: 215–239.

HARTEWIG, KARIN (2000), 'Militarismus und Antifaschismus. Die Wehrmacht im kollektiven Gedächtnis der DDR,' in *Der Krieg in der Nachkriegszeit. Der Zweite Weltkrieg in Politik und Gesellschaft der Bundesrepublik*, ed. Michael T. Greven and Oliver Wrochem, Opladen, 237–254.

HEINEMAN, ELIZABETH (1996), "The Hour of the Woman. Memories of Germany's 'Crisis Years' and West German National Identity," *American Historical Review* 101: 354–395.

—— (1996), 'Complete Families, Half Families, No Families at All. Female Headed Households and the Reconstruction of the Family in the Early Federal Republic,' *Central European History* 29: 29–60.

HERBERT, ULRICH and AXEL SCHILDT, eds. (1998), *Kriegsende in Europa. Vom Beginn des deutschen Machtzerfalls bis zur Stabilisierung der Nachkriegsordnung 1944–1948*, Essen.

A Selected Bibliography

HERF, JEFFREY (1997), *Divided Memory. The Nazi Past in the Two Germanys*, London.

HILGER, ANDREAS (2000), *Deutsche Kriegsgefangene in der Sowjetunion 1941–1956. Kriegsgefangenenpolitik, Lageralltag und Erinnerung*, Essen.

HORNUNG, ELA (1999), '"Penelope und Odysseus". Zur Paarstruktur von Heimkehrer und wartender Frau in der Nachkriegszeit,' in *Eiszeit der Erinnerung. Vom Vergessen der eigenen Schuld*, ed. Ulf Brunnbauer, Vienna, 65–83.

KLUNDT, MICHAEL (2000), *Geschichtspolitik. Die Kontroversen um Goldhagen, die Wehrmachtsausstellung und das 'Schwarzbuch des Kommunismus'*, Cologne.

KUHN, ANNETTE, ed. (1986), *Frauen in der deutschen Nachkriegszeit*, Düsseldorf.

KÜHNE, THOMAS, ed. (2000), *Von der Kriegskultur zur Friedenskultur? Zum Mentalitätswandel in Deutschland nach 1945*, Münster.

MEYER, SIBYLLE and EVA SCHULZE (1985), *Wie wir das alles geschafft haben. Alleinstehende Frauen berichten über ihr Leben nach 1945*, Munich.

—— (1985), *Von Liebe sprach damals keiner. Familienalltag in der Nachkriegszeit*, Munich.

MÖDING, NORI (1988), 'Die Stunde der Frauen? Frauen und Frauenorganisationen des bürgerlichen Lagers,' in *Von Stalingrad zur Währungsreform. Zur Sozialgeschichte des Umbruchs in Deutschland*, ed. Martin Broszat, Munich, 619–647.

MOELLER, ROBERT G. (1996), 'War Stories. The Search for a Usable Past in the Federal Republic of Germany,' *American Historical Review* 101: 1008–1048.

—— (1993), *Protecting Motherhood. Women and the Family in the Politics of Postwar West Germany*, Berkeley.

—— ed. (1997), *West Germany under Construction. Politics, Society, and Culture in the Adenauer Era*, Ann Arbor.

—— (1998), '"The Last Soldier of the Great War" and Tales of Family Reunions in the Federal Republic of Germany,' *SIGNS* 24: 129–145.

—— (2001), *War Stories. The Search for a Usable Past in the Federal Republic of Germany*, Berkeley.

MÜHLHÄUSER, REGINA (1999), 'Massenvergewaltigungen in Berlin 1945 im Gedächtnis betroffener Frauen. Zur Verwobenheit von nationalistischen, rassistischen und geschlechtsspezifischen Diskursen,' in *Geschlecht hat Methode. Ansätze und Perspektiven in der Frauen- und Geschlechtergeschichte*, ed. Veronika Aegerter et al., Zurich, 235–246.

NAUMANN, KLAUS (1998), *Der Krieg als Text. Das Jahr 1945 im kulturellen Gedächtnis*, Hamburg.

—— ed. (2001), *Nachkrieg in Deutschland*, Hamburg.

NEUMANN, VERA (1998), *Nicht der Rede wert. Die Privatisierung der Kriegsfolgen in der frühen Bundesrepublik. Lebensgeschichtliche Erinnerungen*, Münster.

NIETHAMMER, LUTZ and ALEXANDER VON PLATO, eds. (1983), *Lebensgeschichte und Sozialkultur im Ruhrgebiet 1930–1960*, 3 vols, Berlin, Bonn.

OSIEL, MARC (1997), *Mass Atrocity, Collective Memory, and the Law*, New Brunswick, London.

PETÖ, ANDREA (1999), 'Stimmen des Schweigens. Erinnerungen an Vergewaltigungen in den Hauptstädten des "ersten Opfers" (Wien) und "letzten Verbündeten" Hitlers (Budapest) 1945,' *Zeitschrift für Geschichtswissenschaft* 47: 892–913.

POIGER, UTA (1998), 'A New "Western" Hero? Reconstructing German Masculinity in the 1950's,' *SIGNS* 24: 147–169.

POUDRUS, KIRSTEN (1995), 'Ein fixiertes Trauma – Massenvergewaltigungen bei Kriegsende in Berlin,' *Feministische Studien* 13: 2, 120–129.

ROSENTHAL, GABRIELE (1987), '. . . *wenn alles in Scherben fällt . . .*' *Von Leben und Sinnwelt der Kriegsgeneration*, Opladen.

SANDER, HELKE and BARBARA JOHR, eds. (1992), *Befreier und Befreite. Krieg, Vergewaltigungen, Kinder*, 2nd edition, Munich.

SCHORNSTHEIMER, MICHAEL (1995), *Die leuchtenden Augen der Frontsoldaten. Nationalsozialismus und Krieg in den Illustriertenromanen der fünfziger Jahre*, Berlin.

STOEHR, IRENE (1997), 'Der Mütterkongreß fand nicht statt. Frauenbewegung, Staatsmänner und Kalter Krieg 1950,' *WerkstattGeschichte* 17: 66–82.

THIELE, HANS GÜNTHER, ed. (1997), *Die Wehrmachtsausstellung. Dokumentation einer Kontroverse*, Bonn.

TEO, HSU-MING (1996), 'The Continuum of Sexual Violence in Occupied Germany, 1945–49,' *Women's History Review* 5, no. 2: 191–218.

Notes on Contributors

Birgit Beck is Lecturer (*wissenschaftliche Assistentin*) for Contemporary History at the Historical Institute of the University of Berne/Switzerland. She is finishing her doctoral thesis on *Rape committed by German Soldiers during the Second World War*, based on the files of the German Military Courts, and has published several articles on this topic.

Frank Biess is Assistant Professor at the History Department of the University of California/San Diego. His research focuses on German Social and Gender History, especially on postwar history and German–American relations and gender history. His dissertation 'The Protracted War. Returning POWs and the Making of East and West German Citizens, 1945–1955' (Ph.D. Dissertation, Brown University, 2000) will be published soon.

Belinda J. Davis is Associate Professor at the History Department of Rutgers University/New Jersey. She has worked and published on German history in the twentieth century, the history of the New Left and on gender history. Her current research deals with *Political Fantasies in the German Federal Republic, 1962–1983*. Her most recent book is *Home Fires Burning. Food, Politics, and Everyday Life in World War I Berlin* (Chapel Hill, 2000).

Marcus Funck is Lecturer (*wissenschaftlicher Mitarbeiter*) at the Department of History and Art History of the Technical University, Berlin/Germany. He is currently finishing his doctoral thesis on 'Feudal Warriors and Military Professionals. Noble and Bourgeois Officers in the Prusso-German Officer Corps, 1860–1935.'

Karen Hagemann is in the academic year 2002/03 the DAAD-Visiting Professor for German and European Studies at the Munk Centre for International Studies of the University of Toronto. In Germany she teaches at the Department of History and Art History and the Center for Interdisciplinary Studies on Women and Gender of the Technical University, Berlin. She has published extensively on Modern German and European History, Gender History as well as Cultural and Social History (18th–20th centuries). Her most recent books are *Gendered Nations. Nationalisms and Gender Order in the Long 19th Century*, ed. with Ida Blom and Catherine Hall (Oxford/New York 2000); '*Mannlicher Muth und Teutsche Ehre'. Nation, Militär und Geschlecht zur Zeit der Antinapoleonischen Kriege Preußens* (Paderborn, 2002).

Elizabeth Harvey is Senior Lecturer at the School of History of the University of Liverpool. She is working on a project on *German Women and Nazi Germanization Policies in Occupied Poland.* Her research focuses on twentieth century German history, gender history and the history of youth. Her publications include *Youth and the Welfare State in Weimar Germany* (Oxford, 1993); (ed. with Lynn Abrams), *Gender Relations in German History. Power, Agency, and Experience from the Sixteenth to the Twentieth Century* (London, 1996).

Sabine Kienitz is research fellow at the University of Tübingen/Germany. She is working on a project entitled *War Disability and Constructions of Masculinity in the First World War and the Weimar Republic.* Her publications on nineteenth century German and gender history, social movements and migration include *Sexualität, Macht und Moral. Prostitution und Geschlechterbeziehungen Anfang des 19. Jahrhunderts in Württemberg* (Berlin, 1995).

Christian Koller is Senior Lecturer (*Oberassistent*) at the Department of History of the University of Zurich/Switzerland. He started a project on *Foreign Rule. The Carrier of a Political Term in the Age of Nation/Nationalisms.* His research focuses on the history of racism and nationalism in the nineteenth and twentieth centuries as well as on the history of sports and on historical semantics. His recent book is '*Von Wilden aller Rassen niedergemetzelt'. Die Diskussion um die Verwendung von Kolonialtruppen in Europa zwischen Rassismus, Kolonial- und Militärpolitik (1914–1930)* (Stuttgart, 2001).

Thomas Kühne is research fellow at the Department of History of the University of Bielefeld/Germany. At the moment he is finishing a project entitled: *The Myth of Comradeship and the German Soldiers of the Second World War, 1918–1999.* He has published extensively on German military and gender history as well as on German political history in the nineteenth and twentieth centuries. His most recent books are *Was ist Militärgeschichte?*, ed. with Benjamin Ziemann (Paderborn etc. 2000); *Von der Kriegskultur zur Friedenskultur? Zum Mentalitätswandel in Deutschland seit 1945*, ed. (Münster, 2000).

Notes on Contributors

Birthe Kundrus is Senior Lecturer (*wissenschaftliche Assisentin*) at the Historical Institute of the Carl-von-Ossietzky University in Oldenburg/ Germany. Her research focuses on gender history in nineteenth and twentieth centuries Germany as well as on German colonial history. Her publications include *Kriegerfrauen. Familienpolitik und Geschlechterverhältnisse im Ersten und Zweiten Weltkrieg* (Hamburg, 1995).

Robert L. Nelson has recently submitted his doctoral thesis at the University of Cambridge/Great Britain on *Gender-specific and Racist Representations in German Soldier Newspapers of the First World War*. He has just received a Postdoctoral Fellowship at the University of British Columbia, Vancouver/Canada.

Susanne zur Nieden is research fellow at the Center for Interdisciplinary Studies on Women and Gender of the Technical University in Berlin/ Germany. She is currently working on the *Persecution of Homosexuals during the Nazi Regime*. Her publications include '*Sehr selten habe ich geweint'. Briefe und Tagebücher aus dem Zweiten Weltkrieg von Menschen aus Berlin*, ed. with Ingrid Hammer (Zurich, 1992); *Alltag im Ausnahmezustand. Frauentagebücher im zerstörten Deutschland 1943 bis 1945* (Berlin, 1993).

Bianca Schönberger has recently submitted her doctoral thesis at the University of Oxford on 'Mobilising "Etappenhelferinnen" for Service with the Military. Gender Regimes in First World War Germany'.

Stefanie Schüler-Springorum is Director of the Institute for the History of German Jews in Hamburg/Germany. Currently she is working on the *Condor Legion in the Spanish Civil War*. She has worked on Jewish History, the history of National Socialism and on Spanish history. Her publications include *Die jüdische Minderheit in Königsberg/Pr. 1871–1945* (Göttingen 1996).

Irene Stoehr is research fellow at the University of Hanover/Germany. She is currently working on a project entitled *Peace Discourses and Gender Constructions in the Federal Republic of Germany, 1945–1963*. Her publications on twentieth century gender history include *Emanzipation zum Staat? Der Allgemeine Deutsche Frauenverein/Deutscher Staatsbürgerinnenverband 1893–1933* (Pfaffenweiler, 1990); *Frauenpolitik und politisches Wirken von Frauen im Berlin der Nachkriegszeit*, ed. with Renate Genth et al. (Berlin, 1996).

Index

Note: Significant information in endnotes is indexed in the form 123n5, ie. note 5 on page 123

Index

Index

Index

Index